THE FIFTH BOOK OF PEACE

Maxine Hong Kingston

THE FIFTH BOOK OF PEACE

Alfred A. Knopf   New York   2003

THIS IS A BORZOI BOOK
PUBLISHED BY ALFRED A. KNOPF

Ensos by the author.

Library of Congress Cataloging-in-Publication Data
Kingston, Maxine Hong.
The fifth book of peace / by Maxine Hong Kingston. — 1st ed.
p. cm.
ISBN 0-679-44075-5
1. Kingston, Maxine Hong. 2. Vietnamese Conflict, 1961–1975 — Veterans — Interviews.
3. Authors, American — 20th century — Biography. 4. Draft resisters — Fiction.
5. Hawaii — Fiction. 6. Peace.
I. Title.
PS3561.I52 F44 2003
813'.54 — dc21   2002034103

Manufactured in the United States of America
First Edition

Thanks to the Lila Wallace Fund and the Rockefeller Foundation.

TO VETERANS OF WAR,

VETERANS OF PEACE

To Jose Grier

Peace

Maxine Hong Kingston

CONTENTS

FIRE | 1

*The author tells about herself running through the
Oakland-Berkeley hills, which are on fire. All her material goods,
including her novel-in-progress, are burned. A true story.*

PAPER | 43

The history of lost Books of Peace, and the quests for them.

WATER | 63

*A re-creation of the burned book. A fiction set in Hawai'i,
where Wittman Ah Sing and his family seek sanctuary
during the War in Viet Nam.*

EARTH | 239

*A nonfiction during which the author and her husband live in
temporary homes while their new house is being built. She sends out
a call to war veterans to help write a literature of peace.*

Epilogue 399
Permissions Acknowledgments 405

FIRE

If a woman is going to write a Book of Peace, it is given her to know devastation. I have lost my book—156 good pages. A firestorm blew over the Oakland-Berkeley hills in October of 1991, and took my house, things, neighborhood, and other neighborhoods, and forests. And the lives of twenty-five people.

I almost reached my manuscript, typescript, printouts, and disks in time. I was driving home from funeral ceremonies for my father. I have lost my father. He's gone less than a month; we were having the full-month ceremony early, Sunday day off. Never before had I driven by myself away from Stockton and my parents' house. I turned on public radio for the intelligent voices, and heard that the hills were burning, toward Moraga, toward Walnut Creek. It's not my poor sense of direction, I told myself, but the newscasters in confusion. The pcrimeters of the fire were different from station to station, from taped news to live news. North of the Caldecott Tunnel, south of the Caldecott Tunnel, east, west of the Warren Freeway. I pictured wildfire far up in the hills—ridgelines of flame spilling down, then running up sere-grass slopes. I have seen it at night—red gashes zigzagging the black. Impossible that it cross ten lanes of freeway and take over settled, established, built city.

Behind me, my sister-in-law Cindy was chasing me at ninety miles per hour. My family believed that I didn't know about the fire, and would drive into it, and not be able to find my way out on the altered, burning streets. Like all the Chinese members of our family, I have an instinct that left is right and vice versa. Too easily lost. Cindy, who is not Chinese but Arkie, ran out of gas at Tracy.

In a half-hour, halfway there, forty miles to go, I was speeding over the Altamont Pass (where there be ghosts and accidents; it is the ground upon which the stabbing happened at the Rolling Stones concert, after Woodstock), and through the windfarms. Some windmills turned, and some were still. Here the winds and all seemed normal; I had no evidence that hurricanes of fire were storming on the other side of these hills but for the radio. "Forty-five houses have gone up in flames." "About a hundred homes." "A hundred and fifty structures have burned." The numbers would keep going up—nine hundred degrees, the temperature of molten lava; twenty-one hundred degrees, the temperature of kilns; thirty-five hundred houses. "Winds of forty-five miles per hour . . ." ". . . sixty-five-mile-per-hour firewind . . ." ". . . record heat and winds . . ." "Foehn winds." "Northeast winds . . ." I would have to look up "foehn," which sounds like "wind" in Chinese, as in "typhoon." "The fire has jumped the junction of Highway Twenty-four and Highway Thirteen." It's blown over and through ten lanes. Ten lanes are not wide enough firebreak. It's on our side of the freeway. ". . . dynamite College Avenue." ". . . draw the line at College Avenue." ". . . helicopters and available cropdusters chemical-drop the Claremont Hotel." "If the Claremont Hotel goes, explodes, the fire will burn to the Bay." "No cars have been trapped in the Caldecott Tunnel." Once, a propane truck had exploded inside the tunnel—a giant flamethrower pointed at Oakland.

NO TANK TRUCKS

WITH HAZARDOUS MATERIALS

ALLOWED IN CALDECOTT TUNNEL

A police car was parked sideways across my exit, Broadway Terrace. I drove fast to the next exit, which was blocked by a Highway Patrol car and flares. They are setting up the roadblocks moments ahead of me, I thought. If only I had driven faster, I might have saved the book, and my mother's jewelry, and my father's watch, and his spectacles, which fit my eyes, and his draft card, which I had taken from his wallet. "This card is to be carried on your person at all times." He carried it safely for over fifty years.

When I got off the freeway, I was somewhere in downtown Oakland, and driving too slowly through complicated traffic. It was the middle of the afternoon, about two o'clock. Too late. Too late. The sky was black. The sun was red. Leaves of burned black paper wafted high and low among the buildings. Ashes from a forest fire were falling and blowing in downtown Oakland.

In the middle of my U-turn, the radio said that Broadway and/or Broadway Terrace was on fire, and that there was looting on Ostrander Street. Parallel streets—big Broadway Terrace for cars, little Broadway Terrace for walking—eucalyptus and pine trees and apple trees between them—a tree-high, two-street-thick wall of flame. Mass fire. I said out loud, "No. No. No. No." Ostrander is—was?—a one-way road through a small woods on a hill. On my walks to and from the Village Market, families of quail would surprise me. They walked ahead just so far, as if leading me, or as if I were giving chase, then took off running into the bushes, and flying up into the lower branches of the oaks and pines. Once, on Ostrander, I stood amazed at the center of a storm of birds— hundreds of robins, jays, and chickadees—flying touch-and-go, on and off treetops and roofs and grass, circling and crisscrossing singly and in schools, and never bumping into one another—better than the Blue Angels. I love looking out at Oakland and seeing a crane extend itself over the city. So—their flyway can sweep this far west, and they rest at Lake Merritt or Lake Anza or Temescal. Anne Frank saw cranes out the sky window. Another time, riding BART, as the train came up out of the Bay into Oakland, I saw twelve angels wheeling in the sun, rays of white wings and gold light. "Swans!" I said loudly; the other passengers had to see them too. "Look. Swans."

It can't be too late. All I want is a minute inside the house—run to the far end of the living room, to the alcove where my book is in a wine box, take one more breath, and run upstairs for the gold and jade that my ancestresses had been able to keep safe through wars in China and world wars and journeys across oceans and continents.

Where Broadway meets the start of College Avenue, at the California College of Arts and Crafts (where Wittman kissed Tañia; but I'll get to that), only a few feet from the sign pointing up to Broadway Terrace, the police were herding cars down and away to College Avenue. I stopped at the light, left the car, and ran over to talk them into letting me through. Even though the light turned green, the line of cars I'd blocked did not honk; nobody yelled. I wished for a hand gesture to communicate Sorry, to use in traffic situations. Sorry. Thank you. I asked a policeman, "Are you absolutely sure I can't drive up there?" He answered that no cars were allowed past this point. I thought, May I go to my house on foot, then? I got back in the car, drove diagonally across the intersection, and parked in the red-curb stop for the College Avenue bus. The police shouldn't write tickets on this terrible day. Twenty-eight dollars, worth it. Have mercy on this car that could very well have been left here by someone who had escaped the fire and was getting a drink of water, parking as close as she could to home.

I stood at the curb plotting how I was going to fade past the police, and got in step with an African American family with many children crossing the street. I told them I lived on Golden Gate Avenue and was trying to go up there; where did they live? They lived on Brookside, which winds around Golden Gate. I asked, "Were you officially evacuated? Has our area been officially evacuated yet?" They didn't know, but they had been back to their house. The father said, "The police will escort you home if you tell them you have a life-and-death situation." The mother said, "They drove us to our house." I asked, "What was the life-and-death situation you told them?" "We couldn't find our son. Our son was missing." The kids, all about junior-high age, were smiling and safe; I couldn't tell which was the one lost and now found. An unfinished book is nothing as important as a child. I told the family that I was trying to save the manuscript of a book I was writing. Said out loud in the open to actual people, who did not get excited, my plight did not seem to have enormity. "I've been working on it for years," I said. About one and a half to two years of pure writing, not counting thinking and imagining. Is one and a half to two years much? It depends on which years. Didn't Rilke write *The Duino Elegies* in six months? Or was it six hours one wide-awake night? He did it about ten years before his death at fifty-one. The happy family and I wished each other Good luck and Take care.

While the policemen—the Oakland cops aren't as big as during the Viet Nam demonstrations—were busy, I walked through the barricades into the defined fire area. Householders were staying, hosing down roofs and dry lawns. A flare of fire fell out of the sky and landed behind a man intent on watering his property. I motioned to him that he should look to his rear, but he stared at me as if I were a crazy woman, pointing at my own butt. I didn't try to shout over the helicopters; they chopped up sound and the air, and whupped up heartbeats. Anyway, only now, as I write, am I coming up with words for the things that were making wild appearances and disappearances. That flame went out; another fell out of nowhere onto his roof. Even if he saw it, he couldn't have reached it with the spray from his garden hose. I ran on.

I felt afraid when there was not a person in sight. I ran up the center of the street, between the houses, locked up tight. I wanted to run faster, through and out of this deserted place. But I was trying to breathe shallowly. The car radio had said that poison oak was burning; I coughed, thinking of breathing poison-oak smoke, which must blister lungs. The air smelled poisonous—toxic polymers, space-age plastics, petrochemicals, refrigerants, Freon, radon. I am breathing carcinogens, I will die of lung cancer. I held my long white hair as a filter over my nose and mouth and ran at a pace that allowed me to control my wind. I passed side streets without deciding to turn left into one. Many streets end in culs-de-sac, or loop around. I would lose time backtracking out. I wished for a photographic memory to recall the map of this area in the *Thomas Guide*. But the *Thomas Guide* only blurredly indicates the snarl of these streets, lanes, paths, and steps; they curl around boulders and oak trees and Lake Temescal and hills. From now on, wherever I live, I will pay attention to which streets go through exactly where. Pages of ash were floating high up, and also skimming along curbs. I did not stop to try to read them. Someone once told me about a child who lived at the time of the burning of a great library. He caught pages of burned paper, and read Latin words. At Margarido, a long, wide street, I turned left toward the heat and fire. I hoped that I would see again the enormous old ginkgo tree that fountains up and up—wings, gold, autumn. I passed a man and a woman leaving their house, and a homeowner on his rooftop wetting it down. None of them could answer me: whether or not this street was officially evacuated. I arrived at the edge of the golf course, which was lined by a row of eucalyptus trees. Their tops were on fire. This is crown fire, and flames jumped from tree to tree. I imagined myself running under the eucalyptus trees, but, before I reached the open field, the trees dropping fire on my head, and me exploding. More eucalyptus trees lined the other side. (My husband, who should be at my side helping me, would tease, You're always afraid that things will explode. " 'Be careful,' " Earll mimics me. " 'Watch out. It's going to explode.' " But I have seen and/or heard for myself the explosions of an automobile motor, a sewing-machine motor, my electric typewriter [a cat pissed in it], a toilet, mother spiders, tules. In Phoenix Park in Dublin, I made Earll get away before a dead cow, its big stomach expanding, blew up.) Eucalyptus trees have big wood-cells filled with eucalyptus oil. The bangs I was hearing were houses, cars, and trees blowing up. If I made it across the golf course (Private Robert E. Lee Prewitt, the hero of *From Here to Eternity*, was killed on a golf course), I would come out at the corner of Broadway Terrace and Ostrander, amidst the fire and the looters. I turned about. Is this retreat, then, and am I giving up on my book? I let the possibility that the book was gone — my book gone — enter my ken. I did not feel bad; I did not believe it was lost. I had not stopped trying to rescue it. The same men were still watering down their houses, which their wives and children must have evacuated. The sky was darker now, and the air hotter. The sun was ugly red. ("Ugly red" are Judy Foosaner's words; she's a painter, we're "friends since girls." She was down in the flatlands, and watched the cars exploding up on the hills. I'd thought until she said "ugly red" that to a painter all colors were beautiful.)

Gravity sped me downhill, back to crowds and industrial-strength buildings. I found my red car — no ticket — and drove down College to Chabot Road, which was barricaded. Chabot Road was my familiar turn home. It was not right that it be an impasse. I left the car there, surprised at the free parking. Again, I became invisible to the police, and walked for home. This way seemed almost normal. I should have come up these known streets in the first place. As always, there was a stillness at St. Albert's College; either the monks had evacuated the seminary, or they were staying hidden. You hardly ever see them in the garden or out on the tennis courts anyway. The atmosphere feels full of prayer. The row of elm trees — grandmother tree, grandfather tree — stood unharmed. This was the first tree seen by me as a child, and is more magnificent each time I find another one. Some people call them Chinese elms, some call them American elms. Here was a stand of nine elms, here before I was here, and meant to outlast me. I do not remember touching them, each one, the elephant bark, the horned-toad bark, the crocogator bark, as I usually do; I must have rushed past. Their jigjag leaves were a strong green, though October was ending, and my fiftieth year was ending.

The strange shifting light — the winds were blowing the weather and the time of day crazily up and down the street — stilled at St. Albert's and started up again at Chabot Elementary, shadows swinging across the asphalt and through the cyclone fences, backstop, and jungle-gym bars.

Why do we raise children on ground barren of trees and grass? We are teaching them to endure a world like a cage, a jail.

Chabot Road tails up and off into hills and forests, and Golden Gate Avenue, my street, starts to its right. This corner—I am traveling northeast—is a natural border between man-built city and wildland. Flats and hills, chapparal and forest also meet here. All influenced by underground rivers, and by fault lines. The wind changes its blowing; the climate turns. At such a place, you enter and leave ecosystems. *Leina-a-ka-'uhane*. I was at a border of the fire, the built city behind me, and ahead black ground. I walked onto it. I could disappear, I thought. If I had continued walking northeast, up the hill, I would've come to the place where the fire killed nineteen people. The slopes on either side of me had just burned. The ivy, dill, vetch, pampas plumes, and coyote bushes do not exist anymore, except in my mind.

I have been at controlled burns. Farmers weed fields by burning them down to fertile ash and black earth. The harvest fires in the cane fields run at you, and suddenly stop. The burning kansaa, the prairie grass of Kansas, smells like baking bread. The Forest Service clear-cuts trees, then napalms, then seeds. Storms of wildfire are as normal as timely rain. The reason for this fire is five years of drought.

Golden Gate, my street, begins with a small cement bridge marked "Narrow Bridge," which goes under a steel bridge for the BART train. It's a wonderful surprise when, overhead, up in the air, the train appears out of the trees. The Concord line was not running today, the radio had said. The girders were smoking. Were they usually this red? Was the bridge rusty, or red hot? I stood still and thought about whether I should go under it. The metal could melt or crumble, the loosened structure break apart, drop, and hit me on the head. I only worried for my head, had not a thought for other parts of my body. The head looks out for itself. I needed to see around a bend to look for my house. I didn't see any houses on the other side of the bridges, but wasn't sure if you ever could from here anyway. I threw myself straight forward, and felt the heat from above. I ran through a gigantic kiln, which has since recurred in nightmares: I am flying up into the hot ceiling, and can't wake up. The concrete walls that support the trains and the freeways boxed me in. I was a long time under the BART rails, then under Highway 24 West, then Highway 24 East, then Broadway—immense wide slabs of concrete and steel that could fall and squash me entirely, like the Cypress Freeway, which "pancaked" thirty-five cars and the people inside them during the earthquake two Octobers ago.

I came out into a changed world. Its color had gone out. Its dimensions had stretched away here, shrunk there. New mountains and canyons vistaed as far as I could see. To my left, close beside me, a mountain appeared, terraced with streets on which burning cars sat on every level. To my right, below, opened a canyon; I could see its entire contours—a black, defoliated wedge. The canyon contains just the College Prep School, has held it from harm. Clean two-by-fours at roof angles poked up to the canyon's rim, where I was standing. The frame of the gym or auditorium they were putting up had not burned; they could keep on building it. Suppose I were to go on, take myself farther into the fire scene—might I see my house, earn it, cause it to be, after all, there? What with the tricky distances, beyond the next turn could very well be my house. Walking in the center of the street, I stepped over power lines. I was entering a black, negative dimension, where things disappeared, and I might disappear. The only movement and color were flames. I sidestepped burning logs that had flown here; they must have been chunks from houses. The houses cast off logs before falling into ashes. Suddenly, I saw a whole two-story house with high-peaked roof— I have never seen this house before, not from this side; I was looking at it through invisible, gone houses—an enormous house standing squarely inside a flame. A red-orange diamond enhoused the house, the crystal within a crystal. So—a house can burn all at once, not simply be eaten away corner by corner.

I kept looking down at my feet to puzzle my way through the tangles of power lines, and looking up at a wavery, flickering, blinking scene. What I wanted to see, what used to be, popped in and out of sight, alternated with the real. The hot ground was reeking mirages that cheated the eye with blear illusions. A thing would appear—a chimney, an oldened wrought-iron gate, a ceramic pot—but it did not cue the next thing, the thing that should be attached to it (house, fence), to appear. Things were out of the order that was in my mind. Memory was off. If only I had paid better attention—I have to be more awake—I would not be losing the detailed world. One more bend, and yet one more bend, but my cedar-shake roof did not rise into sight.

I came upon and recognized a tiny white house with wood siding, which looked water-stained or chemical-stained. The poorest house in the neighborhood has survived. I hadn't met its latest owners; it was always changing hands. This small house on a corner lot was affordable entry into our good neighborhood and the housing market. The houses to the side of it and in back of it were gone, and it now seemed to have a huge yard. Happiness rushed back and forth between it and me. The tiny house nicely fit its place in my mind, and gave me my bearings. My house, the next smallest, should be at the other end of this curving, winding block, with only the crest of the hill in the way.

A fireman was puttering with a long yellow fire truck, parked beside the stone retaining wall that held an upswooping street and a hillside of houses. I could not see if any houses were still up there. The fireman did not warn me from stepping through the mess of wires and cables and flat hoses, black serpents and white serpents that had fought, and lay slain. I tiptoed amongst them. Jackstraws—one touch, misstep, trip, and be zapped. I made it across the street—a wire did not wake up and jump me—to say Hi to the fireman. It takes this much upheaval for me to get over shyness. I thought of saying but didn't say, "What a mess, huh?" or ask, "How're things going? Is your truck broken? Where are the other firefighters? Do you know where the main fire is? Why are you here all by yourself?" He might feel embarrassed. I did not bother him with inquiry after my address either. We stood quiet together awhile. I asked, "Which direction did you come from?" He said, "It came down that way, very fast," pointing northeast, up at the hills. "And blew back up, then down again from over there." At my house. The firefighters had taken a stand at my intersection. The fire almost surrounded them, fire in back, then in front of them. They retreated to this rampart. We were standing at the wall of our devastated city. "We didn't get water up here."

The fireman did not stop me. I went on. A bicyclist got off his bicycle to walk alongside me. We hesitated at a maze and thicket of power lines, some piled waist-high and others dangling eye-high. Where to straddle over, where to limbo under? The street was webbed in knots and nets of lines. I remembered learning in Latin class that the triton-and-net was the most dangerous weapon, the one to choose for war games and war. In dreams where I try to fly, I am halted by electrical lines, which shoot ahead of me and cut off the free sky. Where had such a plethora of lines dropped from? Our utilities weren't buried underground, but the sky had never seemed hatchmarked and crisscrossed. Through the knot, I saw Mrs. Fessler's Karmann Ghia. Its paint had been seared from red to white. Tears of melted glass hung from the windows, the eyeholes of a baboon skull. Cables draped like black hair over its low forehead and weeping eyes; the interior was a black hollow. The tires were gone, burned off. Where is Mrs. Fessler? She is all right, please. She was at church; or her son came for her, and they drove off in his car. The simmering ground was flat, no mound of ashes that could be a small human body. There—another recognizable house: the house-in-the-gully—how many lots away from mine is it?—crouched under the flames, and had made it, alive. So—firewinds blow over the top of the earth. You can see why people lived in tunnels in Viet Nam and Okinawa. (But months ago we bulldozed the desert sand into the trenches, and buried Iraqi soldiers alive. I had read an impossible number—seventy thousand. "A turkey shoot.")

The fire had reached from the foot to the armpits of the phone poles; crossbars were hanging by a burning arm. Atop its white metal flagpole, higher than the utility poles and away from trees, on a mound in a clearing, was the American flag, limp and singed, but still there. Its primary colors (which don't occur much in nature) had dulled, scorched in the dark air. The wind stopped; I might have been in the eye of its swirl.

I have ambivalence about the Flag. It is a battle flag, a war flag, and I don't like being patriotically roused and led to war. The Red, White, and Blue stands for competition and nationalism. I want it to stand for peace and cooperation. I get scared of my fellow Americans' going crazy as it waves. Because of that dramatic unburned American flag, our part of the fire would keep appearing in the news. A CNN reporter called our area a "picturesque burnscape." A reporter for a college paper interviewed me, and translated my burbling: "So, you saw the Flag, and realized that you transcended the fire." I was dismayed—he was a writer, yet locked inside the Flag symbol: You have the Flag, you win.

I did not have a sudden moment of knowing that my house and all that was in it were no more. I stood there reasoning, If I can see that flag from here, then I am also looking through the place where my house was. I was laying eyes on it without registering which piece of blackened land amidst all this blackened land was exactly my piece. The landscape was utterly changed. I had come to the ash moon of a planet that passes through the sun.

I had flown a flag too, a white dove on a sky-blue silk field, UN colors plus orange beak, green leaves, brown branch, brown eye. I appliquéd and embroidered two peace flags at the beginning of my country's continuing war against Iraq, and hung one out the upstairs front window, the other out the side, toward the peaceful neighbor, to hearten her. Christina Simoni was the only other neighbor who put up peace signs, made on her home computer: across the top of the picture window, EVERY SOLDIER IS SOMEBODY'S SON; and across the bottom, OR DAUGHTER. She was answering President Bush, who made a speech— "our boys"? "our sons"? "our side"?—that didn't make sense, wasn't true, so I forget it. He kept ejaculating, "Euphoria!" On another day of our country's mad fit, Christina hand-lettered a new poster—WAR IS NOT AN ENERGY POLICY. We were two households with such ideas, amidst neighbors who tied the trees and poles and gates with yellow ribbons. The giant eucalyptus tree at our crossroads was tied. Some middle of the night, it was untied (not by me), and never retied.

My Book of Peace is gone.

Suddenly, I felt rushing at me—this fire movie is about to run in reverse; smoky ghosts will hurry backward into rising houses and trees, refill them, and pull them upright—I felt coming into me—oh, but here all along inside chest and stomach and all around me and out of the smoking ground—Idea. Idea has weight and life; I can feel it. Ideas are pervious to firebombs, which shoot through them without harming them. Americans own too many things. I can feel Idea because I am thingless, and because of my education, thinking, reading, meditation. I heard the monk and teacher Thich Nhat Hanh say the Five Wonderful Precepts, which are the moral foundation of Buddhism. Having ethics, even intentions and aspirations, turns you in the right direction, toward some lasting idea about good. I am a manifestation of Idea, food that makes blood, bones, muscles, body, self. I stood alive in the fire, and felt ideas pour into me.

I know why this fire. God is showing us Iraq. It is wrong to kill, and refuse to look at what we've done. (Count the children killed, in "sanctions": 150,000, 360,000, 750,000. "Collateral damage." The counts go up with each new report. We killed more children than soldiers. Some of the children *were* soldiers.) For refusing to be conscious of the suffering we caused—the camera-eye on the bomb went out as it hit the door or roof at the center of the crosshairs—no journalists allowed, no witnesses—we are given this sight of our city in ashes. God is teaching us, showing us this scene that is like war.

I'm not crazy; I'm not unpatriotic. People who've been there, who saw Hiroshima and Nagasaki after the A-bombs, the Ong Plain and Huế after the firefights, compared our fire to war. Oakland Fire Captain Ray Gatchalian, Asian American, Green Beret, Viet Nam vet, Panama vet, said, "When I went up in the helicopter the day after the fire, I couldn't even film, I was so stunned. You have to remember, I went to Mexico City after the earthquake where hundreds and thousands of people were displaced, but when you see your own environment, people you know, whose homes were burned to the ground, I was stunned, in total shock. That day, one house burned every five seconds. Seeing it the next morning, it brought me back to the shock and horror of Vietnam. When I looked down on the devastation that day, I thought what an opportunity this would be to bring busloads of people and busloads of children and tell them when we, as a country, decide to go to war against somebody, this is what we are going to get. When we decide to send our military and our bombs into a country, this is what we're deciding to do."

My Book of Peace is gone. And my father is gone. Fatherless. And thingless. But not Idea-less.

My father is trying to kill me, to take me with him. At this morning's funeral fires, we burned gifts and provisions for him, but it was not enough, and he's angry. He wants more—my book, all my books, my house, and neighborhood—and is taking more—my cities, Berkeley, where I teach, Oakland, where I live. In the incinerator at the Chinese Cemetery, we burned blank paper to him, a symbol of everything, like money. He wants writing, and real things. (In the Ur-draft and again just now, I typed "tings," which is my name, Ting Ting, my father-given name.) This heat that covers me and my territory from hot ground up to the sun is anger, the anger that had been one man's task to civilize. Now that my father is dead, this energy is loose.

It discharged out of his too-old body, which had no illness but time, leapt sky-high, and divebombed earthward, me-ward. My father is now part of the father-god of the Americas, who hunts his children, spears and fishes for us with his lightning yo-yo. BaBa is not focusing his terrible new death powers. He is carpet-bombing. He can't catch me, small and alone, driving and running here and there, Stockton, Oakland, back and forth across the Berkeley-Oakland border. I had taken belongings most full of his mana. He wants back his spectacles, which fit my eyes, his wristwatch, his draft card, the Cross pen that I had given him, the brass spindle for spiking gambling tickets and laundry tickets, the bamboo match extender-holder he invented for lighting firecrackers. His brass ashtray from the 1939 World's Fair. I had made an arrangement of these things on my kitchen desk, and they'd evoked him. But mostly he wants my book. "I have always wanted the life you have." My father started saying that to me when I became a published, paid writer. He was wishing to have many poems come to him, and to have readers. My mother—Brave Orchid—tried scolding him into poetry: "You used to be a poet. Where are the poems, poet?" He would wonder, "How is it that I can like poems so much, but can't write them anymore?" In China, he had written six tomes of poetry, "each one this thick." My mother held up her hand, thumb and forefinger wide apart. Poetry comes out of the country—the ground and the people—but he couldn't hear the voices so well in America as in China.

At the blanketing ceremony three weeks ago, we, his children and children-in-law, two by two, everybody married, holding a piece of printed cloth between us, walked up to the coffin and spread it over his body. We blanketed him with layers and layers of colors and flowers as in a fairy tale. I put the fountain pen my son had given me into BaBa's breast pocket. Then Earll and I pulled the coverlet up to his chin; it felt like being young parents again, tucking the baby into bed.

Today was the day for wearing red. I was wearing my new red carnelian necklace through the fire. MaMa had told us to spend about $20—"a lot of money"—on something beautiful and red to wear on this day. Shopping, keeping an eye out for red, you see it everywhere you go, and get pulled back into life. At a death, you don't want to live anymore; you want to follow the dead, loved person. Finding and buying a red object, you leave the black and white of the grave. Get up, get out of the house, live. A ray of sunlight lit on the necklace in the gemologist's window, and I walked straight into the shop and bought it, though it was twice $20. At this morning's ceremonies, we wore red blouses and red shirts, red vests (vest, *boy sum* in Chinese, "heart protector"), red ties, red hats. We compared who bought what, for how much, and the shades that people consider red, such as hot pink. MaMa tied bunches of juniper leaves with red ribbon, the crinkly paper kind that squiggles and curls. They were for us, the daughters and daughters-in-law, to wear in our hair. My youngest sister, Corrinne, tied hers across the top of her head, and looked like a Santa elf. She has some silver hair; we all have silver hair now. I pulled mine into a ponytail, attached the juniper and red curls over an ear; our mother would not be able to scold me for having too much hair and wearing it wild. My other sister, Carmen, said that in her next lifetime she will have thick hair: the hairpins and juniper hurt her scalp. She got scolded for wanderfooting about the cemetery looking for the lost grave of our great-uncle the river pirate. Heeding the rituals argued out by the constantly scolding old women from China—wear hoods and sashes, black hoods; no, white hoods; no, black hoods; eat, bow, eat, bow; no, not toward the chicken, you stupid *ho jee* boy, toward your father; buy yellow candy; no, not lemon drops, you stupid *ho jee* girl, Brach's butterscotch—turning in the directions that you're pushed and pulled—you infer Heaven. Its distance from Earth is a month's walk away. Kneeling in the grass, my kind cousin-in-law from China instructed us, who were standing, "Say bye-bye to BaBa, *la*." The movements of ceremonies indicate the direction and timing for escorting BaBa on his journey away from us to another, farthest-away home. For twenty-seven days and nights, he has been climbing and clambering up a steep mountain, the back of a dragon. He scrabbles forward, turns about and walks backward, and sees us again, eats with us, and looks down at the earth and the trees that he planted. He is lonely, missing his body, and us. Our every wish against his leaving makes it hard on him. We have to persuade him on and on. Climb the mountain, go through the double door into the sky, all the great nothing.

We shouldn't have let them push him screaming into the MRI machine. I hope he was not hallucinating that he was being tortured, that Immigration had caught him. The tube for wafting oxygen under the nostrils, then the light plastic mask had been enough; we should have declined the loud respirator, which pumped air into him. How to breathe like Buddha when the machines are forcing you? They tied his wrists and ankles with strips of cloth to the bed rails. He had been racing in and out of doors, from room to room, up and down the basement stairs, back and forth and around on the paths of his garden, unconscious of us and this reality. He was searching for something, lost money that he himself had hidden. He said, "I don't understand where I could have put my birthday money—ninety gold pieces." Carmen had given him a silver dollar for each of his years; he called this treasure "gold." A White nurse said, "It took three of us to hold him down. And one was a big Black man." His eyes were shut tight. With a foot of slack in each rope, he kept moving, arms rowing, legs pedaling. I held his right hand; my brother Norman held his left hand; he pulled us both along. My hand covered his; when he taught me to write and draw, his hand had covered mine. I said to him, the last words I said to him were, "Okay, okay. You rest now, BaBa. Rest. You have been a good BaBa." Too late to discuss any bad fathering. Norman also said, "Rest, BaBa." We didn't know the Chinese word for "relax." Maybe there isn't one. I considered "I love you," but that would be an American sentiment unnatural for me to express, and for him to hear. I should have said: "Thank you, BaBa, for working hard for us. We love you."

These ideas—that the fire is to make us know Iraq, and that my father caused the fire—came to me when I stood still in the center of devastation. For 360 degrees, everything was flattened except chimneys, columns of chimneys two and three stories high. Each burned-away house had left its tombstone. (In the earthquake the October before last, chimneys fell into piles of bricks beside standing houses.) Hearth-and-flue out in the open looked like the incinerator for communicating with the dead. All around me, in valleys and on the hillsides, were hundreds of entrances and exits between worlds. The way to the other place is wide open, and it has many, many mouths, consuming our things, and us, and issuing visions and thoughts.

You can send messages and gifts to people who have died. My mother, Brave Orchid, says to write the deceased's name on the package, and "c/o Seiji Goong Goong." Seiji seems to be everyone's grandfather, a kind of postman who delivers mail in Heaven. "Send whatever you like," she instructs. "You can even write letters and poems." Then you burn them in the incinerator at any Chinese cemetery, not necessarily the one at French Camp. Your addressee doesn't have to be buried there or be Chinese. Postmaster Grandfather Seiji will know where to find him. My mother most approves of sons' sending things to fathers and grandfathers. Women's offerings seem to get routed to in-laws. She scolded me and my sisters for participating in the burning of the gold-and-orange leis that we had origamied and strung. "You shouldn't have burned the paper. It's not your business to burn paper." Behind Mom's back, Corrinne, who is a lawyer, and I passed the spangly train hand to hand into the fire. The boxes of air whiffed into flames.

It was a mistake to have the red ceremony today—too early. We did it just because Sunday is convenient. We shouldn't have hurried our father. BaBa had three more days on this side of the sky door, and so he set fire to Oakland and Berkeley. We burned paper in a small fire in the walkway in front of his house, and jumped over it; he was not to have followed us. The Berkeley-Oakland fire will burn for three days.

From a side street rode another man on a bicycle. Now a bicyclist was protecting me on either side. "Are you all right?" this one asked. I must not have been looking all right. How to answer him? I could not tell the news that my father was dead, and what's more have to explain that he had not been killed by the fire. Nor did I feel like pointing out the black space—right there—that had been my house and possessions. It would make me cry to talk about the neighbors and our *communitas.* We had blind-chosen one another at random, and were not trying for it, but we'd gathered a community. It is over. No more chances to improve on and appreciate what we were. Too late. I never joined the Christmas caroling organized by peaceful Christina next door. I hadn't gone to any of Randy and Sue's Halloween open houses. They went door to door inviting one and all to come trick-or-treat and party. They carved three dozen jack-o'-lanterns, flights of jack-o'-lanterns that lit every step of their cement stairway, which is that pyramid next to the flagpole. Last year, vandals knocked, kicked, threw the pumpkinheads into the street, where cars ran over them. I hoped that Sue and Randy and their kids had been planning to set up the Halloween House next week. Los Días de los Muertos. Ching Ming in October. The wind that came with me out of the Valley and over the hills and Mount Diablo was the east wind, the Diablos.

I answered the bicyclist, "I was working on a book. It's lost." How strange, the book was the loss bearable to say. "I lost my book," I said to a stranger, just met. He tapped me on the forehead and said, "You're alive, and it's up here." I decided to take this touch of a human finger to be a blessing upon me, and his words to be testimony. I can trust a bearded man with silver hair like mine, a veteran of my own age and times, to tell it as it is. But he wasn't right on. It's not up here in my head; I feel Idea at center, heart, stomach. And it is all around and underfoot.

The other man, who had been walking his bicycle alongside me, asked, "Do you want a ride on my bike? May I give you a ride?" I reached for the Coke cup attached to a handlebar. He said that the water was dirty, and proffered me a wet facecloth, and again a ride. I covered and wiped my face, wanted to suck on the cloth but did not. I got up sidesaddle on the crossbar; we did not wobble and topple like kids pump-riding. The bike turned heavily back toward the way we had come, and I rode face forward, carried through hot wind, coasting downhill above the Bay and the white city at its edge, like a mirage. I was above the devastation. So—these streets were named Golden Gate and Ocean View because there was a time, and now again, when you could see the bridges, the islands, the ocean, Mount Tamalpais. I felt high up in the sky. It was full of birds and helicopters hauling bags of water, like storks bringing babies.

The bicycle ran over power lines. The tires rolled over them without a sizzle. We did not get electrocuted. The rubber tires were good enough insulation. The power was off; the firefighters couldn't get water up here because the electronic pumps were burned dead. Transformers had blown up. I felt safe, going back over territory I'd already explored. And nothing left to burn. I looked for but did not find Olde English "A"s painted on the street. Two World Series in a row—it's a tradition— neighbors painted green-and-yellow "A"s in the middle of the road and on garage doors.

Moving easily past my neighbors' property, I thought about dead bodies; I looked at the ashes for shapes of bodies. The ashes were flat, and the chimneys and black trees stood bare. I heard the ground crackling and simmering. Twenty-two people were murdered days ago in Killeen, Texas, and twenty-five people would be killed in this fire. My mind was already working out the numbers, and the morality of fire vis-à-vis massacre. Even if the number of people killed is about the same, our fire is not as bad, not tragic, because not evil; fire is morally neutral, an accident, a storm of nature. But what about that poor soul who shot twenty-two people in Luby's Cafeteria? Could he help it that a firestorm raged through his brain?

I got another look at Mrs. Fessler's Karmann Ghia, and saw her chimney from basement on up; the wide firebox was held by a narrow column of bricks above and below it. The floors are gone. The grove of Monterey pines and redwoods is gone. Mr. Fessler died some months ago; he did not have to see this. Vera Fessler was born about eighty years ago in Turkistan, raised in China, and educated at Berkeley. She and her husband, chemist and oenologist, also at Berkeley, used to take walks many times a day. The quality of life is high where elders can walk as they like, and bid everyone Good morning, Good afternoon, and Good evening. Mrs. Fessler wore her ancestral jewelry, which featured words, Chinese pictographs and Finnish runes, wrought in jade, gold, and seashells. She flew the black-eagle flag of the Romanovs. Her floor had fleur-de-lis tiles in honor of her French ancestors. My neighbor on the other, Ocean View side, Eva Varga, was also a "vidow"; she came from Austria or Switzerland, and was often calling my attention to my trees branching over and dropping needles down her chimney. Next to the old couple lived a young couple, whose baby girls were born here—twins! The first time they came trick-or-treating, they saw me—long white hair, Chinese face and skin, black dress—and gaped, eyes and mouths wide open. One twin asked, "Are you a real one?" The other twin, speechless, handed me her bag of candy. She was propitiating me, a witch. I answered, "Yes, I am a real one." Halloween is for the children to go out and meet strangers. "A good one," I added, "I am a good one," and gave these identical baby chicks lots of candy and smiles. We were integrated in a way that I've not seen in other places: rich people and not-so-rich people lived side by side. Big houses were hodgepodged with little houses, a villa next to a cottage, a mansion next to a bungalow. Some of us were owners, and some were renters. We did have a go-around once with a petition to zone out renters, but few people signed it. Now I am passing the empty site of a house where many African American adolescents lived and visited. Another Black family, also with many relatives and friends, lived on the other side of the big eucalyptus tree; their house was famous for its Julia Morgan roof, yellow tiles arranged like snake scales, like sea sand. Counting me, we were at least one person-of-color per block. Not bad for Rockridge, which had once had a law: "No person of African or of Japanese, Chinese, or any Mongolian descent will ever be allowed to purchase, own, or even rent a lot in Rockridge or live in any house that may be built there except in the capacity of domestic servants of the occupant thereof."

With my back to the bicyclist, I did cry. I was proud that no other loss but the community made me cry.

I saw again the house that was a flame inside a flame. The house was prey, wholly swallowed by an orange translucent python.

Now that I'm on the move, the bicycle moving, the wind and the scene moving, is Idea still here? I'd forgotten to keep noticing Idea. Yes, it's here, I can feel it, a solidity at the center. But would it exist if I were killed? What if "Idea" were just my life, me feeling my life? (Be extra careful of my life.) Can ideas really exist as cloudsouls, hovering, waiting to be breathed in? I'm the only one who knows about and works on the Book of Peace. Its idea depends on me—small, slow, forgetful. Things gone, Idea remains. Old Father Williams said, "No ideas but in things." I'm saying, "No things but in ideas." The bicycle wheels went round and round, birds were circling, and my thoughts were going around. "No things but in ideas." "No ideas but in things." Things—red wheelbarrows, white chickens, rainwater—all gone, Idea remains. Ideas *cause* things. I am alive because of Idea. A book exists before its words. Remember. An actuality surrounds and permeates words and things, and exists in their absence.

Needing instruction—a law of poetry—on how to bring into being word and world, one of my hands let go of the handlebar, and reached for my *Collected Williams*, which had been on the right side of the middle shelf of poetry books. I keep making that reaching gesture toward books that aren't there anymore. Another of my post-fire symptoms is that I can't read.

Very high up, in the good air, birds that seemed entirely black or blackened were wheeling in tight circles and wide circles, clockwise and counterclockwise. The birds were of various sizes and species. Turkey buzzard, hawk, crow, pigeon. The straight-flying birds, goose, mallard, are behaving weirdly, whirling. Aristophanes' Whirl. *Whirl is king.* What happened to the birds at Lake Temescal—the great blue heron that stood hunch-shouldered on low branches, the red-faced goose-duck, Big

Red, who lived under the willow tree, the cormorants and the wood-duck coots? I pictured mass fire sloshing up and down the basin, and the lake boiling.

We rode through a black-and-white *Guernica* of trees—black skeletons, negatives of trees, caught in poses of agony, killed and reaching for air. Unable to run, they clawed upward, begging, praying. They died in fear. The fire had filled all this space; it had covered the trees. It was now racing wherever the sirens were screaming.

I passed again the little house that changes hands. A side had burned off of it. From my perch, I saw through the balusters on top of the retaining wall that the houses on the hill had not burned. I waved to the lone fireman with the truck. I said, "Thank you. Goodbye." He said, "Good luck. Take care."

Here I come—Samantabhadra, bodhisattva of contemplated action, charging on her flying elephant, bicycling out of the smoke—out of dreams and thoughts into action. Right action is effortless. See? No pedaling. You get help. Samantabhadra crosses the wide boundary from imagination to deeds.

I was returned to College Avenue and my red car. I appreciated the unburned city, its hard planes and solids, the straight lines, the bright logos that label and advertise each thing so there's no mistaking what it is and what it's for. The loud artificial colors excited happiness in me. I shook hands with the man who had given me the bike ride. He was Ed Murphy, an employee of the city of Oakland; he had red hair, and his bicycle was red with whitewall tires. Baskets, clips and clamps, and brackets were attached to the bike both back and front, accessories of his own invention.

I drove to friends' houses. Nobody home. I drove back and forth across Berkeley, North Side, South Side, and told myself the L.A. joke: You can always live in your car; you can't drive a house. I had a bag of funeral food in the back seat. I sat waiting on friends' doorsteps; nobody came. Two men with beards offered me their studio: "Come inside. Make yourself at home. Use the telephone." They left, trusting me with their place and valuables. The TV was on loud; the fire in cool red-orange miniature was on every channel except one, which was broadcasting a football game. The on-off power button was nowhere to be found, nor any wire from TV to wall plug. I muted the volume.

I called my mother. I couldn't call my husband; I didn't have Earll's current number memorized. He was in Virginia doing Chekhov, play-ing Sorin in *The Seagull.* Typical: he's playing; I'm working. I shouldn't be calling MaMa with bad news; but upon hearing her say, "What's wrong?" I blurted out, "MaMa, my house burned away. My house is all gone. I'm all right." She reacted the same as when I woke her and told her BaBa had passed on. (I heard a man's voice announce in my sleep, "Your father has passed on," just before Carmen phoned and said, "BaBa has died.") MaMa had sat bolt upright, held body, hands, face tight, big eyes wide, and said, "I am so glad. I am glad." All is as she wills it. "He is a lucky, lucky man. He suffered for only two and a half days and nights. He didn't suffer. He was entirely healthy. His every drop of spit was clean. There was nothing wrong with him. He walked to Jene Wah and played pai gwut, and walked home. He played very well; everyone said so. Then he went unconscious. No use my accompanying him to the hospital." She hadn't seen him for his last two and a half days. He was already gone; he wasn't himself. "He did not die of an illness. He died of age. He died of time." She talked on and on, leaving me no room to say how I felt. "I am glad." O well-gone. Now she said, "I'm so very glad he didn't live to worry about you in the fire."

"The entire house, MaMa, and everything in it. Burned away. All gone. My writing too. My book that took years of work." People through-out the building must be hearing me yell Chinese. I yelled into the phone and her ear; her sight and hearing were fading. She's going deaf because she really doesn't care to hear me, or anyone. She likes to talk, not listen, even to music or Books on Tape. "Oakland and Berkeley are on fire, thousands of houses, cities, burning right now, MaMa, and the firemen can't stop it. People have been killed." Chinese don't say "burn *up*" or "burn *down*"; the idioms for "die" have to do with "up" and "down."

"I'm glad. I'm glad," she kept saying. "I'm so glad it wasn't you. The house doesn't matter. Things don't matter. Don't *hun* things." *Hun* is the very sound and word for pain at loss. "Hunger" must come from that same groan from the guts.

"I almost got there in time, MaMa. I tried to save everything. The books. My book. The jewelry, your jade bracelet, the one with the brown flecks." Like the age spots on her hands. "And the three jade bracelets Joseph brought from China." They cost pennies, but my son, her grandson, had bought them. "And the gold necklaces."

"Don't *hun* things."

"And BaBa's coins, and his eyeglasses, and his watch. And the jade heart." Jade pendants pacify the breathing, and jade bracelets calm and protect the pulse.

"Why were you keeping so much jewelry in the house? Money belongs in the bank, and the jewelry in the bank room."

The money was BaBa's loose change. "Any day now, I was going to roll it up, change it to paper, and bring the money to you." There had been $300 in quarters, nickels, dimes, and Susan B. Anthonys. My father-in-law also had Susan B. Anthonys strewn and cached throughout the house and car. I hope toward the end I won't go crazy over money. Oh, I see: the Chinese for "buck" is *mun*, ten bucks, ten *mun*, as in "money." Must be.

I can't say numbers to my mother. No matter what the price, she yells at me, "Too much." No matter where I go, "Too far." I've been tricking her for years with small maps and globes. "See, MaMa? It's very near, less than one inch from Stockton."

I confessed, "Remember the pure true gold ring that Grandfather won at the Gold Rush?"

"You lost it."

"I had a plan, MaMa. My plan was: first, run for my work, run into the front room, save my book, then run upstairs for your jewelry. I couldn't accomplish any part of the plan. I took too long reaching the house, and it was all burned when I got to it. I drove and ran as fast as I could. But. It was too late." I said "but" in English. Chinese does not have such a strong adversative, or it's rude to use one.

"Your BaBa saved you!" she yelled. "He kept you busy and safe here. If not for him, his funeral, keeping you home in Stockton, you—I know you—you would have been in a cloud of reading or a cloud of writing. The house burns, the city burns, you wouldn't notice. Sirens go off, you don't hear, you don't wake up. Smoke and gas fill the air, you don't smell it."

"I was going to run inside the house."

"*Wey!* It might have fallen on you. And exploded. Your BaBa saved your life."

Now, that's the right way of seeing my father, not the father-god of the Americas who hunts his children and burns things with his anger, but BaBa, who used his funeral to save my life.

"Ah!" my mother continued. "I see why your sisters and brothers sat quiet, not having conversations, not doing anything, sitting and sitting into the afternoon. They were worrying over you. I asked, 'Why aren't you talking? What's the matter with you? Everybody gone quiet. If you don't have anything more to say, leave. Don't stay in this terrible, barbarian, wild neighborhood. What are you waiting for?' They said they were waiting for Cindy. I saw her hurry out. She went to look for you, didn't she? They were trying to trick me. George's family went home, came back. Norman's wife left, visited her sister, came back. Joe came home off work, quiet. He knew about your fire. And his wife had driven off fast to catch you." My youngest brother Joe works communications at the Stockton Police Department, the same work that he did in Viet Nam, dispatching cop cars like deploying ships, planes, and helicopters. "They just now left, family by family. The little kids were also too quiet. It's not like them, and it's not like your brothers and sisters to be together and not talking."

My brothers and sisters and I started conversations nearly half a century ago, and are continuing them. When each one was born—another one of us!—we urged language out of him or her as soon as possible, to tell memories about the life and world before this one. So much to ask and say about this world too, we talk all at once, loudly giving one another our ongoing takes and views. In English, we discuss Mom and Pop, and protect one another. At parties, we get back in our huddle of siblings, leaving out everybody else, husbands, wives, parents, children, and friends. One of our children, Cher, said, "You're not just happy to see one another, you're really, really happy." Six like minds. All sane.

"They were sad from walking the mountain today," I said. "They were thinking of BaBa."

"No, they were thinking of you."

I liked very much hearing that my noisy family stilled in imagination of me. All along, I'd been held in their minds. It must have been terrible for them, having lost their father, and possibly now me, eldest sister.

"Where are you?" my mother asked. "Come home."

Simultaneously, I was saying, "So—they've all left. Are you alone, MaMa?"

"Of course, I'm alone. Who wants to be with me? Old dying woman. Who would stay with me forever? Nobody."

She's been going out into the garden and yelling at the sky, scolding BaBa for leaving her. She has called herself an old dying woman my whole life; she was in her forties when I started hearing her fears for me, then for each of us—that we would be orphans. You two orphan girls, no one will adopt and raise you. Three orphans. Four orphans. Five orphans. Six orphans. I can't get used to it; she still scares me every time she says that she's going to die. And it will happen, she will die. I cannot bear for her to die. Mothers ought to be immortal. "I want to go be with your father. I'll be with your father in two, three months at the most. No longer than that."

"Don't die, MaMa. We can't bear to hold another funeral right now. It's a lot of trouble. Live a long time. Live to a hundred, MaMa. I want to be an old lady with a mother."

"Huh!"

"Who's staying with you tonight?" I asked. "Someone will be there before dark." As our last task at home this morning, we filled in the calendar for the rest of October and November until Thanksgiving with turns staying overnight with Mom. To make up for living farthest away—eighty-five miles—and for staying in Hawai'i for seventeen years, I signed up for the most nights. I took the dates that were inconvenient for everybody else. She had told us that a new widow can't gad about to people's houses and the shops and markets and the Chinese Multicultural Senior Center for a month, maybe forever. The reason why is that the cronies would get upset if she were to bring death, ghosts, widow-fate, trailing after her into their homes and businesses.

I said, "Do you have something to do until somebody comes back?"

"I'm going out in the garden and yelling at your father for abandoning me. 'Why are you in such a hurry?!' We were the Jade Girl and the Cowboy. He always called me Jade Girl. To the many people who know us, I was Jade Girl and he was Cowboy. Jade Girl and Cowboy are eternally together, she before him, he behind her, crossing the River of Heaven. She always crosses the sky ahead of him; I took their order of going as an omen, that I would die first. Oh, will he get a scolding. 'Cowboy! What's your hurry, Cowboy?!' "

I pictured my mother standing in the space open clear to the sky amongst the leafless tangerine, pomegranate, and pear trees. She will look up at one cloudsoul and call, "Cowboy!" She will call him by his other Chinese names too; I've never heard her call him by his American name, which is Tom. Another of his names is Maxine's Father, not

Carmen's Ba or George's Ba but Maxine's Ba. "Take me with you. You have no heart, leaving me all alone. Wait for me! How can you leave me?!" She'll do the talking, and he won't reply, as always.

She continued, "Months ago, he was already plotting his leavetaking of me. He told me his plan: 'You go back to China. Americans don't cherish old people. You take the money and go back to China, where you can buy slave girls to take care of you.' Your father wanted to send me back to China."

I felt agony, that his life in America hadn't taken. He'd been here since his teens, and he died regressing to a weird fantasy of China. What happened to his knowledge of history and current events? And he forgot us, his children—that we could take care of him and MaMa. He was not perfectly well before dying. He lost facts, lost money, erased us. "MaMa, he was saying impossible things. That wasn't a plan. He was not all right, talking like that."

"All the more to yell at him about. To teach him, your grandmother had to beat him even when he was a grown man married to me."

"What was she teaching him?"

"Not to smoke opium, *la*. Your grandmother hit hard. She was two hundred pounds. She had to do all the beating herself. Your father never saw his father."

Oh, no. She's changing the father stories, and it's too late to ask him.

"How is it that my father and my grandfather didn't meet?"

"By the time your father got to Cuba, your grandfather left for California. They missed each other. You think life is so easy. Your father was caught twice by Immigration in New York, and put in jail, and deported back to Cuba. He stowed away, and was caught, and stowed away again, and was caught again, and by the time he settled in New York, your grandfather was at the other side of America and leaving for China. He got home, holding his Western-style shoes to his chest; your grandmother gave *him* a beating. He didn't make any money; he made more debts."

So—BaBa had had to make up from scratch how to be a father; he had never had one.

"Did they write each other letters?"

"They wrote each other poems! Ah Goong laughed and cried, reading your father's poem. He said, 'Listen to this. Listen to this:

My ship has sailed into port.
I have come to land —
Beautiful Country.'

"The third time your BaBa landed in New York — safe — he saw a newspaper headline: 'Lindbergh Lands in Paris.' Your happy father yelled to Lindbergh, 'So — we both did it!' Whenever I suffered, I'd read his poems, and go to sleep with the book open on my chest. He wrote six tomes of poetry — all lost."

"How did they get lost?"

"BaBa's nephew Juan coveted the book box. He dumped the poems, and took the box. Your father wrote to me to send him the six books, and I had to tell him that his mother burned them."

"Oh." My father had six books burn, unpublished.

"MaMa, you wait until somebody gets there before you go out in the yard." I was picturing a drive-by shooter shooting through the cyclone fence. Or throwing his coat or hinged boards over the barbed wire, climbing over it, and beating her up.

"I'm not afraid of dying. I don't overly love life too much. I'm not afraid of poison-sellers. When a brother or sister, somebody, gets here, I'll say, 'Take me to Maxine!' " She tries to scare away the drug dealers by openly watching them and banging doors. She knows their cars and bicycles. She once knelt at the fence and spoke into the ear of a man who had been clubbed almost to death. She said, "You okay?" He was robbed of $2,000.

My mother yelled at me, and I yelled at her. "Take care!" "You take care!" My mnemonic for "take care" sounds like "darling." Dok lai. "You're all by yourself?!" "You can't stay all by yourself." "What about you? Come home. Sleep at home tonight." "It's getting dark." "The sun will be down soon." "Get back in before dark." "Where are you? Where will you sleep? Sleep at home tonight."

I lied that I was going to sleep at — already was at — a woman friend's house. It crossed my mind to sleep on the burn site. I had napped under the oak at the cemetery across from the hospital where my father was dying.

"Is she a good person? You aren't in the den and lair of a bad person, are you? Do you know her?"

"You know her," I said, "surname Chin, la."

"*Sing* Chin, *mo.* Tell her I thank her for taking care of you."

My mother does not understand my life. I am not taken care of. It is I who have to take care of everybody else. Earll, as Sorin, will stay in Virginia for the run of *The Seagull.* The show must go on. I'll hold a grudge against him for neglecting me, nonetheless. (Virginia was burning too, forest fires in two parts of the state. And a fire backstage that sent the asbestos curtain slamming down in the middle of Sorin's scene with Arkadina.)

"I take care of myself, MaMa."

"I will sew and hem and crochet everything anew for you. I'll make placemats and runners again. I'll embroider and appliqué pillowcases. And you need curtains and quilts. And I'll knit you some more hats and slippers. And I'll needlepoint the heirloom again." She had made six reproductions of the piece of canopy that she had woven and embroidered for her bed in China. Each of us children had been given a unique, elaborate version of Dragon and Phoenix, who are a married couple. Across the top, in the sky: "Good Morning" as if the heavenly pair spoke English. My father used to tease her, "You could write English that long ago." We heard often how she'd pulled this cloth off the bed frame and run from the attacking Japanese. Hiding under a pile of oranges, she rode a boat through the Pearl River Delta. A Chinese soldier pointed a gun at her and ordered, "Don't move. Stop eating." Other people shook with fear, and even men cried. But she kept on eating. "Nobody tells me not to eat. Shoot if you're going to shoot." She told us, "I didn't love life then; I didn't have children. Don't love life too much." Twice, she ran inside grand hotels to escape mobs, including policemen and soldiers, trying to steal her money. They'd spied her stash when she paid bribes and paid for tickets. She paid again and again to get on the USS *President Taft.* And arrived in America, bearing our heirloom. My replica of it had a poem by BaBa, who signed himself "Idle Old Man" or "Old Man with Time." My mother wrote-sewed her name too: "Made at her leisure by Chew Ying Lan." Brave Orchid.

"Don't *hun* the Dragon and Phoenix. I will sew it again. And *you* have hands. You can make anything. You can make all of it again, better than before."

She was referring to my book. What an odd idea, that books come from the hands. Then and there, my hands began to hurt. Carmen's and

George's and Joe's arms hurt. Nights when the pain in my hands keeps me awake and it's too late to be working, I hold my hands and arms as if cradling a baby, and am relieved. I said goodbye, interrupting my mother. I could hear her voice saying in English, "Lucky. Lucky," as I set down the receiver. (I'd called long-distance from the strange borrowed studio, and forgotten to pay.) I'd said I was at Bessie's house, so I went there. Awake and asleep, I saw red flames behind and through my eyelids.

First thing in the morning, Monday, I took two friends with me into the burn. I wanted to see for myself that my book was actually completely burned. There might be remains; at the center of the thick stack of paper, pages might be readable. Bessie Chin, my friend since the first week of freshman year at Cal, and John Crow, who assists me with paperwork for free, dropped everything to help. Bessie took off from her job as librarian at Redwood High. Earll phoned me at Bessie's; he said, "I can't believe that you tried to get through the fire." He doesn't know me. We'd been married for twenty-eight years. If I'd asked, or told him to, he would've left the play and come home.

We could not go the way I'd gone yesterday. The roadblocks now were more widespread, and stricter. The police and volunteer police, who wore yellow shirts and hats with yellow insignia printed up overnight, shut every through-street on College Avenue. The gates in the long wall of the College of Arts and Crafts were locked. The boundary was hardening. Without discussing it, my friends and I— veterans of demonstrations—stepped away from the bottlenecking crowds, walked around the police, who were busy answering questions, and entered the fire zone. The fire was continuing, no news of containment. We are in urban wildland. This is both an urban fire and a forest fire, according to the news: "Forest fire within the city limits." "Urban-wildland mix." "The fire of the future."

Trying to outflank the barricades, which had been set up here and there within the fire area, we climbed higher and higher northeast into unburned forest. We enjoyed being inside a family of redwood trees, and shared lore about them: "They don't burn." "They live in the path of the fog." "Giant creatures living on fog." Redwoods drink the fog through hairy bark and evergreen leaves like little hands with many, many fingers.

Buddhas have infinite hands, raying everywhere, forever. "In past incarnations, we were trees." "Are redwoods the trees that need thousand-degree fires to crack open the seeds for regrowth?" "They have shallow roots, and stagger." "They live in families; they hold one another up with interlacing roots." Californians love exchanging knowledge about redwoods. Another meaning of the fire is that it returns the city to wilderness.

We trespassed across backyards, whose friendly owners helped us down off of fences, out of flower beds and tomatoes, and gave us directions to reach unpoliced lanes, paths, and steps.

Approaching from the south, we came to the burned hill in back of my house site. Over there was my backyard, and there's the eucalyptus tree, hub of five streets. We ducked down against the hillslope. Police cars and television trucks encircled the tree—Command Headquarters, Fire Central.

A military chopper buzzed us. A loud voice overhead commanded, "It is illegal and dangerous to remain in this area. Leave the fire zone immediately. Repeat. Leave at once." Noise, wind, orders. I have an instinct to disobey. I don't take orders. Bessie hunkered down under a bush. Its leaves were burned off; you could see her through the branches. She looked like a Viet Cong. She had put her red backpack under another see-through bush a ways off. Decoy.

When the helicopter gave up and flew off, we stood and walked over the hill. Stepping out into the open, we went by sidewalk to approach my gone house from the front—up the flagstone walkway and in where the front door had been. We did not go through where the walls used to be.

There was more to my house than I had seen yesterday. The stone archway for the front door remained; it stood upright, and its dusty-rose color had not much changed. On top of the lintel sat the bathtub, nakedly up in the air for all to see. We stood under the arch, under the bathtub, and looked down at the footprint of the house. It looked like the low ruins of pueblos and heiaus. From the brick-and-stone threshold, I stepped down inside the foundation, a pit of ashes. My feet were touching down beneath where the floor had been, down in the crawl space. I walked inside the footprint, and thought out which room had been where, which top-story room had fallen on which bottom-story room. The upstairs ashes were a middle layer, and the roof ashes the top layer. There was an obvious pathway to a wall that made a corner. It had an opening in it that had been a window. This was the northwest part of the house. *Leina-a-ka-'uhane.* Place where spirits leap into the netherworld. Jumping-off place. Bessie went that way, and I followed her; you get drawn to the solid. We were in the dining room. I suggested that we dig near the window for my jewelry, which had been in a nightstand upstairs. I felt protected by the corner wall. I delayed knowing about my book, and having to tell about it. No sooner did I imagine my jade heart than it appeared, green and gold on a cushion of ashes. I held it flat between my palms, wanting to heal it against my skin. It was hurt; green veins had grayed, and there was a black burn in its setting, the very middle of the gold flower. I willed life force—the pain in my hands, pent-up chi energy—from out of my hands into the jade. When Mother gave each of us our jade, she told us about the symbiosis between true jade and human flesh. "Wear it on your chest. It breathes with you, and beats with your heart. You're healthy, it grows greener. You breathe easier. It lightens your heart, and it becomes more beautiful and green." Jade for a peaceful heart. Jade, a sign of being Chinese. You see someone wearing jade, you know he or she is Chinese. My jade heart has returned to me; I have to pacify the world.

On the pads of my fingers, I picked up and rubbed a dust, like pollen, like mola, with which Indians blessed the noses of deer. It was the ashes of the thick gold chain for my jade heart. I thought gold was an element that could not be transmuted, created, or destroyed. So Chinese gold, which is double the karats in regular gold, is an alloy. That heavy chain had become a puff of pure gold; a bee could carry it. *Gum hay*, gold jewelry, gold air. Not wanting to go to the trouble of saving specks of dust, I mixed them broadly amongst the warm ashes. Too bad. I'd anticipated Bessie and me having the fun of uncovering nuggets.

Throughout the day, out of the camouflaging ashes, emerged jade bracelets. One had turned black, two were shades of brown and gray, and there was half a circle of white that looked like a tusk. I could tell by the size of each piece which had been which. The jades were of various qualities; the fire burned at extremely different temperatures from one spot to another. I put the whole circles, warm, on my wrists. I shall wear them—fire jewelry. We also found an inch of gold links, some garnet beads, and a chunk of rose quartz that had been in the backyard. Its lavender and pink lights had gone out. The garnet beads were enmeshed in a web of gray metal.

I seemed to be inside my recurring dream about chasing after jewels and money. I reach for trails of gems and coins, which keep moving, proliferating, and vanishing ahead of me. They change as I touch them and pocket them, and change again when I try to count them. Dream questions: Should I steal this treasure? Who owns these antique pendants and olden chains of double eagles? Finders keepers? My psychotherapist, Rhoda Feinberg, says that the dream jewels are my values. That explains why traditional Chinese jewelry doesn't feel right on me. New-age plastics and metals are affordable and mine. I need to make my own jewelry, or buy it, not merely inherit or find it.

I thought about the diggers who tried to find the gold tablets that Joseph Smith claimed to have read, then witnessed sink back into the American ground. They dug up a feather and other proof at the very depths Smith predicted they would be found. The gold tablets, however, sank downward just ahead of the shovels.

Looking over at Bessie digging amongst the ashes, I thought: *Woman in the Dunes*. We will live in the ashes forever. I tried jabbing quickly into them, to catch up with my valuables. Fire flared alive. We were stoking it. The ground itself was burning and breathing. The soles of my boots heated up, and burned my feet. Hotfoot. I walked about on cooler, undug ash, and stood teetering on the cracked foundation. I didn't say "Hotfoot" to Bessie and John; it felt shameful to joke. John's feet were bleeding; he was wearing zoris and no socks. His feet and the blood looked very clean, as if he'd been cut rather than burned. "Never mind," he said. Bessie's nose was bleeding red-black blood. We are inhaling burned insulation, which is spun glass. I have walked upon live volcanoes, and gone down inside vents where green ferns quiver with cooling dew. Volcanoes are not this dry and dead.

"I found your book," said John. "Your book's over here." He had been looking for it while I was fading away with the jewels in the corner. I stepped up and over broken foundation, and down into the space that had been the sunken living room. It was all right to step on nails pointing upward; they crumbled underfoot. The alcove, where I'd last been writing my Book of Peace, was yet an alcove; it was outlined by the fieldstone-and-brick chimney and a piece of stucco wall that had folded over. I'd just had this corner renovated, with a complex-paned window and window seat, bookshelves, and cabinets. (The original rain-gutters had been mistakenly tilted so that rainwater ran into the walls and dry-rotted them.) This reading nook was the northeast corner of the house. A blowup of Gauguin's two beautiful women coming out of the jungle bringing red and pink fruit or flowers had entirely covered the wall lit by morning sun. John lifted the other, windowed, folded-over wall about a foot. I got on my hands and knees, and looked inside the tent. There was a black block of pages. I put my arms around it, and slid it out. The print was an intense black against the black paper, like carbon paper, and legible. But this isn't the Book of Peace. It is the page proofs of my old book *Tripmaster Monkey*. On the title page, in the colophon, Monkey's black eyeballs stared out of his black mask. I lifted a page. It flaked into pieces. The next page was also readable, as long as I didn't move it or touch it. Inside this block of ashes, flakier than puff pastry, are all the words of an entire book, but you can only read them once. I took up a handful of the block, and put the chunk of it inside my ceramic jack-o'-lantern, which was round and smiley as ever, though the glaze was now crackled. It had been sitting on the patio table, the top of which was made from a cable spool. The table had burned from the bottom; its legs burned shorter and shorter, and lowered the pumpkin, unbroken, down to the soft ashes. This must have been how ashes of a book could land unscattered.

I then found for myself, and laid eyes on and touched, the ashes of my Book of Peace. The unroofed sun shone extra brightly on a book-shaped pile of white ash in the middle of the alcove. I had been working at the table with the hand-stenciled flowers; the pages had been to the right of the computer. The ashes of my Book of Peace were purely white, paper and words gone entirely white. The temperature here in the middle of the alcove had been hotter than by the wall. I held in my hands the edges of pages, like silvery vanes of feathers, like white eyelashes. Each vane fanned out into infinitely tinier vanes. Paper had returned to woodgrain. I touched the lines, and they smeared into powder. I placed my palm on this ghost of my book, and my hand sank through it. Feathers floated into the air, became air, airy nothing.

Of course, I had put my Book of Peace into more than one form. Some of it had been in the garret computer, and some in the downstairs computer. But you had to be an expert to guess which mangled piece of machinery was a computer, which the television set, the small TV, the radio, the nonworking Victrola, the other radio, the tape deck, the lawnmower motor. You couldn't tell by location either, because explosions had blown things to odd places. I handwrote the Ur-draft of my Book of Peace in red-trimmed black ledgers that I'd bought in China and Canada. They had utterly disappeared, like the thin china, some of the tines of some of the forks, coins, most of the walls, and other things I can't remember.

I touched the ashes again and again. I led expeditions—brothers and one sister, sisters-in-law, nephews, nieces and niece's boyfriend, brother's neighbors, friends, friends' sons with trucks and gas masks, and, at last, my husband—and talked story to them about the fire, how it swooshed down those hills and whipped up that street there, then skimmed that street over there, how I found fire jewelry in the ashes.

Two of my brothers, Norman and George, chorused in song and dance, like a football fight-song. "Flames to the left; flames to the right." They made me feel, We are funny and special. Father dies; look to brothers, though younger than me, to be fatherly. When Earll got home, I drove with him to the burn so he could see what had become of his home and belongings. He was not interested in digging; he took my word for it that it was impossible to find anything more. He says that he is not attached to material things and money. Which is what I liked about him in the first place. He kept some pieces of house—marble from the hearth and some twists of glass. He misses the photographs of his parents and grandparents, all gone.

George also took melted glass, and phoned for me to save him some more. He liked the interesting forms and colors. I hadn't wanted glass until George did; then I collected glass. I got hoardy, didn't want to give him the best pieces, though he's the one who knew to see them as beautiful. He took the biggest blue-green-violet chunk. I have no idea what it had been originally. He keeps it in his office. (George and Putsy have on their mantel a teacup blackened and chipped from the Earthquake and Fire of 1906, saved by Earll's grandmother.)

Each time I returned, I hoarded more things: The fireplace grate that hadn't changed whatsoever. The spike, now crooked, for gambling tickets at Bing Kee and laundry tickets at New Port Laundry. The string-holder, once heavy black steel, for dispensing a cone of red string; I'd looked forward to having blessing strings for everybody for the rest of our lives. (My father snapped string apart with a quick move of his fingers, a trick I never mastered.) Two dollars' worth of coins stuck together. (It's okay, MaMa, to let on that I kept money and jewels in the house; my readers do not steal, burgle, or rob.) Pieces of terra-cotta, the warrior statues I'd brought from Xi'an. They looked like the original warriors during exhumation—a head, a hand, a torso emerging out of the earth. The face of my mother's statue of Kuan Yin, clean and shining white, as if broken in an earthquake and not a fire. Monkey with his paint burned off. The Santa Clara wedding vase, the lizard's foot almost detached from it, the mica dimmed. Knives with handles missing, handles with blades missing. Forks with every other tine missing. So, a tine-width apart, the fire had been different. Spoons bent as if by telekinesis. Shards of the cheap Chinatown dishes. The thin fine china had evaporated. Fire-marked outdoor rocks. Whole flowerpots. More pink-veined black marble from the fireplace. A faded Christmas-decoration dog that Carmen had given me. (I got so excited, I dropped it on the cement floor of the vanished garage. I kept the pieces.) A metal box for cough lozenges that now looked like a tiny undersea treasure chest. Miniature swords from an ancient battle—yet-usable letter-openers. Rusted and encrusted health balls that still tinkled and chimed. Drawer pulls. Lids of bottles embedded in glass. A crucifix with the Jesus burned off. A scythe with no handle but a lovely curve. Ashes of various textures. Beads and shells that turned into powder when I looked at them later, continuing to crumble away. A heavy piece of steely metal that I pulled out of the hot earth, smooth and silver-bright upon discovery. Being lifted into the air, it iridesced, shivered with rainbows—waves shimmering up and down, and out, as if soul and life were passing through and leaving. I am left holding a dull, broken piece of metal.

I quit collecting stuff when I realized that I could end up carrying all of it, the entire contents of the lot, all of the ashes, even the burned dirt, to Bessie's garage and basement. I cried when deciding not to take the stump of the crab-apple tree. I left a grove of Monterey-pine trunks. I didn't dig for the tulip bulbs I had planted; either they cooked in the ground, or will come up in the spring.

But I kept a yellow plastic nozzle that didn't belong to me. It makes me happy to look at it. A stranger, a Good Samaritan, had tried to save my house. My hose hadn't had a nozzle, and he or she had brought and attached one, sprayed my house, and fled. Who was this neighbor? The uninsured Korean American neighbor whom Norman knows from the Rad Lab tells about being mesmerized watching my house catch fire; he did not see his own house go up behind him. Eva Varga, the "vidow" next door, says about someone, "I told him to vater *my* house, and he vatered *your* house."

A few days after the fire—on my birthday—not able to read or write—I went to a conference on "Dream" in Salado, Texas. I could've canceled appointments, and people would have understood. But there's a stability about keeping my calendar and commitments. Besides, I had interesting dreams to report: I am digging up a crashed airplane. The dog's legs are burned black and red. The people have disappeared, all turned to ashes. I'm hoping that they were taken by Martians or New Age Venusians to other times and places. The voice of the man who narrates my dreams says, "Intimation—intimus guts." I follow a path to a region where there live beautiful black-haired, curly-haired animals, gorillas, buffaloes, and some large thing, immense, hooved; it does not step on me. My mother is making—*gwoahing—joong*, Chinese tamales, but there is a net over her hands/hooves. (My mother will die soon; she will bounce back into the electrical grid out of which all beings sprang.) I say, "It's okay, MaMa. I can gwoah the joong." She envelops me with her eyes, and turns—she is an enormous cow or elephant—and goes toward the door that leads outside. I am being left with deep love. A black wildcat, like a hot, growling, hissing furnace, lives in dark forest and in a broken cage and inside of me. I am filled with power. Black Elk empowers me. Through dream, I access—know about and thereby have—deep life.

The conference began with movies. We have the technology to film and show others our dreams. We watched three of Kurosawa's *Dreams.* In luscious light, when it rains and suns at once, a boy accidentally comes upon the fox spirits' wedding. For this sighting, his mother locks him out of the house. In a nightmare about war, soldiers with German shepherds march forever in and out of a tunnel. Not knowing that he has been killed, one soldier runs away from the platoon of ghosts, then at last joins them. In daylight again, a boy sees fairies in a terraced peach orchard. The emperor and empress sit at the top, and row after row of sparkling nobles sit beneath them. Peach blossoms rain down, and a rainbow halos over all the scene. The scene was like an altar of dolls that Japanese girls set out on Girls' Day.

Harry Wilmer, the director of the Salado Institute for the Humanities, brought from Europe a videotape he'd made of a woman who studied with Carl Jung. She is not called an analysand but a student, and students become teachers. The magisterial ninety-year-old woman,

Baroness Vera von der Heydt, narrated a dream she had many years ago. Jung helped her understand it, and it guides her and gives her strength. Fish in a tank on her left jump out and dive into the tank on her right. Gifts are coming from the subconscious to her conscious self. Jung had a dream at the age of three that he remembered and worked on into his eighties. It fueled him all his life. (God sat on the church and shat. His turd fell through the roof.) My recurring dream from smallkidtime is that bombers and missiles fill the sky, steadily moving, like words on a page; I can prevent the bombing by finding the Three Lost Books of Peace. Three Books of Peace came into existence, it's said, when Chinese civilization began, and were somehow lost. We must find them. We need them. Now.

In dream, we arrive at Einstein's time/place. Free of chronological order, everything happens at once. Awake, trying to record dreams, we have to unscramble the superimpositions and juxtapositions and enjambments. Start anywhere. Harry said that since dreams are mostly visual, we can get at them by drawing them rather than by writing them. Divide the paper into three parts: "Dreams have three acts." Harry sat at an easel, and beside him stood the dreamer, a woman at the podium before the plenary audience. She told us her dream while he illustrated it with Magic Markers. She is standing on a pier, looking out to sea, and sees a fisherman in a boat. With the sun shining brightly, the fisherman catches on his line a whale of a fish. The fish swings through the air and lands in her arms. With the triptych beside her, she answered questions and listened to ideas from the scholars of dreams. "No," she said against certain interpretations. She spoke confidently about her dream, what each thing is and means. Her voice was full of authority—it comes to her as she communicates the dream. At Harry's invitation to respond to her, I said, "You are lucky and strong. Good work. You've had a wonderful, wonderful dream." I complimented her on being able to dream it. I was sure she had the same feeling I did when I saw my animals. The fish in the sun is id energy, life force, health, chi power, which coursed through her.

Steven Weinberg, "Big Bang cosmologist," "working cosmologist," and a Nobel Prize–winner in physics—we bravely included a practitioner of the hard sciences—challenged the methodology of dream studies. He said, "If you dream people were on to something, I'd drop my work right now and go for it, join you. But your methods are not scientific. There is absolutely no evidence of a connection between dreams and physical reality." He went on to explain unified field theory. Here's my understanding of what he said: Physicists are working on a theory that will account for the cosmic and the minute facts of the universe. The "pi meson field," which causes energy inside the nucleus of the atom, is a particle in cosmic rays. There is laboratory evidence that it exists. The pi meson is not the ultimate finite unit; it is composed of quarks and antiquarks. Know the interrelations between and amongst the infinitely large and the infinitely small, and you will have an idea of the whole shebang. Unified field theory will answer these questions: Is the universe infinitely old? Was there a first moment? What happened before the Big Bang? Are there universes? Is ours but one Big Bang universe in one bubble, while other big bangs and total universes occur in other bubbles? When the unified field theory—the theory of everything—is accomplished, there will be no more physics. I think: So explosions (and implosions) billions of times bigger than a nuclear-bomb blast happen all the time. We blow up the earth, it's natural.

A psychologist from France stood up and said, in tears, "I beg of you, please, sir, Dr. Weinberg, open your mind. Our evidence is necessarily anecdotal. We must accept the anecdotal as scientific. There is so much at stake—the psyche of the individual. Dream is the portal to the soul. Do not close the door."

I didn't join in the argument, not having ready words or confidence to say: The unified field theory seems to me to be a theory about theory. Science deems repeatability to be good evidence and sound method. But a dream happens once, witnessed by one. The universe is also only one. *Universe—one turn.* The Big Bang happened once upon a time. You, Dr. Weinberg, will find what you set out to find—the theory that will describe everything, all. You have the pre-vision that there can be— has to be—such a thing in reality as the unified field theory. Unified field theory is your dream, and you will make it come true.

The team of sleep doctors from Stanford didn't participate in our agonizing over methodology. They had a concrete answer—technology. They'd invented and were selling a machine that induces lucid dreaming. Nine hundred dollars. For me, $700. This light on a timer flashes into one's dream via this sleep mask, and cues the dreamer to be conscious while asleep. You can direct and manipulate your dreams. Their examples of lucid dreams had to do with monster chases and sex fantasies. People need a machine to have sex fantasies! So they can enter the dream further. Better to go out amongst real people and try to find an actual lover and beloved. I know a way to have a flying dream for free: leave the windows open, and crosswinds will blow on you. Your body will feel as if you're flying through the air, and your mind will travel to high places.

Behind my hotel, The Inn on the Creek, there was a sweet-sounding stream. I could get to it from my patio. I borrowed a bathing suit from Harry Wilmer's wife; I didn't care about fit. Walking barefoot on green grass banks, I found water that didn't have catfish. Six or eight enormous ones were resting in the shadows and root caves of a waterside tree. Sharp black horns poked from their heads. I got into the water. Let this unknown river take me where it will, like Loren Eiseley in *The Immense Journey*, when he became one with the watery planet and time: "I was water." "Common water." I floated on my back, heading slowly downstream toward the Salado Creek Bridge. Cars and pedestrians were traveling back and forth through the town overhead. Water rushed sounds into my ears and thoughts. The sky held many individual clouds, floating with me. I hadn't noticed clouds for a long time—five years of drought. American Indians say, "Clouds are our ancestors." Of course, that is scientifically correct; my father had become minerals, essence, elements. Father in clouds; Father in moon. I felt looked after by my father, by many ancestors in the sky. My father followed me here, and was watching over me. BaBa came with me to Texas! He is soft and light and calm now. I said, "Perfect." Joy so surprised me, I stood up in the stream and spoke out loud: "It is perfect, and I am happy."

On the patio, through the glass doors, I heard the phone ringing. My friend the Quaker poet Phyllis Hoge Thompson called me to say, "If a woman is going to write a Book of Peace, it's given her to know devastation." Oh, say that again. "If a woman is going to write a Book of Peace, it's given her to know devastation." I've got to hang up and write that down. Goodbye, Phyllis. She just gave me the first line to the Fifth Book of Peace. (I've lost the Fourth; this will have to be the Fifth.) And the fire's aftermath also gave me the method of how to write it—with others, in community. I went outside and sat at my little patio table, where the notebook from Africa that Bessie gave me lay open, and wrote the sentence down.

I was the last speaker of the conference. It was the evening of my birthday. (Thich Nhat Hanh calls "birthday" "continuation day": "We aren't born, we don't die.") The title of my lecture was: "You Tell Me Your Dreams and I Will Tell You Mine." I told dream experts gathered from all over the world that it was my birthday, and that I had lost my book. They had to help me find it.

I told them how John Cronin, one of my former students, English major, kind of a dream specialist, and graduate of a six-week course in hypnotherapy—you see his ad on milk cartons—flew up from his house trailer on the Pacific Palisades in Malibu and hypnotized me. He had a plan to retrieve the burned book. "You picture the computer screen scrolling up your book. You read it off the terminal into a tape recorder, and we transcribe it. Voilà." His plan scared me. What if I got stuck in that word-for-word version? I suggested that we go on a journey and see what we would see. John said, "The hypnotist and the person hypnotized both go into trance."

So, in that dream, we walk side by side on a path I choose in the forest. I keep lofting up through the green canopy for an overview, to see how far we are from the ocean. I see it—the Pacific—within flying distance. Blue with high waves, whales singing and sounding and spouting, porpoises leaping. John says to get back down on the path and walk where it would take us. We walk a ways and come to a stream. "Collect some of its water," says my ally. There on the green grass banks—a ray of sun sparks it—is a glass vial in the shape of a heart; its stopper is also a glass heart. I lean over and dip the heart into the clear river.

A spotted owl is sitting in a redwood tree. "Bring them along," says John, "and let's go home." I collect: the water-filled glass heart, the spotted owl, and the redwood tree for the owl to live in, and walk for "home." It is my house whole, as before the fire. We go to the alcove where the Book of Peace was, and I plant the redwood—perpendicular to the ceiling beam. "And the spotted owl stands guard," says John. I unstopper the vial of river water, and wet my computer and papers and bookshelves and books, the walls and ceiling, the table and chairs, and Redwood and Owl. A cornucopia of water and light fountain out of the bottle, and wet the room and everything in it. A crowd of people come to be with me. They are people from my lost book. I pour water over them. The queenly Hawaiian woman whom I called Tūtū in my book says, "When you have questions you need to ask, and talkstory you want to hear, come back to us. We'll answer you."

I gave John a piece of fire glass that he called a glass bird.

I asked the audience of Dreamers to help me write. Please send me anything you find about lost Books of Peace, cities of refuge, tactics for stopping war.

My fellow Dreamers stood and sang "Happy Birthday" to me. They asked after my mother, Brave Orchid. I told them that when I met my aunt in Singapore (which is near the home of the Senoi, a tribe of people who live according to their dreams) she asked me, "How is your mother, and what is she dreaming?" I was able to answer her, and so connected two women who had not seen each other for fifty years and would never meet again.

I told the conferees an important dream—maybe we can call it a vision—which my mother had after my father died. Living alone, MaMa got locked out of the house. This part isn't a dream. She actually got locked out, and spent the cold night out in the yard. She covered herself with the dog's blanket. She didn't fall asleep all night. Suddenly, many beautiful children, boys, surrounded her. She was so happy, she could hardly bear it. She drew crosses on the boys' heads, and also on herself, her chest. Frogs/toads jumped and sat and played. Flowers bloomed on the front porch, which was like a temple or an altar. People, all kinds of people, were around the tables of food. They ate, using forks. She asked for chopsticks, but the food was not real to her. Then a beautiful lady appeared; Kuan Yin walked along the porch, placing flowers on the stairs and railings. All was clean and shining and full of colors. MaMa took off the dog blanket and knelt in praise until sunrise. Then she slept in the sun.

The Dreamers—I told them I'd lost my home and things—showered me with gifts: flowers, a yellow and a white "Friends of Jung" polo shirt, two pairs of shoes that fit just right, purses, an amulet from Alaska, boxes of clothes a daughter had outgrown. A married couple gave me a Japanese doll dressed in a bright-red-and-white kimono; she looked as if she came out of Kurosawa's dream. Harry gave me a philosophers' stone, a piece of pyrite, fool's gold, stuck to "an ordinary rock" from the Jungfrau in Switzerland. "Combined, they represent the transformative power of changing lead into gold, not ordinary gold but the pure gold of spirit." Everybody promised to mail me dreams for the book-to-be.

PAPER

Supposedly, a long time ago in China, there existed Books of Peace. They were Three *Lost* Books of Peace, lost in deliberate fires. Ch'in Shih Huang, who built the Great Wall, a military achievement, burned books. Book-burnings go on to this day and age—the Cultural Revolution, the destruction of six thousand temples in Tibet—six thousand libraries. At kingdoms' rise and fall, the new king would cut out the historians' tongues. Writers had to set fire to their own books, and be burned to death in the book fire. Historians whose tongue stumps were cauterized lived on. They made dumb gestures that could not express subtle, complex ideas, such as descriptions of the way the world has never been but might be. One legendary historian who had eidetic memory wandered through battlefields of killed and wounded people. His agony never ceased, because it was inexpressible.

A thousand years ago, on the Silk Road in Western China, the mayor of Dunhuang ordered books burned to keep them out of the hands of the invading Xiaxian tribe. Heroic readers saved twenty horseloads of books. Recently, in the Dunhuang caves were found twenty-five manuscripts of music for pi-pa lute and the little barbarian reed pipe. And I have heard that it is possible that a Lost Book of Peace was among the books taken away on horseback. A Book of Peace existed, then, until the eleventh century, in the Sung period. Diana T. Wu, professor in the business school at St. Mary's College in Moraga, pooled these facts at a dinner party. A miracle—at the end of this millennium in capitalist America, a conversation turned to locating the Chinese Books of Peace. I am not the only one who knows of them.

Tibetan refugees had a choice whether to carry food or to carry books. Some of those who carried books died. Some of those who carried food also died. A lama in Berkeley started the Dharma Publishing Company, which is finding and reproducing destroyed Buddhist texts. Some of the books are strips of unbound paper in red boxes. Every year, more books are presented to readers at the Ceremony of Peace in Dharamsala.

Everybody I met who was traveling to China—tourists, students and teachers on exchange programs, people on business—I asked to do me the favor of looking for the Three Lost Books of Peace. They would keep their eyes and ears open, and be able to see China better. One of my students said, "The story of our generation is that we're always on the move. We travel to every state and country, and do not commit to any one place, to Aristotelian unities of time and place. The setting of our novels will be everywhere." Not one of the other students contradicted her. Having things to find for me should help root them. Listen for any whisper of Three Lost Books of Peace—a line, a reference, allusions, words such as "peace," "pacific," *ping, wo, wo ping, ping ho, ho ping. Ho* is pronounced with the sound of an exhalation of breath. Listen to talk-story all the way through. And should you hear what might be a quote, a phrase, a stanza from the Three Lost Books of Peace, take note of it and the circumstances of your discovering it. Was it in a classroom, in a work camp, in the city, the countryside, at a private gathering of family and friends, a public assembly, in a viable temple, in the north, the south, Beijing, Tibet, Taiwan? And who said the line? What was his or her character, and relationship to you and others? Then we will know how the book lives. That it lived through the Cultural Revolution and the Tiananmen Square massacre.

Counting Taiwan and Hong Kong, I have been to China seven times, and have seen for myself "turtle books" and writing on bones. Turtles brought writing out of the sea; the Chinese said you could read the patterns on their shells for words. At the Forest of Steles, I walked amongst thirty or forty gigantic stone turtles, as big as Volkswagens, carrying monoliths on their backs. The indestructible steles were carved with poems and laws—the hexagrams of the I Ching!—which were inked, and used to make printed scrolls that were distributed throughout the land. Some of the turtles stood on pedestals adorned with ocean waves. One turtle seemed to be a bench, but it was a book; the stone tablet slid out of its carapace.

I asked Wang Tao, called Xiao Wang, Little Wang, our translator twice in China, whom I remet in Great Britain after the Tiananmen Square massacre, "Xiao Wang, have you ever heard of Three Lost Books of Peace?"

He exclaimed, "Oracle bones!" Working on his Ph.D., he found five hundred oracle bones in the basement of the British Museum. "The bones have 'war' and 'peace' cut into them, and the paint in the grooves is still bright." The Chinese read "war" and "peace" in the colors of clouds and in bones, which are clouds solidified. Little Wang and I conjectured: Had the ancients thrown the bones like dice, to make decisions, to divine? When a bone came up Peace, what efforts did they make toward peace? When it came up War, did they attack peremptorily, or did they take time to think and plan? Had words—"marks"—been a transformative force that moved Heaven and Earth, caused war, caused peace? At temples nowadays, people throw shells, cups, and sticks over and over again until they come up with the fortune they want. Little Wang said in delight, "On some bones, they wrote, 'It did happen!' "

Writing on bones, turtle shells, pottery, sticks, and jade began at the start of history, the Shang dynasty, also called the Yin dynasty. Shang pottery was black; Santa Clara pottery is black. Shang and Santa Clara have been named Black Pottery Cultures. The first king of the first period was Hong, the same Hong as our name, as we Americans from the village of a thousand Hongs pronounce and spell it. Hong had an epithet—Hong the Completer. The Peace hexagram is number 11 of the I Ching, which also began during Shang. There isn't a War hexagram. I did not get the Peace hexagram on a throw of coins. I had to turn the pages to it. Hexagram 11—Peace—T'ai—is beautifully balanced, three firm, bright masculine lines on the bottom, three dark, feminine lines resting on them.

The I Ching, itself a wise person dressed in a yellow book cover—he had sat on top of my tallest bookcase, higher than my head—advises the good person to "divide" chaos to make harmony. In the book of the I Ching, the image for the interconnectedness of all beings and things is ribbon grass. "When ribbon grass is pulled up, the sod comes with it." "In times of prosperity every able man called to fill an office draws like-minded people along with him, just as in pulling up ribbon grass one always pulls up a bunch of it, because the stalks are connected by their roots."

When I was in Taiwan asking after the Three Lost Books of Peace, scholars, historians, translators, even poets told me that they were *not* lost. They nicely tried not to condescend to me, an unread person of the West. The mother of a poet said, "You are connected by karma to China." She and the translator spoke that very same word—"karma." She was claiming Chinese Americans as infinite kin of the Chinese. The same causes caused us. We are not lost in America. The Taiwanese gave me lists of books. "See? Peace books. Not lost." "And there are more than three. Here's a long list off the top of my head." I heard: The Book of Songs. The Book of History. The Book of Rites. The Spring and Autumn Annals. Confucius. Lao Tzu. Mo Tzu. Mencius on social utopias: "The king and people would hunt on the same land." The Duke of Chou, who gathered the I Ching, perhaps *was* the I Ching. "Now banned on the mainland." Sun Yat Sen's Three Principles. Tao Yuanming. Wolfgang Bauer. Chuang Tzu, Yang Chu, Shang Yang, Li Ssu, Ch'u Yuan. Ch'u Yuan is Ch'u P'ing, the peace martyr in whose honor we make joong and race dragon boats; he lived over two thousand years ago, during the Warring States period.

When I mentioned Books of Peace to Shu-mei Schorr of UCLA, she said, "Oh, Sky Books. You must mean Sky Books. T'ien Shu." Sky Literature. She explained that there came a time when the sacred object that made a king was not a shield or a belt glowing in a well, but a book. The reader-king applied the ideas he read, and he and his people became united with the way of all things, the Tao. Such miraculous books were canonized as "Sky Books." A Hundred Flowers bloomed. (Mao Tse Tung did not invent that metaphor for free speech. He was harking back to the Zhou period, 1122–221 B.C.) And the Chinese are seeing the coming of books-from-the-sky again, now.

To this day, in Chinatowns everywhere in the world, there are statues of Gwan Goong, god of war and literature. Usually he's astride his red horse, but often he's reading a book. Finally knowing to ask, What book is that?, I found out that Gwan Goong is reading Sun Tzu's *The Art of War*. Gwan Goong is studying his sometime enemy. *The Art of War* lives and is popular now—new English-language editions come out all the time. It's used in military academies and business schools for training soldiers and capitalists. I glanced through the latest edition— chapters on how to set fires, how to burn down a city, directions on the use of fire as a weapon, outflanking and trapping armies with fire.

Scholars argue that *The Art of War* is about preventing war: How *not* to have war. How to win without fighting. Sun Tzu's highest value was peace; he advised going to war only when all other ploys failed.

If *The Art of War* is such a good book, why isn't it called *The Art of Peace?*

My own *Woman Warrior* is being used as a text at the United States Air Force Academy in Colorado Springs. "It gives a mythos to the women military students," says their instructor James Aubrey. I have to make up for that. The roots of "warrior" are in "quarrel," "error," "worse." I've been pretending all this time that it means "one who wars against confusion."

Another time that the Books of Peace may have appeared and disappeared was the wonder-filled T'ang period, A.D. 618–907. The Chinese explored and contacted the rest of the world. T'ang Ao found thirty fabulous lands. Tripitaka T'ang brought the *Heart Sutra* from India; it is a chant about emptiness (peace?), and started Buddhism in China. Empress Wu sent ships on rivers and oceans out from the Center, the Middle Kingdom, loaded with art and calligraphy—books—to show to faraway people. The ships were sailing museums and libraries that exhibited and disseminated wonders; they were not trading ships, and they were not battleships. They were not ships for collecting. Things from these ships have been found in Arabia, Turkey, Tibet, Korea, Manchuria, Thailand, and the Americas.

T'ang Ao was gone for so long that his daughter, Little Jug, incarnation of Fairy of a Hundred Flowers, went in search of him. She searched twenty-nine fabulous lands—island paradises, mountain paradises, cave paradises. In each place, she heard that he had come and gone. She found him, a captive in the Land of Women, rescued him, and brought him home. Together, they wrote about the societies—communes, utopias, hermitages—whence they learned solutions to human wars. For example, in their collection: Those in the Land of Sexless People do not reproduce or die. Another country practices no discrimination between species; man and animal are equal. There is a race of people whose feelings show in clouds; they value revealing their innermost feelings. There's a market where customers haggle to pay the highest price, to give profit to the other person. They'd say, "These oranges are so lovely, you're charging too little for them."

And in the Land of Highest Peace, it's against the law to sell food to hungry people. Food is always set out, and foreigners, the homeless, eat free of charge. Just think: it's wrong to sell food. Feed the stranger. *I* walk into restaurants, dine, sign my name, and leave, fed and satisfied. Everyone should be able to do that. We shouldn't be keeping points, who gets to eat and who doesn't. Organize the civilization so that whenever you're hungry, you see a place at a table, you pull up a chair, and eat as at home. I would dearly love for a witness or even a storyteller to come forth and relate that at a lunch-counter sit-in in Louisiana or Mississippi — it must have happened once — a restaurateur cooked a wonderful meal for a sitter, and generously served it to him or her.

One of the people from whom I sought Books of Peace told me definitely, "China has no utopian literature." But he had gone through the Cultural Revolution, been "re-educated," diseducated.

I got to the San Wei (Three Flavors) bookstore in Beijing, founded by an idealistic couple, Madame Liu Wan Sheung and Lee Shi King or Giang, who met in labor camp. Throughout their imprisonment, they dreamed of someday opening a bookstore. "We can begin civilization again." On street level, readers browsed at open stacks, and sat at small tables arranged for privacy. You didn't have to buy a book; you could read it here, your own living room and club. A bust of Lu Xun was centered in the middle of the store. Upstairs, on the second floor, was a tearoom with tables along lacy balustrades. You can assemble with a few or many friends. People with opposing politics come here; they can't label the bookstore as being of any one faction. San Wei was closed after the Tiananmen Square massacre, and the bookshop owners' daughter taken in for questioning; it opened again. It closed one other time, for earthquake repairs. San Wei gave me a reading party. Chinese readers know me as Tong Ting Ting. Many people came. I was an occasion for them to assemble. My translators amingle in the exciting crowd, I couldn't converse with smiling, nodding Madame Liu; she held my hands; she held me in her arms. My audience talked to one another while I was reading to them. The ones who understood English conversed during the translation; the Chinese-speakers spoke during my English. Madame Liu said, beaming upon the happy, loquacious party of readers and writers, "They're glad to see one another. They can't meet very often." It was safe for them to come to my reading; an American can say anything. And the din confounded any bugs.

I queried the tearoomful of people about the Three Lost Books of

Peace. I asked carefully, not to show up anybody's poor scholarship, not to make them admit in front of colleagues that there's a classic they didn't know. A few tough souls said outright, "I have never heard or read of them." "There are no references in Chinese literature to Three Lost Books of Peace."

Two learned men—Wang Meng and Mr. Yang—conscientiously questioned me about the Three Lost Books of Peace. "Where did you first hear of them?" I tried to remember. I've known about them always. They must have been in my mother's talkstory—in her war stories—but then I would hear "Three Lost Books of Peace" in her voice, in Chinese. They were not mentioned in or among my father's books bound and re-bound with laundry-wrapping paper. I would be picturing them, my father's finger pointing to the words "Three Lost Books of Peace" and knowing they were on this page or that page, recto or verso.

Mr. Yang, great translator of *Red Chamber Dream*, asked, "Which word are you translating as 'peace'? There are many words for 'peace,' many ways of saying 'peace.' " He is a tall old wiseman with bright-white hair. Wang Meng, the ex–minister of culture (he was deposed after Tiananmen), has jet-black hair. The hair of musicians and poets, people who have galvanizing thoughts, halos all around their heads.

"Of course," I said. To show that I was not entirely illiterate, I said some words for "peace": *ping, p'ing, ho ping, an* (as in *tiananmen*), *t'ai ping*. No, it can't be T'ai Ping, which is the name of a war—two wars, one in the second century A.D. and one in the nineteenth century A.D. Wars for peace.

"K'ang," a listener added. K'ang Yu Wei (1858–1927) advocated a "little peace" ("*xiao ping*"). Land should be organized into grids, a hundred minutes of longitude and a hundred minutes of latitude per community. Networks of ten thousand "fields" would progressively coalesce into a world state. Armed forces would be internationalized, and war and warlike sports directed so that adversaries would injure one another and take prisoners but not kill. K'ang made lists of borders and boundaries, and suggested closing the distances between species, between men and women, between the healthy and the sick, between the rich and the poor. He distinguished thirty-eight kinds of suffering in six main categories. He made up a new money system, and reorganized time, and predicted that the Era of Great Equality would begin in 1900. "Philosophers who understand music and language" would create a world language. It would have elements of Chinese, which is "easiest," only one sound per meaning. The vowels would be French and Italian, which have the most beautiful, clearest sounds. Sing Italian. There would be a Ministry of Utmost Happiness. K'ang wrote about the life and ideas of Abraham Lincoln.

Ping. P'ing. Peng. Ping shu. Ping see. We said "peace" and "Peace Books" in various ways. I tried to hear the okina, the glottal stop, and to make it. In my Say Yup dialect, *peng* means "level," "even," "inexpensive." Yes, same in Mandarin, "equal," "ordinary." "Great equality is the means to highest peace." "King and ordinary people hunt deer on the same level land." "San Ping Shu," I said, picking up how to say "three" in their Northern dialect from the name of the bookstore, San Wei.

"I also remember 'Three Lost Books of Peace' in English," I said. "Maybe I heard it from an English-speaker or read it in a book written in English." Lin Yutang? Pearl S. Buck? Arthur Waley? And it wasn't "Peace Books" but "Books of Peace." There was the pomp of that preposition between two mighty nouns. (I never told the Chinese that the narrator of my dreams speaks English.)

Wang Meng gave his voluminous smile, and tapped himself on the head. My father used to do that, and the man at the fire had tapped my head. "You yourself imagined Books of Peace. And since you made them up, you are free to write whatever you like. You write them yourself."

Oh.

I asked Wang Meng, who's about my age, how he accomplishes so much. After banishment, he republished twenty books, and wrote and published more. How to make up for lost time? He held out three fingers, counting, thumb holding down each finger, the way my father counted, the way Chinese do. He was making a series of mudras. "Drink Chinese tea. Stay happy. Don't work for the government." Everybody laughed.

I have been mandated by the ex–cultural minister of China to write Books of Peace. I made it up, I write it. And he said I was "free." I first heard Wang Meng say "Freedom!" a decade ago. He opened the conference of Chinese and American writers with one word: "Freedom!"

People laugh and smile when they discuss my lost books—riddles, Taoist jokes. "If they are findable, they are not the lost books." Asian people can laugh at loss, like the Thai passengers who laughed when our Garuda plane was indubitably about to crash in a hurricane. Landing was aborted three times. The trickster pilot was able to pull up again and again and again, and landed the plane on his fourth try.

I met a Berkeley Taiwanese poet in Hong Kong, Wang Ching-hsin, name-in-poetry Yang Mu (and probably another name when he was a rock star). He had an idea about numbers. "There could be five Books of Peace. Seven Books of Peace. 'Three Books of Peace' does not mean exactly three Books of Peace. Three is a symbolic number. It just means there were a lot, more than one." And on the reformed Chinese language, he said, "Taiwan and Hong Kong use the old characters, and are ninety percent literate. Actually, Taiwan is 100 percent literate. But China, using the new simplified system, is only fifty percent literate. Yet Singapore is going for the new system."

I said, "Too many 'x's and 'q's and 'z's." My father was relearning writing Chinese until he died.

Yang Mu chided Americans also for not revering words. "There's no superstition in America. The *San Francisco Chronicle* made up a word—'Baysball'—to write about the World Series. Big banner headline—'Baysball.' And just at the top of the very first inning, the earthquake started." He chortled his badboy chortle. "Your earthquake was because of Baysball." He's so Chinese, such a poet. Words have sacred power; mess with words, you start an earthquake.

So—I have asked the Old World to teach me. I met three cultural ministers, and wondered why we don't have a Cabinet-level position like that here. I learned: it is my responsibility to pull the Book of Peace out of nothing. I'd been hoping to get a jump start, but not a quote, line, or word of it did the Chinese have.

At Hong Kong University of Science and Technology, I held office hours for students to ask and tell me things. The campus buildings are those stacks of giant Lego blocks beside Clearwater Bay. To soften some lines, chicken feathers edge the risers of an outdoor stairway—a cascade of chicken feathers over Legos. One old building remained to be demolished; the evicted tenants left a graffito in English: NOT HAPPY. The first student to visit me was a young woman who said "peace" in words I hadn't heard before: "*Tai ping ching.*" "I asked an old scholar for bone knowledge, and he told me, '*Tai Ping Ching*'"—*The Classic of Highest Peace.*

The Classic of Highest Peace, a second-century Taoist text. Chang Tzu/Chueh, "the good doctor of great wisdom," healed people using "water and words." Strange: Searching for books has led me to bones, water, clouds, choreography. Taoists walked in patterns on and around pyramids. "People approaching one another will let their arms hang by their sides, and put them together only in greeting." Joy is the means to peace. "Joy prevails even among worms and flies." "Help a ruler to go about joyfully all his days, and he will not suffer harm. No one will suffer harm. Greatest, brightest joy and highest peace prevail among all beings." The joyful ruler, though peacefully sleeping, yet preserves order, spreads joy, brings highest peace. Chang and his students had dialogues like Socrates and his students. "Have you stupid fellows understood, or not?" "We have." "Giving one thousand gold pieces to the state is less valuable than a single important word."

Peace begins in thought. Thoughts enworded go from mind to mind, and mind makes the world. Peace, illusive, abstract, negative Yin, dream, would take a long writing-out to make real. Its book has to be longer than war books—longer than a bumper sticker, longer than a sound bite. As we read, neuropeptides in the brain grow longer, longer than in nonreaders. Thought becomes body. Sudden fast change is a method of war. The logic of peace has to be spoken out at length.

Another cultural minister, not Wang Meng, replying to our gentle hints about Tibet, said, "Buddhists are peaceful. Too peaceful." Was he signaling that the Tibetans ought to rise up and defend themselves? That peacefulness invites aggression? That peace is a bore?

I need to confess another manuscript—one more set of papers—a scroll—burned in the fire. My mother's writing. I had stolen it from my mother. It was sitting next to my photocopying machine. I had just finished making a copy, and intended to return it to her at the red ceremony but forgot. I had taken it from the false bottom underneath the cupboard in the pantry. A few days after my father died, I led my brothers and sisters in rifling and emptying all his secret hiding places that we could find. One was above and another below the basement windows. The keys are nails that lift out; the two-by-fours of the window frame unlock and slide apart like a Rubik puzzle. Behind the sill were toilet-paper tubes filled with silver dollars. There's a proverb that begins, "If a daughter steals her father's writing . . ." I can't remember the outcome of this conditional phrase. The jade pendants under the cupboard were gone, given away to us and granddaughters and daughters-in-law. (It surprises me to see hip American kids—"cool Asians," as my niece Karen Hong, née Karen Newkirk, names her generation—atavistically wear jade, and tattoo themselves with calligraphy.) Nothing in that cache anymore but paper. A scroll about the size and shape of half a roll of toilet paper. The cheat sheet for Immigration. Fake paper village of MaMa's fake paper husband. (Our fake name is the same as our real name.) Sneaking this paper in and out of hiding, she studied it while seasick on the USS *President Taft*. She came through Angel Island, not Ellis Island; she has corrected that story since my father's dying. I smelled the scroll, and imagined my mother rolling and unrolling it, memorizing it for interrogation. In her strong handwriting and drawing were layouts of a village and houses of that village, and names and dates of relatives and neighbors. Overlooking the village was a mountain, labeled in the simple characters for Peace Mountain or Peace Hill. I once got to the village; I saw a hill of that shape. It does exist.

Immigration scroll in hand, I found MaMa sitting by herself. I sat in my father's chair beside her. "MaMa, look what I found in BaBa's secret hiding place. These papers are important. Let's give them to the library in Berkeley, which will treasure them."

"That's mine!" My mother snatched the scroll out of my hand. She huddled with it, her knees up to her chest, protecting her papers in the cage of her body. Squinty-eyed, canny, wily old crone. And I was her enemy. "You've hurt us enough. You ruin us. You can't have this too. They hate you. You must know, they hate you. Oh, how they hate you."

Who? Who hates me? Why?

"The Han people, the T'ang people hate you for writing books. You endanger them. You tell immigration secrets, and ruin families. They have bad lives, it's your fault. They hate you. They won't talk to you anymore. They're never telling you anything. You tell on them. You point them out."

So they read me, they hate me. They think I hate them, and snitch on them. I cause the suffering that I write about. I make money off of Chinese people's hard lives. I sell them out. I exploit them. The capture of the *Golden Venture*, the jailing and deportation of boat people—my fault. I shouldn't be writing. They will give me no more stories. Stop writing.

My mother was speaking on behalf of the Chinese people, "we."

"We want you to leave us alone. You've done enough harm to us." All over Asia, people confidently say "we." Each naturally speaks for all the rest of the nation family. Americans say "I." I can speak for no one but myself, my opinion, my point of view.

"Stop your writing and Immigration will stop hunting us. You've wrecked the immigration routes to get to America. Oh, you have done your harm."

I tried to defend myself. "I only wrote about the outdated immigration. Everybody already knew those secrets; they aren't secret. I told the old tricks that aren't useful anymore. There's no Immigration at Angel Island anymore. Coming into the country has different ways now—through airports. I don't know the present-day tricks and maps, so can't very well give them away, can I?"

She didn't hear me. She was crouching in her chair, holding the paper to her, like holding one of the babies that had died. Husband gone. Here for fifty years, and she did not feel safe or belonging in America. I had to leave her unbearable presence. I got out of her way, walked out of the dining room through the kitchen to the back porch, where I paced in air. So people talk about me, and it's gotten back to my mother. They say that I betray them. I meant to honor them, and keep their history, but I hurt them. They'd rather I write PR, do them some good, not bad-luck tragedy. I'm sure the people who hate me haven't read me. They are nonreaders.

When I came back, my mother had hidden the scroll. "MaMa, those papers are important to history. Donate them to a museum. Give them to the Angel Island Historical Society; they're restoring Island, and you can help. Bessie's donated her mother's papers, just like yours, even thicker, to the library at Berkeley. BaBa's commentaries on my books are there. You can safekeep your papers with BaBa's." My father had responded to my writings; poetry returned to him as he answered me.

"No. No. You will have us deported. Deported."

"They're not going to deport you. They're not going to deport us. You're safe here. Your stay in America does not depend on that paper."

I could not put sureness into my voice. Norman had just been worrying about getting security clearance to do some architectural work at the Rad Lab, now named Lawrence Livermore Laboratory. (Norman is a resident of Livermore, and head of the Livermore Beautification Committee.) He had been top-secret Q security in the air force during

Viet Nam, yet was having to decide, should he forgo the job or expose our parents to one more security check? Corrinne, a lawyer, says that they would never deport the parents of six excellent Americans. But she's the youngest, maybe overconfident.

"You don't understand. You don't understand anything," she said, and I said, "*You* don't understand."

When I returned to Stockton for the next funeral ceremony for my father, MaMa told me she had burned the scroll. "The paper is gone. I burned it. We don't need that paper. Everything is okay now." She had cleared up the trouble. All is safe from me. "I burned the paper."

I didn't believe her. She was lying. I know her, she can't do things neatly. Pots boil over and food burns. Both stoves on fire. Food on fire. I used to think all mothers cooked thrillingly like that; I cooked like that. Hot oil and hot water flying onto walls and floor and ceiling. I looked for and did not find a mess of ashes about, no black smears anywhere, no charred spot on floor or ground, no signs or smell of recent burning in the oven or buckets or sinks. I rummaged the house, and easily found the scroll amidst the clutter in the upper right-hand drawer of her dressing table. I'm very good at finding her hiding places. She is a messy person; she thinks she can camouflage mess amongst mess. I burrowed down through a few layers of stuff, and there was the scroll. I put it in my pocket and took it.

I stole it, and brought it to my garret, where I kept my new photocopier. I would duplicate the scroll and return it to her. As I copied it in sections, matching up torn parts, I recognized some words—the word "generation" again and again. "Elder brother" and "little brother." Many brothers. Maps of streets, paths, lanes, and the detailed layout of one of the houses, the Great Door, the back door, numbered steps, numbered windows. I thought, I'll take my time translating the paragraphs of narrative, written in her hand, later. She'd labeled a parabola "Peace Mountain" or "Peace Hill." When she saw the photographs I took of such a mountain or hill, she said, "That mountain still there?! So they didn't dig it up and remove it after all. They were always making plans to level it." The Great Doors, with thresholds raised as on a ship, were small, and to me the streets were alleys.

In our genealogy book—the real lineage, not the fake info for Immigration—are maps of cemeteries with mounds and circles where the paternal ancestors are buried. My father's book shows what Chinese people are interested in; my mother's scroll shows what American Immigration is interested in. There are twenty-seven known generations of Hongs; the book is the size of a ream of typing paper. The last time I asked my mother for the Hong genealogy book, she handed me a thin booklet. She'd deleted "all the bad people," keeping the teachers and poets, and recent generations, relatives she knew personally.

Immigration scroll and genealogy book—gone.

Now, the nights I stay with her, she helps me remake my lost book. She tells me what to write and what not to write. "Your father told you not to harm anyone in your writing. Don't tell our Benefactor's name, or anything that would hurt his reputation. Don't tell about the gambling house." Too late. To set the record straight, our Benefactor was not my father's boss; they were partners. "Your father made half the profits at Bing Kee." Which means my father was co-owner of the gambling house where he worked, not just bookkeeper.

She tells me about another woman warrior, "better than Fa Mook Lan," a strange and sexy story, which she breaks off when one of my brothers enters the room. "Men shouldn't hear such wet, salty stuff." Ming Hong, which translates into Bright Sugar, not the same Hong as our name, disguises herself as a man, and wins first, second, and third places in the imperial exams and archery contests. As a doctor, she cures the king. The king's daughter throws the red ball at Ming Hong, who catches it and has to marry her. Already married to a man, she marries a woman. Her enemy discovers her feminine shoe, and takes it to the king. Her father-in-law, who's been having yearnings for her/him, takes the mighty archer, doctor, scribe in a carriage to a whorehouse, and exposes him/her. Meanwhile, Ming Hong's husband, away at war, lives through many adventures. He comes home. "This was the best play I ever saw," my mother says. "I liked it so much, I bought the book and memorized it. Strange, isn't it? I was only twelve years old, and I still remember the entire opera." We get a tape recorder, and my mother chants in full voice for an hour straight. In a climactic aria, Ming Hong counsels the king on how to be a good ruler.

MaMa also tells me her real ancestry, not the fake genealogy on the scroll. My mother is a descendant of the last Sung-dynasty emperor, Sung Chew. Chew Brave Orchid is twenty-two generations after Sung Chew the Artist-Emperor. She's not making this up, it is documented: My father wrote it in her funeral eulogy. He wrote on the back of one of

Norman's blueprints, which he hid whenever she came near. "He was writing a speech about me for himself to deliver. He expected me to die before him." I asked her to write the word Sung; it is the great historic civilization, all right, the age of calligraphy, the time of the highest quality of life ever anywhere on earth, the air and every resource for human nourishment better than now. The Gobi Desert was smaller, and the Great Wall went through healthy forest—not windy desert, as at the sections of wall I've seen.

But my mother only tells about the fall of Sung. Refugees fled south by boat and on foot. They came from beautiful Hangchow, the capital, to Gwong Moon, then to Nguy Moon. To Gwo Loo, to Soo Kai with many mountains. The enemy trapped them at a river. "The wind knocks down the ships," she says. The Sung women jumped into the river and drowned, and the men jumped too, rather than be killed by the conquering army. My mother visited that river and saw three temples made of wood in remembrance of Sung Chew. She also saw lions with globes that were almost falling but didn't fall from their mouths. And a general on horseback with swords. A theater. A stone.

An edict went out to kill the Chew princes. A woman named Lum saved two of the boys by claiming them as her sons. She said to the soldiers, "This is Tai Lum and Xiao Lum." Big Lum and Little Lum. In gratitude, we are to venerate and give gifts forever to the Lums. "You carry their shoes," says Mother. "You meet Lums, you carry their shoes." (Among the many Lums I've met is a grandson of the Oglala Sioux medicine man Black Elk. Lum and I vowed to carry each other's shoes. Black Elk taught: At the sound of thunder, all beings, four-legged and two-legged, stand and hear the silence. Be silent. Be the silence.)

My mother's people arrived at Ng Fook Lai, Place of Five Contentments, and started the village of Ancient Wells. "They lived like Inchins," said my father—that is, in caves and tents. They built the plaza where every night my grandfather would talk story about orphans, and make the old ladies cry.

My mother remembers walking to the castle where the Sung emperor—well, he must have been a descendant of the emperor—was ensconced; she did not see him. I saw a brochure of the only tourist attraction near her village, a castle fortress with stone walls, "where the Sung emperor fled after he was deposed." If I had known he was my ancestor, I would have visited there.

Yu/Ngok Fei, whose mother tattooed on his back "Above All Save the Nation," was a Sung general. He failed to save his country. Gwan Goong also ultimately lost the Three Kingdoms. It was during the Sung period that Gwan Goong was deified as god of war and literature (and gamblers). China adores nonvictorious warriors—they are honored so well that we forget they lost.

The conquerors who chased the Sung to south China in 1127 A.D. must have been Mongols. Kublai Khan was the next big emperor, and named his dynasty Yuan. Oh. My mother often talks about the Yuan enemy. And Juan, my father's nephew—in Cuba? in China?—who threw out his six tomes of poetry and kept the book box. And Yuan is the enemy of Ming Hong, the new woman warrior I just learned about.

Life—the life that precedes and flows into mine—has been one long war, forever, that I have to sort out. I'm still trying to figure out which refugees ran from which world war.

"Write about unemployment," my mother orders me. In recurring dreams, Mother, at her most powerful, middle-aged, large and solid, asks: "What have you done to educate America? Have you finished educating the world yet? You go educate everyone." My job, my calling, my reason for being, my assignment and charge from Mother: "Educate America. Teach everybody." My niece Cher Nicolas, who has become a middle-school teacher, raises her fist: "Teach America!" Generations.

One of the nights I stayed with MaMa, I was sleeping on the sofa, and woke up and saw her walking in the dark to my father's desk. The rolltop desk is also our altar with pictures of grandparents, incense, candles, plastic fruit and flowers. She was speaking. "Your father just told me—he wrote words—his exact calligraphy. I have to write it down. Let me show you." She said the words my father was saying. Strange sounds. She repeated them again and again. Deep guttural sounds from the dead. "Oh, so scary," she said. She turned on the tensor light and, encircled by the dark, she wrote, taking dictation from my father. She was bent over, writing, not caring about hair, clothes, shoes, glasses. I was watching Creation. I fell asleep, and when I awoke in the morning, she was surrounded by writing. "Page twenty!" she yelled. Scattered on the desk and the dining table and in my father's rocker were the pages of her writing.

Carmen took Mother's writing to a Hong auntie to translate. Auntie read it and said, "Your mother should forget about these things. You say to her, 'Forget.' " MaMa (and BaBa) listed grudges: The land in China was land that Father's brother had taken from him. Twenty of the lichee trees are ours; only ten belong to Uncle. In China, she, Dr. Brave Orchid, worked for ten years "carrying soil," "carrying earth." And in California, she had had to work in the tomato fields and canneries, for Western Tomato. Word traveled back to the village, where the people said, "Impossible. Lan has soft white hands. Unbelievable—she's doing farm work?!"

MaMa and I warn and argue, argue and warn: The relatives are trying to give the land back to us. It's a trick. Don't take back the land. We take the land, we'll be landlords and have to fix the roof. Now that Brave Orchid is almost a hundred years old, she shouldn't be flying to China to reclaim property. We don't owe anybody anything. Land, debts, lichee trees, boat passages, schooling are paid off. No, we won't fix their roof. No, we won't buy them another water buffalo. Ting Ting doesn't owe them money either. (I caused big uproar in the villages; I missed giving red envelopes to some removed cousins and in-laws and descendants of second and third wives.) All of us work hard, and owe nothing more. Let them have the lichee trees. Those trees were dear to him, yet Father was saying, "Let them have the lichee trees." At sixteen, he had stayed awake every night of harvest time guarding the lichee trees with a gun, which cost $200. Hang on to grudges. No, let them go. Remember. Forget.

The Fourth Book of Peace, the book I was working on—156 good, rewritten pages that burned in the fire—was fiction. I was making up characters who use peace tactics. It had to be fiction, because Peace has to be supposed, imagined, divined, dreamed. Peace's language, its sounds and rhythms, when read aloud, when read silently, should pacify breath and tongue, make ears and brain be tranquil. I'd gotten to the place in my narrative where a Hawaiian woman appears and gives a prayer for humanity. I had taken many runs at a scene in a world where such a prayer is real. I hadn't gotten near the happy ending yet, which would be a happy ending to the Viet Nam War. That happy ending was to be reached with no violent action, no violent conflict, no apocalyptic climax.

After the fire, I could not re-enter fiction. Writing had become a treat for my own personal self, as it was when I was a kid and it first came to me, for nobody to read but me. Say any manner of thing. For my own benefit. Retreat into the Yin mother darkness. Oh, the necessity and comfort of writing "I . . . I . . . I . . . I . . . I . . . ," the selfish first person, author, narrator, protagonist, one. Freedom—to write diarylike, okay to be formless, no art, no good English.

Fiction cares for others; it is compassion, and gives others voice. It time-travels the past and the future, and pulls the not-now, not-yet into existence.

The garret where I wrote, which was just my height, burned. A sign. I do not want the aloneness of the writer's life. No more solitary. I need a community of like minds. The Book of Peace, to be reconstructed, needs community.

Ralph Ellison died. He never wrote a novel again after he lost his work-in-progress in the electrical fire that burned his summerhouse. He had written 360 pages over twenty years. The firefighters couldn't get water there in time. People would ask him how much time he had lost. He replied, "You know, I'm not sure. It's kind of blurred for me. . . . Let's say I was disoriented, but I worked on it. I don't know how long the inter-ruption was. Maybe four or five years. It wasn't as if I weren't working. I was trying to reimagine the situation. The characters are the same and the mixture of language is the same. But nuances are different. After all, when I write I am discovering things."

I hope that Ellison knew this blessing by Robert Louis Stevenson: "All who have meant good work with their whole hearts, have done good work, although they may die before they have the time to sign it."

The narrator of the fourth Book of Peace was Kuan Yin, who has mercy on all characters. She drops treasures and obstacles on them, flies in and out of their consciousnesses, suggests things for them to do—that they make love, make peace, make joy, and honor, and justice, and be good. She sees far into the long Chinese past and a short distance into the American future. She does not let bad things happen to anyone.

Through Father and Mother, I am related to Hong the Completer and Sung Chew the Artist-Emperor. *Letterature D'America* mentions a writer named Maxine Hong Fiction—must mean me. I should be able to write again about the time during war when Earll and I took our son, Joseph, and left to live in Hawai'i. . . .

WATER

When the peace demonstrations turned violent, and doves and hawks were using the same tactics — revolutionary and governmental provocateurs infiltrating parades and vigils, Governor Ray Gun ordering the National Guard and helicopters to tear-gas and shoot up People's Park and Berkeley (they killed James Rector, and blinded an artist) — Wittman Ah Sing and Taña made up their minds to leave America. Lew Welch, the poet who called himself The Red Monk, guided them in his poem "Chicago."

> You can't fix it and you can't make it go away.
> I don't know what you're going to do about it,
> But I know what I'm going to do about it. I'm just
> going to walk away from it. Maybe
> A small part of it will die if I'm not around
>
> feeding it anymore.

"It" is Chicago; "it" is also Viet Nam. Can't love it, leave it. Butting heads against the escalating war gives it energy. Don't think about it anymore. Quit reading the news about it. Curiosity also makes it grow. Let it go. Leave it behind. Lew Welch came to California. No sooner had the Ah Sings met him than he disappeared in the north woods.

As a special treat, and to make the leaving bearable and fun, Wittman and Taña, and their son, Mario, flew away by helicopter from the Berkeley heliport at the marina. The noise of the blades and motors loud, you didn't have to say and hear too many heart-hurting goodbyes. We're going on a tourist ride, and will be back soon. The helicopter banked, its side window beneath you, like undersea viewing in a glass-bottom boat. Look at them—friends and family waving, throwing kisses, flashing peace fingers. They don't know—Wittman had not declared himself to them—that they are sangha, community. GrandMaMa PoPo was wiping her eyes. Does she have a premonition that this journey will be forever? It is forever for an old person. We may not meet again. Wittman's ex-girlfriend Nanci seemed to be crying, and Mom too, but actresses do that for the crowd. They're proud of the ability to weep, to have the gift of tears. But they must be sincerely sad that Mario, the only child, is going away.

Our people are bonded to us forever; they're caretakers of stuff and things given away at the potlatch farewell party. "You can have anything in the house," Wittman and Taña and Mario had said to one and all. "Keepers of my belongings belong to me," they said, hugging the taker. Because of marriage, there were two of many things—sets of text-books, hot coils for instant coffee or tea, Crock-Pots. Mario, who was four, gave away his baby toys, let his child friends own them now. Taña's witchy friends from the College of Arts and Crafts accepted her crystal ball and her globe of the ancient world. (She'd given away the taxider-mied bat when they baby-proofed.) Wittman was not much attached to stuff, trying to live by The Red Monk's advice that even fifteen things are too many. Be open-handed; be free. Let the bookstores and libraries take care of the books. Read them and give them back or away. To be free in America: rid yourself of impedimenta. American karma: owning too much stuff. Own stuff, and the stuff starts owning you, the caretaker of burdens of heavy furniture. They were raising their kid without TV.

Well, last night's potlatch giveaway hadn't been like *Zorba the Greek*, where the crones grabbed the old lady's possessions while she lay alive on her deathbed. Our crowd has no acquisitiveness. His peculiar stuff not moving, Wittman had to urge it on people. "When you wear it, think of me." "Use it up; it won't take up space for long." "Pass it on to somebody who needs it." "Yours. Pass it on. No backs." Taña told people that her paintings and sculptures would be more famous if the plane crashed tomorrow. "And you will be collector and patron in the cata-logue of my retrospective. Be my Stein and Toklas, who recognized Picasso and Matisse and Cézanne at the start." (Gauguin wrote "studies" and "documents" for others to paint and sculpt, should he not live long enough.) At last, all of her art was taken. Some friends said they were borrowing and would return it when she came home. It takes skill to give gifts.

Farewell. Farewell. For a time, tears on crying faces were visible. You could communicate with facial expressions; you could read lips. We love you. We miss you. Have a good time. Do you also keep seeing PoPo's wrinkles and tears, and rays at the sides of her eyes, and smile lines at her mouth? Could be optic memory at work. Mom and the aunties—a dozen aunties—continued goodbying with their dancers' bodies. Caught your kiss. Throw it back. Go. Go learn hula. Wittman felt honored and loved that such a crowd had come to see him and his wife and child off. Flying above my people—look hard at them, hold them in the eyes, hold them in the heart. He was living right, that he cultivated these people of all kinds into family community. He liked himself for keeping everybody he had ever met. Make whomever you come across your own. There's Lance and Sunny Kamiyama, each with an arm about the other, and their outer arms waving. Yale Younger and Black Li, White friend and Black friend, flashing Peace with both hands. The kung-fu gang were power-saluting with their whole chi-strong bodies. Look upon PoPo and Lincoln Goong Goong as if for the last time. And Ruby and Zeppelin, Mom and Pop, aren't so young either. Appreciate them. There's Judy Louie. And Louise, who worked at the department store. Sure are a lot of singletons down there. Mr. Sanchez, the employment counselor. Why don't they get together as lovers in whatever combinations? Mr. Sanchez and Judy; Yale Younger and Louise; Black Li and Judy; Yale and Mr. Sanchez; Siew Loong's kung-fu club and Taña's art witches and the showgirl aunties. Taña's mother, father, and stepparents—White people have families after all—were Back East, and had written and phoned in their goodbyes.

"Goodbye, everybody," Taña said. Mario yelled, "Bye-bye! Bye-bye!" Taña unheld hands with Wittman, and waved with both of hers. She was crying, and got Mario crying. An ape will also cry when another ape cries. They will stop weeping when friends and family are out of sight. A new interesting life will engross them. On to fair adventures and the future. It's easier to be the leaver than the ones left behind, who return to the ordinary life, missing you. The helicopter went higher and higher and toward the sea.

Always ambivalent, Wittman, escaping America, felt bad forsaking his people. America is over. He hadn't had the nerve to break that news to the *campesinos*. He hadn't formulated his political thinking well enough to try to convince others to escape too. Leaving them behind to keep fighting the ongoing, endless war. He hadn't told it that way to Taña and Mario either. You don't want to scare the kid. And Taña can enjoy this trip as a belated, affordable Hawaiian honeymoon. They had return tickets, just in case. . . .

The helicopter righted itself, left-banked, right-banked, left-banked, laterals, then straightened out and off. Riding a helicopter is especially fun because this distance above the ground is the height of flying in dreams. Mario sat in front with the pilot, who showed him the controls and let him touch them. They circled the Bay—goodbye to each bridge, bye-bye to San Francisco—Coit Tower, where Mommy and Daddy got married—and peeled off south to the airport.

From the helicopter to the shuttle bus to the main terminal, Wittman and Taña carried the Gold Mountain trunk, each taking ahold of a leather and brass handle. The Gold Mountain and the Sandalwood Mountain sojourners had been giants. The trunk was itself heavier than the stuff in it, mostly Mario's and Taña's—all they now owned.

Wittman had an altercation with the check-in clerk about this ancestral traveling trunk. He argued mathematics. "The true way to measure volume is length times width times height. Your computation— *adding* length and width and height—you come up with a meaningless number. Girth is not a measurement in geometry." His way of being a father was to set a good example—be a man of principles.

"How much is the surcharge for excess baggage?" Taña asked, and solved the problem. What a confident White American she is. And what a Cheap Charlie China Man he is. Then they were side by side in a bulkhead row, which they got because of traveling with a kid. Holding hands for takeoff, Mario in the middle with the tangle of hands in his lap, they left the land, flew away from the Americas, out over the ocean, away from that long, long shoreline, the tide and the edge of the continent and the Western Hemisphere. They removed the armrests, pushed the seats back, and made a sofa. Squeezed together at the window, they watched San Francisco, the white city, move away, and the white waves smooth out into blue water. Sudden sun sparks—lines of light—darted and darned—a storm of needles—glinted in the water and all the air, and for quick moments inside and through the plane. "Dragonflies," said Mario. "Dragonflies and water spiders," the effect lasting until they went into the clouds.

They were headed for the piece of land that is the farthest away from any other land. No need for passports, of course, to go to Hawai'i, but their passports were at the ready, just in case. They might have to skip the country, keep going west to the East, to Japan, which has a constitution against arming for war. In Hawai'i, give the U.S. one last try, the fiftieth and last state, barely America. The Ah Sings were traveling on family passports, each in a photo with the other two. Utter commitment, nobody can leave anybody. Gauguin goes to Oceania with his wife and kids.

It was a theme flight; Hawaiian music played constantly. "Aloha," said the stewardesses, who changed into hibiscus-print muumuus for the food service. These were not baggy-sack muumuus but like the cheongsam, like the ao dai. A purple orchid bloomed on each food tray, and passion-fruit juice flowed. You could smoke after the "No Smoking Fasten Seat Belt" signs went off. But Wittman had quit already. The literature in the seat pocket advertised and promised Paradise. What should Odysseus do, traveling with Penelope and Telemachus, if he meets Calypso?

"When are we getting smaller?" asked Mario, looking at his out-stretched hands, looking at his mother and father. "We aren't small yet." Oh, he thinks that airplanes really do get small up in the sky. He hasn't learned perspective. His little boy's way of seeing so delighted Wittman that he wanted to trip out with him instead of teaching him the real world. He broke facts to him reluctantly.

Wittman asked, "Are you saying that airplanes get small when they go up in the air—so they *can* go up in the air—and all the people inside get small too?"

Mario nodded Yes. "Then they get bigger and bigger and come down. I saw them do that before."

Tough Taña said, "We and the airplane are the same size in the sky and on the ground. We are not getting smaller. Airplanes in the sky look small because they are far away. They're really always the same size. They looked smaller and smaller because they were getting farther and farther away. People and airplanes don't get smaller and bigger; they stay the same—they only *look* like they're shrinking and growing. They *seem* to change size." She certainly is a strong mother, making her son fit for real life. Wittman's policy of child-raising was not to ask the kid if he liked chocolate or vanilla better, in order that he not fall into dualism.

"Oh," said Mario. "Oh. I *thought* the airplane and people inside the airplane get small in the sky. But. We are going far away all together."

Under their feet the bulkhead floor, which had legroom and kid-room, became strewn with toys and picture books and cereal and juice. Mario lined his Hot Wheels and bulldozer in rows of traffic, and made motor and gear-shifting and braking noises. No, the cars did not shoot at one another. They were raising their son with no television and no war toys. It is not true that kids naturally make up war games, play war, turn sticks, rocks, cooking utensils into weapons, and point their fingers like guns.

Out of and above the clouds, Taña took off her shoes and tucked up her feet, partly under Wittman. She took out her sketch pad and drew the clouds, and lines of water. In the fields upon fields of clouds were openings, and there was the ocean. Taña caught shapes in ink as the plane moved. "You can't make mistakes drawing clouds," she said. "Wait awhile, the wind blows, the sun moves, the clouds may become like this later." Curved lines and straight lines streamed along, and when she got to the edge of the paper, she drew new clouds on top of the beginning ones. She colored them with yellow and lavender pencils. "Look for this color, and this color," she instructed her family. "See them?" Wittman and Mario looked in the pure-white clouds for yellow and lavender.

"I see them," said Mario. Wittman thought he saw the yellow. Of all the practitioners of the arts, it is the painter who is called artist. She guides your seeing, draws a wonderment, you look for it in life, and there it is.

She said, "Look, Mario," and dotted the paper twice—a cloud face, puffy-cheeked like Wind on old maps, appeared and looked back at him. Squiggle-wiggles, a line, pairs of dots—herds of animals and crowds of people emerged, peeking from trees and houses and palaces with columns. All the journeying of travel is transition, place changing, time changing, Planet Earth and light moving. Place moves, time moves, we move. Usually, Mario did not handle transitions well. "Can't like it," he'd cry. It breaks your heart, he tries to stay happy, to like whatever's going on, what's supposed to be good for him. But the inside of an airplane is a still place, and the time aboard a long, steady time; he felt safe. Air travelers are suspended above troubles.

"It's a good time to think out our life, and plan, Wittman," said Taña. "I have a resolution and plan for the rest of my life: I'm not going to do anything I don't want to do. From now on, I'm only going to do things that I like." Spoken like the White woman she is.

Wittman felt envy, that she could think up such a vow. She had had the upbringing of a blonde American person. One reason you espouse yourself to a White person: access to more of the world. He said, "Artists shouldn't be married to each other. One should do the art, have the life in art, and the other make the money." Poet and playwright, he's the artist too.

"I agree," said Taña. "An artist should be married to somebody who is satisfied to make money, and feed the artist, and wash dishes."

Off to start a new life in a new place, they will be the first generation to solve make-a-living, getta-job. Wittman's parents, both retired now, still argued over who should make the money while the other one played. They still held the Great Depression and World War II against each other. He didn't support the family; he left her for Europe. Mass unemployment, the wartime draft—no excuse. And she's bossy, wears the trousers, doesn't need him. Liberated Taña did not want, existentially, to be a wife, a woman who had to be husbanded. And Wittman did not want to die the Death of a Salesman or be the Man in the Gray Flannel Suit.

"I have a plan," said Wittman, "a compromise whereby each of us is unhappy for only half the time. Why don't you make the money for six months while I'm the artist, and I hump my lump for six months while you're the artist? Take turns."

"Okay," said Taña. "You go first. I mean, you get a job first."

"Why not you?" he said. "Why don't you go first?" He knew her, she'd get six months out of him and count on inertia to keep him slaving away. What's the point of being married if you have to do all the work?

Taña said, "The artist in a new place will have the new eye for just a short while. I *need* the fresh eye. I have to have my first, fresh impressions. They last for moments, and things become ordinary and unseeable again. This move to a different angle and light opens the eyes to see new colors and new lights. I'll *see*, and catch the brightness before I fall dull again."

"I need that too," he said. "A playwright—and poet—needs to look as if for the first time too."

"But your work doesn't depend on the *eye*. I need to practice and train my eye." He pictured her with just one of them. "A playwright and poet doesn't have a specific natural organ he has to keep exercising the way an artist or a musician does. The *eye*. The *ear*. You could do what you do while you're at a job. It's good for you to have a job, so you have something to write about."

"I do too have a natural specific organ—it's my entire body, and brain. My body needs lots of room and time."

"I need the right-now time," she said. "And the morning light. And God's light." That means she wants all the livelong day. She went on, "Another reason I ought to be doing my art first is that you've had your time off already, unemployed."

Aha, there's his argument. He was not "unemployed"; he was on Unemployment, which is itself a job. It's a lot of work to give the appearance of active job-seeking. "I bought the plane tickets on my Unemployment. My Unemployment money and the red packet from my PoPo is paying for this honeymoon. And I'll be continuing Unemployment in Hawai'i. Trudging to the Unemployment office is work. I'm working already. I'm the one bringing in money. So—you go first, get a job first. And I live the life of the artist." He could keep on talking, outtalk her, but marriage had changed him. Fatherhood had changed him. He was not so much a talker anymore. No more tripping out. And he had something to write—the poem, the play that would stop war.

"I'm living the life of the artist first," she said.

"I'm living the life of the artist first," he said.

"I contributed to the marital effort by selling my Porsche. PoPo's gifts are to *us*, not just to you. I've put in my equal share, more than equal. My painting will eventuate in money. The sooner I show, the sooner I sell. I'll go first."

"Marital effort" is a legal term justifying community property, which is the law in California. Each espoused one puts in half the work, and gets to take away half the resulting wealth.

"We can both go first as long as the savings hold out," said compromising Wittman. So sad, when job and true life's work don't go together. "We'll both take off. Here's the plan: we both live lives in art, together, and make the next decisions when the money runs out." Let's try for the ideal—man artist and woman artist loving each other and working at creation together. They would both stay home every day, not like most married workaday couples, who hardly see each other. No matter if one's on swing shift or night shift or the dawn or dusk commute, the spouse leaving for or coming home from work (typing her life away at an insurance company) hates the slugabed spouse.

Berkeley people, they planned short-term. Six months ahead was farsighted for them, longer than a semester. Revolution is imminent; any day now, capitalist competition will end. At least, Congress will pass the Guaranteed Annual Living Wage Bill. At worst, the world will end. Westmoreland will drop the Bomb on China, Russia will launch its missiles right through NORAD, we send our nuclear warheads back at them, and there goes the world. The Porsche money and the Unemployment money and the Grandma money should go a long way in Hawai'i, a place where fruit grows on public trees, and the weather is unvaryingly just right for sleeping on the beach. No need for winter blankets and expensive coats and boots. Take a vow of poverty and parsimoniousness, and you'll be all right. Wittman nicked the entire folder of complimentary stationery with the airline logo.

From behind the *New York Times* across the aisle came a woman's voice: "That's exactly what we need, more haoles and kachinks coming to Hawai'i to live on Welfare. The tourists are bad enough, but—hippie colonists!" It was a Hawaiian-looking—that is, beautiful—woman flying home.

Knee-jerked, Wittman said, "Pardon me? What did you say? You say something to me? You saying aloha to me? I'm not a Welfare cheat. Unemployment is not Welfare. Unemployment is getting some of my own earnings and taxes back. I paid into the system."

"And besides," said Taña, leaning over him for the confrontation, "even if we were going on Welfare, I'm pro-Welfare. I'd rather my taxes went to the poor, to feeding unwed mothers and babies, than to napalming them."

The Hawaiian beauty lay down her East Coast newspaper. She really was lovely, lively black hair floating and blowing in the airjets. Her dark eyes were outlined with blue-black stripes like Kathakali and Chinese-opera face; her skin was a perfect tan, like Pilipina or Chicana. She corrected the lazy hippies, "AFDC and Defense are separate budgets. States and counties and the feds pay for different parts of Welfare. Using up Unemployment money doesn't take away from Defense."

"Are you sure?" asked Taña.

"Yes, I'm sure. I'm an attorney. I just got my LL.D. from George-town. I clerked in Honolulu, and I'm prepared for the Hawai'i bar exam in July. I do not appreciate hippies coming over to live off of us."

"Oh, you're a lawyer," said Wittman. "Will you be my lawyer? I need to get my Unemployment transferred over. I could use your help staying out of the military too." Get a free consultation off the rookie lawyer. "I'm a draft dodger. Will you hide me?" Like "Will you marry me?"

"Hide you? I could turn you in."

"But let's say you do that, you turn me in. I land in jail, you put me in jail, you'd be giving me time, leisure, ultimate Welfare. I'll live the life of Tolstoy and Dostoevsky and Thoreau. I'm going to ask for solitude."

"Solitary," said Taña.

"Same thing. I'd be by myself, safe from armies chasing me through jungles and rivers. Come on, you can't turn in a brother. I don't know Hawai'i. What you ought to do for me is to tell me places to hide, how to find refuge, where the underground railroad is, and the safe houses, and contacts. Now, don't be hasty rejecting me. You have to get straight with what you fundamentally believe about war and the War in Viet Nam. You can't want to ship my ass over there to cluster-bomb people who look like you and me, huh?"

Taña was getting annoyed with Wittman, acting out the on-his-own fantasy again, impressing the pretty girl, bragging about his draft evasion. She addressed the other woman: "This is your chance to be like Miep hiding Anne Frank. And her whole family, and more people on top of that. How about us staying at *your* house?" If your husband has an interest in another woman, you just move in, friendly, bringing the kid with you.

Bruno Bettelheim chastised the Frank family for hiding all together. They should have split up, each one on his or her own. But what's the use of living if you have to go it alone?

Look at that child asleep at his parents' feet, so especially cute—it did look Hawaiian; it looked like a baby Viet Cong. The cuteness of babies is their protection. But that defense isn't working. We're baby-killers, and so are they. The Viet Cong are wiring babies with explosives, using babies for booby traps. During the Indian wars, the slogan for exterminating the cute red babies was: "Nits will become lice."

"You mainland people," said the attorney-to-be, "you take advantage of our aloha. You come to our country with the prejudice that we give, give, give, and you take, take, take. 'Aloha' does not mean only giving. It is giving and receiving. Giving and receiving love. Reciprocal generosity." Wittman had been told: Cold hard English does not have a word for "aloha."

Mario was awake and listening. He said, "I will feel aloha when I get to Hawai'i, and grow bigger." How can you not welcome him into your heart and country? The Hawaiian lady gave him a loving smile. She had been pronouncing "aloha"; though said meanly, that lovely word in the mouth melts hostility.

"May I draw you?" asked Taña. "You are beautiful. And I would love to draw you." Wittman was (again) amazed at women. A man never says to another man, "You are beautiful." Women are always complimenting one another on hair, clothes, health, looking rested, niceness, general attractiveness. They make up for men's not noticing, or not speaking up. "I love that expression on your face. May I draw you? You can just go about what you're doing, reading, talking with my husband." Taña's hands were making drawing motions. The woman, Polly, said Okay, and Taña traded seats with Wittman to get a good sight-line. She drew as if touching the face gently, stroking cheeks and chin, blackening the eyebrows and lashes as if putting on liner and mascara. She made no erasures, honestly setting down every response to her model. Taña loved drawing hair; you can't go wrong drawing hair. Her pen squiggling and curlicuing any old way, a corresponding hair goes that way too. The crisscrosses and curves made moons and stars in a night sky of hair that filled the background to the edges. Most of the picture was nude skin, Polly's large face full of the intelligence of reading. With her palm and finger pads and a little spit, Taña rubbed the umber skin. People passing down the aisle looked at the drawing, looked at the model. A naiad of the ancient world is flying home, and this airplane is at her service. Taña drew her for a long while, taking time and care. It matters how long an artist spends drawing someone; painstaking work or slapdash effort shows. Everyone fell silent. The little boy napped on the floor. Wittman read *Noa Noa*, his field guide to Oceania. "My beautiful solitude," wrote Gauguin. "My beautiful poverty."

"I'm done," said Taña, and held the portrait up for her subject to see.

The shading of the nose was just right, light makeup straight down the center and darker makeup on the sides, a theatrical trick to improve people with broad noses.

"I like," said the beauty. "I like" is what people in Hawai'i say when they are encouraging you to give them something. "May I have it?" she translated. Hawaiian people are good at helping you give them things. They are a giving society. A giving-and-taking society. Taña signed and dated the picture, and handed it across the aisle to Polly. They thanked each other. Gauguin hadn't given his artwork away to the Tahitians and Marquesans he painted. He shipped his paintings off to Paris for sale. A model-mistress burglarized his studio and stole paintings of herself.

Taña's model put the picture in her briefcase, and, as long as she had it open, gave out her card. She was Poli'ahu Nona Keoua of the Big Island. Poli'ahu is the caressing goddess of snow on Mauna Kea.

An announcement came over the loudspeaker to pull down the shades for the sake of movie-watchers, mahalo. Thanks. Mahalo. The movie was *Hawaii*, adapted from Michener's novel by Dalton Trumbo, author of the great antiwar book *Johnny Got His Gun*. Trumbo has been forgiven—he's off the blacklist. The little family rented one set of headphones to pass amongst them. Polly turned on her reading light, and continued with the *New York Times*. (Westerners take all week to read one.)

Ocean water covers the screen. The first people are coming from Bora-Bora. They pray to fire, Little Mother Pele, and Mana and Kāne, mother and father of the universe. They make a human sacrifice to Ora, and set sail. In the middle of one of the boats is a stone with white hair, Gentle Kano. A prince sings the Chant of Migration; then the omniscient narrating voice says: "After thirty generations of worship of Kāne, it was a Time of Changing Gods." And sailing toward the Hawaiians through thundering, moving water, ocean storms, constant movement—around the Cape of Good Hope, through the Strait of Magellan to Evangels to Lahaina, Māui—come Max von Sydow and Julie Andrews. These most haole of haoles—White people—speak about bringing "enlightenment to the heathen and primitives in Awahee." We slow-zoom to their first view of the Hawaiians: a group of white-haired elders, kahunas and kapunas. Amongst them, Gentle Kano, the rock, sits on ti leaves. Above the deck of the missionary ship, hoisted in a sling, hovers Ali'i Nui Mālama, a fat angel, saying in a slow deep kind voice, "Aloha-a-a. Aloha-a-a. Aloha-a-a." From snowy New England across more water comes Prince Kioka, returning from Christian college to marry his own sister. Offscreen, one of the haole missionaries marries a native; the others talk about his "whoring after the heathen." Ali'i Nui Mālama commands Julie Andrews to teach her to write, more important than going to church. "First write. Teach. Now. Teach me." (Written Hawaiian is less than two hundred years old.) Mālama speaks English in an accent that you've never heard before, soft, majestic, maybe unique to that actress. She writes laws and reads them aloud to the English-speaking whalers and sailors. She writes to the President of the United States. Prince Kioka teaches children in the Hawaiian language; his love scene with the princess sister is in Hawaiian, and subtitled. The choir in the Christian church sings Hawaiian hymns, also subtitled. You could learn a lot of Hawaiian words watching this movie—*kapu, heiau, 'ohana*. And pidgin too: "I no do nothing bad." Julie Andrews holds the dying Mālama in her arms, and speaks the voice-over in the funeral scenes: "Of her bones was Hawai'i built. . . . Our greed is what kills them—arrogance, lust for their land. . . . Land given by God to Hawaiians." The wind wails and lows in mourning. The Ali'i Nui's royal consort knocks his teeth out on the Kano rock.

Mario had the earphones at the part where the tidal wave runs over buildings and villages and the hurricane blows down the church. "Can't like it!" he cried, tearing off the earphones. He jumped into his father's lap and hid his face in his mother's stomach. They assured him, "It's only a movie. It's not real." He hadn't been upset watching the bad sailors and whalers torch huts, like hootches in Viet Nam. He hadn't had the earphones. It's violent noise that gets to kids.

"That movie and the book are full of stereotypes," said Polly. "Noble savages. That actress isn't Hawaiian; she's Tahitian or some other South Sea Islander. The weather and the geology are the only good parts."

"And the film is centered on the haoles," said quick Wittman, "when they were a minority of the population."

"We shouldn't have become a state. Business interests voted for being a state."

"I would have voted against being a state," said Wittman. "I'm almost a Hawaiian person myself, you know." He could work up a case for Hawaiian ancestry; his apocry-full PoPo came from or through Hawai'i. Free-choose your ethnicity.

"We have a saying," said the real Hawaiian. " 'Kachinks and katonks want to be haoles; haoles want to be Hawaiians; Hawaiians don't want to be nobody.' Like in the movie, haoles come over and make us wear clothes; now they laze on the beach with no clothes on, and we do the labor. The slavebor." Though she wasn't directly name-calling, her listeners felt sticks and stones.

Taña said, "I'm not Anglo haole. I am of Dutch and Indonesian descent." Wittman often heard Taña tell people, "Don't call me Anglo. I'm not English." Now she would have to start saying, "Don't call me haole."

Then, because they were intelligent people of their time, they argued about the war. Not giving in to the inertia and lethargy of air travel, they covered the implacable reasons for Viet Nam: The domino theory. International Communism. North Viet Nam, backed by Russia, China, and Cuba, attacking South Viet Nam. We're in too deep to pull out. Honor our commitments. We are winning; count the bodies. Count hearts and minds. The President's secret plan; trust him. Don't trust him.

Taña fell asleep. Maybe being apolitical could end the war.

Polly, a lawyer, the *New York Times* in hand, was a much better debater than Wittman, who was boycotting newspapers. Listen to Johnson speaking to our troops at Cam Ranh Bay: "The trouble is that there are only two hundred million of us and nearly three billion of them and they want what we've got and we're not going to give it to them."

Who are the Them he's talking about? He can't come up with three billion unless he's counting every Oriental on earth.

Tall, barefooted Wittman hunkered on his airline seat. "Seriously, Miss Keoua, we're on vows of almost poverty. We're bringing savings, and we'll be renting and spending. We won't buy a house, we won't grab your land. Your Robert Louis Stevenson said, 'Earn a little and spend a little less.' That's us." That tenet was engraved on the pedestal for the Española, monument to Robert Louis Stevenson in Portsmouth Square, San Francisco Chinatown. Scots and Chinese understand each other in regard to thrift. "Seriously, may I consider you my lawyer? If I get caught, would you defend me? Come on, quit being a devil's advocate. I warn you, you play devil's advocate, you start believing some knotted things." Poor girl, poor mermaid on her way home from dry law school, stuck next to a talker.

"I'll give you advice," she said. "I warn you in advance: don't get into trouble. Dumb haoles and kachinks drop their big-city survival skills the moment they land in what they think is the country and Paradise. You're going to an urban, modern, twentieth-century place. Act like you're street-smart in New York."

"Street-smart in San Francisco has got to be as good. So—we'll be safe?"

"It's not up to me. It's not up to you. You go Big Island, Pele will hide you if she likes you. Every island and every jungle, the same. Too kind jungle." Or did she say, "Two kine jungle"? The closer they were getting to Hawai'i, the more she was getting her pidgin back. "Wilderness rain forest one kind jungle. High-density Waikīkī city, another kind jungle. But you get refuge only if the place wants you. It's not up to you. *You* don't choose. They—we choose."

Time and space suspended, at the margin, Polly let on, she has worries. "I've been away too long. I'm anxious, Madame Pele won't have me anymore. I'm haoleized. And I'm trying to fly home with a planeful of haoles. The last time I went Big Island, she punished me. She hit me in the eyes and the head. The most terrible pain, so I could not see. She was not letting me gaze at her. She gave me head pain—for getting educated. I got a haole intellect, so she hit my brain. She kapu my mind—my mind belongs to her. She does not like competition. She is especially competitive against women. I hope she'll take me back. She'd welcome me if she could understand, Hawai'i needs lawyers to save the *'āina*." *Āina*—land, earth, property, estate. Not just any land, but the sacred land that is Hawai'i.

After being at sea and in the air for more than five hours that seemed forever, they came to the archipelago on this planet farthest away from other land, the most isolated islands on earth. Currents of water and wind converge at Hawai'i, the center of the Pacific Ocean, the middle of the Ring of Fire. Power forces pull certain people here. Down out of the high clouds they came. Pressed up against the cold windows, they watched clouds like icebergs break apart and show blue water and sky, thin and flatten just above the sea, and pile up near land, like drifts of snow. The islands looked like candy drops on doilies, frothy rims of surf, circles of tides. They passed the Big Island first. Madame Pele was allowing Poli'ahu to approach; else she'd tear open the plane, suck her out of it, and throw her into the ocean. And there's Maui, where Charles Lindbergh, who named his son Land, is buried. And Molokaʻi of the sheer cliffs that kept out conquerors until Kamehameha. And Oʻahu, with mountains in the center tapering down to the beaches—Water Margin with the ocean for moat. Inside Diamond Head Crater is military equipment—jeeps, supposedly camouflaged but standing out in the bright-green grass. Then out over the ocean again toward the leeward side and the Waianae Mountains, and back around, lowering and landing in Honolulu. In *From Here to Eternity*, the Japanese planes came leeward too. Then Pearl Harbor and the Kaneohe Marine Corps Air Station. This side of the Honolulu International Airport looked like an air-force base—covering the ground were death planes with no markings, like the terrible plane that prowls the countryside around Travis Air Force Base. And many fighter jets, like darts parked in rows. So—it's here they take off to and come back from Viet Nam. We are at a staging area for the war.

The stewardesses went up and down the aisle and collected the ag-inspection form about plants you were importing and (optional) what business you had coming to Hawaiʻi; they gave away the champagne prize for the closest calculation of the time to the midway point, sprayed the cabin with insecticide, and said their alohas and mahalos. The plane landed safely, everybody applauding when the wheels touched down. Taña wished Polly well on the bar exam. Maybe we meet again. The islands are small. Waiting in the aisle for the slow disembarkation (keep saying your alohas), suddenly you felt the air change—it was real air, alive, warm. Diesel fuel could not spoil the air. At the door, no jetway, you stood at the top of the open steps and felt the tradewinds and the kissing raindrops, smelled flowers and pineapple. Two rainbows arched across the heavens. God's footprints. "Ānuenue," people said. "Ānuenue." Rain welcomes us, and we welcome the rain—the same in arid California; the same in China, where rain is Dragon. The name of the caller to the Water Margin is Timely Rain. Polly had been in the black-and-white cities of Back East, and Taña and Wittman had been in California's brown and soft gold. Suddenly they were shifted to the ultimate other end of the spectrum—orange, red, purple. And six hundred shades of green.

The Wiki-Wiki bus took them to the terminal. Polly went to Domestic Flights for the Big Island. Wittman carried Mario piggyback, and Taña carried most of the carry-on. Looking for Baggage Claim, they took a turn to a place they were not supposed to go. No other people were about. Through immense windows, like glass walls, they saw an airplane very near them, next to the building. And there were rows of coffins on the ground and a row of coffins on the conveyor belt for luggage. The conveyor belt was not moving. Each coffin was draped with an American flag. An armed marine at attention guarded the score of coffins. Wittman and Taña looked at each other and did not comment, did not want their son to know about soldiers killed in Viet Nam, and their bodies being routed to hometowns all over the U.S. Mario pointed at the scene: "What's that?" Holding him, Wittman said, "Those are coffins, and there are dead soldiers in the coffins. They were killed in Viet Nam, in war. Their bodies are being flown home to their families." Fear and trouble went into the boy's eyes and face and body. "I can't like it," he said. Wittman set him down, knelt to his height, looked into his child's face, and promised him, "When you grow up, there will be no war. You will not have to be a soldier. You will not go to war, because there will be no such thing as war." They should find Japan Airlines, change their tickets, and fly on to Japan, that country which has learned its lesson about war. But they had just come off of a long flight. And other, nearer places in the Pacific they'd heard of—Guam, Kwajalein—were military bases.

Outside Baggage Claim, the air of Hawai'i again touched them, and surrounded them, and went through them. Hawai'i breathes you as you breathe it. The air carries you. The family of three held hands, and though weighed down by luggage, they floated. All is moving, hair and clothes, wind and air fingering and stroking skin. *Noa noa.* All is fragrance, essence. *Nhó , nhó.* Remember.

Dole Pineapple had a dispenser like a water cooler fountaining free all-you-want pineapple juice. In the heat, they drank. The body became a cool tube of sweetness. Dole pineapple juice was the best thing you ever tasted. "I like Hawai'i," said Mario, dribbling juice.

They walked toward Ground Transportation along the breezeway, where the wind blew in and out of them. Sojourners were being welcomed home with leis from neck to nose, tourists kissed and garlanded by professional greeters. Such aloha nowhere else; the farther west you go, the more aloha. The Ah Sing family, having come to the farthest-out unknown place they'd ever been, had nobody to welcome them. So they greeted one another, kissing and hugging. "Welcome to Hawai'i, Wittman." "Welcome to Hawai'i, Taña." "Welcome to Hawai'i, Mario." "Welcome to Hawai'i, Mommy. Welcome to Hawai'i, Daddy."

At the Hawai'i Visitors Bureau booth, they found an ad for Rent A Wreck cars, with a lease-and-buy option. Almost financially ahead already. To get to town, they took a taxi, its trunk lid wide open over their luggage. Used-car lots and palm trees lined the highway from the airport to Honolulu—it looked like Los Angeles. Bumper stickers said: RESTORE THE MONARCHY. All windows down, the heavenly atmosphere prevailed. The double rainbows rolled and wheeled ahead of the car, which drove toward dark and light greenery in the distance. The sunlight was red and the earth that was unpaved was also red. "Acid colors," Wittman and Tañia agreed; dropping acid had made them vulnerable to purples and oranges, and now they'd followed the luring rays to their source. The city of Honolulu was high-rise concrete and steel, but trees and green hills and green mountains poked through. The ancients and people today built structures in the bottoms and sides of valleys; green ridges pointed up through the subdivisions of housing. The underlying, upcropping island was manifest everywhere.

Rent A Wreck was on Kapiolani Boulevard. (Oakland has a Kapiolani Drive; it's on the Mills campus.) They rented a '61 Valiant, white with red upholstery, on Tañia's driver's license. Wittman's was expired; the SSS wouldn't be able to trace him through the Motor V., which is the primo-uno locator of people for the draft and jury duty. Tañia drove, setting out for the nearest water, Waikīkī. Mario stood in the front seat, between his parents, and conducted the radio music and the movements of the traffic. "Cars, music, go together!" he yelled. "Move! Together!" They were in a Polynesian musical, cruising the Waikīkī strip with fellow drivers. The orchestra leader, Mario, and the coconut palms waved to one another. They rode past the zoo to the fountain at the foot of Diamond Head, around the fountain, and back Ewa way to the top of Waikīkī, and around again. Past the pink Royal Hawaiian Hotel, and the Natatorium, like a bath from an ancient civilization, where Johnny Weismuller and Duke Kahanamoku, Olympians, once dived and swam—THE WAR MEMORIAL. Tañia found a parking spot, and they walked toward the ocean, crossed the street, the sidewalk, the grass, and sand. Mario's parents lifted and swung him between them over curbs and ironwood burrs. They walked around sunbathers reading and sleeping. To the Californians, Sans Souci was but a tiny strip of beach, like a sandbox. We are used to long, wide beaches and tide flats running along two continents—*Norteamérica y Sudamérica*—forever.

The island is very small; all is sky and water. They took off their shoes and waded into the water, holding Mario up like a baby ape between them, arms long and legs lifted above the waves. "Fish bite," he kept saying. In water clear as air swam schools of silver-and-white fish and sharp shadows of fish. Suddenly a yank, a pulling away, and sand was rushing out from underfoot, and the water was deep and overhead, brine in eyes and mouth. Wittman lost ahold of Mario. Where is he? Carried out to sea? There he is, Taña's got him, sitting in the surf, and water washing over them. Mario tried to stand, and a wave knocked him down. He was so surprised, he forgot to cry. He held on to his penis. Years later, he will say that his father knocked him down and held him under, and tried to douse and drown him. Which was what Wittman remembered *his* father's doing to him in the San Joaquin River.

Sitting in the ocean, their backs to the city, they saw the sea uptilted and the horizon high above. An island in the center of the Pacific Ocean lies at the bottom of a tube of water. A blue-green wall of vertical water moves and rises. And there are pools within pools, depths within depths—patches of liquid turquoise, and army colors, maybe bottom-rooted forests or floats of seaweed, and dark blues, and a blue that matches the sky. The ocean continues the sky. Getting up, you fall back into water that keeps variously moving. No repeating movement to hang on to. To make the ocean horizontal again, your mind has to insist on perspective. Make a carpenter's level of the horizon. And the noise—you could hear nothing but ocean, sounding into the ears, overturning balance. This very same ocean crashed against Kerouac's MeeMaw Mountain, but his ocean and mountain made words. The ocean constantly drums ears and diaphragm, but the people living beside it seem not to hear the ongoing bass roar. Soon the newcomers won't hear it either. In a few days, they will have to remind themselves consciously to listen before they can hear it. And an hour after that, they will forget to remind themselves, and so not hear it anymore.

The little family came dripping out of the water, pockets and hair and ears filled with sand and water. This was not a high-surf beach, but the tamest sea of the island, just a tourist beach at Waikīkī. The sand had been trucked in, and was combed and brushed daily by a street sweeper. They sat on a seawall drying out. The surf reached for their toes.

They saw three wounded men, clothed, playing in the water. One held his splinted arm up in the air as he jumped up and down, his other arm holding on to a man with one leg, who hopped in the waves. A man with his chest in bandages, and a bandage around his head, kicked water on his friends, grabbed them, and pulled them farther from shore. They whooped and splashed, jumped on top of one another, then let themselves fall into the water, and rolled around in a laughing dog-pile. They were cavorting, happy to be alive, out of Viet Nam alive.

The little family in damp clothes got into their car; the rushing warm air would dry them off. They drove past public beach pavilions with outdoor showers, foot-rinsing spigots, barbecue pits. "Look. A ramada," said Taña. "It's for people to live under. We could live there. We don't need anything to live in Hawai'i—we can sleep on the beach with shelter provided." She was a tourist in Paradise, full of hope and naïveté, forgetting what she knows about America—crime, rape, mugging, laws against loitering and overnight camping. On Christmas Day, the governor will evict a shantytown on Sand Island; Hawaiians will leave carrying a decorated tree.

Around Diamond Head they went; it was a green-and-brown wedge, otherwise not diamondlike, a dormant volcano with one side blown off. Ocean on the right and mountain on the left, they came swooping downhill on the northeast part of the island. Wittman and Taña kept guessing at this spot and that spot: "That's where Burt Lancaster and Deborah Kerr rolled around in the surf." Tucked amongst the uproaring rocky shoreline were coves with beds of sand pulverized by waves for eternity, many possible places for making wild love. No privacy, though—surfers, cars, vans everywhere. And had *From Here to Eternity* been a black-and-white picture? Or had they seen it on a black-and-white TV? Or is it that Hawai'i is so rich in color, so bright, that elsewhere fades?

The day clear, Lāna'i and Moloka'i appeared like purple-gray whales or long, flat clouds on the water. And among the many tiny islets offshore, Rabbit Island did look like a rabbit's head sticking out of the water, long ears laid back. Either that, or the entire rabbit is on top of the water with its rump in the air. Or rabbits live out there; you can almost see them. Keep going in that direction and you'd come to Viet Nam and China.

They were driving into the dark, and thinking about finding a place for the night, when a FOR RENT sign appeared on property across

Kāneʻohe Bay from Chinaman's Hat. Oʻahu, whose brim they were driving around, seemed mirrored in miniature by this conical islet which you could pretend was a hat worn by an underwater giant. Yes, they'll stay here tonight, and maybe live here. It was so quickly and suddenly dark because they were now on the windward side. The Koʻolau Range blocks out the sun. From Kamehameha Highway, they turned onto a dirt road into Tong's Village, Kahaluʻu. On either side of the road loomed dripping jungle, elephant-ear leaves as big as people, vine ropes, the smell of eucalyptus like back home. The road led to a wooden house that looked like the kind children draw, makeshift and temporary, no foundation but short stilts on cement blocks. Lights were on, and they got out of the car. The dark mass out there was gum eucalyptus, all right: buttons and moon leaves covered the ground. A Chinese-looking man answered their knocking. He was very quick and nervous, opening the door instantly. "Who are you? Who are you? I'm Mr. Tong. Who are you?"

Taña gave their first names and last names, and showed Mr. Tong their child, who stood in front of his parents, children able to protect with kidcharm. She stuck out her hand, and he shook it and shook it. "How are you? How are you? How are you?" He shook Wittman's hand and Mario's too.

A habit that the Ah Sings had gotten into was that the White person in the family did the negotiating, went out ahead into America, particularly the rental market. Taña said, "We just got off the plane and want to settle in Hawaiʻi, and need a place to live. Have you got a house for rent?" Wittman wished she hadn't given away their business right off. He should've been quicker, said that they were moving from Honolulu to the country or from another island to this one, passed himself off to this Hawaiian Chinese American as a fellow local.

Mr. Tong said, "I got. Let me show you da kine unit." He rushed out the door with his flashlight, and scuffed into a pair of shower shoes among many shoes on the porch, his entire shoe wardrobe and his wife's shoe wardrobe. He must like us; we look like trustworthy people. Or something's wrong with the unit, he's so eager.

"Walk this way," he said. They followed him on an ever-darkening path. Wittman and Mario did the Groucho walk, and when their leader turned, straightened up. Mario ran to catch up with him as he played his flashlight about. "Bufos," said Mr. Tong. Brown toads were sitting big-eyed and touching the ground with their hands. Mario hunkered to look at them; toads and boy smiled wide smiles. Mr. Tong flashed his light at puddles and ruts and up into the vines. Side paths forked into the jungle. The sound of trees brushing together, banana leaves and bamboo leaves rustling sounded like ocean. You could smell the sea, and earth, and ripe fruit. Stars had come out directly overhead. The solid blackness, blacker than the rest of the ordinary night, was the Ko'olaus, no lights on the face of the mountain. They were in a well. The lights overhead were stars, and the lights on the ground were the star eyes of the bufos. Some jumped and some sat still, entertainers in the spotlight. The mud had manifested them, eyes, smiles, lumps of live mud jumping for the fun of it. "Are bufos special to the Hawaiian people?" asked Taña. Wittman felt proud of her for not being squeamish. "No, no. All, all animals special." But toads *are* special, bringers in haiku of the eternal present moment. Beware of Hawaiians leaving out information.

Mr. Tong, walking and talking, leading the way, said, "This my village—Tong's Village. My wife and I, we sold lunch-wagon sandwiches at the university. I bought one broken-down house, fixed it up, rent it for higher than monthly mortgage, buy anadda house, fix it up, rent it out, buy, fix, buy, fix, anadda one and anadda one. Pretty soon— one whole village. And the village get beeger and beeeger and beeeeger. I give you secret of success—you be rich." Wittman recognized him, a Chinese old guy passing on his immortality to Chinese young guys. Humbly, he suggests that if he, with his poor English and small capital, can make it rich, then anybody—you—can too. These successful guys' advice usually has to do with real estate; real estate is real to them.

"Look, look," said Mario. "Her eyes are shining." He was eye to eye with a bufo. "She's looking inside me, and I'm looking inside her. She's all light. Are my eyes shining too? Do humans' eyes shine too?" They had to tell him the truth: his eyes were not fluorescing, but maybe, if he were sitting where the toad was sitting and the moon and flashlight were just so, they might.

They continued walking on the path overhung with elephant-ear leaves and Spanish moss. On the ground and in round-headed trees with gnarly branches appeared five-petal flowers—cream-yellow stars, burgundy-wine stars, pure-white stars, red-and-white candy-stripe stars. They had arrived at the source of *noa noa* and leis. The air was perfume. These must be the frangipani you read about in Stevenson and

Conrad and Maugham and Melville and Jack London. What Gauguin painted and called *tiares*. And the smell, the essence is *noa noa*.

"Are these frangipani?" Wittman asked.

"Plumeria. *Maké* flowers," said Mr. Tong. "*Maké* means 'death.' Maké trees grow in cemeteries." Throughout their time in Hawai'i, no one will say whether plumeria is the same as frangipani. Gauguin defined *noa noa* as "the fragrance of a bygone joy, which I breathe in the here and now." In darkness, smell—the mix in the air of flowers, fruit, ocean, earth, a whiff of sandalwood for which Chinese named these islands the Sandalwood Mountains—was the most real thing.

They arrived at a little house that was like the landlord's house. You went through a thicket of bamboo, and there it was. "You can rent this one. Ninety dollars a month, and ninety dollars deposit, first and last months—one eighty." Ninety dollars was exactly the same price they were paying back home, but for an upstairs apartment only. Here, a whole house, their first house, a unit unattached to anybody else's. "Can you show us the inside?" asked shrewd Wittman.

They followed Mr. Tong up the steps, and everybody took off their shoes on the porch. The veranda was practically an extra room. Mr. Tong unlocked the door to the dark house. "You can have Hawaiian Electric turn on the utilities tomorrow." He didn't ask if they had jobs, probably assumed that an able-bodied, Chinese-looking guy with a kid must have a job and work hard.

All was clean and bare, ready for beginning anew. The main room had windows on three sides. A door led to two rooms that could be for anything you please, and a bathroom. Another door opened up to a large kitchen. And a porch for indoor-outdoor living. What more would you need? "We'll take it," said Wittman. He did not have to consult privately with Taña. When first they met, and could read each other's minds, they had transmitted back and forth images of just such a house, and explored it together. It seemed they had stood and talked like this before.

"Good," said their landlord. "We be neighbors." He shook Wittman's hand, shook Taña's hand, shook Mario's hand. "One eighty."

They rummaged through a backpack, and wrote out travelers' checks. Mr. Tong said to make it payable to Tong Hui. That was the first time they heard *hui* in Hawai'i. It sounds and means exactly the same as the *hui* in Chinese. It means "community," "association," "people coming together for mutual benefit." If you ask where the word *hui* comes from, China or Polynesia, nobody knows or will say. Linguists teach that any two languages can have seventy-five similar words and they can still be coincidences—not proof that the peoples are related. Hawaiians were connecting themselves to the Jews via the language of the Kabbala. The Mormons claimed Polynesians to be one of the lost tribes of Israel.

Collecting rent was exciting to Landlord Tong. "I charge rent only a little bit more than monthly mortgage payment. The house pay for itself. I get equity long-term. And you—the tenant—get a deal too. You live in the house, no down payment. Win-win."

And he did a social service too: he gave public subsistence. A lot of the people living in Tong's Village were on Welfare, which sent him their housing allowance direct. "You like to know how we spend this money? We send three kids to college: My girl at Lewis and Clark, boy at Orange Coast—top mainland school. One girl at Walla Walla, Washington. You go Orange Coast," he said to Mario. "Surfing, soccer, music, and top education."

Bad Wittman said, "How's your son going to keep his draft deferment at JC, two-year junior college?"

"Our church does not believe in war, but," said Mr. Tong, "our sons cooperate and do their service. They be Conscientious Objector medics. But. Before two years—any moment—it is prophecy—the sky will open and the Hand of God will descend and lift up the chosen. The world as we know it will be over. No more Viet Nam War. No more war."

Mario was looking big-eyed at Mr. Tong. In the unknown spooky dark, this man was saying that a giant was coming.

"Don't worry, honey," said Taña. "Good people will be okay."

"Right," said Mr. Tong. "The Hand of God will smite the bad people. The saved people will fly up in rapture, and sit at the Right Hand of God."

"But," said Mario, "they get *wrapped* into the *air*."

"Rapture," said Wittman. " 'Rapture' means feeling very good."

"We don't fight man's war," said Mr. Tong. "We fight God's war."

"We shouldn't fight any kind of wars," said Wittman.

Landlord Tong gave them the keys and their address, which was a long, hyphenated number on Kamehameha Highway. Wittman walked back with him for the car, and drove the Valiant to their house and abode. Taña set the Gold Mountain trunk for dining. With careful artist's hands, she arranged their three plates, three cups, and three sets of utensils, and the food: Sacramento almonds from the plane, dried fruit, a loaf of San Francisco sourdough bread from SFO, candy bars, and water with Tang crystals. They sat on the rolls of their sleeping bags for chairs, and ate dinner.

In *Noa Noa*, Gauguin wrote about his first night in the country after leaving the capital. He was in the uncivilized part of the island, where they did not use money. A native gestured and called to him, Come eat. He declined, and hid indoors, ashamed of having refused food and wanting food, but not able to catch a fish or dive for shellfish or climb the tall trees. A little girl left cooked vegetables and fruit wrapped in freshly picked leaves at his door.

The Ah Sing family unrolled and unzipped the sleeping bags in the middle of the living-room floor, and opened them out one on top of another. Sheets were all the blanket you needed in this weather. The three of them got in the bed. Lonely Western custom to banish a child to his separate room; they would not do that to Mario their first night in a strange house in the middle of nowhere, out in the Pacific Ocean. They would establish themselves in the center of the house. They would hold the space. A large black window loomed in front of them. At the smaller windows to the sides, banana leaves like people with tall heads and long hands and fingers and war bonnets were peeking and trying to get in. The winds made loud whispery breathing noises. You could almost make out what they were saying. Mario got between his parents with his toy cars in the tunnels and hills and roads of the sheets.

Taña locked the door. They had not locked their doors in Berkeley and Oakland; existentially, they were trusters. Paranoia can attract criminals to you. She brought out a drawing tablet, and aligned on it marijuana and its paraphernalia.

"Taña, you didn't tell me, you're transporting dope. You shouldn't have risked getting us in trouble, Taña." Wittman had quit smoking as a political action.

"It's a farewell present," said Taña. "Our friends laid it on us at the heliport. I couldn't very well refuse."

Well, a fat pouch of gift marijuana from loving and beloved friends wishing you the best had to send you out on a happy trip. Unlike street dope, dealt for money, root of evil. Another reason for leaving California was that the time of free grass and legal LSD was over. A stranger walking by on Telegraph Avenue or in the Haight would have handed you a tab or a cookie for free, as if looking out for Gauguin. Those good high days were no more.

"It's really really intense here tonight," said Taña, "and I want to touch down, and catch up with the jet lag." She nicely joined some papers and pinch-rubbed onto them the high-quality leaves, without stems or seeds. Wittman appreciated her deliberate movements, which were slowing time down already. She rolled a neat, tight joint, and put it in her puckered mouth for a sealing of spit. She lit up with a big inhale and passed him the joint. He couldn't very well let her trip out all by herself. And he didn't like the state of her high and him straight. Might as well reel in his jet-lagging self too. Mario between them said, "Tell me a story." Wittman and Taña, taking turns, made one up in tandem:

"Once upon a time, before you were born, there was a homeless knight and a homeless lady—a princess—a homeless princess. They did not know each other. The knight had left his country because the king was being bad and making war. The knight did not want to go to war. In fact, he did not want to be a knight at all. So he left his country and wandered to a faraway land. He did not carry weapons, neither lance nor spear nor gun. But he did keep his horse and armor, and he rode his horse to the faraway land.

"Meanwhile, the princess had left home too. She had lived in the enemy country that the bad king was making war upon. It was the custom in her country that a princess was supposed to marry the knight who brought her the most amazing gift. But she did not like any of the gifts, which were plunders of war. Plunder means 'stealing,' Mario. The princess did not like any of those plundering knights. So she left for a faraway land.

"The Homeless Knight and the Homeless Princess each had many adventures on his and her own. He came face to face with monsters, and did not kill them. He spoke with them, and taught them to speak. He talked himself out of danger. You can always talk yourself out of danger. When you see danger facing you, little boy, you will know what to say. We'll practice. We'll rehearse.

"The Homeless Princess came upon singing creatures and swimming creatures and flying creatures. And she sang with them and swam with them, and they taught her to fly. She did not shoot them or catch them with a hook or cook and eat them.

"One day, all by himself and all by herself, each one came upon a green hill. On opposite sides of the hill, the Homeless Knight and Homeless Princess climbed a path in the grass. At the top they found a house that had nobody living in it. There were no shut doors and no shut windows. The house was always open to the outer world, because it was safe. Animals and birds and butterflies came and went, and the sun and rain too. And the sounds of the ocean and the trees. Through open windows and open doors, Princess and Knight spotted each other—and met!

"They said, 'Welcome. Welcome home. Make yourself at home.' "

"The house was so empty, they could use any room for whatever they pleased. If they felt sleepy in the living room, why, they could make it their bedroom. There were no secret hiding places for monsters to hide. The house was so bare that Knight and Princess never fought over housework. The house was so bare, they had a little boy, who filled it with toys. The house was so small and open that everybody in it always knew where everybody else was, and they were always close and cozy and cuddin'."

"Mommy, I feel happy, Daddy."

"Everyone was happy."

"I went through the open door, and there was Wittman!"

"And there was Taña!"

"And Mario!"

"And Mario! And they lived happily ever after in their new home."

A new moon—new situation, new moon—smiled through the clouds. The new moon is all smile. Can you see the round head of the Cheshire Cat? The leaf-people in headdresses also peered in, waving and beckoning and waving Good night. The night circled by, and seemed to go on and on. The new moon moved to new places in the sky all the long night.

Wittman floated off the floor, his feet turning toward the left, as if he were being wheeled away. Startled, he jumped up—and flew through the roof and into the sky, and out low over Kāneʻohe Bay. He shot out to the ocean—Chinaman's Hat below, the new moon above, its thin, bright wake on the sea. On the other side of Chinaman's Hat, he looked back at the open ring of the Bay—"I see the whole curve of the Bay"— and was out over the ocean, high over our planet, like a water jewel, and past the moon. I am awake. In fact, he's never been in a more alert state. Everything felt hyperreal. He had a sense of knowing the truth, aware of everything, even his doubts and having smoked dope. "Taña, are you awake? Mario, are you awake? Taña. Mario. Are you guys awake?" They did not answer; they were far away back there on earth. He was not making this up, and not controlling the story. He was blown along, moving fast, being blown by something like a time wind. He was looking at the earth from above—and all around the North Pole was a rainbow, perfectly round and ringing the continents at their tops. People and animals were riding and walking on that bridging rainbow. Oh, he has gone far out in space/time and is looking at eons before the Eastern Hemisphere plate and the Western Hemisphere plate parted, and those are mammoths down there. Time and space are impossible one without the other. The material stuff of the universe is all here forever, neither created nor destroyed, just moving with the Big Bang, which happens all at once, is still happening now. Wittman flew in for a closer look. He went through the mist of the rainbow, the shimmering of before-images and after-images, and sunlight refracting in water and ice. Earth's halo reflected in microcosms of arcing, streaming halos around always-moving beings, people and animals, who travel everywhere. He was definitely awake; he couldn't be making up such detail. The rainbow was also the shine from the turquoise and jade and red coral and jasper that these proto-Indians and proto-Chinese were wearing and trading. Their feet stepped on solid earth—land bridges. And, of course, land bridges were two-way. The mastodons went back and forth; the people went back and forth. There is no telling who was indigenous to where, whether human life originated in Asia or Africa or the Americas or Australia. All is connected to all, and I am conscious of that, and I am conscious that I am conscious. Which is escalating joy.

At another certain distance from earth, in our own time, he saw fires and the spreading black pall. The burning of Viet Nam. He came zooming in like a jet plane, at that terrible speed. And saw war fires, strange reds; the black palls were merging. Those shadows influence lives. People were depressed and thought it was their own psyche or the weather.

(He quoted Defoe: "During the plague, moods were greatly affected by the weather.") Ghosts, the spirits of people being killed, were flying about. Disembodied people hovered near; they are very interested in our doings. They try to advise us, and urge us to do this and that, to further the activities at which they'd had their chances. They envy us our strong, working bodies and materiality; we can carry out dramas, and manipulate and affect and effect the world. The proportion of matter to nothing is minuscule; it's a miracle to have a physical self, and to meet up with this wife, this child—sea turtles well met in all the ocean.

Wittman must have been awake; he could think and doubt. He wasn't seeing anything he hadn't read or heard about before. He was able to question, Am I seeing objective reality? PoPo slept on a pillow that was an arch of wood. The hump presses against the nape of the neck, the acupressure point for memory. (Why people rub the back of their neck: they've forgotten something, and are trying to remember.) On the bridge pillow were drawings of people traveling by foot and on horseback and by palanquin, and a monkey going somewhere too, and an elephant. In a museum at Stanford, another proof of a rainbow land-bridge: a Costanoan "dream pillow." The Costanoans lived—still live—in what is now Berkeley. Like the Chinese, they slept on a rainbow decorated with pictures of migrating people and animals. Some went this way, and some went that way, east to west, west to east.

But Wittman knew, he and his family had not outraced the life-covering pall by coming to Hawai'i.

For a nano-moment, maybe eternity, he shot so far out that he was unconscious of himself. Nothing. Then light. And time. Back to thinking and observing again, he knew with certainty that he was a thousand years old. He was on an immense journey that was now in its thousand-and-first year. A speeding up, a slowing down, his last three lifetimes flashed by. Sucked into, caught, held in time, he lost his high perspective. Brought down from the vantage point from where he could see all things (and wished to fix them), he was pulled into a specific human-scale drama. Wittman was in a post office in the Wild West of about a century ago, after the American Civil War. An eyeshade banding his forehead, and sleevebands and paper cuffs at arms and wrists, he was sorting the mail that had arrived by stagecoach. He was entirely caught up in figuring out which letter went into which slot, the handwriting of names and addresses, and the alphabetical order of the pigeonholes. Utterly absorbed in this task, he was living, moment by moment, an entire long life.

The door opened and shut, and there came and went the smell of horses and rain. In walked Tañe, looking the same as ever, Caucasian, same hair, but netted in a snood. She was dressed like *Little Women* and *Gone with the Wind*, black frogs up the wide skirt, bodice, and collar of her brown velvet dress. Her kid gloves were a sienna-terra color. Wittman came out from behind the counter, and they walked toward each other, looking into each other's eyes. It's you, all right. He was at once attached to her and wanting to escape her, to be with her and to part. Stuck. Right there in public, he clutched her by the shoulders. She said, "I do love you," or "I don't love you." He could not get exactly whether she said "do" or "don't." And he couldn't very well say, "What? What you say? You love me? Speak up." The negative is a very small sound, a mere hum of the nose. He nodded. "I love you too," he said, and so clambered on the wheel with her again for life, for another lifetime, for many lifetimes.

Suddenly the time wind came up again, and that marriage with Tañe sped past in a blur. They parted ways without having to say good-bye, and he was relieved to fly off. But he landed in the post office once again. He heard Tañe's voice, "Oh, we're at the post office again." This time the workers were dressed in khaki uniforms, and Tañe was behind a teller's cage. It was a banking post office, and probably in Alaska; the town had that prefab look of a frontier outpost. (Many people migrate, like the golden plover, between Alaska and Hawai'i. The University of Alaska and the University of Hawai'i have exchange programs.) You could see backward through the window, UNITED STATES POST OFFICE, and the main street; people whom he recognized were going about business. Wittman and Tañe must be here in the Yukon because of her chanting of Robert Service, that ballad about being out in the Great Alone. He walked past the other people to the front of the line.

"I'm tired of working at the post office," Tañe complained. "You should be at work supporting me, Wittman. I made a mistake marrying you, a man who doesn't love me enough to support me."

"But you're the women's liberationist. You want to work; you want to bring in the money. You keep saying you don't want to be a mere housewife." And she's the White person in this interracial marriage. They know the system, it's theirs, let her work it.

"That doesn't mean that you stop working. I hate this; you've turned me into a shrew nagging, 'Get a job.' "

"I am working. I'm a poet. A poet works. And you benefit. I take you out amongst the artists. We have a bohemia of friends."

"No, you don't. You hang around the bohemians and the demi-monde, and I work. It's not fair. You're being a poet at my expense. I don't want the life of the woman supporting the poet. You don't love me. You just hang around for the luxuries that I provide."

"I never asked you to provide for me."

"Somebody has to go to work. I couldn't wait around for you to get a job. I took a job so you wouldn't be trapped and unfree. And you don't appreciate it. All you do is play. All I do is work."

"When you met me, you told me you liked the way I was non-conformist. I'm not a sell-out to the bourgeois ordinaire workaday world."

"I changed my mind. I grew up, okay? I want to be the non-conformist. I didn't know better, to get the free life for myself, not just marry it."

"You said you wanted to be free to leave the house and work like a man."

"Does that mean that you get to stop working like a man? A woman feels loved when the man works for her."

"I'm leaving. You don't have to support me anymore."

"Go, then. Go. Go."

The people in line didn't yell at them to get on with business. They were in the slow days, when each customer had a satisfying visit with the clerk.

"Here. Take your mail and go." She pushed divorce papers across at him. He lifted his hands so as not to touch them. See what a longtime plotting schemer she is? She got this post-office job for the satisfaction of personally and officially hand-delivering his walking papers. He turned about and ran out of the post office. Got away from her. The ability to fly into the air out to sea and off the planet had abandoned him. He forgot that he could ever have flown. He had to live moment by moment this life of being married to the postmistress.

All of a sudden, Taña rolled over and whacked him in the mouth; her thumb plugged him. Years and stars whirled by, and stopped—thwack—she held her hand up for him to kiss, and jabbed him. Knocked him back to his body, sleeping on the floor in Hawai'i.

He lifted Taña's hand off his face. "Taña, wake up. I've got to tell you something." A privilege of being married is having someone you can wake up and tell your trips to. "Taña, are you awake?" "Yeah, yeah." "You just brought me back from the most far-out trip. We've been married two times before this marriage. To each other. We've been married forever. The only person I've been married to in all my incarnations is you. There is such a thing as reincarnation. I've had direct experience of it. I don't think it's the dope. We've never had a good marriage, and we have to keep reincarnating and being married to each other until we get it right." She made sleepy noises. "Divorce will not liberate us. We have to keep marrying each other. We were mail clerks in our penultimate lifetimes. Were you there? Did you dream about being in a post office?" Of course, two people whose heads are together night after night, year after year, would be in each other's dreams.

Taña sat up. "What are you saying? You're saying divorce? How many times have I told you, you can't hold me accountable and get mad at me for what you dreamed. I can do anything I want in your dream, and you can't get me for it."

Then Mario was up, and they couldn't talk about divorce anymore. "I remember," said Mario, "I was three people." He held up his fingers. "One, I was caveman. Two, I was cowboy. Three, I am me here." He'd also been an animal; he's forgotten already. At Tilden Park, he had looked at a bush with red berries and said, "When I was a raccoon, I ate those red berries."

"Hey," said Mario. "Wait a minute. I'm on the edge of the bed. Why am I on the edge? All night I was in the middle between you and you, Mommy, Daddy."

"No, I'm the middle one."

"No. I was. For sure."

Each of them had felt a being on either side of him or her. "Somebody was on *this* side *and* somebody on *this* side." Somebody. Who?

"*Both* sides."

"I was awake a lot, and didn't change places and didn't see anybody change places."

"No, I was the last person awake, and asked, 'Who's awake?' And nobody answered."

"No, *I* was the last asleep. I talked to you guys until you didn't talk back anymore."

"Me too. I did that too."

The place was haunted. The three of them huddled together in a family hug.

Roosters crowed. Many roosters were calling, "Wake up!" Their fierce, healthy, individual voices set one another off, calling, answering. "Awake! Awake!" "What a da-a-ay!" "I can cro-o-ow louder than yo-o-ou." "O. O. O. O. O." "Awe. Awe. Awe." "Aloha-a-a." Ah, our ancestors awoke every dawn to cockcrow. The newcomers to the country threw on clothes, found their shoes, and went out to look for the roosters. The jet lag was in their favor. Resolve to keep that jump on the day. We are awake at too few dawns.

They followed the rooster songs through bamboo and banana groves, green and yellow hands of bananas, guava and papaya trees, and buffalo grass with Job's tears. (So Job's tears grow pearly gray in nature; they're dyed into love beads.) The various fruits were not organized row upon row as in agribiz but wildly jumbled. Taro voluntarily grew in ancient beds. Houses exactly alike were spaced among the greenery. If the jungle were flattened, the village would look like migrant labor housing in the Central Valley.

No one else was up, no rushing out into the day. Tong's Village was sleeping in. No commuter traffic into town. These are signs of poverty, but lush foliage, rich nature, trees hanging with fruit—"Eat me"— disguised the poverty of the poorest area in America.

Every rooster lived in its own separate cage, and on the eave was lettered its name: Pedro, Romeo, Adobo, Champ, Boy, Amboy, Bong Bong. They must be Pilipino fighting cocks. They were stretching and crowing as you watched, pluming and ruffling fiery-orange and green-black feathers. They looked at you with yellow eyes. Mario called them by name; he could read already. "Hi, Bong Bong. There's Boy. Hello, Boy. Hello, Romeo." Stretching their entire selves, craning their necks, spreading their feet, they cock-a-doodle-dooed from tiptoe to crown-comb, and out the wide-open beak. The urgency and effort of calling reddened their faces. Maybe they were not fighting cocks, none wounded or crippled like in *The Day of the Locust*.

Out of the nearest house came a Pilipino-looking guy, a Manong, but bigger and darker than back home. "What you messing with the chickings?" he said.

"We're just listening to them," said Taña. "They have beautiful voices and colors. Are they yours?"

"Are they your pets?" asked Mario.

"I like their names," said Taña. "Is there a Juliet? Is one of these hens Juliet?" The hens were loose, scratching about outside the cages.

"We are your new neighbors," said Wittman. "We live over there." He gave his name, and his wife's and son's names.

The man, extending aloha, said that he was Black Pete, and his wife's name was Mary. He said, "You like fish? Wait here." He was blacker than any Black person. It must be the Hawaiian sun. He went inside, and you could hear him and Mary cluck-clucking away. Pilipino language must come from their raising chickens, that quick bok-bok-bok. Black Pete came out with a bucket of water that had a fish swimming in it. Fresh. Alive. "Anadda day, you come, Mary fix you clams, eel, blowfish." The giving culture has not died.

Mary appeared in the kitchen window. She looked and sounded like a tough man, smoking, praising her husband and the nice fish. "Black Pete only get one lung, you know. Seventy years old, he can dive fifty feet on one lung of air. No gear. Free-dive. You come diving with heem. And come go out to Chinaman's Hat and chum for sharks. You catch blowfish, bring 'em back to me for cook 'em for you good. Can poison you with one taste, but I know how fix 'em. Kāneʻohe Bay has plenty clams too."

"And all this fruit in the trees? Is it free? Does it belong to nobody too? We can pick it?"

"Help yourself."

"Pick guava and mango and papaya, otherwise fall and rot. Coconut too. Not banana but. They belong to da kine." "The kind"—Landlord Tong.

So, walking back to their house, the little family did help themselves, picking guava and papaya and mangos. Nuts and fruit they'd never before seen grew way high and also at picking level. Many just-right fruits, not too insect-bitten, had dropped. They would forgo the coconuts until they could find out how to open them. Taña took a long stick and pushed papayas off, which Wittman and Mario caught. Mario set the bucket with the fish far from where the fruit would fall. The fish was not food. Mario said, "She is my pet. Her name is Linda." Wittman held him up to pick tomato guavas. People living here should always be happy.

Dawn lit the mountain range—the Ko'olaus are immense green stage curtains for some epic drama. In its draping folds and creases, twenty-three long, long waterfalls, silvery, glassy ribbons of water, fell and fell. It had rained, and twenty-three waterfalls were spraying and spattering uncountable rainbows, spangling big rainbows and tiny rainbows inside main rainbows, rainbows within rainbows. Diamonds leapt out and vanished. Winds lifted and dropped the water, which waved like strands of DNA, like Rapunzel's hair. Yes, resolve to get up early every day, and not miss any more dawns. The full sun came up out of the sea—roseate, golden ocean. And shooting stars made meteoric lines that streaked the sky, and lasted. They're jet trails caused by the planes taking off from the Kaneohe Marine Corps Air Station.

If you could see far enough past Chinaman's Hat and over the horizon to where the airplanes were going, there would be Viet Nam. The planes were flying straight out from KMCAS to go there. The dawn is so fragile and quickly gone anyway, and we want to blow it up. We want to answer it with a matching glorious bang.

For the benefit of their child and the beauty of this first dawn in Hawai'i, Wittman and Taña said in unison:

> The sun rose on the flawless brimming sea
> into a sky all brazen—all one brightening
> for gods immortal and for mortal men
> on plowlands kind with grain.

Back at the house, they emptied the Gold Mountain trunk, and put its contents here and there. Taña cut up the fruit in the kitchen, where she displayed the one pot, the pan, the spatula and wooden spoon, and the coil for heating water. Counting aggregately, their things came to only six: art supplies, clothing, cooking utensils, toiletries, paper (passports, driver's license, money, books), and bedding. Wittman rolled up the sleeping bags and sheets, and that took care of housekeeping. Father and son pushed the trunk to a corner, and that was the breakfast nook. They had their second meal in this new land, which provides the food. They had new foods to name — Pukey Papaya, Mandrake Mango, Guapo Guava.

Taña reassembled her easel out on the porch. Here would be her studio, in air and light.

Mario could have had a bedroom, but he unrolled his backpack on the closet floor and said, "I want this coziest room to be mine." His sleeping bag fit just right; its foot was against a tiny door that led to a crawl space and outside. Linda in her bucket was next to his pillow. "Linda and I are moving in here."

Taña said, "Today, I'll see what images are coming here to me. I'll be out in my studio." She was dressed besmeared with the colors of her palette.

"I'm going to make friends," said Mario. "I'm finding the kids of this place."

Wittman would do practical things, see about Hawaiian Electric, return the Valiant for the cash deposit, check out the hitchhiking. With an expired driver's license, he would have to drive flawlessly; every California man is a great driver. They said farewell on the porch, like normal Americans, wife and child saying goodbye to the workaday husband/daddy. "Drive carefully," said Taña.

At Kamehameha Highway, Wittman decided to turn left; he would continue going around the island, go to Honolulu the long way, all around the rim. He would circumnavigate the island. Be alone in it. The Windward Side is the farthest away from the U.S.A. mainland. Jungle vines and enormous leaves almost met overhead. The sun seemed to have gone back down. The island was doing its optical illusions.

The people here junk their cars along the highway, and the jungle rusts them and takes them apart. Vines twined and hung from the jib of a crawler crane, and trees grew inside its cab. The jungle is winning; the red earth absorbs cars and earth-moving equipment. A backhoe's bucket, dead on the ground, was filled with water and grasses. Wittman drove out of a tunnel of greenery, and saw the surf line on his right again, and the Ko'olaus on his left. The Ko'olau Range is the solid center of the island, the top of a long, broad mountain risen from the bottom of the sea. There is no way into it. No roads or terraces on that implacable mountain range. No mountain climbers on its face — people don't scale it like El Capitan — and no caves to hide in.

Wittman was alone on the road, and could've driven on the wrong side if he'd wanted. Then one car went by, then another. The commuters waved to him in greeting. They were on their way to work in Kāneʻohe or Kailua or Honolulu. They must think him strange, going in the opposite direction. He passed Waiāhole Station, and a road leading toward the mountain, maybe to a town named Waiāhole, but as far as he could see, no town. Maybe the closed-up banana stand and gas pump and store *was* Waiāhole Station. This was the second banana stand he'd passed; the other was in Kahaluʻu.

He drove on, and the terrain changed. Some places, a row of houses one-house deep lined the shore. At the foot of the mountain range were pastures with horses. The climate was dryer now, normal, more like northern California. Ironwood trees with tassels of long needles grew among eucalyptus. Wittman pulled into a parking lot at Kahana Bay, a gray, overcast beach almost like Stinson Beach. Only one other vehicle, a van, was parked at the other end of the lot.

Wittman got out into cold wind, fog, sprinkly rain, and walked barefoot toward the water, stepped painfully on ironwood burrs, and reached the gray powder sand. Sun lit up seaweed kelp vines strung with big yellow-brown bulbs like lightbulbs, some floating in water and some grounded. The seaweed bulbs are not transparent enough to look through and see the world ambered. (In this time of finding natural highs, people made kaleidoscopes to frame and fracture sightings.) The sand fleas bit Wittman's ankles. The waves were flat and came from and went far out to sea. Sand crabs brushed ahead of the waves, and rushed into and out of holes. The edges of the waves were like tiny white horses prancing. They were also like many many fingers dancing and playing piano. There were no birds in the sky, only the planes coming into and taking off from Kaneohe Marine Corps Air Station. No surfers either, the waves too flat. You follow a wave, and it goes out and out and out. From the reef, another wave comes in and in and in, soaks into the sand, ends at your feet. Now and forever, the waves are coming and coming and coming, and going and going and going. Always. Always. Always. Now. Now. Now. The rate of change, water changing earth, is the pace of evolution. The changes are so slow, they seem stopped, stuck in the nothing sky, and time, which is nothing, stuck between past and future; we want to break out, blow it up, explode into the infinite. Wittman was aware of emptiness, and afraid. There probably isn't reincarnation; the people you love will suffer and die. Tibetans teach that upon feeling a strong emotion, such as fear, you shouldn't say, "I am afraid." Say, "There is fear." "There is fear," said Wittman aloud. Oh, that is worse—fear is an emanation from this place, trying to get me. He counted the waves, watched for a largest ninth wave, lost track. As a conscious being, he had the job of keeping an eye on all this—the kelp, the grasses, the sea grapes. You want to do something about it, find a use for it, fish it, shoot it, eat it, blow it up.

Suddenly into the sky sailed a pair of magnificent frigatebirds, gliding on the winds. *Fregata magnificens.* Man-o'-war bird in Southern California. The sky held two 'iwa. Male and female soared together and soared apart. Each pointed wing spanned the height of a tall human being. The 'iwa gyred, now black against the sun: now glinted a white breast, now a red throat. They are the birdpeople that fly in hope-filled dreams.

At the other end of the curve of beach was a group of people. They had an encampment, blankets on clotheslines and stakes making a tent or a windbreak. To be here this early, so much equipage, they might have spent the night. A row of fishing poles were stuck into the ground with lines out into the water. Wittman could not hear them over the sound of the ocean and wind. All was hazy in the rain that came and went in layers of gauzy scrim. Their hair blew smokily around their heads.

He ought to go over there, introduce himself, have a closer look, not miss anything. They might be rare real Hawaiians. Be respectful and quiet. But maybe he should leave, not disturb them on their territory at the edge of the world, at the edge of the day. It would be nice of them to invite him over to their fire, which they knew how to keep lit in this coming-and-going rain. But he shouldn't obligate them to give him their catch of food. And he was in no mood to hear racists say, "Go home, kachink. Yankee, go home." He got up, squatted down, got up, walked around ironwood burrs, walked to and backed up from the waves, examined his own footprints, like Friday's.

Two black creatures were bobbing in the water. Seabirds? Seals? They bobbed closer—people, one prone and the other supine, talking with each other. They stood up and walked toward him. Wittman straightened up, and went to meet them partway. Close up, he saw: Twins—each so beautiful, God made two.

Two Hawaiians, wet with ocean water and now rainwater (*wai* and *kai*—salt water and fresh water), invited him to join them. The guy said, "Eh, bradah, you like come go eat?" Four verbs in a row, all movement their language, like the wind and the ocean. And you—brother—the honored subject of all those verbs, addressed as brother upon meeting.

"You stay come, then," said the girl.

Stories warn not to eat anything on the strange land, or else you get trapped, fall under spells. But there are also consequences for refusing food—making enemies, insulting the worth of offerings, going hungry, not becoming part of the place. Wittman walked between the mermaid and the merman. The gathering of the tribes continues, and he has been invited to dine. He went along on his bare haole feet, stepping on excruciating ironwood burrs. They slowed down for him, and ah-ed him. What you say in pain, and sympathy for another's pain, is *auwē*. Instead of "ouch" or "ow" or "aiya," the sound they make here is "awe-way." They pointed to a blue bubble in the sand. It looked like the plastic stuff when you were a kid for blowing bubbles with a straw, tougher than bubble gum. Be careful—Portagee man-o'-war. Following the tail, they marveled at the length of it. "One Portagee man-o'-war can wrap your body around and around." "Once, I swam into a fleet of da kine." "In the water, that blue stripe flips up like a comb, like a sail." "The tail wrapped my arm. Awe-way. Pain all over, shooting through the lymph glands, you know, so hard to swim." "Get to land, and piss on 'em, or call your friend piss on 'em." "Also for coral cut and sea-urchin spine, piss on 'em and pour Adolph's Meat Tenderizer on 'em. Da kine grows inside your skin." The girl was as tall as the guy, the two of them with lush curls of black hair, hers to her waist and his to his shoulders. Both spoke with deep, rich voices.

Wittman's hair was long too, but flat and tied back in a pirate tail. Theirs was loose and floaty. The wind dried and lifted it, and it rose above their heads. Wittman was glad that he himself was tall, though inappropriately dressed (black T-shirt and blue jeans).

The girl said, "I, Lilinoe. He, Edmund Lele." And in a friend-making voice asked, "What's your name? What your name be?" She spoke in two ways; he heard it.

"I, Wittman Ah Sing."

In the movie, Ali'i Nui Mālama and her consort were husband and wife *and* brother and sister. But that was in the olden days—a custom among the royalty for purposes of consolidating power. Wittman, who didn't have a sister, saw an ideal: a relationship of equals, a man and a woman perfectly equal.

"What school you went?" Lilinoe asked. "I went Roosevelt. He graduated Kamehameha." She was telling the newcomer from maybe not too far away that she lived at the Hawaiian Homestead housing at Papakalea, and went to the school that had been English Standard. And Edmund Lele was one of the elite Hawaiian kids, having gone to the second-most-endowed school in the country. (Yale was first.)

"University of California," said Wittman. He didn't say "Cal"; he didn't say "Berkeley."

"What high school, that is?" said Edmund Lele.

"Sac High, Sacramento High School in California. I'm from California. That's the high school in the middle of the city, not too rich, not too poor." There. He categorized himself for them, and he demonstrated that he recognized that they were placing him.

From the Gypsy-like encampment, the smell of meat cooking and the sound of string music wafted down the beach. His mouth watered at the barbecue char smell. Savages, thought Odysseus/Wittman; they eat heavy meat for breakfast. Maybe they live here, too much stuff for a picnic. They had appeared like in a Chinese movie, where gods alight and become extraordinarily good-looking people who walk amongst us. In Hawaiian stories, it's mountains that get up and interact with us. The camp was the bright color on this gray beach, as if a spotlight shone on this group, or came from them. Sheets of flower-patterned cloth tied to trees and stakes made apple-green-and-violet-pink walls. All of the people looked at their guest; he stay come. Are they wondering, Who is this man in black at leisure on this workday?

There was a tremendous amount of food. The brick barbecue pit provided by the Park Service was fired up, and a couple of hibachis—a mixed grill—beef, fish, chicken, pork. Steak *and* hamburger, fish from the Bay and tako poki and laulau and lomilomi salmon. More food than the half-dozen people here could eat, as if they were awaiting many people with many tastes. A giant with a black eyepatch manned the barbecue and the hibachis. On the picnic table were more piles of food—rice and rice balls and bread and char siu bow, which here they call manapua. Bags of potato chips and Frito-Lay corn chips. And many kinds of salads. Potato salad and baked potatoes and potatoes au gratin. Cold cuts, Spam, Spam on the barbecue and Spam cold. Pineapple and coconuts. Coconuts cracked open for the meat, and coconuts with a hole for the milk. And cool chests and washtubs full of sodas and beer, Primo. It seemed many meals for many days.

"Is this a lūʻau?"

"No, no special occasion."

Wittman's escorts walked him into the grove to a woman on a lounge chair. A haku lei with fern points crowned silver hair fanning about the large face that regarded him with unconditional kindness. Beside her, a girl cross-legged on the lau-hala mat was slitting and shredding ti leaves with her fingernails. Edmund Lele said, "Tūtū, this Wittman Ah Sing. Wittman, this Tūtū. Grandmadda." He also said the grandmother's long name, full of "k"s and "l"s. She held her visitor by both hands and lifted herself to kiss him on one cheek and then the other cheek, fully and warmly, then turned her face each way for him to kiss. They are very affectionate people, loving right away, no boundaries. "*Aloha nui*, Tūtū," said Wittman, taking a linguistic chance that they actually talk as he heard in the movie. He called her Grandmother, and was instantly grandson of this family.

The girl bit the spines of two ti leaves, knotted the stalk ends together, stood, and put the new lei around Wittman's neck, the knot against his nape, and the fringed leaves flat on his chest. He had to bow and kneel to receive the lei. The girl also kissed him on either cheek and said, "Hi, Wittman." Four kisses already upon meeting, eight counting his in return. How affectionate they are. They have a culture of affection.

And all the while, a troubadour at Tūtū's other side played on six-string ukulele a music that accompanied, commented upon, and sometimes seemed to direct moods; it expressed the feelings of now this one and now that one, and now of the group. Life was at last a musical. Such a small instrument, and it carried over the sounds of ocean and wind. A gourd with ribbons tied around its neck or waist sat nearby; it was the shape of Kano the rock in the movie. (The immortal who spies on us left his water gourd.) The musician picked it up with his feet, and pounded percussion on the earth.

Grandmother presented each person to Wittman, introduced the heralds again. "Edmund Lele you know. And Lilinoe also you know.

Hea, Calvin. *Hea,* Tremayne. *Hea,* Princess. *Hea,* Pua from Moloka'i."
Calvin, who was cooking, waved his spatula like a scepter. Tremayne, on
ukulele and gourd, wagged his eyebrows. Pua of Moloka'i was the girl
who gave him the ti-leaf lei. Princess was a woman who was sitting outward at the picnic table with her back to the food, smoking a cigarette.
She got up and gave him a smoky kiss on the corner of his lips.

"Come eat," Tūtū invited and commanded. "All come eat." She
held out her hand for Wittman to hold. He helped her up out of the
chaise throne, and escorted her to the head of the picnic table, facing
the sea. She had the presence of an actress onstage, hugely moving from
this exact place to that exact place. She had the large features of an
actress too; you could see her face from distances. Her high silver hair
waved and blended with the general silver-gray of the sky. It's wonderful
she is big; so much kindness exists. (Taña often said, "Fat models are the
most interesting to draw." Wittman readjusted his aesthetics.) A mountain had stood up and become her. If he had known the terrain, he could
have looked about and seen which mountain was not there. Tūtū
motioned Wittman to sit at her right, Princess on his other side. He felt
surrounded by expanses of dark skin, sparkling with salt crystals from
ocean and sweat. The cloth walls of this pavilion were their pareu dresses.

The men came to the table, and before sitting down shook their
guest's hand, other hand on his shoulder, almost a hug. Calvin, who
brought over platters of meat, sat at the foot of the table, nearest the
barbecue, and the ukulele boy and the lei girl on either side of him.

The Hawaiians were extraordinarily beautiful, every one of them,
including the men. They were like ideal Chinese, but skin more sienna
than yellow, non-slitty big eyes, double, triple lids. Their nose has a
bridge. They're like Pilipinos, but large and tall. And their hair is like
Blacks' but not nappy-kinky, their skin black, but not that black. They
almost look Caucasian, but tan. They're like Mexicans and any kind of
Indians perfected. In fact, they are Native American too.

Calvin presented a whole fish to Wittman, the guest. "Fresh kine,
just now swimming in the Bay."

"Please, you say grace, Wittman," said Tūtū. "Continue prayer you
been praying." Oh, she thinks I was praying, kneeling on the sand. Fallen
among religious fanatics and proselytizers. The island is full of them,
rudely putting him on the spot to take a stance vis-à-vis God. These are
not pagan heathens but missionaries, inquisitioners. He should say,

"Grace. 'Say good night, Gracie.' 'Good night, Gracie.' " Monkey would dive into the potato salad with both hands and big maw mouth, and talk and eat. But Wittman, the daddy, had been teaching his own kid table manners. The first rule of improv is: say Yes to anything that the other players suggest. Improv grace. Whom to address? For political and historical reasons, democratic American, he would not say Father or Lord. We are not children or feudal serfs. Taña would address the Goddess; he can't do that. Last night he had tripped way far out, and did not see a giant or giantess organizing the universe. Automatically, under peer pressure, his head bowed in prayer pose. He peeped at his tablemates; their eyes were downcast, and no one peeped back. "You," he said. "You. Kind, surprising new friends well met under the sky beside the Koʻolaus on this island in the Pacific Ocean. Thank *you* for the munificent food. Thank you for knowing to distribute food to everyone, even feeding the stranger." Yes, the people here caught, bought, and cooked this food, and it's they who should be thanked. "Thank you. May we always be prosperous and safe as we are right now. Don't let harm ever come to a one of these trusting people. Don't send them to war. Don't pick Edmund Lele's and Tremayne's numbers in the draft lottery. I cast a kapu over them—you—and over all my family and everyone, that bombs never fall on anyone here, nor anywhere." This grace is not graceful, not much of a grace under fire, but not bad for the first and only grace of his life. "Amen," he said, like in the movies.

But they did not start eating. Tūtū continued prayer. He hadn't prayed enough; he hadn't done it right, she had to correct him, and pray more. He was her warm-up act, and she was to do the main praying, and they were going to go all the way around the table. "O Lord, our Father," she began. No Pele, no Ku, no Lono. "We thank Thee for Thy generosity that descends with the head-tapping rain and the cane-tapping rain and the face-touching rain." She said those rains in Hawaiian and their English translations. And it was raining. "We are grateful for the food-growing rain that makes this bounty from the earth and the sea. Help us to embrace and be worthy of all you give us—pain and loss, sickness, death, and war. Teach us to grow in our love for one another and Thee. We thank Thee, thank Thee, thank Thee. Amen."

She was saying to go about with the attitude of thankfulness, to take on the most terrible problems with aggressive thanking. God respects us by giving us the worst suffering.

I can't do that, thought Wittman.

Next Calvin said, in the speaking-to-God voice: "Please, God, take care of the sons in war. Do not let them be hurt or killed. Nor hurt or kill others. Bring them back home safe. Take care of daughters in war. Get one granddaughter fool girl join up army for makeup makeover. Please don't let her get killed or wounded. Don't let her come back worst, she not be one Nightwalker, nightwalking on this ocean here or on Viet Nam ocean forever." He spoke to God like a lawyer, defended the grand-daughter against monkey's-paw loopholes. Coming home does not mean in a body bag. "Protect the sweet and happy boys and girl, they come back grown up sweet and happy men and woman. By'm'by, she come return to home, to here, one good kind wahine woman, one beau-tiful woman, beautiful already without makeup. May she win the war, and be happy. You the God, make all this come true. Amen."

And each of them had a turn. Princess, who had put out her ciga-rette, prayed, "God bless all those far away at War in Viet Nam." She chanted a list of men's names and one woman's name. "And help us love and forgive our enemy as ourselves. Especially the families, women and children, in the tunnels. God, the Americans are making bombs with da kine plastic shrapnel that does not show up on the X-ray. Help us understand Thy will, that we may carry it out. Bless the families of war-riors who sacrifice gladly. Amen." Human sacrifice. They come from a tradition of human sacrifice with ritual cannibalism.

As soon as she finished, Wittman spoke up, to tell Princess and everyone the good news: "Back home at UC Santa Cruz, the peace movement has raised the money to buy a sonar machine that can detect the shrapnel. There is such a machine; it has been invented. And mem-bers of the peace movement are delivering it to Hanoi." No one argued with him about giving traitorous aid and comfort to the enemy. They felt good; we invented an antidote to un–X-ray-able shrapnel.

The talk of horrible weapons did not spoil appetites. The 'ohana gave the food their devoted enjoyment. The meat was still warm, and the salads and drinks cold. They'd gotten work done, praying: teaching and learning, telling of plaints and fears, facing terrors, giving news to God and to one another. They'd expressed themselves, and now could eat and laugh in the coming and going rain. No one here had yet lost a relative to Viet Nam.

The surprising rain tickled them. They laughed—here we are, people who don't know to come in out of the tickling rain. "*Kilikili*," they said. *Ka wai kilikili noe* is fine, misty rain that tickles in the many ticklish parts of our bodies—neck, insides of arms, ears, feet. Stay in it and laugh.

Language-loving Wittman was learning vocabulary. '*Ohana* is like *hui*, but *hui* is people organizing for business, whereas '*ohana* is "family," originally "family gathering for prayer." '*Āina* is the land, the specific earth of Hawai'i; it is part of the motto of the state of Hawai'i: *Ua mau ke ea o ka 'āina i ka pono.* "The life of the land is preserved in righteousness." These people are *kama'āina*, children of the land. And they will adopt—*hanai*—the stranger, who can then belong to this country. Words you hear every day in these islands—'*ohana, hui, hānai*—have to do with coming together as a loving community.

"Ah, Ah Sing," said the Tutū, informing the table. "Old kama'āina family, Ah Sing. The oldest Pākē kama'āina family."

" 'Pākē kama'āina family,' " mimicked Wittman.

"Longtime Chinese resident child of the land. Land child."

Oh, you don't have to be Hawaiian blood, you can belong to the 'āina.

"Ah Sing, sugar pioneer, brought beeeeg millstone for grinding cane. Twice, he gave up and took away the millstone, came back, went away. You see the sugar chimney nearby? Spreckels Sugar boats brought the cane from Ewa side to here." Wittman had passed a brick ruin, that very chimney. "We have Ah Sing in our calabash—yes, we do."

He had thought that Ah Sing was a made-up American name, his parents' stage name. Everyone at the table was giving him that happy look that we get when we find another one of us. We got you connected up with us, you long-lost calabash cousin.

"We Pākē too," said Calvin. "Long time ago, Pākē old man all alone, he marry Hawaiian widow with one dozen keikis, and hānai the whole family. Most everybody get one of those Pākē grandfathers." You have aloha, give and take aloha, you be Hawaiian.

Tremayne chanted, "I twelve and hapa percent Chinese, twelve and hapa percent Pilipino, twenty-five percent Portagee, twenty-five percent Samoan, fifty percent Hawaiian, fifty percent hapa haole. . . ."

"Wait a minute. You can only have a hundred percent," said Edmund Lele, straight man.

"Doubt it. My sistah get two hundred."

Everybody in Hawai'i is avidly interested in race, tells race jokes, and keeps track of what races I am and you are.

"I have a son," said Wittman. "My keiki is half Pākē and a fourth Dutch and one-eighth Irish and one-sixteenth Indonesian and one-sixteenth Cherokee." Surely, blood flows backward too, and the father gets some race from the son.

"Princess won Miss Cosmopolitan," said Pua, "*and* Miss Black Hawai'i. She won against da kine Popolo girls from Hickam and Scho-field. Princess of O'ahu! And Lilinoe Narcissus Queen!"

Lilinoe said, "Princess and I went to the Mainland sponsored by the Hawai'i Visitors Bureau."

Princess said, "Wherever we went, shopping centers coast to coast, and in the Midwest, America's Heartland, the Popolos said to us, 'You are the most beautiful Afro-American women we have ever seen.' We said, 'We aren't Negroes,' but they wouldn't believe us. We had to keep saying, 'We aren't Negroes.'"

Wittman didn't like her conceit. She was like Latinas back home who said, "I'm of Spanish extraction, not Mexican." Would it have hurt to let the Blacks, who are forging a new aesthetic of what's good-looking, take pride in this ideal beauty? Look at her—anyone would want to be the same kind as her. But race is in the eyes of the beholder; if you look at her and think Black, then she looks Black. You think Italian, your eye searches out the features that are to you Mediterranean, such as olive skin, aquiline nose. Noses and lips are a degree more or less flared or flat or wide. We differ but shades and fractions of an angle from one another. Whatever race you're thinking, you can see it.

Edmund Lele and Calvin picked up guitars; the sounds of tuning went with the plink and plunk of a raindrop here and a raindrop there. Princess stood tall and still, held up her arms, and moved to the same wind that moved the palm fronds. The waves undulated behind her. She held out her arms and danced toward Wittman, looked directly and softly into his eyes, held the gaze. Singled out, he felt chosen and lucky. "You and I. Only you. Only you." Her mien was full of feeling for him. She was not smiling but seriously giving in to beholding him, beloving him. I love you. The in-love kind of love. I am in love with you. Her eyes were pouring love into his eyes. In public, shamelessly. He thought about looking away, but it would be impolite. How can I bear this much demonstrativeness? And how to return in kind? It must be good manners to give love—aloha—back to her, to let her see emotions well up. I love you. I love you. Does a returning love show in his eyes? It must. He has brown eyes, she has brown eyes, easy for warmth to flow back and forth. There were not the negotiating complexities of looking into Taña's blue eyes, like skies and seas. These eyes were of the warm, deep earth. But they're putting on an act and a show, aren't they? Aloha, part of the hula and the culture, nothing personal. In-love is personal, unique to me and the one person meant for me alone. Lilinoe and Pua stepped to either side of Princess and danced too. At a certain place in the music, all the women gazed upon him, the beloved. Their bodies and arms drew him, pulled away, yearned and withdrew, then almost touched him again. They passed their opening and closing hands over their hearts, and extended them to him, and touched their hearts again. In an open-handed, strewing, sowing movement, they poured kindness into him. His soul—'uhane—he has a soul—filled with aloha, and he was Hawaiian. At the end of a dance, someone would shout "Hana hou!"— "Encore!"—and they danced it again.

The cultural revolutions and the Illegal Religions Act had not killed off the hula.

Word-needing Wittman asked Tremayne to translate please, and he did: "You are freshly adorned as the cool dew-laden plants. . . . Love alights like mist over the lei I've woven for you. . . . Flowers thrive in the water, softened and drenched by the rain. . . . Sweet the fragrance of the maile, kept fresh and moist in the misty rain." Maile are plants, and they are goddesses of the hula. The rain kept changing, and the people sang mele to the rain of the moment. At one point, Tremayne said, "There is no translation for that. You can't say that in English." Polite guest Wittman did not say but thought, I am amongst nonreaders. Anything can be said in English; just use more words is all.

Suddenly Tremayne pounded the gourd, resounding the earth. Tūtū, who sat upon the ground, danced from that root position, her torso and arms reaching for the ocean, the sky, the mountains. She clicked the rocks in her hands like castanets.

Calvin stepped with authority on the ground and danced slap-knee men's hula, at once singing in a deep-cave voice. Tremayne translated: "Hold fast to an idea, hold fast to the tapa blanket of mist. Listen here, O Mist, nestling now on Ka'ala." Touch the head with two fingers at mana'o, "idea." Hold the stomach, hold *mana'o* fast. All were moving, men and women, their faces to the face-tapping rain, the trees, the ocean, the wind. All the 'āina was dancing.

> *Kīpū i ka mana'o,*
> *kīpū i ke kapa o ka noe;*
> *'auhea wale 'oe ek'ohu,*
> *kīpū maila i Ka'ala.*

What idea is it that they hold fast? The 'āina. Aloha. Hawai'i. Hawai'i herself, where everything makes love to everything.

The air was solid with music; you could walk on it. It penetrated body and soul, slackened heart strings, and loosened tears. That macho China Man Wittman wept unstoppable male tears. Good thing it was raining again—warm tear-camouflaging rain.

Tūtū got to her feet. Sassy and frisky, looking side-eyed at this man and that man, she hula-hula up to Wittman. "My top half belongs to God. My bottom half belongs to me, and gives me plea-suuure. Better not sit on that man's lap—make hard feelings." And everybody sang, "What is the work of 'Anapau there? Rotating the hips is the work of 'Anapau there."

Merely sitting, Wittman took many roles—the audience, the adored, the honored, the witness of wonders. Seated on the ground, he looked up at the dancers against the sky, and was worshipper, adorer. Fed, loved, entertained, he'd better reciprocate. But he couldn't very well lay money on the lau-hala and tatami mats, like on a Native American—the Indian kind—blanket. They weren't dancing for money. If he hadn't come along, they would have danced for themselves. He'd offend them if he paid. It was his turn to perform. He would tell them true things.

He declared his love. The first truth was that they were beautiful, one and all, men and women, beautiful, and he loved them. Say so in so many words. Don't die without letting them know. "You are all so beautiful. You are beautiful. I like you. I love you."

They laughed, pointing at him. "You," they said. "You the one, beautiful." "You. You."

"You," said Wittman.

"You. You." And in song: " 'Only you. Only you.' "

Next, he told them the vow he had invented for his keiki son that war would end. He resaid his promise. "For you, Edmund, and you, Tremayne too, no draft, no war."

The third giveaway truth was that he himself was a draft evader. "I'm evading and dodging the draft. My draft board, which is in Oakland, is especially after people from Berkeley. I'm hiding out here in your 'āina." He had placed himself in their hands, in their arms.

The children of this land told him ways to keep safe:

"No use go up those mountings. Those not deep caves, only shadows, and no path up. Go outer island. More better hide out on Big Island. City of Refuge, Big Island."

"More more better go Kaua'i. Ko'olau the Leper hid from the United States Army for two years on Kaua'i."

"When they found him dead at the pass, he was holding his rifle; he had no fingers but. Not one trigger finger."

Wittman had heard about Ko'olau the Leper from Jack London of Oakland.

"His full name be Kaluaiko'olau. His wife, Pi'ilani. She stuck with him, and wrote a book all about his life."

"He said famous last words. He said, 'My only command to you, if we are together and I'm in trouble, then bury my gun with me, that we lie together inside the womb of the earth, because I won't use the gun. I'm the only one who used it, and if I go, we (the gun and I) go together, and my work and its work is finished in this world.' "

"As for your keiki, we get Kill Haole Day last day of school. Don't come go school that day."

"Or get Hawaiian friends walk him home, he be okay."

"You be passing Sacred Falls soon. Don't eat the mountain apples or any kind fruits on the way up. You climb to the falls, and walk down, *then* can eat."

"Don't carry pig in your car when you drive over the Pali, or else the car act up and die. No ham sandwich or baloney, any kine pork. Even Spam." They told car adventures that happened on the Pali. "The throttle wide open but. Nobody stepping on the gas pedal, in fact, both feet on the brake." "Four simultaneous blow-out flat tires." "The steering wheel went stay locked." "And sure enough, there was a can of Spam in the trunk." (They didn't mention a pig goddess, or joke about pink skin or ham actors.) "You go over the Pali, you take care yourself with ti leaves. Wear 'em over the heart and genitals."

"If the ghosts bother you too much, you put out beer and fruit for them on the doorstep. And sprinkle the house with Hawaiian rock salt. You be okay." Same as Chinese, but wine and rock sugar. "Don't eat kukui nut, only a little bit taste. Diarrhetic and emetic, that candlenut."

"Never eat da kine puffer-up balloon blowfish—it is so 'ono, but. You can die with one swallow. Even so, some people, Japanee specially, like try risk 'em."

They warned him about the bad places in the ocean—the Potato Patch; the Toilet Bowl, which can flush you. "And at the gooood surfing—Pipeline, Sunset—be careful of the locals. Watch out."

"Don't go stay Wai'anae side. Dangerous. Da kine gang up you, beat you up, by'm'by kill you, and steal your car. Take the inland route, through the center of the island."

"Never stay at the lū'au past ten o'clock. The fighting begins. Watch out."

"Beware of Kaena Point, which sticks out in the northwest corner of O'ahu. Pass it by. The northwesternmost place of every island and district has *leina-a-ka-'uhane*. It is the leaping-off place of souls. The *puka*, hole, between here and another place is wide open in the northwest. You can disappear, and people will say, 'He gone *leina-a-ka-'uhane*.' But no road over Kaena Point anyway. You got to go inland, *mauka*." *Mauka* is toward the mountains. *Makai* is toward the sea. The other directions are Diamond Head and Ewa.

"I know about getting-off places," said Wittman. "We get the kind on Main Land. One is the Golden Gate Bridge. And another is the north woods where the poet Lew Welch disappeared."

"Before you mudslide Jackass Ginger, examine the mud for razor blades. Bad boys embed them in the earth of the slide." Warnings about razor blades were pandemic; the whores of Viet Nam were said to have razor blades in their vaginas.

Pua and Lilinoe had a special warning for Wittman's wife. "At the ladies' room at the Waialae Theater, there is a green ghost in the mirror." "It's happened to me and my girlfriends, combing our hair. We saw in back of us—the Green Lady." "We turn around, no one there."

But we see her inside the mirror." The shivering girls rubbed their arms. "Ohh, chicken skin. Feel my chicken skin."

"If you meet a strange woman"—they say "shtrange"—"a shtrange woman, sometimes young, sometimes old, and she asks a favor, a drink of water or gin, or she wants to sell you something, you give it, you buy it. She may be Madame Pele, who not only rises up in the volcano fire with fire hair and smoke hair and yellow sulfur hair but walks up to you like an ordinary lady."

"She knock on your door, you be kind to her, next eruption, your house not burn, and your family saved."

"Don't pay to get in the Polynesian Cultural Center. It's a tourist trap. It's a trap for Polynesians too. Missionaries convert the people of Oceania—Fijians, Tahitians, Maoris, Tongans, Samoans, Hawaiians—and collect them in a fake, unauthentic Polynesian village. Everybody has to do everybody else's dances, especially Tahitian, because the tourists like da kine action hips. You like go see for yourself, see the show for free, take your wife and keiki, go around to the fence to the far side of the tikis, and ask for Fiji Joe. He get you in free. Fiji Joe's skin black like a Popolo, but not Popolo. Mormons prejudiced against Popolos, you know, because they black, and Ham black. But Polynesians can make it into Heaven because we supposed to be a lost tribe of Israel. Many words, Hawaiian and Hebrew, the same." So—it's one of the entertainments here too, as in California, to swap Mormon stories. Wittman delighted in the Hawaiians' mixing pidgin and good English. He would use this language too.

"Da kine Mormons can convert you behind your back. You be dead, you not even *there*, they make you one of them. I know a man married a Mormon. He told her, 'You better not baptize me after I die, or my ghost will come haunting you.' "

"Mormons take interest in us for our genealogy meles. They put the lineage into the computer, and try to link up everybody with everybody. And they'll baptize your whole line, ancestors, you, everybody. Doesn't matter dead, posthumous baptism, they get."

"You know why those temples have indoor pools and tubs, not only baby founts? For baptizing, that's why. They get you, you live for eternity in Mormon Heaven with Mormons."

"There! We talk story everything we know for to take gooood care you."

They ate dessert again, and at their urging, Wittman ate another meal, and another dessert. He was just about living with these leisurely people. He should be on his way, but what was the hurry? No business to accomplish, only to enjoy one another's company. Lucky met. Well met, unbearable to part.

"I must be on my way," said Wittman again. "I want to get all the way around the island, and back to my wife and keiki, before dark."

They assured him that it doesn't take long to go around the island. It's a three-four-hour island. Please stay, no hurry, have more food, talk more story.

"I have to get the rental car back, and my wife and keiki will miss me." That's how to get out of an enchanted place: evoke the wife and kid, remember them, and let the wahine sorceresses know you're married and a father.

The generous Hawaiians said, "Take food for your wife. Take food for your keiki." He accepted paper plates full of meat except for pig, wrapped with Saran Wrap (made by Dow Chemical, who makes napalm). The foraging and hunting father would come home successful.

The Hawaiians thanked Wittman, and he thanked each of them again and again. By now old friends, the women kissed him on the lips. The men hugged and shook hands. Tremayne hugged with the ukulele between them. Tūtū said, "We'll remember you, and name this day the Day of the Pākē Guy in Black." He had found another grandmother; everybody has a right to a full complement of living grandmothers. Each and all vowed aloha. We shall love one another always. However far away I go, you will be beaming me to be happy.

"Fare thee well," said Wittman, saying words he'd only read. "Fare thee well. Fare thee well."

"*Aloha oe.*" "*Aloha pumehana.*" "*Aloha nui.*" "See you by'm'by." "Aloha."

Wittman walked away, and each time he turned to look back at those unusual people, they were waving to him and looking after him. The trees also waved, the world waving goodbye.

He drove on, feeling lonely, and sorry for all the lonely people. Aware of emptiness, he turned on the radio, which had Viet Nam news. He turned it off. Another of his vows-to-live-by was to stop reading newspapers and listening to or watching news until the war was over. That would be news: THE WAR IS OVER. Allen Ginsberg declared the war ended already. What was being broadcast were numbers that kept getting higher, and putting you into despair so you didn't want to live. It's not good to be well informed. Being up on current events adds to the war, and makes war real.

For a stretch, Wittman was alone on the road through what seemed an uninhabited part of the island. Suddenly a convoy of jeeps and tanks and personnel carriers with their headlights on came toward him. The U.S. Army were on maneuvers, occupying Hawai'i. On their way to Viet Nam. Some of the soldiers had black makeup on their faces, and leaves on their heads. The vehicles and the people were in dull drab matte camouflage. The Pentagon considers olive and tan to be earth shades, but here earth is red. What kind of country are they going to dressed like that? In dead colors. Nobody can see me, ha-ha. Feel sorry for soljers. They should be in college. It's the poor, the uneducated who have to go to war, the poor fighting the poor. It's hard to read those faces moving past, masked with blacking, the Black soldiers too. He spotted Chinese American–looking and AJA-looking faces. In Berkeley, you hardly saw any soldiers, and never weapons, rifles, military vehicles. At the demonstrations at the Oakland Induction Center, you mostly saw civilian kids, young, dumb, duped kids walking over your lying-down body to get to the war. Now here they were, each with his own rifle. Flatbed trucks were hauling big guns like cannons, probably for launching grenades. Jet bombers in the sky, picnickers on the beaches, Wittman had come to the center of operations for the staging of the Viet Nam War.

A soldier flashed him the peace sign! Looked right at him and held up two fingers. And another soldier gave him the peace sign. Wittman flashed one back. Half a truckload of GIs saw him do that, and flashed him—Peace. Peace. Peace. Peace, brother. Peace—the hip, cool signal of our generation, the antiestablishment, the flower children, the peaceful. Truck after truck, not just one guy sneaking a peace sign but truckloads. A long convoy wishing him peace. One GI and another and another held up his fingers in the hand sign we give one another in solidarity and peace. There's Wittman, with his long hair and as much mustache and beard as a Mongolian can grow, like Uncle Ho, a VC-looking guy in a rebellious black T-shirt. And they're trading signs with him, approving of him, wishing him peace. They must mean: Keep it up. Have a good time. We don't begrudge you. Be free. You work for peace and freedom your way; we'll work for it this other way. Good for you.

You got away. (Lew Welch: *"Look, / if nobody tried to live this way, / all the work of the world would be in vain. / And now and then a son, a daughter, hears it. / Now and then a son, a daughter / gets away."*) We'll free the Vietnamese, and be back and live like you, be hippies then. They didn't yell at him, "Go back to China, Commie. Gook. Berkeley scum." They quietly flashed the peace sign. Underground-resistance-working-from-within infiltrators. They do mean peace. They're a peace-keeping army, defending the peace, going to pacify Viet Nam. Wittman cast a white light around all those troops. Be safe. Come back without getting killed or killing anyone.

Wittman saw where the convoy had come from—a man-made cleft in the mountainside. He would not have seen it but for this sign:

KAPU

KEEP OUT

PROPERTY OF U.S. GOVERNMENT

So—the Government put a kapu on this part of the 'āina. They're mixing church and state, declaring a military site to be sacred land, and vice versa. Just for that, Wittman's going in. He made a left turn across the other lane, and through the cleft and into the mountain. It behooved him, a taxpaying citizen, to check out his own property. He kept on driving on the red-dirt road for a ways into the Koʻolaus. There are ways in, then, from off the rim. The car made red dust in the air, which could be seen by any guards. The cleft—*mawae*—opened into a spacious valley. He pulled over, parked, and got out. Continuing on foot on tread prints, he walked between red hillsides. Red dirt, the same color as the international orange of the Golden Gate Bridge, stained his sneakers. Ahead was a wide valley in the wings of abrupt green mountains. He was inside the island.

PROPERTY OF U.S. GOVERNMENT means it's my property, my territory, my valley, my mountains. This land is my land. I am an American taxpayer walking on my land. Nobody kapu my 'āina. Nobody kapu me. If an MP tries to arrest me, I'll say I'm a civilian citizen; I don't salute or obey anybody. *He* should be following *my* orders. I'll say, I'm new here and don't know what *kapu* means.

BOOM! BOOM! BOOM! BOOM! BOOM! Suddenly, booms surrounded him, filled the air and the ground. Was it the valley clapping open and shut? BOOM! BOOM! It was coming from inside the island—and also the air and the sky—and his own diaphragm drum. BOOM! BOOM! BOOM! Regular, steady punch-booming filled all space. The time and space between booms resounded with echoes. Wittman walked farther in, for more view of the valley. He saw no can-nonlike machines, no people, no bomber overhead. He saw the green skin of a section of mountain to his right explode, blow apart, fly apart. Underneath the green skin was red earth like meat. BOOM! Chunks and gouts of red rock flew outward like starbursts. It came to him what was going on: missile target practice. He looked to the left side of the valley, where rocket bombs must be coming from. But jungle, forest, meadow were still, nor did he see rockets shoot past. They went by that fast, at unseeable speed. He did not think to duck or hit the deck. So the target was a mountain of the Ko'olau Range, O'ahu herself. BOOM! BOOM! BOOM! BOOM! BOOM! BOOM! Pieces of green skin and red-meat dirt chunks broke apart and fell, broke apart and fell, blew through the air in flowering starry sprays of red earth, followed by sound. BOOM! BOOM! BOOM! BOOM!

Wittman turned about and walked out of there. No, the explosions couldn't be natural or legal. He ought to report this strangeness to the authorities. Tell somebody in charge what was going on. At the car, he took out his tourist map, and marked the spot of the bombing he had wit-nessed. A disproportionately huge section of the map of O'ahu was pink, which according to the key meant that it belongs to the military. The U.S. government kapu the island. The island was an aircraft carrier, a launching pad, an armed satellite, and its purpose was to funnel our every destructive resource to Viet Nam. Wittman drove out of there. The booming continued until he reached Kamehameha Highway and could not hear it anymore. The mountains somehow locked up the sound.

At Laie, he recognized the Mormon enclave, a Mormon temple like a pyramid for pharaohs, and the Polynesian Cultural Center. Two black tikis with mother-of-pearl eyes and teeth stood at the entrance directly beside the highway—Trader Vic and Trader Joe. Above fences and foliage was a majestic, magnificent roof, resplendent with brown-and-white carvings. How bad can this place be? They're showing that the people of Oceania to have had more than a grass-shack architecture.

Then he was going around the end of the Koʻolau Range, and joining the traffic on the north shore, Sunset Beach. To his right, the waves were pounding the highest of any he'd ever seen. A hand-lettered sign on a phone pole on his left said: Pupukea. He crossed the highway and drove up the mountain. Very soon, he was going over ruts on a steep, unpaved incline. At the top of the hill, a State Park Service historical marker announced that Pupukea was a *heiau*. A heiau is a high place of worship. There was a small parking lot with no other cars, nothing much up here, no attraction, no gift shop or building. That open ground must be the heiau, the flat top of the hill, a clearing surrounded by scrubby trees and bushes. Wittman parked alongside the sign, and walked on a narrow dirt path toward a low wall. He walked carefully along the outside of the wall, and felt for vibes out of the ground underfoot and out of the ceaselessly massaging air. So this is holy space, special ʻāina. Breathing quietly, he felt for the quality of the atmosphere with all his skin, and looked sideways for sneaky ghosts. Yes, there did seem to be a weightiness, a heavier air, a density of gravity, a silence. He heard and smelled the wind and the ocean, and traffic. Energetic things had happened here, heightened by everybody high on kava. Piss and blood had watered generations of these grasses. Wittman tried reading the landscape for human history. The low rock wall was man-made, stacked without mortar. It enclosed and outlined rectangular spaces, like the foundation of a meeting hall with side chambers, like the footprint of a pueblo. Or the heiau might not be a ruin but always thus, rocks marking the outdoors for ceremonies under the sky and rain, directly in line with the sunset.

Wittman followed the almost overgrown footpath through the scrub and brambles to rusty barbed wire. He stepped over the barbed wire, and stood at the sharp edge of cliff. He sat with his back against a phone pole. If he fell or jumped or was pushed, he'd land on the highway of cars and trucks. Below was a strip of a town, shops, market, Sunset Beach and surfers, then ocean until China and Viet Nam. Just follow the Tropic of Cancer. The ancient people could have looked up here and seen a theater of blood, unless they'd been forbidden to look.

Wittman hunkered down amongst beer cans and Coke cans and cigarette butts. Last night, a necking couple were up here partying and shivering at ghosts. Or bad boys, drinking and smoking, dared the ghosts to throw them off the cliff. The old barbed wire was left from World

War II, strung by Prewitt and his brother soljers in *From Here to Eternity*. You find barbed wire like this all along the California coast too, to fortify against Japanese invasion. The Pacific Rim, rimmed with barbed wire.

He got up, and walked the rest of the length of the heiau. Here and there on the walls and on the ground were stacked single rocks, one on top of another, in careful, thought-out balance—rock snowballmen, fat Venuses, wats, towers. Some rocks had been placed a long time ago, and some recently, wrapped in fresh ti leaves and set just so. Some ti leaves were flat like bookmarks between rocks. Each set of rocks had a different personality—a short, stocky body with a pebble head; a tall, precarious pillar; a skinny man all vertebrae; a tiki. Some figures seemed definitely men, some women. What were these stacks of rocks for? Maybe it was a game: each player would come along and add one rock on top, see how high you could get the pile without toppling. Wittman picked up a stone that appealed to him, and chose which figure he would help build up. He decided on a column of four rocks with a funny crookedness that looked like a tall, thin man like himself. Holding his stone with thumb and forefinger of both hands, he placed it—a hat—on the skinny guy's head, gently settled it, and let it go. It stayed put; he did not tumble the pile. He had joined the dialogue of rocks. It could be that the purpose of rock arrangement is to teach the correct attitude toward the 'āina. Kneel to pick up a rock; bow to the rock man to give him a head or a hat. The island is so tiny, each piece of it is a special, valuable jewel that you handle attentively. Each rock was placed by human intelligence and human hands, not nature's gravity or wind or time. A couple of rocks were on top of the "State Park" sign.

At the end of the heiau farthest from the sea, Wittman saw—how could he have missed it earlier?—a dirt mound, like a pitcher's mound, smooth and packed down—encircled with a peace sign made with plumeria flowers. A long, long lei of classical yellow-and-white plumeria garlanded the circumference of the mound. Another strand of lei was the diameter, pointing straight to where the sun would set, and two near-radii completed the forking, raying peace sign, the old "Ban the Bomb" sign. A group of Hawaiian hippies or yippies had been here last night or early this morning and held a peace ceremony. They were turning this ground where unknown, mysterious violences had occurred into a peace heiau. Shtrange. He hadn't noticed the mound or the peace lei when he came, as if it had been done behind his back while he sat looking down at the ocean. Heartened, he went on his way. He had come to the right country after all.

On he drove through Sunset, and deliberately passed the turnoff going south into the center of the island. Too soon to be going back already. The island is too small. Turning south would take him to Schofield. He knew about Schofield; he was carrying *From Here to Eternity* as one of his field guides to Hawai'i. He kept driving along the north shore. On the map the road was marked clearly with a blue line with but a minuscule sixteenth-of-an-inch break, and connecting up with the red lines to Honolulu. Surely, he could bump this Rent A Wreck Valiant across that space.

Soon, the road was a dirt one-laner with no other traffic, no road signs, but definitely a road, all to himself. He rolled up the windows against the clouds of dust that his tires were churning up. The ocean on his right became fiercer, too fierce for surfers. The waves had pounded away any beach, and were hitting bare vertical lava rock. The road kept narrowing like a funnel. Cactus grew on the mountainside.

A wooden shack sat on the widest part of a finger of land that pointed out into the ocean like a natural pier. The sea had salted off the paint to a brownish-gray wood. A porch shaded uncurtained windows on either side of the open front door. This could be Robert Louis Stevenson's think house, or a place like one of those cabins up in Alaska which the owner leaves unlocked and stocked with food and firewood in case a lost wanderer needed haven. Wittman stopped the car; he would go in and ask whether he should turn back. How much rougher does this road get before connecting up with the highway? A haole man with a black beard came out of the dark room and stood in the doorway. Wittman jumped over the tide pools, running over to meet him. Who lives in such an out-of-the-way place? He would talk story with the hermit of the place, and see how he afforded his life. The beard was a peace sign.

Zing!

He knew he was being shot at. Looking up, he saw the man taking his rifle down from his shoulder. He stood very straight, staring at Wittman. Wittman shouted, "I just want to ask directions. I'm a tourist. I don't want to break into your house." If they could only have a word with each other, he wouldn't want to shoot him. "My name's Wittman Ah Sing." Identify yourself, and he'll realize he's shooting at the wrong person and stop.

Even as Wittman spoke, the man lifted the rifle to his bearded cheek. Wittman ran to the other side of the car. Zing! He'd never been shot at before. Zing! Zing! Puffs of sand leapt into the air. He wanted to peek but kept his head down below the car windows. I don't feel scared, he thought; I'm not panicking. Zing! All was quiet except for the zinging bullets, and the sound of the ocean. The man did not speak, did not tell why he was shooting at him. The many movies Wittman had seen offered no guidance as to how to stop this situation. Nothing in his life led up to this. Zing! It shouldn't be happening. Shooting is not real; shooting is fiction.

The bearded haole man must be crazy. A crazy haole living with a gun at Kaena Point. This has got to be against the law, a crazy shooter living uncivilized out in nature instead of in a mental hospital. Wittman reached for the handle and pulled the door open, and crawled in, crouched low beneath the steering wheel, stepped on the gas pedal, turned the key. The car started. But it did not move. Its wheels were spinning in sand. Zing! He let up on the gas, then floored it. The wheels did not grab. Zing! As long as he heard the shots from a distance, the shooter was not sneaking up on him. Don't look at him; it sets them off to be looked at. Move, Valiant. Oh, God, Taña and Mario waiting for him, and he never comes home. Killed. Shot to death. He opened the door, hung his head down over the side, and looked at the tires. They had not been hit but were in ruts of sand. He got back in the car and grabbed the books that he was going to leave here and there for readers to find. *From Here to Eternity, Noa Noa,* and Jack London's *Stories of Hawaii.* He crawled out of the car headfirst like a snake, and shimmed and wedged the books under the rear tire closest to him. He pulled himself back into the car. He took off! Gathering traction and speed, he turned around, and sped away the way he had come. Zing! Zing! Zing! Wittman drove hunched down without seeing the road. When he had not heard the zinging for a long while, he sat up and joined the traffic that suddenly reappeared, and followed it toward Schofield.

After getting out of danger, he became scared, knees shaking, foot having a hard time evenly controlling the gas. He could have died, his shot-up body dropped from the cliff into the ocean, the sharks eating it right now. And the sunken sea-rusting Valiant a reef for the fish. Kaena Point really is a point, and the ocean does spit on the spit of land. Everything had been hyperreal, the haole madman and his shack sharp against the sky. He should have recognized the jumping-off place. The finger of land points it out—the northwesternmost part of the island. *Leina-a-ka-ʻuhane*. He had been expecting the site where souls vanish into a netherworld to be a place of mist and fog.

Then he felt exhilarated—he'd competently gotten the car out of the sand. And he had had more concern for his family than for himself. He's a family man. For their sake, he could not be killed.

What's wrong with Hawaiʻi, that nobody has called the police or the army on that mad haole shooter? Probably everybody, including the army, which is right around the corner, avoids the jumping-off place. Well, he wasn't going to be the one to call the cops on the shooting hermit of Kaena Point. Never call the cops.

So he drove the inland route after all—into Wahiawa and the military zone. He passed the long, low one- and two-story buildings that were GI offices and GI housing. He recognized them from James Jones' descriptions. They had verandas and lawns, purpled from the jacaranda trees. It didn't look like you could launch a war from here. Somewhere on this side of the Waiʻanae Mountains is the rock pile where the soljers serving time were tortured, and the stockade where Prewitt and Maggio listened to the weird Wobbly guru, Malloy, and practiced taking beatings. The guard beat Blues Berry to death. "All this occurring in a peaceful nation not at war." " 'There ain't no peacetime army.' " Reading *From Here to Eternity* accurately would stop you from joining the army. James Jones should have used the full epigram as the title: "*Damned from here to eternity.*"

Wittman hated the book for being gook-filled. "Gook shirt." "Gook shirt." "Gook shirt." "Gook shirt." "Gook shirt." "Gook shirt." "Gook shirt." Seven times Jones calls the aloha shirt a gook shirt. He wrote "gook" 30 times. "Gook waiter." "Gook maid." "God damn gook." The "God damn gook" is Choy, the Hawaiian Chinese American who runs the diner. He talks like this: "Herro, Prew. Me hear you move 'closs stleet some time soon. I think so maybe, eh?" We don't talk like that. Choy says, "Marine Corpse." Only a reader would sound out all the letters in "Marine Corps." James Jones names the people of Hawaiʻi: "the gooks," "his Chinese shackjob," "Kanaka maids," "the gook maids," "a gook beachboy," "the gook waiter," "the Chink handling the boat," the "Chinese proprietor" with a daughter at Stanford, "500 gooks . . .

inscrutably alien." (Melville in *Moby-Dick*: "God hates the inscrutable.") " 'MacArthur's gook boy scouts.' " "A gook wife and hapa haole brats." "Greasy Filipino wife." " 'His wife is a gook, she don't count.' " " 'Filipino nigger brat family.' " ". . . condemned by his nigger family to foreign service for the rest of his natural life." By "nigger," they don't mean Black but Filipino American. "Black gook." "Gook draftees." You can be drafted into the U.S. Army and you're still a gook. Good thing *From Here to Eternity* got ground into the sand.

Miles of cane fields rolled by, and miles of pineapple—the militarized agribiz zone. Prewitt sees the pineapples as an army. A GI is in "rank and file like 7,000 other pineapples." He is in a totalitarian hell, a fascist parade going on forever into bad eternity. The bluish spikes are swords or bayonets. The young green pineapples look like grenades, bumpy, just the size that fits the hand. It seemed that Dole grew grenades for the army. Signs along the road said that the fine for stealing a pineapple was $50. But you could stop at the A-frame sticking out in the fields of this one-crop farm and look at the Dole Pineapple exhibit and have a complimentary drink of pineapple juice and a chunk or slice or spear or ring of pineapple. Wittman did not stop; he wasn't going to be appeased. The cane was tall and wild compared with pineapple. You could hide in the cane.

Wittman passed Pearl Harbor. Keep evading the military. And there, up on the hill, was Tripler Hospital, pink like the Royal Hawaiian Hotel. Here's where I came in. The buildings, the freeways of traffic, the city chopped up soul and mind that had begun to expand, having been awhile in nature. Wittman had circumnavigated the island. Including stops, it had taken less than half the day. The island is that small. He's used to continents. Well, O'ahu is the size of the Bay Area, and there were months at a time when he never left the Bay Area. Life on an island should be manageable. It would teach him to focus and concentrate.

He dropped off the Valiant at Rent A Wreck on Kapiolani Boulevard, left some of the picnic food for the workers, kept some to feed his wife and child. Now to hitchhike home to Taña and Mario. He walked to Waikīkī, and along the Strip for a while. Attracted by the "International" of the International Market Place, he walked into the hodge-podge of shops and stalls, didn't like it, walked out, walked back in. Give it a second chance. Like Chinatown but worse. A live banyan tree, pruned, roofed, with stairs up its main trunk, was used as a restaurant for two. "Dinner for Two." What a fantasy—Somerset Maugham–type native boys climbing up and down serving wealthy folie-à-deux lovers hidden behind the thatch. Right now, nobody was up there, fairy lights off. Taña's got to see this queerness, so they could scoff at it together. Beneath the tree were the treasures of Hong Kong, Taiwan, the Philippines, Thailand, India—plastic leis, oysters guaranteed with pearl, Day-Glo coral heads.

Wittman got out of that fake market place with its fake alleys and fake wares, and stood on the ocean side of Kuhio Avenue. He had had his hitchhiking thumb out for a short while when a parade of ten or a dozen peace marchers came along, going the same direction he was going. They were walking in the street, along the edge of the traffic, single file, stretching out the length of their parade. They did not have a parade permit, which would have gotten them a police escort and a lane closed to traffic. To the credit of the tourists and citizens of Honolulu, nobody gave them the finger or yelled or honked at them or tried to run them down. Wittman felt grateful and at home to see them. My people. They were the smallest demonstration he'd ever seen, the bravest, maybe the first Viet Nam peace march in Hawai'i, where they remember Pearl Harbor, and the 442nd, and the Pineapple Army, and night marchers, and probably secret warrior societies. It was an honor to be present at history, the birth of the peace movement. These few people are walking for peace on this island that has ROTC in high schools, plutonium warheads secreted at Sand Island, convoys exporting weapons and bringing back the dead and the wounded, and an economy obviously based on military spending. The peace marchers walked at an even pace, moving in concert. Their demeanor and attitude created an atmosphere that made the cars slow down for them. A bubble of peace moved with them along the street. There was but one banner: Sister Corita's "War Is Not Healthy for Children and Other Living Things," the curving sunflower in orange, green, and yellow, a nonaccusatory message, not specifying which children or who was harming them. Flowers bloomed on muumuus and aloha shirts, and real-flower leis wreathing heads and necks meant that this day was special. Back home, the love-ins, be-ins, teach-ins were culminating in riots. A small group is better for peace marching than noisy, exciting dragon crowds. You could see each face, and wonder and think about that person, what brought him or her out here. They were not freaks but ordinary everyday people assembling, respectfully suggesting that we stop the War in Viet Nam. Ladies in muumuus walked ahead of and behind long-haired men; their hair was tied back in the style of patriots of the American Revolution. A couple in bathing suits walked barefoot; they were vacationers off the beach. The blonde women with long hair wore haku leis, and looked like Eve and Primavera. The dark women looked like Gauguins. People in Hawai'i are healthier than Mainland people. Nobody wore a football helmet to defend against clubbings. One man wore a business suit, like Dr. Martin Luther King, Jr., and the dignified civil-rights marchers. (Things began to change when Stokely Carmichael marched in bib overalls.)

Of course, Wittman had to join in; he got in step behind the last person. Their energy field easily included him. But as he walked deliberately through Waikīkī, he saw that he was in the Land of the Lotus Eaters. Look at them—picnicking, swimming, necking, reading, tanning, unconscious that they were sunbathing on a weapons station. At Fort DeRussy, the peace demonstrators stood in vigil at the curb, their backs to the "fort," which was an R&R center. The demonstrators weren't enough bodies to obstruct the wide entrance, a sweeping driveway and lawn. They were on the sidewalk, property of the city and county of Honolulu, not the federal government. No military personnel were in sight; maybe they were under orders not to recognize demonstrations. The peace march was being officially ignored. Wittman stood straight with arms to his side, a bag of lū'au food in either hand. The motherly woman next to him looked up and smiled. He gave her a smile back, and tried to pass that smile on to motorists. A bare-chested man driving a convertible gave him the finger. Wittman did not react, though he wanted to. Be strong in nonviolence. Violence shoots through the air with the flip of a finger, let alone a gun.

A car honked. "Key of G," said the guy demonstrating in a bathing suit. "Most car horns are in G." Another car honked them. A long honk, then blast, blast, blast. No, it wasn't normal traffic. They were honking against peace. You could tell by how they lay on the horn, and the hostile expressions on faces. But here was a honker honking merrily in support. That carload flashed peace signs and yelled, "Right on!"

A car almost went up onto the curb, and the honker yelled, "Oddballs!" Encased as they are in metal skin and body, people in cars are impervious to peace vibes.

For a long while, the demonstrators stood there, and passersby paid them no mind. You get self-conscious doing nothing in particular with no lines to say. Embarrassing, so public, standing out, showing off. Making up a new ritual—like a corny nontraditional wedding, like amateur hour—gives you red face, red ass. "Nail stick up, hammer it down." "Deviant crab, back in the barrel." We're rudely offending vacationers on getaway from cares and woes.

They walked in an oval in the swooping entranceway of Fort DeRussy. The peace walk is also embarrassing. It's not a march, which would be orderly and manly. Trying not to walk like flower children, the young guys slouched, bounced to a beat in their heads, kept on trucking. The group left the fort and walked on to the next street corner. They stood along the red stripe for the bus stop, but were obviously not waiting for the bus. Wittman shared the rest of his lūʻau food.

The demonstrators went for quite a time not chitchatting. They must be practiced Quakers and/or Buddhists. The smiling woman next to him was Phyllis. Next to her was a blonde girl in doe colors and fringes, then the man in the summer-weight business suit, neat and clean-cut, which was appropriately Japanese American. Next to him was the girl in a bikini and the guy in swim trunks who could hear the music in traffic, then a tall man with a dark beard, and a small man with a sunny beard and sunburned face. An Asian-and-Polynesian-looking woman in a muumuu and a lau-hala hat with a haku lei band visited with another housewifely woman, haole. There was a Hawaiian-looking girl in an empire-style muumuu. Oh, joy, one real indigenous person to give our cause authenticity. And at the other end, the front, the leader, a haole guy with a lei. Maybe he was a preacher or a union organizer. He was the one lifting the Sister Corita banner. "Oh, boy," said Phyllis from under her straw hat. "Isn't it terrific? Eleven of us. Eleven people showed up. Good turnout. Terrific. Good for us." She laughed. "Twelve, counting me."

But two more people joined them. Oh, no—Communists. The Reds had arrived. They stood next to Wittman, who was now antepenultimate in line. The guy carried a pole with a huge red flag. The flag was so big and so red, it co-opted the parade, as if Communists were sponsoring the whole thing. They're always doing this, tricking you into being their political bedfellows. You can't chase them away or lock them up; you can only protect yourself against their convincing ideas by remembering: they believe in violent revolution, international warfare, killing people as the means to a fair world. The Communist was a tall, angry youth in a brown beret; he propped the flagpole against the instep of his heavy boots—workman or combat storm-trooper boots. His little companion also wore a brown beret and dyke boots, and looked like Arlo Guthrie's mute girlfriend in *Alice's Restaurant*. Too many people were in hats; in this hatless age, they looked like a gathering of eccentrics. Brown berets were the uniform of some foreign war. The trade winds blew the flag; the girlfriend held its edge and moved it aside as if she were coming out from behind a stage curtain. The Revolutionary Communist stood with his profile to his fellow demonstrators.

"I wish they wouldn't join us," said Phyllis, then leaned over and said to the Communists, "I'm sorry you had to join us. Did you have to bring that flag?"

The Arlo Guthrie girlfriend said, "We compromised at the meeting, we wouldn't bring the flag of the National Liberation Front. And we didn't."

Phyllis said to Wittman, "We're it, then. That flag is going to scare away any more demonstrators. We're it."

Wittman's particular dislike for the girl Communist wasn't only political; it was sexual. She was probably Chinese American, and rejected Chinese American guys for this Sinophile haole. Trying to be winning, she said, "My name's Melanie Toy. He's David. I'm a Maoist. He's a Marxist."

To prevent her from lecturing on what the difference was, Wittman talked: "I'm a veteran of demonstrations. I was at the Viet Nam Day demo. I heard the most famous of Communist haranguers—M. S. Arnoni. We were a crowd of one hundred thousand people on Sproul Plaza and on the grass. Arnoni was in a World War II death-camp prisoner outfit. He yelled, 'Are you committed to Viet Nam?!' The crowd yelled, 'Yeah!' He yelled that question three times. 'Are you committed to Viet Nam?! Are you committed to Viet Nam?!' The crowd yelled louder and louder, 'Yeah! Yeah!' *I* yelled, 'Yeah!' I felt the sound of a hundred thousand human voices rolling and bouncing off the walls of the buildings, on which the face of LBJ was projected. Arnoni shouted,

'How committed are you? Will you go to Viet Nam? Will you fight for the Viet Cong?!' The crowd went dead silent. A few people waved blue-and-red flags with a yellow star—sort of like the state flag of Arizona—but I didn't hear them volunteer to go fight for the Viet Cong. No Viet Cong brigades were forming, like the Tibetan Brigade. The crowd didn't boo or hiss. They were troubled, quiet. Arnoni depressed everybody, doves and hawks, Communists and non-Communists. He revealed hypocrisy and cowardice, and lack of alternatives, and lack of thinking things through. I felt the heart go out of that crowd. That was my last mass rally. You can't argue and articulate principles; all you can do is boo or cheer." The Reds of Hawai'i neither booed nor applauded, and Wittman went on talking.

"Then the spotlights X-ed a psychedelic bus driving slowly through the crowd. Faces with face paint were at the windows. People in army-navy surplus clothes rode on the roof. I got the impression of maybe toy machine guns mounted up there, but they could've been loudspeakers. The bus drove up to the platform, and Ken Kesey and Wavy Gravy and the Merry Pranksters got out, and jumped and climbed up onto the platform. Kesey played he was the Catcher in the Rye; his daughter was running toward a dangerous place, yelling, 'You chain me up. You chain me up.' He breathed in and out, in and out, on a harmonica, and chanted, 'It's my fault. It's my fault. It's my fault,' on and on until the crowd booed him off. The Pranksters got back on the bus and drove away."

" 'Mea culpa,' " said Red Melanie. "That's Catholic."

Red David seemed to have made up his mind to ignore the talker. The Quakers, of course, practiced silence, as did the Japanese American man, who was a Buddhist minister.

"We marched to the Berkeley-Oakland border on Alcatraz, where the Oakland motorcycle cops were in one line and the Hell's Angels on bikes paralleled them. My part of the demonstration didn't turn back, but walked along the row of Angels. I think the Hell's Angels were for us, between us and the cops, though some people said they were guarding Oakland against us. It was ambiguous as to whether they were antiwar. They'd asked to be sent to Viet Nam as a platoon, but Allen Ginsberg fed them acid on the eve of Viet Nam Day, and they were maybe converted to peace. I heard a radio announcer say, 'Stay tuned, violence expected.' But there wasn't any violence."

Cars honked, and you could tell they barely refrained from running up on the curb and mowing down the peaceniks and hippies and yippies and Commies. The people waiting for the bus moved over and clustered to one side, not to be taken as part of the demonstration. In the beautiful weather, the cars and buses had their windows and tops down, and people yelled, "Take a bath, dirty hippie." "Hippie scum!" "Go back to Russia!" "What are you? A boy or a girl?" "Fuck you!" "Assholes!" "Traitors!" "Get a job!" "Get a haircut!" "Cowards!"

Jesus and Gandhi and Martin Luther King, Jr., taught us to be peaceful, silent, loving in response to ignorance and anger. But the hyper, sunburned kid yelled back, "Fuck *you*! Baby-killer!" People tried to calm him. "Calm yourself, Raleigh," said the leader with the banner. "Cool it, man. Take it easy." "You can't hold a discussion with a passing car," said the Buddhist.

A carful of athletes and cheerleaders yelled in unison, "Love it or leave it!" Raleigh chased after them. "But. But. But. You. You. Fuckers. Come back here and say it to my face." The Buddhist minister walked him back to the curb, an arm about his shoulders. The outburst of pedestrians into traffic started more cars honking. The nice ladies counseled Raleigh: Don't provoke. Don't be provoked. They patted his arms. "Okay. It's okay. Okay," they said.

Phyllis said, "Raleigh's come to the Quaker house a few times. There are people who could use psychotherapy before trying silence."

Wittman asked if most of the people here were Quakers. Was this demo sponsored by the Friends?

No, only she and the dark-bearded man were Quakers, "weighty Quakers."

The Buddhist was not only a minister, he was the bishop, but he was here as himself, Robert, not representing the rest of the Buddhists. One of the neighborly ladies was a Unitarian and the other was with Catholic Action. The man with the Sister Corita flag was with Hawai'i Resistance, which met at the Wesley Foundation. What was it about religion that got people to remain staunchly peaceful through the long war? Once a week, every Sunday, people gathered and reminded themselves, "Thou shalt not kill." No codicils, no riders to that commandment. They did not have to invent from scratch what to do at every war.

But you have to admire the nonreligious individuals. They're able to take a stand without the help of an institution. They come to their stance and actions through their own reasoning.

Civilian men—you could tell they were not military by their hair—
yelled from the passing cars. They singled out the women. "Go home,
where you belong!" A car blocked the cruising traffic, slowed to a stop
in front of the picket line. The driver said, "Why don't you ladies get
out of here before you get hurt?"

A man with a pair of Doberman dogs in a convertible rounded the
corner. He wore impenetrable sunglasses. "I'm back from Viet Nam,"
he shouted to Phyllis. "And I'm all right. I am all right." He was reporting to Mother: the war wasn't that bad, and she need not be concerned
for him.

"That's good," said Phyllis. "I'm glad you're all right."

During their stand on the next street corner, Wittman ran his class
credentials by the Reds. "I'm an artist of the theater, and accept Unemployment compensation. I'm a renter. Come the Revolution, would you
execute me for a bourgeois capitalist?"

"You shouldn't take it personally," said Melanie. Red David did not
deign to answer the obnoxious, disingenuous naïf.

"I'm a poet," said Phyllis. Admiration and envy coursed through
Wittman. Oh, the feat and deed, coming right out and naming oneself
poet. He took a good look at her, and saw that she had an epicanthic-
lidded eye. Her mark-of-the-poet was one Chinese eye. "The Russians
and the Chinese are imprisoning poets like me, writers of love poems.
They're interpreting love poems politically, and forbidding them."

A woman on foot crossed the street. They watched her come
through the traffic. She was in a flower-print A-line dress that was too
long, hemline down to her knees. She was a military wife meeting her
husband on R&R. The army advised wives not to upset their husbands
by wearing miniskirts. She ran up to the demonstration and walked up
and down the line of picketers. She was in the gutter, and looked up into
their faces. She crouched and bent, as if she had a stomachache. Pain
seemed to shoot out of her. Her face contorted; she opened and shut her
mouth. Her eyes were wide. She opened and closed her arms across her
stomach. Her hands went up to her face, her cheeks, her mouth. She got
words out: "How could you?! How could you?!" She stuck her face into
the face of each demonstrator. "You're killing them! You're killing him!
You kill my husband. He's giving his life for you. How can you do this to
us? Why?! You are guilty!" She was screaming and weeping. "You're
guilty! He's not guilty! You're guilty of the killing!" She pointed at the

demonstrators but did not jab or touch them. Her nose was streaming, and she did not wipe it. She was inside that nightmare where nobody understands, and she could not talk them into understanding. She could not make them feel her pain, any pain. She let out noises, then words again: "People are dying! For you! You're guilty! He's not guilty! You're guilty! You are cold. You betrayer! Betrayer! Betrayer! Don't do this to me. Answer me! Answer!"

Raleigh said, "We're trying to save your husband. We're not against him. We want to get him out of Viet Nam. We're trying to bring him home."

"Liar!" she screamed at him. She turned to passersby. "Look at them. Betrayers! Help me. Help me."

A woman in back of the demonstrators cried, "Hurt!" She hurt: she wanted them to hurt. "You stand there smug, when my son is at the war. Hurt!"

"How could you?!" screamed the other woman. "How could you?! Cold!"

"Enemy! You are the enemy! Worse than the enemy!" screamed the voice at their backs.

Raleigh said, "I didn't do anything. LBJ drafted your husband, and your son, or they volunteered. I didn't tell them to go; did I tell them to go?"

The two women were in frenzies of weeping. They bent over, groaning, and jerked themselves upright and yelled. They pulled their own hair and cheeks. They were doing to themselves what they wanted to do to the demonstrators.

Phyllis said, "I have three sons, two draft-age, and my youngest will be draft-age in months. The only way we can protect them is to teach them peace values. Then they'll know to think to take care of themselves."

"My son is fighting for your coward sons."

The other woman wailed, "Too late! Too late!"

The military wife and the military mother held their arms crossed over their breasts. It is the most panicking terror and agony to be told what you should have done when it's too late. The mother pushed between Phyllis and Wittman to yell in their faces. They felt her spittle. They felt the tremors of her body. The two women stalked back and forth as if they had to piss or shit or hit.

"My son is not a volunteer."

"I'm sorry," said Phyllis.

"You traitors are costing us the war. We're losing. Losers!"

"You can't win a war," said Raleigh.

"You don't understand."

"You don't understand."

Raleigh and the wife yelled into each other's faces, "You don't understand!" Fear arced high, amplifying like feedback out of control. Raleigh cried tears of frustration.

The two Communists stood impervious, looking over the women's heads. The Buddhist bishop looked sad. The weighty Quaker man talked quietly to Raleigh, trying to stop him from arguing with the women. The wife and the mother turned on the young women. "Slut!" "Hippie slut." "Dirty slut." The faithful wives were hating the free-love hippie whore chicks. There were whores in Viet Nam too.

Wittman was not singled out. In Hawai'i he looked like the average common person.

Slowly cruising at vacation speed, careful not to hit the two hysterical women, came a car with two Afro-American men inside. Intelligent about city streets, they sized up the scene. Wittman made eye contact with the guy on the passenger side and said, "Peace, brother. Welcome to Hawai'i." The Black guy answered, "Peace, brother," a quiet voice amidst the shouting. He called me "brother." Here comes the real thing; the Bloods have arrived from the freedom rides, bringing, embodying the ideas of Dr. Martin Luther King, Jr. The chosen people of America—marked by their entire skin—they take on the most awful conditions, and overcome. The other guy, the driver, gave Wittman the power fist. Was it a salute of solidarity, or "up yours"? That ambiguity was what had gotten them in trouble at the Olympics. Wittman returned a raised fist and said, "Say, can you give me a ride? May I please hitch a ride with you-all thataway?" He thumbed in the direction they were already headed.

The driver said, "Hop in." Oh, joy. Here I go with my people. Wittman got into the back seat, and waved goodbye to his brief community. "I'll be back," he said. "I'm just taking a break." He'd put in his stint for now. "Phyllis, I've got a son too. I'll raise him the way you said."

The driver was Clifton Anderson from Missouri, and the fellow passenger was Sheraton De Clair or Declare, also from Missouri. Wittman introduced himself as "Wittman Ah Sing from Berkeley"; his benefactors had picked up a man of political action. "I just now raised the peace movement in Hawai'i to a dozen souls," he reported. "They're inexperienced about keeping quiet and going limp. We could use your help." He and Blacks had to have the same politics. ("No Viet Cong ever called me 'nigger.' "—Muhammad Ali) "You're welcome to join our vigil when you come this way again. Are you military guys?" Both of them had short afros like soldiers. The few Black people in the islands are military.

"The army of the Lord," said Clifton. Oh, no, fallen among the religious again. The island is full of Christians.

"We're VISTA volunteers," said Sheraton, "sponsored by our Methodist church."

Missionaries. From the government *and* the church. The missionaries are still coming, and now they're Black. Say one word to convert me, I'm getting out.

Sheraton said, "We're on our way to Kahalu'u, the poorest area in the U.S. We just came from the airport. This is our first day in Hawai'i."

"Me too!" said Wittman. "We're on the same life-path and route. I flew in yesterday. This is my first full day here too. And I live in Kahalu'u. I'm on my way back there now." What a small world. My karass. Brothers of the open road. "What a great way to evade the draft. You've got it made. What a smart plan, covering all the bases—the religious exemption *and* the indispensable-service exemption. VISTA workers get deferred and exempted like Peace Corps, right?"

"I haven't been planning like that," said Sheraton, who was turned around in the seat listening to Wittman. "How about you, Clift? You have motives like that?"

Clifton didn't answer. A shutter in his wide-open eyes looking at Wittman via the rearview mirror closed. Shields in Sheraton's eyes also slammed down. How do they do that?

Wittman blurted and blabbed out his secret. "I'm a draft dodger myself, on the lam and underground. I read *The Conquest of Violence* by Joan Bondurant. That's Dr. Martin Luther King, Jr.'s favorite book. Have you read *The Conquest of Violence*?"

No, they hadn't read it. They're probably the kind who don't read but the one book, the Bible.

"VISTA trained us in organizing," said Sheraton. "I believe in organizing for power. We're going to organize the poverty out of Kahalu'u. The people of Kahalu'u have a valuable resource—one another. Organized, they pool and multiply their talent and wealth. Together, they'll think up what they *want*. They're *in* want, but when they *know* their wants, they'll begin to generate and create fulfillment. Once a person learns organizational skills, he'll be able to live anywhere—a slum, suburbia, jail. Turn that slum, suburbia, jail into community. Into home. I expect to be happy living in Kahalu'u." He was admitting he was *for* happiness—so uncool, when the times were so unhappy. "By organizing everybody, I can make any place—public housing, a corporate office, any job, a city block—a viable homeplace. When I learned my organizing, I stopped being lonely and afraid. I will never have to live alone, get old alone, die alone. I won't be a lonely old man in an old-age home; I'll just organize my fellow old folks to be my community."

Clifton, the driver, said, "When the VISTA job is over, and if the war is still going on, I'll resist the draft. I'm not a draft evader. I'm not a draft dodger. I don't believe in dodging and evading. I'm a draft *resister*." He looked Wittman eye-to-eye in the rearview mirror. "Do you get the difference? I keep my draft board and the SSS informed exactly where I'm at, and what I'm doing. My every activity on the outside of the army is political activity. Everything I do, I'm resisting. I'm practicing for my confrontation day with the army. I look forward to it; I'm not evading it. When my number comes up, I'm going straight to my induction center. They'll call out my name—Anderson, Clifton. That's a crucial moment, when they call out your name. You're supposed to take one step forward. That one step is a very symbolic step. It means that you are volunteering of your own free will even if you've been drafted. You're assenting, I am a soldier. You're obeying your first order. I'll use willpower, that I not take that step. I'll resist. I'm practicing not to take that step. My telling you about it right now is practice. I *think* about not taking that step. I am developing a resistance state of mind. Everybody else will step forward, so I naturally will want to step forward too. My good friends rehearse me; they call out, 'Anderson, Clifton,' and I freeze. You take a step, and that's the step that takes you from walking the walk of a free man to walking the walk of a Government Issue. The army may try to coax me or ridicule me or threaten me, but I'm forewarned and prepared. I will not step forward. Then they'll see that I heard my name but am purposefully not stepping forward, and they'll arrest me. They could jail me then and there. Or they could dangle me, send me home for two weeks or an indefinite time. I know a guy who didn't hear from them for nine months. They want you to stew over the possible consequences. Jail. A record. Unemployed from now on. Losing the vote. A lot of people can't take the suspense. They'll leave for Canada, or they'll induct themselves. Me, I'm withstanding the pressure. They call me up again, I'll resist some more. I'm resisting evil. 'In times of evil, resist evil, even if you have no hope to stop it.' "

Sheraton chorused with him, " 'In times of evil, resist evil, even if you have no hope to stop it.' " He explained that this was the motto of the Resistance; it was first said by Robert McAffee Brown, the chaplain at Stanford.

So multicultural Wittman rode through Honolulu with two idealistic Black men. When he got to know them better, he'd ask them about soul. What precisely is soul? And did they detect his? Over the Pali they went, and stopped at the Lookout for a look, when a surprise wind blew upward out of the cliff—wind can come *up* a mountain—and another wind blasted out of the Old Pali Road. They leaned on the wind without falling. It held them up. It spun them. They laughed in amazement, lying prone and supine on the stable wind. They ran with and against it. Great invisible creatures wrestled them, roughed them up, and with dextrous fingers unbuttoned shirts and pulled T-shirts over heads. Two men with curly nubs of hair on their chests and a man with no hair on his chest played like boys who find themselves in miraculous bodies that leap and run and just about fly. Head down, arm out, they ran for touchdowns into the wind, through the wind tunnel, and on to the Old Pali Road. Then the air went still. The cantilevered road wound along the face of the mountain, and bent out of sight. Boulders had fallen and broken the cobblestones-and-tar pavement. Through cracks and holes, you could see the depth of the valley under your feet. And before you as you stood at the low wall was the windward side and the ocean. Kings and queens on horseback and in carriages and palanquins had traveled this road to and from their summer palaces. Chinese must have built this road. Look up the history of any hard-made road, the Chinese built it. The road curved through noa noa—green and yellow guava, torch ginger, yellow and white ginger aflutter with yellow and white butterflies. At the inside wall grew Job's tears and buffalo grass. Good thing nobody leapt over that wall to take a piss. You would fall through the space between wall and mountain down into the valley far, far below. No kapu signs: look out for yourself.

Climbing up a side gorge, they found a big round metal thing that was the nose of an airplane, and next to it a piece of wing, and a propeller blade, and a rotary and axle. An airplane had crashed up here, maybe shot down in World War II. But any Rising Sun insignia had disappeared. They picked up still-elegant gears, and each considered taking a piece of airplane for souvenir. But respect kapu. Travel light. Bad luck. History. Treat this place like a national park, where it's against the law to carry away anything. They left the reminders of death and war, turned about, and went down along the stream, back the way they'd come.

They drove windward to the music of Hawaiian radio KCCN. Heartstrings loosened by slack-key guitar, they arrived at the Hygenic Store, where Kahaluʻu began. The whitewashed wood-frame hutch, bigger than a banana stand, had a barn-type door that was wide open all day, and a false-front proscenium that said HYGENIC STORE. (Mainland spelling: "hygienic.") The three odd-colored men went inside and bought sodas, greens, bread, cold cuts, and milk, familiar brands that were shipped and trucked in. Bringing an especially large number of items up to the counter, the good customers introduced themselves by name to the clerk. She did not give them her name in return, but treated them like any tourists passing through. Sheraton informed her that they were going to be residents, her neighbors, regular customers, about to open up a rec center in the Quonset hut in back of the store. "VISTA and all the churches in Kāneʻohe are sponsoring us and the Drop-In Canteen." The clerk did say that she'd heard "da kine."

Wittman followed the VISTA workers around behind the Hygenic Store to check out the Quonset hut. World War II had left Quonset huts all over Oʻahu. The doors were padlocked; they peered in every window, but couldn't quite see through the dark and dust. The shadows could be piles of junk, unnecessary stuff that people had stored and forgotten, or the promised Ping-Pong table and record player with stereo. They were counting on sports and music, and books to segue the dropouts into getting their GED. The Quonset hut was a luxury of space on this minuscule island. The first project for organizing Kahaluʻu would be a fixer-upper clean-up party. These two VISTA workers had to touch you and make you laugh—they believed that the dropout youth of Kahaluʻu would be turned on and turned around by housecleaning. Wittman volunteered to teach reading and writing, to do antidraft counseling, and to help put on a show. Those were about all the skills he knew to give.

Clifton and Sheraton were also going to live in Tong's Village. So Wittman came home like any workaday daddy, home from the day's commute with bags of groceries and some new friends.

Goodwife Taña at her easel on the porch was surrounded by girls modeling for her or watching over her shoulder or also painting. They were scrunching and smooshing, jabbing and twiffling her brushes on expensive paper. Taña, wearing her palette of colors on Wittman's old shirt, was concentrating on a group of three girls posed sitting on the floorboards. Gauguin painted a picture like that, except that these girls were wearing XL T-shirts over cut-offs. They held themselves just so for Taña to appreciate and record. The low sun that goes down so early at the bottom of the Ko'olaus backlit the girls, and made halos—haku leis of light around each head. It was the time of God's light.

Ambivalent ape Wittman felt envy-of-artist-working. He had squandered the day—all he'd done was go around in a circle—while she harnessed Creation and Time. A couple of girls sitting on the railing played with Taña's long golden hair, spreading a blonde cape of tresses over her shoulders, braiding strands, unbraiding them, and marveling at the crinkles and curls of blonde ringlets. They had crowned her with a lei of yellow-and-white plumeria. Titania and her brown fairies. Taña did not like people fussing with her hair, but she was suffering the girls' fooling with it in return for their modeling. (She never let Wittman look over her shoulder like that.)

At the approach of the men, the tableau broke apart; the kaleidoscope was turned and shaken. The girls quit their poses, pulled the flowers out of their hair, tried to stick them in other girls' hair. Right ear, taken; left ear, available. "She available." "Not. You available." "You." "You." "Alicia loves Duncan." "Not. You love Duncan." "O-o-o-h, Taña stay married to one Popolo!" "Which one yours, Taña?!" At their daring, they scattered. "Awe-way!"

Gone is the Oceania of Gauguin, when his models and everyone rested in perfect silence hour after hour. That quiet way of being is over. These girls are speedy, everyone getting speedier.

"Dad! Dad!" Mario, sounding Hawaiian, called from overhead. "Look at me, Dad! Come look see heah in da eah, you know." Plop. A coconut cannonball landed at Wittman's toes. Thank God, it was not his son fallen out of the tree. His tiny boy was at the top of a coconut tree, holding on to it with one hand and his toes. He had enormously big feet. His other hand pushed at a coconut, to throw down to or at his dad. "I can see the ocean from up heah. I can see the top of you' head, Dad. You like some mo' coconut? I t'row anadda the kind down for you."

"Come back down, Mario. Come back down slow."

"My name be 'Ehukai. Now call me 'Ehukai." A wind came up. The tree moved; a frond, bigger than a grown person, could scrape the boy off. The fronds could close on him like shears. He wrapped his arms and legs around the hydra neck, and rode that tree.

"Wait until it stops blowing, then come down, 'Ehukai," said his mother.

"Try wait," he said. "Try wait, Mada." He was already speaking the language of the kids here. The wind and the tree weren't shaking him out of it.

"Okay, 'Ehukai," said his father. "We have enough coconuts. How about coming down?"

Their son, now 'Ehukai, scooting down, knees bending and straightening like a frog swimming, was saying, "Hardah stay come down than go up da buggah." He'd chosen a tree that somewhat inclined. Smart boy. He climbed down as far as Wittman, stood up on the tree, and flew into the arms of his father, who caught him.

"Now, tell me about 'Ehukai. Who and what is 'Ehukai?"

" 'Ehukai—that's me. Da kine—the kind people—my *hānai* family—found me and I found them today. They *hānai* me. 'Ehukai is my real true name. I am *'ehukai*, you know. See?" He pulled his hair up, and bent down for his mother and father to look at him. "See the red? Like the kind rooster comb. *And* like the top of the wave when the red sun *comb* it. That's *why* I be 'Ehukai. 'Ehukai *goes* with how I *am*." There are Hawaiians called *'ehu* people. They have reddish-brown skin; their hair is black at the roots and shades out to red at the tips.

Wittman noticed that his son's Chinese black hair had turned brownish, with a hint of red. Orangutans and mutt dogs have orangy hair like that. In the presence of Black witnesses, Wittman accepted the colors that nature gives. He'd brought his mixed-race kid to the right place. He got straight with his offspring's outgrowing the name he'd given him.

"Are you a Hawaiian boy now?" Wittman asked.

"I am hapa haole, hapa Pākē." Half White, half Chinese. So— Hawai'i has given him the words for who and what he is. Back home, they'd call him "Eurasian."

God's light went out for the day. A day goes by fast in Hawai'i. Time is tricky here. You walk for hours along the rim of a volcano or the shoreline of the ocean, but return in minutes, following your own footsteps. You speed across a parking lot or a forest, but take a long time, forever, recrossing it. You come to Hawai'i for a vacation, to live a vacationer's life, temporarily evading the nine-to-five, just until the war is over, and the next thing you know, your kid is grown, and you are old. The ancient people didn't like time going by too fast either, and tried to do something about the hurrying sun. Māui lassoed the sun, dug in his heels, and braked its speed across the sky. Then his mother could get more work done. New land is still forming and coming up out of the sea, and time is not firm; the people are still singing Creation chants.

Since they had been in Hawai'i for one day, one day longer than Clifton and Sheraton, it was up to Taña and Wittman to welcome them and give them aloha. They cooked dinner for the newest immigrants, and made only one faux pas: Taña offered their guests an after-dinner toke of pot, or would they like it in their tea? Clifton said, "No, thank you." Sheraton declined too. "No, thank you, ma'am." The shutters in their eyes definitely closed. Their host and hostess were too familiar, expecting Black people to be liberal, dope-smoking, law-breaking nonsquares. They ended the evening uncomfortably. "Aloha, Brother Clift," said Wittman. "Aloha, Brother Sheraton." They did say Aloha and Brother in return.

To get control of life in Hawai'i, the immigrants got down to work on their projects. Taña kept her studio outside, on the lanai; an artist should not live in her studio, because of toxic chemical fumes. At day's end, she cleaned the expensive brushes that should last forever, wrapped her palette board in plastic, aligned the tubes and bottles according to the rainbow, blacks and whites at either end, in the order she'd invented as a child. She also had lots of cheap brushes that she didn't clean; that profligacy should show up in her strokes as freedom. She taught the girls, who came over every day, hanging out, to clean the good brushes, to recap the tubes and bottles after each dip, squeeze, or pour for economy, and also not to breathe unhealthy fumes. Pads and blocks of paper were aligned by size on the porch floor, where the rain didn't hit. It is a Hawaiian and Japanese and hippie custom to live on the floor, which can be chair, table, bed. On one window ledge, shelf, sat the porcelain cruet of water for mixing ink and paint, and on the other, the electric pencil-sharpener. Constantly sharp pencils are a happiness. It's wonderful to be married to an artist; she touches and places a thing, sets it so you can see it out of its general ground. You don't have to entertain her.

Another reason for having the lanai studio was to insist upon the society that does not steal. To live trusting and unparanoid. Our hearts and house are open, and the world is good.

Taña became the odd, bountiful White lady who shows up amongst poor children, and pays attention to them, gives them things, invites them into her home, and shows them marvels. She can change their lives. Her palette arrayed all kinds of browns, and the colors that make up brown, purples and reds, lit up with yellows and oranges and greens. She mixed skin colors, and talked to the girls she painted. "Your face is a different color and tone from your arm. See?" She wanted to show them their beauty in detail. "More red in your face, rose and orange. And blue in your lips—and coral in *her* lips—and yellow on your arm. Do you see it? You have to really look, and you'll see. There are many, many colors in your face. And it keeps changing in the shadows and the lights. The skin on your face is different on your forehead and around your eyes, and different on your nose and the wings of your nose, which stand out in planes if you put color here and here and here. O-o-oh, your face is a beautiful color. Ah-h-h, you are beautiful. You have so many expressions. Your feelings change your colors too." Giving teen-age girls cosmetic hints can keep them from volunteering for the military, which recruited women with promises of makeup and makeover classes. "See how many colors go into making skin color, even a haole face, which is not chalky-beigy pink like the flesh-color crayon."

The Volunteers in Service to America organized some Kahaluʻu people to clean out the Quonset hut. The churches came through with the Ping-Pong table and a dartboard, and a sound system. The empty floor space should get people inventing how to fill it. Dropouts, who were all boys, started dropping in, especially when there were refreshments. They played chess, stoned and unstoned, but were not curious about the old books, many of which were stamped "Discard." Clifton and Sheraton would mention the GED, and the boys left, politely saying goodbye. When they dropped in again, the VISTA workers gave out info about Selective Service, but the boys thought they were recruiting, and left. Next time, Clifton and Sheraton got right down to giving them the three questions that the army asks Conscientious Objectors: (1) What are your values? (2) Where did you get them? (3) How do you live them out?

To get the kids off spray paint—they snorted saturated rags—you have to replace dope with a natural high, such as engaging in sports, swimming, surfing. But Kāneʻohe Bay was not a swimming or surfing beach. The children had impetigo up to their knees from wading. And no bus commuted to jobs in Kāneʻohe, Kailua, and Honolulu, let alone to recreational beaches. People lived here who'd never left this side of the island. "I don't think they're putting us on—there are Hawaiian kids who've never been swimming," the VISTA workers reported to Wittman. "Just like Black kids." But, as luck and noblesse oblige would have it, a retired admiral of the Pacific Fleet, who lived on a spread *mauka* of Tong's Village, opened his swimming pool to the drop-ins. The admiral's daughters and niece, home from college, volunteered to offer a summer swimming program.

Wittman's independent project was to work on perception. His specialty was observing life. The way of seeing the world—even one person's seeing of it—could cause it, could change it. Seeing would be his important job. End the war by knowing it to be over. Change yourself from your inside out, from your guts. Only change oneself, and the world will change. It's all connected, all related to all. Reality comes into being *because* of our being. My being. Which is most amenable to change. I am and I see; therefore it is. Mind creates what's out there— the ʻāina, the war, everything. Hawaiʻi, small, manageable earth, ought to be easily affected and effected. *See* the world peaceful and the war will end. Wittman had such faith from having been raised Chinese.

On the Windward Side, reality dissolved. It rained and rained and rained. As at Kahana Bay, the people named the rains. Cane-tapping rain, taro-tapping rain, leaf-bruising rain, flower-spoiling rain. But here it rained military rains—"bullet rain," "rain that marches like American soldiers," "dishonorable discharge," "rain that attacks like American soldiers," "rain like the feet of soldiers forming a rainbow pattern." The thuds and thumps in dreams and waking were rains of coconuts on the roof.

Taña drew the rain in graphite lines of gray, shades of darker gray that were the Ko'olaus. Crosshatches of rain blew one way and blew the other way, layers of rain, rain on land, rain on ocean. The horizontal lines were bamboo bending down on roads and streams. She was drawing the "dark rain like a new house before it has been made"; that is the rain like long grasses. She ran her watercolor paintings under the faucet.

The rain that rained on them in Kahalu'u was *ua-po'ai hala*. Kahalu'u has a famous rain. It is red rain in the sunshine, and it rains near the house. It can rain in one spot and be dry next door. The great curving leaves are echo chambers, amplifiers. "It's only the rain," you say to reassure the dreamer of loud nightmares.

In the sexy rain, of course, you make love. Winds blowing you away, rains washing you away, hang on to a fellow body who makes you feel you have a body too. Make love, calling each other's name. Reel in the soul. But not on dope, which blows the mind and loosens all holds, erasing distinctions between life and death, incarnations, yourself and others, past and present. Fuck to be grounded, rooted, earthed. Touch and be touched. There's a certain sex trip that happens in Hawai'i: He touches her breasts and feels that they are his. She takes his penis and feels that it is hers. And the borders between us and the 'āina overlap; we are the mountains and the ocean and the sky mating. She becomes immense, and he is spread out on her, a ship riding the night ocean.

"Taña, you're so large," said awed Wittman.

"I am not. I weigh exactly the same as before we got married. I weigh the same as in high school."

He didn't mean fat. They were misunderstanding each other. They could lose each other in this place.

On the Windward Side, rain is a season, but the wind always blows. Trade winds from the northeast and storm winds from everywhere blew through the house, between the boards of single-wall construction. Always noise. Wind caught by ears says all kinds of shtrange things. You can't hear yourself think. The air was alive with myriads of gray doves, living whistles. Wind went through them as they flew, and their wings beat the sound. We human beings are likewise reeds that the wind blows through. All reality was in waving motion. Wall, ground, floor moved. Mushrooms grew indoors in the corners. Cockroaches or crickets three inches long flew through the air on wingspan that was half a foot. Roaches can fly! A molting swarm of fairies shed opalescent wings all over the floor. What revels or battles during the night, and what creatures had they become without their rainbow fairy-wings? Metamorphosed into what? Geckos lived indoors too, holding on to the walls with five fingers and five toes. Tsk-tsk-tsking. (Lizards spoke prophecy into Carlos Castaneda's ear.) Ants ten times as big as Mainland ants. And one of them is carrying away a peel of somebody's sunburn.

Poems and plays were not coming to Wittman. No speech that he could hear came out of this ground. Williams' law of poetry: Listen to the ground of the Americas, and hear and be her voice. But the book is not the art form of the people of this land. It is dance and mele. The ʻāina sings Hawaiian, secret language. A corollary to that law of poetry could be that we not move from our birthplace. Too late, Wittman thought. Haole from now on. Gauguin had said, "I've lost words— abstract or concrete."

Taña gave ʻEhukai a magnifying glass on a string to wear around his neck, to see the ʻāina in its infinite, substantial minutiae. Don't goddamn the mosquitoes. Don't mindlessly whap a tickle on your arm. Look at it. You may see a creature that no one has ever seen before. And it landed on you, of all people. One day ʻEhukai saw the yellow-and-red laughing spider. It smiled at him!

To weigh his family down, and be practical, Wittman furnished their house. He found floating in the water a park bench, sea-weathered wood and rusty bolts, adorned with barnacles. He and Taña carried it along the shoreline and Kam Highway and home, feeling like characters in a French movie. They sang a song from childhood about "the wooden box with the XXX—boom boom boom—afloating in the bay." "I went on out and brought it in, as happy as a king." "Get out of here with that XXX—boom boom boom—before I call the cops." You never learn what the XXX is. They put the bench inside along the picture window; it would do in lieu of a bourgeois sofa. Exploring an abandoned house, Wittman found the metal frame of a bunkbed with two sets of wire bedsprings. Mr. Tong lent or gave him mattresses. ʻEhukai invited friends for sleeping over. Valuable glass balls and glass cylinders floated from Russia and Japan and Australia onto doorsteps on Kāneʻohe Bay. Toys and useful things came in on the tides. It is the karma of Americans that we can never be without things. Wait and see what you get.

Taña took down the window screens, and put them under the house. Screens filter out 45 percent of the light. At night, ʻEhukai said, "They can see *in* but. We can't see *out*."

"Who can see in?"

"Menehunes and ʻaumākua and tupapau and birds."

They took him outside, and watched shadows become leaves and bufos and mountains.

An ʻaumākua is a member of your family, albeit a different species from you. An ancestor has taken on a new form—shark, bird, dragonfly, plant. They bring you news and help. People with shark ʻaumākua are not afraid of sharks, nor would those people eat sharks or be eaten by them. ʻEhukai said that birds were paying attention specially to him.

Wittman and Taña were so city, they thought Kahaluʻu was wilderness country. The beauty of nature covered up poverty. Men hung around the Hygenic Store; they did not seem poor amidst the flowering trees. There was stealing going on, but it wasn't recognized as stealing. A girl sat on Kahaluʻu Bridge, on Kam Highway over Kahaluʻu Stream, wearing Taña's hand-sewn ball-fringe dress. Was that stealing or borrowing? Is it a right of the aloha tradition to enforce a gift? They lived near the dawn; mores seemed newly made.

The garbage collectors came twice a week rather than once a week like Main Land. After three brand-new plastic garbage-containers disappeared, the Ah Sings found a used metal one off the Bay. The children rolled one another down the street in the metal garbage-cans. People went about barefoot; they were shoeless because of poverty, not because of the rain and mud and fashion.

City people in the country are lonely. No crowds, no people walking overhead and talking on the other side of walls, no culture, no restaurants, not enough noise, not enough people. It's too quiet in the country. You get the feeling of not mattering—the ocean and the jungle don't care, and you're haole.

There was a sign on buildings and fences everywhere on the island: an eye and the word "SUSPICIOUS?" and a phone number. Wittman and Taña would stop whatever they were doing and ask each other, "Suspicious?"

They sat on the roof of their house, having climbed higher up the well under the black Koʻolaus, and looked at the black ocean. "What the fuck are we doing here?" they'd say. "Where are we?" "What are we doing here?"

One sunrise, ʻEhukai was coming home from an exploration. He'd gone out early to look for chicken fights—"chicking fights"—and crepuscular critters, owls, which are ʻaumākua of Oʻahu. He awoke mongooses and pet geckos and bufos. He followed trails and tracks and streambeds, named the crayfish and the crabs, and played house in abandoned houses. Parted from his *hoa-aloha* friends, he was running by himself along an old rock fence, and saw something in the dawnlight—an extra glow and shine. He stepped close to it for look-see curiosity. A Menehune. It arose out of or from behind the old rocks. It opened its mouth wide and wider, till it took up the whole face. It turned its head and smiled, following the boy with its gaze. Its head was shining. Its body shone too. It shone everywhere. It saw ʻEhukai, and laughed. Its laughter chased him all the way home.

ʻEhukai jumped into bed between his mother and father, and got under the covers shaking. They were terrified at his terror, held him, coaxed him to tell what was wrong.

"I-I-I-I saw a creature. The King of the Menehunes. Terrible. Terrible. Menehune. Tall as me. Everywhere shiny white. It—he was *crowned*. He saw me. His head with the crown turned at me, and—and—and he opened his mouth wide open, and hollow. Shiny *points* on his head and points on his crown and inside his mouth—and at the bottom of him. He *saw* me. His head turned at me like this. He was going to *get* me."

"It's all right, honey lamb. You poor honey, you have chicken skin. He didn't get you. You're safe with Mommy and Daddy. You're all right."

"How did you know he was King of the Menehunes?"

"He was wearing a shiny crown with points. He didn't have two legs—he had lots of points that moved. He moved on points."

"Did he say anything to you?"

"He didn't talk. He laughed. His mouth was opening and opening. Hah. Hah. Hah. Like that." The boy laughed his own deep, scary laugh. "I saw a Menehune. A Menehune saw me. His mouth opened into a big hole with points, like sharp teeth. I could've died, Mom. *Maké*, Dad."

Raising a kid, you don't want to cause him to doubt his perceptions. You honor his reality. Believe that he believes it. Don't tell him there are no such things as Menehunes. And you don't know that there are not. The 'āina emanates things, and this boy could see them. Wittman and Taña, open-minded about everything, would go hunting for a bristling light out of the rocks, for a crowned being about three feet tall.

Wittman chanted the come-home-after-fear chant that PoPo had done for him. He took his kid-doy by the ears and pulled them back and forth, pulling the fear out of him and pulling him home by the ears. "Come home to Kahalu'u, on Kamehameha Highway, Tong's Village, Windward Side, O'ahu, Hawai'i. Do not be afraid. No harm. No harm. Be safe at home. You are safe at home." He gave the long, hyphenated address number. "Be safe at home with your mother and father, Wittman Ah Sing and Taña DeWeese Ah Sing. Be home, 'Ehukai. Be home, Mario. Be home, Mario 'Ehukai DeWeese Ah Sing. We will always be here for you to come home to. You are safe. We love you." The father was vowing: We will always be together, married parents together, loving each other and our child, no matter what. His son home after fear, Wittman praised him for his skillfulness. "You're a fast runner. You did just right, took a good look at him, named him, and ran fast."

With his own money, 'Ehukai bought five pounds of Hawaiian rock salt, and sprinkled it all over the house, where it stayed crunchy for all the time they lived there.

Children called 'Ehukai come go play. Chameleon boy often go stay with his *hānai* (adopted) families. Maybe they shouldn't have left Berkeley, where Mario would have grown up to be an intellectual, where he was indigenous, fourth-, fifth-generation Californian. Uprooted from the mainland, their child was lured by spirit-soft Hawai'i. The price of war-evading was reality-evading. Their child was paying the price. A child needs his life to be like everybody else's—regular hours, sofa here, bed there.

Wittman never saw a Menehune for himself, but did see a flapping sheet of whiteness fly across the moonlight. Pueo, the white owl, who won the war between the Menehunes and the Owls. Maybe that war still goes on. The 'āina of Hawai'i throws up hallucinations to confound you with what's real and what's not. The island is so small, everything—civilizations, histories, beings—is crammed and juxtaposed and super-imposed on everything else. Mountains and rocks are permeated. Everything is itself and something else. Creatures seem to peer from corners and sides. The *tehoa* sits by your bed, and you lie there alone, naked, on your stomach, one eye open, on the lookout.

Many a low tide, Wittman crossed the highway, sat on the strip of land that appeared, and looked out at the ocean. Study it. *Be* with it. Unstoned. That immensity must teach you something. Learn to live in this foreign country of water and air and lava rock. Watch the waves come in and come in and go out and go out and go out. Right now. Right now. Now and now come in and come in and go out and go out and go out. Right now. Right now. Now and now and now and now. The same now. From the beginning of water, this same moving has been going on for millions and millions of years of countless moments. It has always been now. In the moving water, and in time, the shoreline changes; the reef changes; the fish and people change. Slow, slow, slow evolution. The now contains the ocean, and the ocean contains myriads of events. Scientists have measured the present moment tighter and tighter—a nanosecond, a ksana. Dark infinity behind us, dark infinity ahead squeeze us in the claustro of the present that we can never, ever break out of. So blow it up. Nuke it.

The warplanes flew in and out of Kaneohe Marine Corps Air Station. And the Ocean Institute on Coconut Island was secretly training porpoises to deliver bombs.

One night, Wittman almost saw a supernatural thing for himself—a light far out on the water beckoned him. Two beings were dancing, turning, crossing or going through each other. The light was either coming from them or spotlighting them. A pair of night birds with reflecting white wings? Amphibious sea monkeys evolving from water to land right before your eyes? They were arrayed in clothes that kept changing colors and styles. They grew bigger and bigger, winging like angels straight across the water toward him.

"Eh, Wittman. Good lobster night. You like?"

It was just Black Pete and Mary. They were holding buckets and lanterns. They gave him two lobsters. Taña would have to help figure out how to cook them before Mario made pets of them.

Black Pete kept inviting Wittman to try entering the ocean, to dive deeply into Hawai'i. One morning, Wittman took him up on it. In duck fins, they walked backward into the tide. They spat into their masks with their own personal spit, "to keep 'em from fog up," and fitted the masks over their faces. You push your hair out of the mask, so it seals tight. Wittman lay prone in the water, and saw the sea floor. Breathing through the snorkel, swimming and poling himself along with the spear of his Hawaiian sling, he followed the steady blue flippers ahead of him. The Hawaiian sling works like a crossbow but with a spear almost seven feet long; you pull the elastic tube-band back to a hook, and it's loaded. Shoot by squeezing the long trigger with your whole hand; the spear springs out. It is connected to the rest of the sling with a rope, so you can retrieve it, and the fish. Black Pete's large brown self with the kicking blue feet—his underheel is white—was just ahead. Wittman was inside his flying dream again, flying over forests and mountains and over deserts, and between and amongst fish. Schools of talapia turned and flashed in the sunny currents. A sea turtle stroked by. Wittman wanted to exclaim over it and talk about it. Sea cucumbers rocked on the bottom. There were climates, gold sand falling and sparkling all around, and sudden cool shadowy darknesses. The swimmers entered and left blue-gray rooms and green chambers.

He heard sounds as if many people were speaking in a foreign language. Voices were trying to talk to him, or they were talking about him. They were behind his right ear, and he could almost make out the words. Being a conversationalist, he wanted to ask, "What you say?" and to answer those talkers. He flipped over onto his back, saw sky and clouds, and shouted, "Hey, Pete! This is great! Terrific! Did you see the turtle?" Pete kept swimming, and Wittman swam to catch up with him. The voices were the sounds of his own breathing through the snorkel. He held his breath, and the voices changed—sounds of his blood pulsing, sounds of his mind.

The reef was like the Sierras, and then fish swam across his view. A school of silver-gray fish streamed by. Pete followed them, and Wittman followed him. This is hunting. Multitudes of life-forms lived in the reef—zebra fish, yellow tangs, angelfish. The creatures moved quickly or drifted slowly. A blowfish came toward him, blew up round and spiny, and squirted away. Our human relationship to other creatures: We try to get close to them, and they recede. We're always catching up to them, and they move away. We have to shoot them to get them to stay still. Another puffer came right at Wittman, looked at him out of round eyes and made an oh-round mouth, and puffed itself up into a spiny round ball. A target. Wittman shot it—in its side when it turned about. Black Pete worked it off the spear and put it in his bag, laughing at the puny catch.

Black Pete pointed out holes—pukas—in the reef. He gave instructions on how to catch lobsters: "You see da kine antennas, feelers, stick out of the coral. Lobster cooperate with moray eel, and with you. Lobster geeve you warning. You see one feeler in, one feeler out, moray eel is inside the puka, living in there with lobster. Lobster keeping his eye on eel. Two feelers out, eel not home, you reach in and grab heem." One deep breath, and down they dived. Sure enough, antenna hairs sticking out from this puka and that puka. Oh, the delicacy and aliveness of Nature, life sensitive to life, creatures sending out feelers into the universe to contact one another. Black Pete reached into a puka and pulled out a lobster. Then sudden churning horror and violence— moray eel, worm ouroboros—big open mouth, in-pointy teeth—squinty black eyes—came shooting out after the black hand gripping the lobster, its cavemate, its symbiotic treasure. Slithering, ribboning yards of eel flowed outward and upward, tail—more and more of it—and how much more within the coral cave—and head about to bite Black Pete's hand. Wittman came in close—the Hawaiian sling has short range, rope not long—put the spear tip on the eel, and shot. This moray eel will be the second creature, not counting insects, that he has killed. And he didn't have to kill it: Black Pete had swum out of harm's way, for air. He hit it. He felt the spear go through hide and flesh. But it didn't die. The moray eel crawled and curled and twisted up the spear and the rope at him. Eyes looked at him. Mouth opened to eat him up. It was climbing out of the knot of itself, twisting up the spear, up the rope. Wittman dropped the entire apparatus, and popped out of the water.

He swam for Chinaman's Hat, land. Mokoli'i. Forever afterward, his body remembered the feeling of the spear going into the tough, resisting eel flesh. He climbed up the cone crown of the hat, and sat up there looking into the sea for Black Pete. Near the spot where he himself had exited the water, he saw Pete's black back rise and fall, like a surfacing sea animal. He's looking for me. Wittman jumped up and down and yelled, "Pete! Black Pete!" Water sprayed out of Black Pete's snorkel, like a whale spouting. He lifted his head, saw Wittman, waved, and swam over the reef to the ocean side. Wittman stayed on land to explore the moon side of Chinaman's Hat. He was the only human being on an entire island. The slope of the hat was covered with tall grasses, and the crown was bare lava rock. The island had been a volcano that had fired from its crown. This other side of the island was hot and treeless. Crabs were baked red on the rocks; the live crabs were blue-black. (Black Pete chewed and swallowed crabs raw, shells, claws, and all.) And there were small lobsters baked purple and yellow. On the tiny beach, where no people collected them or stepped on them and broke them, were large whole purple cowrie shells. The sand was fine yellow-white grains, pulverized by the up-dashing waves. Almost invisible white crabs ran in and out of white foam surf. Most of the ground was black lava rock. An inlet of sea flowed into a little cave; at the edge of its cove, a blowhole boomed and sprayed rainbows. Wittman sat with his feet in the blowhole. Rainbows spewed and broke all over him, leaving jewels on his skin. He stood in the blowhole, and felt the surging, sucking water, did not get sucked through the lava tube and out to sea. He climbed out and crouched in the cave, and looked out at the path of his own Friday footsteps. Chinaman's Hat—Water Margin hideout with the ocean as moat.

There was a ledge shelf of lava rock with tide pools—a universe and cosmos inside each one. A cow with fins swam up to him, and smiled with great big eyelashed eyes and big smiling lips. It dived into a crack in the lava, and did not come out again. He could not find another such creature in any other tide pool. Two minuscule spacemen in blue-black leotard space suits—their flip side was silver-gray—maneuvered up to each other. One sent out a cable tube or guts, and they attached up. They might have been having sex. A wave came in and washed them out and away into the ocean. In the largest pool was an orange caterpillar-like critter that spread out skirts, and turned itself inside out. Sensing Wittman's shadow, it vanished. Wittman got into that tide pool, which had no spiny sea urchins, and, very careful not to sit on anybody, lay back in the water, warm as a tub. Head and legs sticking out, he listened to the ocean and the wind, and looked up at the even, one-color blue heavens. Eyes closed, he saw green, rest from the red sun. The ocean flicked wet, cold spits at him, and made him laugh. He said, "This is perfect, and I am happy."

When he got up, he tried circumambulating the island. The north-westernmost part, which would correspond to Kaena Point on Oʻahu, was impassable, any walking space taken up by a thick forest of tangling, brambling trees and brush. The land mass of the island was minia-ture, but the palms were their regular gigantic size. He turned about and went counterclockwise. The side that faces Oʻahu was much the same close up as it appeared from across the channel—bright-green grass, coconut palms, bushes. Inside the bushes were large white birds that looked like seagulls, but there are no seagulls in Hawaiʻi. The white birds sat so still, they were stillness itself. Wittman looked again and again at blobs of whiteness without making out what they might be. Bright-black eyes suddenly opening belonged to pair after pair of white birds. They did not try to run or fly away. Hardly any people come to the island.

Back on the ocean side, he climbed up the hat, and hunkered down on the lava. Checking out the sea for Black Pete, he again saw his back bobbing and his snorkel spouting. The water was wild on the ocean side of the reef—potato patch next to oily doldrums, seaweed jungles next to black holes, blues like melted turquoise, deep blues and pale blues, moving blue immensities, areas of chrome silver, purple, many greens, brown-greens that must be seaweed, and spring green, as if various sea-sons were happening at the same time down there. Sliding and gliding alongside Black Pete was a gigantic dark thing. Wittman leapt up yelling, "Look out! Pete! Hey!" Black Pete didn't seem to hear him, kept swimming, dived. The giant dark round thing glided over the place where he had been, and also dived. There was a whirlpool where it sank.

Wittman went to Black Pete's rescue. Forgetting any of his equip-ment, he jumped into the water toward the last wide rings of the whirlpool. Go down there, and see what happened. He saw Black Pete putting a fish in the sack tied to his waist. A great shadow slid between man and man. Wittman leapt screaming straight out of the water. The dark thing beneath him, then before him, maybe circling him, he ran-swam across the water, and thrashed back to Chinaman's Hat.

Looking down from there, he did not see the thing again. Before sundown, Black Pete came to get him for the swim home. Wittman asked what that huge black thing was. Black Pete said, "I didn't see nothing. Mebbe one shark. Plenty shark spawn between this *moku* and O'ahu. By'm'by, we chum shark." Now he tells me. Swim back at high tide through darkening water among spawning sharks. Black Pete seemed immune to killer sharks; his net bag full of catch would've attracted them. The globular thing hadn't looked like a shark.

A howling came out of the island. The *moku*—the island itself—was singing, howling out of its ground and air. The sound of crying whirled about the island. Ooooo! Ooooooo-ooooo! It was not a human being hiding on the island and trying to scare them; Wittman had explored almost everywhere. Black Pete slid into the water, so Wittman followed him. They went over a set of rocks like Stonehenge, and crossed the shark-spawning channel. The dark thing stayed on the ocean side, too big for this strait.

Safe on the warm sand of O'ahu, Wittman asked about the howling. "What was that Ooooo-ooooo? Like a wolf or a coyote."

"No get wolf, no get coyote in Hawai'i. Bird mebbe."

"Those white ground-birds?" The howling had soared and lowered, moved as though coming from a flying creature.

"Mebbe *moko'ele*. *Moko'ele* da kine man-eating ghosts used to live on every island. By'm'by the people win even Lana'i, Ni'ihau, Ko'oha-lawe. Mebbe the *moko'ele* stay live Chinaman's Hat yet."

Black Pete and Wittman pissed on their coral cuts, poured Adolph's Meat Tenderizer on jellyfish stings and sea-urchin slivers. "Da kine coral keep living *in* you, and growing, living off of *you*."

Then they gathered their wives and son, cooked and feasted on their catch—lobsters, opihi, a redfish, the eel, and the blowfish. The blowfish had deflated; the spear popped it. Mary explained, "Black Pete one expert taking out the poison gland. Folks eat da kine, and die in torture but. It tastes so 'ono, worth it. You like try?" Taña and 'Ehukai said no blowfish please, thank you. But Wittman had killed it, he better eat it. Showing his family how round and cute the puffer blowfish had been, Wittman put the backs of his hands on his own puffed-out cheeks, opened his eyes wide, and waggled his fingers like fins. He shouldn't have killed it. It didn't taste so 'ono-licious. After he swallowed his bit of blowfish, his loyal wife and loyal child partook. They did not swell up, turn black, die.

Taña was now a minority person at a margin, and began to see through the Paradise of Hawai'i. She noticed the men—unemployed—

sitting all day in front of Hygenic Store. They drank beer and sodas, and talked story. Some sat on the fence, like cowboys in a movie, and some on a log. Good neighbor Taña and her son, 'Ehukai, shopping at Hygenic Store, went over to pass the time of day with the friendly group under the shade tree. How's your mother? How's your wife? Your daughter is sitting for me, thank you. Yes, it is a beautiful day, after the kind rain. She smiled, they smiled. Around and about, mynah birds, hands hidden behind their backs, were walking and talking too. 'Ehukai went over to one of the guys standing by the fence, and gave him a pat on the butt. "Howzit, Gomes?" "Gomes" rhymes with "homes," not two syllables like in California. Mr. Gomes, who was the school-bus driver, lifted the boy up on the fence for a sit. He complimented the mother, what a verbal son she has. The men agreed, "The keiki boy *waha nui.*" "We say, he get *hoa wala'au.*" "He get da kine charisma." The smiling man moving on the middle of the log repeated, "Charisma." That was when Taña noticed what he was doing, sliding to and fro, to and fro. He was masturbating against the log. The log was worn smooth in the middle. She got 'Ehukai away from there. Walking home, she tried to talk to him about sex. "I get it," he said. "I get it about da kine."

She reported to Wittman, "I looked down at this fellow — and he was masturbating with the log. He maintained a sociable expression on his face. I kept my manners, so I didn't traumatize Mario."

Wittman took 'Ehukai to Kahalu'u Stream with bamboo fishing poles. They put bread crust as bait on the fishhooks. They sat there side by side, father and son in the buffalo grass and Job's tears. You could easily and clearly see crayfish, bufo, crabs, tiny talapia swimming, crawling, chasing in and out of the plants and rocks. 'Ehukai dangled the string, and before the hook touched the water, a crab stroked the bait with its claws. "Look, Dad! A crab with no eyes." The crab handled the bait, and grabbed the line. They carefully pulled the crab up; it hung on. "Hi, Belinda," said 'Ehukai. "She's Belinda, Dad." They played with Belinda for a while, and let her go. "She does have eyes," said Wittman. "See? They're on stalks. She sees from the tops of the stalks." 'Ehukai himself was a Cancer-crab moonchild; he'd freed the fish Linda.

Time passed. It was not as if nothing happened. Sitting on the porch or up on the roof, you observed village drama. Everyone looking on, a woman swept her husband out the door, across the porch, down the stairs, and through the street. She went inside and slammed the door on him. He went up and down the streets and Kam Highway saying, "Lend me your gun, bradah. I need a gun. You saw how she treat me?! Let me borrow your gun. Come on. You understand. I ask of you. A gun."

An open convertible full of wives drove off to the free clinic in Kāneʻohe, and sped back with birth-control pills. "For to start up fucking affairs."

Whenever Andrew, the Kamehameha School graduate, walked past her house, there was a woman who scolded him, "Kam School grad! Hey you, Kam School boy! Who you think you are? You think you mo' bettah than anybody? Big head, you. What you good for now, Kam School grad? You good for nothing!" Andrew looked straight ahead, dignified, did not reply to her. The VISTA workers did not counsel him; he wasn't a dropout. He seemed a peer who could look after himself, make his own decisions. He'd gone through ROTC, which was in the high schools. He spoke to the Mainlanders in standard English, and confided that he couldn't speak pidgin unless stoned on another island. "I can speak da kine, but first I have to get myself off-island, and ripped." Andrew lived with his little sister and haole mother in a lane outside of Tong's Village. He must have been one-sixteenth Hawaiian, at least. Once, you had to be almost all Hawaiian to go to Kamehameha, but then it was a quarter, then one-eighth, then one-sixteenth. And even as a potential kindergartener, you had to speak standard.

A big family or clan lived up on the hill overlooking everybody. Mr. Tong did not own their house. The shacklike abode was not better than anybody else's but prominent up on the hill, which was covered with waves of grass. An especially tall pine grew at the top, and cypresses, palms, plumeria, bananas, and a lau-hala tree that looked like a monstrous spider. The people up there dismantled and recombined cars and motorbikes. (Another sign of poverty: cars that don't run sitting in the yard.) They were makes of cars that you don't see on the Main Land anymore. Once cars get to Hawaiʻi, they stay. The cooking fires, tire swing, and clothesline made up a stage set for dramas that entertained the neighborhood. A car would creep down that hill in the middle of the night or in broad daylight, a man and once a woman crouched in the back seat or the trunk. He or she had to get out of town. (So went the gossip.) You would not see that person again. Sometimes two cars would come barreling off the hill, one either chasing or escorting the other. The children said that a boy had been strung up in a bag on that rope where the tire hung. The bag with a boy in it was up there for days, and beaten like a piñata. His father and uncles whacked it with a plank whenever they got the urge. Women rarely appeared.

At the stores and banana stands, an excitement sparked at the entrance or passing by of the hill men. Their boys and young men were considered cutest. The girls had crushes on them. It was them the ladies were showing off and getting birth-control pills for. Big Eustace. Gia. Johnny Jesús. Nobody ever said that Gia had a girl's name. Big Eustace came home from Viet Nam, and walked about Kahalu'u in his entire dress uniform. They were more Hawaiian than other folks. They had guns, and shot the gray doves out of the trees, and roasted them on spits. A masturbator would stand up and greet a man from the hill. The Drop-In Canteen was a success because their boys came to it.

The more the newcomers got to know people, the more stuff disappeared. You haven't seen something for a while, can't find it anywhere, and begin to suspect that it might have been stolen. Or you're losing your mind. Or there's poltergeists, because so many adolescents are hanging about. Taña's green glass earrings. 'Ehukai's magnifying glass. Taña's fringed dress. The "marsh"/"mosh" pens from the Drop-In Canteen and from Taña's studio. Taña's prisms. Wittman's infrared aviator glasses, the metaphor glasses that he'd nicked from the Lions Club box. What you steal gets stolen from you. Kleptokarma. Nobody stole books, never books, not hardbacks or art books.

The brand-new office supplies and school supplies were missing from the Drop-In Canteen. The kids must think that it's okay to take from such a public place; the stuff practically belongs to them. They could've asked. They steal pens and notebooks because what they really want is an education. As if they could get an education by stealing school stuff. They think they can get the powers of tools from stealing the tools. They don't know about the long process of learning. They don't make graffiti with the "mosh" pens; they sniff them to make pictures in their heads.

The Mainland folks discussed whether the nonverbal people were giving them a message. Is there a pattern to things disappearing? Is someone fucking with my mind? Are they attacking rich haoles? Yet they didn't start stealing from us until they got to know us. They could be taking our possessions because they like us and want mementos. They want some of our mana. "Mana" was one of the words that connected the Hawaiians to the lost tribes of Israel. They're teaching us aloha manners, reciprocal aloha. Share. This taking is the remnants (but maybe the renascence?) of the old giving culture. They believe in communal ownership. Take from the haoles, who don't know that gifts have to be passed along. It isn't enough to feed the kids or to paint them; you have to give them your personal stuff. Indians used to walk into the settlers' houses and take back the peace pipe. They were helping the rude newcomers to pass the gift along, so it continuously be gift. Capitalists, who have a taking culture, take over a giving culture, and the kids become thieves.

Rationalizing why they'd been stolen from, the immigrants tried to figure out where they went wrong. When the kids say, "I like," they aren't just giving you a compliment. They mean, "I want." Gimme. "I like your earrings." She means, "I *want* your earrings." Watch the kids at the store. Somebody buys an ice cream, and they say, "I like. I like." The one with the ice cream has to hand it over for licks. The kids here are well brought up; they won't eat without offering, "You like?" They must've said, "I like," to us many times, and we ignored them. They said, "I like," and we said, "Thank you," when we should have given da kine whatevah to them. We didn't give fast enough, so they took. Captain Cook's men went wild for gifts, insatiably pointing to valuables, even the threshold beam of the temple; they burned it as firewood.

Taña decided that she would not put up anymore with Yolanda's blatantly wearing her fringed dress. She confronted the girl on Kahaluʻu Bridge: "Yolanda, I want my dress back. I did not give this dress to you." Yolanda looked at her without saying anything. Taña, despite herself, kept talking, explaining herself. "I don't have many dresses, and I like this one a lot. I sewed it myself." "You should've asked to borrow it." "I want you to bring me back the dress, to my house today." And Yolanda did change into shorts and T-shirt, and returned the dress folded on the porch. But thereafter, whenever Taña wore that dress, she felt guilty. She'd taken Hawaiʻi; a dress was the least she could give in reparation. (Yolanda was probably Pilipina.) The green glass earrings had been a birthday gift from Wittman. Taña fluctuated between cursing the thief ("May her ears fall off") and wishing her well ("Wear them in good health, whoever you are"). To compensate for her take-back, Taña bought fabric from the Coronet Store in Kāneʻohe, and taught the girls to bell the bottoms of everybody's jeans.

The well-meaning Mainlanders felt bad that they could not follow A. S. Neill's teachings in *Summerhill*. If a kid is thieving dresses, she needs dresses. You give her lots more dresses, money, food, whatever she needs. Neill gave a kid enough money that he stopped stealing money. You have to skillfully get him to accept the gift, so he doesn't feel poor.

The famous community organizer Saul Alinsky came to support the VISTA workers pulling Kahaluʻu together. In one hour, he gave his fifteen-month training program—"tactics"—to the church and community volunteers and the Drop-In Canteen. They were to think of themselves not as "leaders" but as "organizers." He got the kids laughing over having a "fart-in." The sit-in, he said, is an antique that should be stored in the Smithsonian now that the government and corporations know how to handle sitters. He would not tell the people of Kahaluʻu what their goals should be. The community has to "imagine" the goals for itself. Don't worry too much about means and ends; you'd get paralyzed, and do nothing. (Hawaiians were familiar with "Polynesian paralysis.") Select from tactics available, "then clothe the means in moral garments."

About the upcoming moon shot, he said, "What sense does it make for men to walk on the moon while other men are waiting on welfare lines, or are in Viet Nam killing and dying for a corrupt dictatorship in the name of freedom?"

He too saw the pall of darkness shadowing the world. "There is a feeling of death hanging over the nation."

Alinsky advised heroically going to jail. "Time in jail is time to think, integrate, write." If you are willing to suffer for "the cause," you gain status among your people. Choose your violations carefully so you do from one day to two months prison time. Alinsky was a writer; that was why he could look forward to prison. A writer would like solitary confinement. "An opportunity to reflect and synthesize his thoughts," he explained. "To gain that privacy in which he can try to make sense out of what he is doing, why he is doing it, where he is going, what has been wrong with what he has done. It is here that he begins to develop a philosophy. It is here he begins to shape long-term goals, intermediate goals, and self-analysis of tactics as tied to his own personality." Wittman felt reassured, nothing bad could happen to the writer.

The dropouts of Kahaluʻu got to hear Saul Alinksy say, "Burn, baby, burn!" He couldn't have been recommending that they burn down their neighborhood, like Watts. He must have been using "Burn, baby, burn!" as an example of something, a radical slogan. (He said "radical" instead of "revolutionary." He said, Don't forget that Gandhi was a "pragmatist.") The dropout boys were frightened and tearful. "But. Hawaiʻi is too beautiful to burn. Don't burn down Hawaiʻi. . . . Hawaiʻi is not revolting."

Paul and Mary of Peter, Paul & Mary led a community sing at the Canteen. They sang about fate: "Turn turn turn." And they sang about land, the ʻāina. "This land is my land, this land is your land / from California to the New York Island." The boys sang uncomfortably along, looking down. They quit at the second round of "This land was made for you and me." That song had something wrong with every word. From then on, out and about in Kahaluʻu, the boys mimicked that song, singing and smirking.

Wittman and Taña faced something: the nation that came together through gift-giving has broken down, or never was. It's up to us, the ones who know about potlatches, karasses, love-ins, and be-ins, to give a party. How to change society? Give it a party. What to do, finding another kid in the bushes unconscious on spray paint? (Paint rags here and there and everywhere.) Bring him to the party. ʻEhukai comes home after a fight. "Who were you fighting with?" "My friends." How to civilize the children? Give a party. How to radicalize Kahaluʻu? Give a party. How to repay the girls for modeling? Invite them to the party. The Ah Sings have been here long enough for the neighbors to bring housewarming casseroles and covered dishes, but they haven't. By'm'by, my ass. By'm'by already. They've had their chance; we'll give ourselves our own housewarming party. We'll show them, we know reciprocal aloha. We welcome *them*. Some people here just came over, yesterday, from Samoa, the Philippines, Micronesia, Molokaʻi, other outer islands. As Americans, we welcome them to our country. Integrate them, give them a party. Extend welcome. Invite everybody you know and everybody you run into. Party for the sake of our own kid; heal any wound we caused, yanking him out of native California to this foreign place. Fill the house with warm, well-fed people; they'll nudge out the ghosts and the dank, the Menehunes, and the princess on a horse clopping around and through the houses. We'll perform a house-blessing. Feed and befriend all the people and ghosts.

And it behooves us newcomers to invite feuders to party. Coming into the new place, innocent of its past, its old grudges and human sacrifices, we can change everything, give people a chance to start their relationships over. Acting as if they'd never met before, we formally introduce them to one another. They meet again and begin acquaintanceship on a new footing.

Walking about Kahaluʻu, inviting people face to face—*he alo a he alo*—Wittman and Taña met people who had the same manners as back home. Ladies asked, "May I bring something?" "What can I bring?"

"Just bring yourself," said Taña. "Bring the whole family."

Wittman said, "By the way, about how many in your family?" He worried about the food allowance for all the uncles, aunties, cousins, the whole calabash, whoever happens to be hanging around. It's scary to give a party. You stick your neck out. The rumor was that every party in Hawaiʻi is open to everybody. Any local who spots—"spocks"—a party considers himself invited, and will walk on in. Open house means open house. "No need for to invite. Walk down the shtreet, spock one party, go come join in." Food is key. Enough food for leftovers to take home. Mustn't run out of food. Good food, enough food, the party will satisfy and fly.

Taken off guard, upon being invited, quite a few people, making conversation, lectured the would-be hosts on aloha. "Hawaiʻi folks generous, not like haoles. Only those one or two people whose names addressed on the envelope really, truly invited to a haole wedding. Can't bring the rest of the family. And all they geev to eat is salad and olives, and the cake."

"No, no," said Taña. "It's not potluck." People had to understand, it would not be stone soup. *We* give to *you*. She got maneuvered into a rudeness—"No gifts, please"—as if she had gifts in mind. Perfection: guests guessing what would be a surprise and delight, and freely bringing that very thing. The party was an opportunity for them to return stolen goods. We shouldn't have to tell you, Don't come empty-handed.

They got to see the insides of neighbors' houses, many as bare as their own, no decorations but calendars and magazine cutouts, and fake flowers.

People would not be pinned down, not commit Yes, thank you, or

No, thank you. RSVP'ing had broken down, or was not the custom. "I'll see." "Try wait." "Let me see." "I let you know by'm'by." "Check my calendar by'm'by." "I need go for ask my husband stay working but." Nobody came right out and RSVP'ed No. Two weeks in advance is not last-minute.

Women asking what to wear seemed preparing to come party. "Comfortable aloha wear," said the host and hostess. "It's an aloha party. Aloha for us." Taña hand-sewed for herself a long hostess muumuu.

Wittman tried ordering clams, lobsters, and opihi from Black Pete and Mary, who said, "No. No. We bring."

"Please, I insist on paying you."

"No, they free from the ocean."

"But you work hard for them."

"Not work. I like fishing. I bring fresh on the day."

"No, no, I pay."

"You money no good. You pay, I no come party."

They had an old-fashioned Asian-style go-around about who pays, who gives. Nobody wants to be slow on the draw — that is, drawing your wallet out of your pocket.

For two weeks, Wittman and Taña argued about largesse. Whenever one hesitated, too much food, too many uncountable guests, the other accused him or her of not having enough largesse. Overcome the guests with food. They don't talk, they can eat. Provide. Follow Chinese customs, and it will be close to what other people besides Whites do. (Not long ago in Hawai'i, there were more Chinese than any other kind.) Our largesse will show them we're not stingy haole and cheap Chang. Wittman and Taña kept going to and from Hygenic Store and Bong's Grocery and the banana stand, and hitching rides to Kāne'ohe Town, even to Honolulu Chinatown. "Only two turkeys and one ham?" They rushed to Hygenic Store and picked up all the Spam. You can serve ham and Spam hot or cold. "Only ten pounds of noodles? Not enough. Where's your largesse?" Wittman bought on-sale yams in bulk, and the petite miniature marshmallows to go on top. Taña said that the big marshmallows would show more largesse. Wittman argued that the little marshmallows were more expensive. 'Ehukai asked, "What is largesse?" They explained that it had to do with "larder." They bought every flavor of cake mix and disposable aluminum pans. They made an expedition up to Sacred Falls and brought back mountain apples. Mountain apples may seem ordinaire to the locals, but there isn't anything like them on Main Land, small red-and-white translucent apples, crisp and watery. And you can't very well serve the free papayas and mangos and guavas that the guests could pick outside their own doors. Unless you cut them in amazing shapes and present them on leaves.

They worried about worrying. A party shouldn't be produced in a panic. The bad vibes of anxiety will get into the food. You need to be festive already, and enjoy the planning, the inviting, the cooking. The process shows in the results. Else the party climaxes in the ten o'clock fight.

They paced out the house. At two square feet per human body, seventy-five could squeeze together inside, and twenty-five on the porch and stairs. One hundred people can come in out of the rain at a time. Cooperating, they could trade places with those dining al fresco. In accordance with Asian ways, you honor people by inviting them inside your private home. And the guests give high honor to you by coming in. When they did the inviting, they also did the borrowing of hibachis and Komodo broilers, which people had on their porches and in yards. Neighbors become insiders of the party by offering refrigerator and freezer space, and a heat-up in the oven. They'd be helping out, carrying the food over when they came to the party. They'd have to come. They lent a dozen rice cookers of various sizes. All the peoples here— Chinese, Japanese, Korean, Filipino, Portuguese, Pacific Islanders— have rice with every meal. Even McDonald's has been taught to serve up the favorite grinds—rice *and* saimin *and* French fries.

Everyone was reminded please to bring plates, cups, and utensils of their own, though paper plates and cups, plastic forks and spoons, and disposable chopsticks would be provided. Wittman and Taña took the doors off their hinges and put them on sawhorses, which they found everywhere, under houses, along roads, in the Bay. The window out to the porch was low and wide enough so that the door-table fit through it with a sawhorse inside and one outside. And Taña could conveniently keep that table laden, and reign like Tess of the d'Urbervilles.

This shtrange coincidence happened: prospective guests were themselves also giving a party on that very same day.

The Hawaiians on the hill were giving a lūʻau for Big Eustace, come home from Viet Nam. "You invited." The Samoans were having a "fête"/"fate." "No, thank you," said the immense woman who answered the door of their *fala*. Hers was a forthright No. Mr. Tong and Mrs. Tong were taking their turn hosting the after-church vegetarian supper. You're welcome to join in, and join the church too. They had church on Saturdays. "You come join church, I forgive you five dollars rent. I take good care my tenants. Not absentee." Every Saturday night was a Drop-In Canteen social. They could very well move it over to Wittman's. Well-mannered Wittman had to say, "All of you—you and your party—come over to my party."

And a sixth party was even now happening: The hippie haoles who'd just moved in were having an ongoing, never-ending party. Revolving lights of many colors whirled from their house, on by afternoon for an all-night light show. You could see the psychedelic beams everywhere in Kahalu'u. The night they first saw the lights, Wittman, Tañita, and 'Ehukai followed the wheeling colors and Ravi Shankar–Ali Akbar Khan music—the dawn raga after sunset—and came to a house like their own on the edge of Kam Highway. Its front steps landed on the gravel shoulder of the road. The revolving lamp with color gels swirling primary red, blue, and yellow hung from the eave over the front door, which was wide open. The smell of patchouli, incense, and pot mixed with the noa noa. Mother, Father, and Baby Bear peeked into a dark room and saw doped-up people, young men nodding and passed out on mattresses and mats and on the floor against the walls. Andrew, Kam School grad, had a hypodermic needle hanging out of his arm; he'd fallen asleep without removing it. A rubber tube was tied tight on his biceps. Near him on the *pūne'e* was his girlfriend, the one girl, her hair so blond it was white, cut in a precise Dutch bob. She was clean-looking, but her eyes were rolled back, the sanpaku whites showing; dry white drool powdered the corner of her mouth. Somebody should have pulled the madras bedspread over them. Most of the people wore no shirts, and showed expanses of naked skin, which had flecks of blood. The Shooting Gallery was in business. One of the shot-up people was awake and sitting; he was playing with a raw egg on the floor, fingerpainting it, trailing a tail of blood in the yolk. He was hallucinating the Ur slime at the dawn of life. The turning light flashed through the roseate tie-dyed curtains. The people looked dead; they looked like zombies and vampires.

A bowl of pills like candy sat in the middle of the floor. Back home in California, trippers had been such brilliant talkers that they tape-recorded themselves. Stoned, they rapped all night. Playing back the tape, they were still brilliant. Times have changed; drugs have changed. Hawai'i is a nonverbal place, da kine pidgin not enough vocabulary. The times and places of good trips are over.

Wittman and Tañia quickly drew their child out of the doorway, away from the scary scene. But they did not run off in a panic and traumatize their son. As they calmly walked down the stairs, the dealer, the host, came out. It was Gabriel, the Universal Life Church minister who had performed their impromptu wedding years ago in California, in this small world. And this mountain girl in a muumuu, a naked toddler on her hip, was Gabe's old lady, Lena. The couple were extremely white, untanned haoles with long, dark hair, Gabe's beard a Vandyke. He wore a blessed red string around his neck. The two families sat on the stoop among the zoris, flipflops, tennis shoes, and boots, and caught up with their lives: We had Mario 'Ehukai. We had Raven Full Moon Kali. So this helpless, potentially gentle baby girl is Kali, who dances on skulls. Gabe had done time, at Terminal Island, for possession. "All the good people are in jail." Then he started this operation, the Shooting Gallery, where he provided sanitary, safe, honest conditions. The use of herbs was not only a sacrament and medicinal but a form of civil disobedience. He harvested 'awa like the kahunas of old, and he grew m.j. macrobiotically. "I name it Kahalu'u Pink. Try some. It's nice, so easygoing and sweet-tempered, you'll barely feel it."

" 'Ehukai," said Tañia, "this is the minister who married Mommy and Daddy, and we're living happily ever after." The pretty lights reeling to music with lyrics—"ride a painted pony," "spinning wheel turn"—were advertisement for the Shooting Gallery, open for business, always open house. We're holding. We're dealing. Come and get it. With glad-handing hippies from home, you easily forget anything wrong. Gabe went from body to body, pulling on eyelids, making sure everybody was alive. You couldn't tell what drugs Gabe and Lena were doing, if they were doing drugs themselves; they acted as straight as could be.

Morning of the party, Wittman started smoking the turkeys in the Komodos. In milk cartons, he diluted root-beer flavor and cola-flavor Malolo concentrate. Between Hygenic Store and Bong's Grocery, every kind of Malolo syrup was available. Hawai'i runs on Malolo "juice." The blue was pineapple; yellow was lemon. Bong's Grocery didn't sell liquor and cigarettes on moral principles. Wittman bought Primo beer at Hygenic, and jugs of Gallo red. Expect BYOB. He filled the tub and shower with ice from the ice machine outside the Hygenic Store.

Taña and her girls (Begonia, Evelyn, Alicia, Vilma, Loke Rosie) had been making hors d'oeuvres—pupus—for days. They sculpted food, and filled the freezer compartments of neighboring refrigerators. They filled bottles and cans with plumeria and the ginger flowers like butterflies, and blue ginger and torch ginger, and birds of paradise. As much as they picked, the trees and bushes stayed full. Mr. Tong's daughters were also gathering flowers, and ti leaves, banana leaves, and ferns, which they'd use as platters for their church supper. Taña's girls strung plumeria into leis and scattered single blossoms about the house and amongst the food, and warned that "the sap is poisonous but."

Taña painted a wall black, and made a gallery. She hung her own and the girls' artwork on the walls of every room. The girls' idea of a tree is the coconut palm. Always fill the house with things painted and sculpted and sewn by friends. She named the house after Gauguin's *Maison du Jouir*, and painted its name across the lintel: Hauʻoliʻoli Hale. Like a Chinese, Gauguin painted words on the threshold doorjambs. "Be in love if you will be happy." And "Be mysterious if you will be happy." In Honolulu Chinatown, Wittman had bought four-word poems on red paper: "Come go in peace" and "Heaven Earth full peace." And, oh, glee—a gold word on glossy red—"Contentment." He tagged the house all over with "Contentment," a few upside down, which some Chinese say gives more luck, like a horseshoe upside down. And a joke for any graffiti artist who can read Chinese: "Contentment" is *fook*. The Beatles and Chinese say, "Fook." And *fook day* means "native ground," like ʻāina, like *la querencia*, "the place where my life belongs."

ʻEhukai decorated his closet room with fetishes for protection from the King of the Menehunes—red paper on the door, an ankh roach clip hanging on the doorknob, god's eyes made from chopsticks and yarn, a Thai Buddha on either side of his pillow, a crucifix and a Jesus picture from Mr. Tong's church.

ʻEhukai also collected and broke open coconuts for the milk and for the meat. "See da kine face? Smash 'em in da face." One end of the coconut has three dark spots; if they were holes, it could be a bowling ball. It did look like a hairy head with a face, a wide-eyed hairy-ape man with oh-ing mouth. He stood the coconut with its face up, and hit it in the face with a rock that fit his hand. The coconut cracked, leaking milk. He hit it again, and it broke open—the meat. So 'Ehukai contributed food to the party. A child needs to feel his competence, to learn effectiveness in the real world.

The party givers waited past the start-up time, one o'clock, and gave excuses for everybody's being late. Well, they aren't really late. On Hawaiian time. Can't keep up with the fast time of the haoles. It's an all-day open house, one to ten, drop by anytime, catch everyone, and room for everyone if they'd stagger their arrival and leaving, anytime come, anytime go, lunch, dinner, eat all day. Colored-folk time, Indian time, Hawaiian time—all of us non-Whites take our time. It's our passive-aggressive way against Whites' nailing us down, haoles stingy with time as they are with food. A crowd was walking up the hill, going to the welcome-home-from-Viet-Nam party for Big Eustace.

The first people to come to their party were the regular kids. They dug into the artistically presented buffets. By the time the adults come, the food will look like picked-over leftovers. Li'l Eustace, a waif who hung around the studio and the Canteen, trying to get himself a hānai family, sat at the porch table before a platter of corn on the cob boiled in sweet water, and ate one after another, over the platter, as if it were his plate.

"Are your parents coming?"

"By'm'by."

An adult did come at three-thirty. Jerome Chang—Chinese but Pacific Islander–looking. In place of conversation, he brought a deck of tarot cards and a Chinese almanac. You had to give him credit, contributing entertainment. He asked Wittman for his sign, and Wittman said, "Monkey," his existential choice. Jerome did not ask his hostess for her sign, nor did he address himself to her. A man talks to the man of the couple. Even in America today, a woman gets married and is dropped from male society. Jerome Chang laid out the tarot cards in circles on the ground; the card in the middle was Wittman. "This one, he you now." The Wittman card was surrounded by creepy, violent images, blood-dripping swords, an upside-down hanging man, skulls, burnings (a tower on fire with black bodies jumping and falling from it), cups of blood or wine, a priestess holding a book. Even the good cards looked bad. The kids, superstitious enough already, gathered around, too fascinated by magic. Jerome didn't have wonderful stories that went with the pictures. He read from a pamphlet, which so bored the kids that they drifted away. He correlated the tarot with the Chinese almanac. "I don't trust you monkeys," said Jerome.

"How you like your hamburgers?" said Wittman.

Yes, he liked four hamburgers, one rare, three medium-wells. "Family," he said, by which Wittman understood that his family were coming soonest, by'm'by. But while Wittman cooked the patties, Jerome confided that his wife, a picture bride here via the Philippines, was shy. She let him party, though. He would bring back for her and the kids, one boy, one girl, their plates. It took eight plates—four piled with hamburger and turkey plus salads plus crudités plus chips plus rice and bread and cake, and four to cover. He stacked them up and went home.

Wittman could have told Jerome's fortune: The wife doesn't come to parties because she's too shame-shame to be out with this socially clumsy husband. She's getting ready to dump him. Here for years, she's had a chance to compare him with normal rich Americans. She'll take off for Honolulu, even Kāneʻohe. His only chance to keep her was to tie her down with kids.

Sheraton and Clifton came with some Canteen boys. The log masturbator came with a six-pack of Primo. Young men stood around rubbing their *opu* (belly), which they stuck out bare in cropped T-shirts. (Why do they do that? Hurt? Comforting themselves? Empty? Hungry? Wanting to be pregnant?) People who owned or worked at the Hygenic Store and Bong's Grocery and the banana stand came. So did the sweeping woman and the swept-out man; they were together and brought their kids. Andrew, the Kam School grad, came with his girlfriend.

Wittman stayed by the hibachis, grilling hamburgers and hot dogs and sausages and shoyu chicken, which he kept cutting into to see if it was done yet. Taña bade him over to the table to carve a turkey. Hope they don't think we think we're like Puritans coming to take over the New World. The old acquaintance, Brother Gabe, came with his commune of new haoles. They outnumbered the locals. They looked like the cast of *Hair*—some *were* in *Hair*, which was on its way to Vegas. One moment, they were resplendent—white buckskin fringe, sparkling headbands and love beads, feathers (my birds of a feather), streams of motley ribbons, face paint—but the wind would die, and they fell sad and derelict. Sweaty hair hung lank; buckskin was too hot; bare feet were dirty, boots inappropriate. Gabe called everybody Brother and Sister. "Brother Wittman. Sister Taña. Hey, Brother Clifton. Brother Sheraton." He taught the Black guys the arm-wrestling elbow-to-elbow brother handshake; you shake all the way up and down the arm with a finale of arms upright and hands clasped. Gabe had tattoos—the letter "C" on the pulse spot of each wrist. " 'C' stands for 'consciousness,' " he explained. "Stay conscious." A couple of long-haired dogs were in their retinue; the baby was naked and rolled on the grass with the dogs. They were raising the baby with dogs; they were trying to raise a free child. For Wittman and Taña, at home around haoles—*kama'āina* haoles or mainland haoles, church patrons or hippies, good hippies or evil hippies—haoles are the easiest people to talk to and get along with. Conversation and dialogue goes apace, a reasonable rhythm as to who talks, then who talks. They have vocabulary for bespeaking homesick stuff, and abstract trippy stuff. But the party would count as real when the Hawaiians came.

The men from the hill came down all together at once. Big Eustace was in his army uniform. Gia, the chieftain, wore shorts and a festive aloha shirt, and a straw hat at a tilt. They brought a housewarming gift— a red front seat from a sporty car they'd chopped down. "You use for love seat," said Gia, then set it down in the grass and sat upon it. A woman who'd been on the expedition for birth-control pills sat right down next to him. What an appropriate gift. They understand we're da kine bohemians who don't own sofas. What is Hawaiian and what is hippie merges.

A woman came with the Hawaiians from the hill. She was a seemingly White woman, and she was with a man with two first names, Johnny Jesús. They were not a married couple or lovers. He was a hit man, and she was his agent, who negotiated for hits. He introduced her as the Whale. (Pu'ukoholā is the Hill of the Whale on the Big Island, where King Kamehameha built the temple to his family war god.) "The Whale here does the business part," he said. She was an enormous fat woman, and they called her Whale to her face. She filled her muumuu full. He was a trim, small man in a sport coat that almost covered his gun holster. During a moment alone with their host and hostess, other people within overhearing distance, Johnny Jesús and the Whale told Wittman and Taña how much they appreciated being entertained socially. In return, they offered a welcome-to-Kahaluʻu gift—their services. They would give of themselves, Johnny Jesús' skills. The Whale said, "Anybody fuck with you, you tell me, and I get you Johnny Jesús. For you, special. You want 'em up? You want 'em down? He take care of them up or down." She means, still standing or knocked out, or dead. "For you, forty-five dollars for broke one limb. Five hundred for da kine." She means dead. A life is worth $500. Johnny Jesús said, "Friends," and reached out for another handshake. "They fuck with you, they fuck with Johnny." (Rumor, via the children via ʻEhukai: it had been Johnny Jesús smallkidtime who'd been strung up in the bag and used like a piñata.)

Big Eustace told one and all his plan to go to Police Academy and be a cop in the Honolulu Police Department. "I just change this uniform, that's all. I need pass the psychology part, that's all. Duck soup. I get the psychology of a cop. I one good MP."

The Canteen boys cooked at the hibachis and barbecues. "You like? You like?" No shame, men cooking. There were quite a few guys named Junior, two named Alfredo, and six named Victorio. Five of the Victorios were brothers, and were called Victorio Two, Three, Four, Five, and Six. One more Victorio, Victorio One, was their father. One of the Alfredos was the father of the other one. The cutest boys wore the leis that the girls had made. On the stairs and lanai and on the grass, that day and all summer and year, the boys sang "Hey, Jude." "Betta bettah bettaaaah": the same in Hawaiian pidgin and British Liverpudlian, and the same nostalgia too.

ʻEhukai and the younger boys, giggling, planned and rehearsed, then ran up to the hippie haoles and in unison shouted, "Hi, hippie! Peace! Love! Chi chi! Balls!" Peace—the two-finger V sign. Love—the fuck-you finger. Just when you're feeling good, up comes the Finger. Chi chi—each hand rubbing a titty, or making a grab for your titties. Balls—grabbing their own balls, and lunging at yours. "Peace! Love! Chi chi! Balls!" Two fingers, middle finger, tits, balls. The kids were laughing and proud. "Fut fut your eyeball!" they shouted, and ran off.

Among the volunteers from the Canteen was Rudy Ku, who lived across Kam Highway from the Hygenic Store. He was only middle-aged, but served as elder. He smiled wide, not trying to hide the teeth broken by a surfboard. He'd understood immediately the wisdom of VISTA, and went to meetings and to the Canteen as loyally as if it were his job. He counseled the dropouts in their own pidgin; he spoke to everyone the same. Even here at the party, he spoke to whoever would listen about how all this land—"Yes, the 'āina under you feet"—got lost. He pointed makai, toward the mountains, and named the families, including his own, who had owned the land thataway. And thataway toward Kāne'ohe Town, you know that valley with ranches and estates, old homes and new housing developments (where his fellow volunteer, the retired admiral with the swimming pool, lived), used to belong to your great-grandfather. And the other way, toward Waiāhole, the hills paved with streets and houses, the descendants are right here in Tong's Village. "How the land get lost is by eminent domain and adverse possession. Somebody put a classified ad in the back of the newspaper. The small-print public announcement declares: So-and-so legally owns that property, and is paying the taxes on it. Let anybody—the true owners—step forward, or forever hold your peace. We had our chance. The declaration of ownership of the land stay in the daily newspaper every day for a long time. Years. But you know how Hawaiian people are—don't read newspapers, don't read nothing. Human nature but. Never read the gray small print in the back. And next thing you know, too late, evicted, lost the land, everything. By'm'by you get one lawyer to contest it, too late. The land-grabbers got money, and outlast you in court. They announce our property be theirs. Nobody challenges, it's theirs. We lost Hawai'i by not reading enough."

Wittman wished that the Hawaiians he'd met on the beach would show up, and start Kahalu'u dancing. Be kapunas for us. And he could show off that he knew some ali'i-type Hawaiians. He had wrapped a rock with a written invitation and left it at Kahana Bay.

Taña saw Lena coming toward her across the green grass, standing still, and looking at her with tears welling up and dropping. She was holding her baby against the same wrinkled muumuu she always wore. She set her child down, held out her hands, and walked toward Taña. Taña let herself be looked at, looking in return, and walked with her hands out for Lena to take. She's stoned, thought Taña, and I need to make her feel safe. A woman of the West, Taña understood the trip Lena was on. They were inside a myth, as if their feet had stepped inside the tracks of two women who had been here before them. A lone pioneer woman amidst the men and horses comes upon another woman. In the wild, they recall the china, the linen and lace, teas, civilization.

"Will you trim my hair, please?" asked Lena. And so, right there at the party, heavy Lena sat upon the grass. Taña got her own hairbrush and comb, and sewing scissors. She combed out the long, dark, sweaty hair. Sympathy gets you over squeamishness. Lena probably did take a shower before the party. People from Main Land feel hot, dirty, fat unless they take at least two showers and shampoos a day. Taña cut the bangs out of Lena's eyes, and brushed the sides away from her sun-reddened face. She cut off the bushes of split ends. The wind blew the hair away.

"Curls are springing up," said Taña.

"Not too short," said Lena.

"No, not too short. Long enough to put up." Taña made a middle part, which was fashionable, and gathered it up into a ballerina's knot. She wore her own hair off her neck too. The girls, who were avidly interested in grooming, put a plumeria flower over Lena's left ear.

"We're not legally married," she said. "I'd like getting legally married. You know what I fear? Something happens to us, and the newspapers identify me as a common-law wife. 'Lena Chafee, common-law wife.' Doesn't that sound terrible? I might as well be married; I'm not getting any free love. Easy enough for him to say. How's a mother with a baby going to get any free love? Should I wear my flower on the available side and see what happens? No, no, I better not wear a flower at all."

The naked baby was nestled up against one of the German shepherds. Frisbee, the dog, was gnawing on a dog biscuit. Kali was gnawing on a teething biscuit. They might have exchanged biscuits.

Lena said, "I've got to get off this rock. I've got rock fever. Something's wrong with the place. Don't you feel it? Too many trees, and the leaves are too big. The colors are too loud. Nothing delicate and fine. I miss roses. No roses or daisies or violets, no maples, no aspens. If I had the plane fare, I'd leave him."

A wet wind blew through, and Lena got on her hands and knees to find her cut hair. She crawled over the grass and through bushes where it might have blown. "Help me," she said. Taña gave her the hair in her hand. "They do voodoo with hair. Have you been to the Bishop Museum? They make amulets and bracelets with hair, and curse you." She threw the hair into a barbecue fire.

"You'll be okay," said Taña. "Nothing bad will happen to you. You can't let anything bad happen to you; you have baby Kali to take care of." She offered to babysit while Lena washed her hair. Lena took her up on it, and walked back to her own house.

Taña got her hands on the dirty baby girl, blinking in the direct red sun. Got that soft white-and-pink skin off the itchy grass, and the baby vagina away from the gaze of wise-ass adolescent boys. She carried her to the shady porch, and put her on her stomach on clean towels. The corner with railings meeting would do as a playpen. The girls fed the haole baby, and fanned her with a pandanus leaf. They hung her over the railing for a piss.

Brother Gabe and his tribe brought marijuana as their potluck. They thought of themselves as generous, but rudely and antisocially shut themselves off from the main party. They took over a bedroom for a party of their own, discreetly hidden from the straight people and the little kids. People would disappear into the smoking den, and emerge stoned, for food.

Britt, a graduate student in oceanography, who lived in cheap Kahaluʻu, a midway commute to UH Mānoa and Coconut Island, home base for the *Tuwi II*, the university's research ship, brought and plugged in a TV set. "You guys are so uninformed," he said. "We've landed on the moon. Don't you want to see it? You're so out of it." He herded the children inside for an educational look. The dopers came out to see the moon landing loaded—to see the astronauts high up on the moon while high themselves. "Wow!" "Wow!" "Far out." "Wotta trip." "Imagine that—there's men up there. On the moon. Right now." "We beat the Russians." "The scale of the technology that went into this was only larger in war," said Britt. Well, there it was. Not very good TV reception, snowing in Kahaluʻu, figures moving slowly, and sudden vertical rolls. The blocky, lumbering, slow-motion spacemen stuck the unwaving American flag into the moon. They looked like they were walking underwater. The TV announcer and Britt talked it up. This was the latest in the series of two dozen moon shots by the U.S. and the U.S.S.R.—a dozen Apollos and a dozen Lunas, some more exciting than this one. Luna 2 crashed into the moon, and Luna 3 got photos of the other side. Spaceships exploded and Americans and Russians were killed. "There's men up there—on the moon. Right now. We're never going to be able to look at the moon the same again." Later, when the moon comes up, we'll have to remember to look at the real thing, and see if it's spoiled.

The children ran off. The dopers went back into the dope room. People came through the house, watched awhile, and went on their way to another part of the party. Sheraton said, "Feed the hungry on Earth first, why don't you?" There was one picture that was amazing: the Earthrise, Earth rising from the point of view of the moon, which has a curved horizon. Bright, beautiful, round, full Earth, its curve broader than the moon's curve, and very near, like faces rolling together.

Britt also brought chicken for the barbecue, marinated in a batter of beer and milk, "Swede sauce," after an old Swede back home in Minnesota. He told Wittman a secret. "Promise me you won't tell my fiancée, and I'll tell you something that I can't keep to myself. At the NASA-NSF-USGS conference on the Big Island, where they walked on the volcano lava, simulating the moon's surface, this NASA guy came up to me and—this is strictly confidential, I'm not supposed to tell anybody—told me that the next manned space probe will be to Venus. And I've been tapped. To orbit Venus. He found me by my name tag. They're tapping me to be that man. Can you imagine—getting shot toward the sun. Even if I burn up, it's worth it. I want to do it. I don't care if I never get back. If they tapped you, wouldn't you go? Even if you lose your life out there, wouldn't you do it? All these ghosts and night marchers they keep talking about here—I've never seen one. I'd give anything to see a ghost, just once. It would change my life, and my scientific thinking. I've always wanted something supernatural to come out at me. It would change the laws of science; I wouldn't be the same person. I'm accepting the chance to go to Venus." He had been in the dope room, but he could actually be on his way to Venus too. He had football knees, and could not go to Viet Nam, but he was qualified for a NASA trip to Venus.

Wittman said, "I'd volunteer to be shot off in a rocket to another planet if there were somebody with me to talk to." On the other hand, he recognized a limit: he could not leave his family.

For the rest of his life, Wittman would watch for a manned flight to Venus. But the space missions went outward toward Mars, Jupiter, Neptune, Saturn, never inward toward the sun. Maybe Venus is still secret. He did hear of Britt later on, though: *Esquire* magazine will run a full-page picture of Britt in a series about the decade's most successful men under forty. He'll travel to Africa, where his nickname will be Bwana

Boom. The Africans, like the folks of Kahaluʻu, will watch him going about in headphones, setting up his IGS gravity meter, sometimes inside their houses. The gravity box has a plunger; it looks like he causes the explosions. He'll hustle Africans in a dangerous pool-hall, the way he now plays for money (quarters and dimes) at the Canteen.

Other people came around the cooking fire, and Britt's talkstory segued into Easter vacation on Molokaʻi, the most ghost-filled of the islands. He'd camped in that abandoned church that survived the volcano, and tried to provoke a ghost. The Bible in Hawaiian was open on the lectern, and he read out loud phonetically from it. Nothing provable happened.

The local boys told about an amazing place to try go explore — the flumes. Well-read Wittman had not heard the word "flume" before. Flumes seemed to be tunnels of rivers inside the island. The boys had been in them, and down them, and riding them. "You go Waiāhole-Waikāne." "You know, the Retread Tires sign? Right there, get one path. You go up, follow that path up the mountain. Pretty soon, you hear the flumes."

"Ba-doom. Ba-doooom."

"By'm'by, you come to one hole, an entrance to like a cave. The kapu sign on the iron fence — ignore it. You open the gate — never locked — and go down six, eight stairs. Go inside the cave mouth into the mountain." They say "mounting." "You inside the mounting."

Li'l Eustace spoke with the authority of an explorer who had seen things for himself. "The mouth — the doorway — is for one small person. I duck, and step into the black. My feet feel water moving so fast. Whooooshing. Whooooshing. No see nothing but."

"All my phobias start up," said Andrew. "Claustro, and fear of the dark, and fear of drowning. Fear of heights. The trip is: fear."

"One time I lit a candle in there, and the whooooshing blew da kine out."

"Eeenside, you no see the water or nothing, only cold and speed," said one of the Victorios. "You don't know, outside somewhere it could be raining and filling up the tube. By'm'by, one beeg lava tube of water. Waay eeeenside, you turn around, and see no more light from where you come in. I inside the mountain. The island on top of me."

"You get one banana leaf for a raft," said another Victorio. "Lie down on the leaf on your back or your opu, and ride. Long, dark ride inside the island. The flume will take you into town. All the way to Honolulu. Come out in the city. There, you shoot out a cliff. Ejected. Out da ada sida da island. Get ready for jump."

"How high is the cliff?"

"Ten feet about. You got to watch for the end—for the light growing beegger and beeegger and beeeegger. Get ready for the drop. You shooting out, be ready to jump out of the puka and drop down to the ground."

"I had a bradah caught in a flash flood, drowned dead. The flume gets full all the way to the top." So—they all have the same name because some could die, and another Victorio would live on.

"Tunnels go all over inside the island, connect here and there and everywhere."

"The inside smell like dirt and water—the inside of the Earth!"

"It's cold in there."

"And echoing—ba-doooom, ba-doooom. Cannot hear the bradahs talk."

"I heard da kine commandments."

"Yeah, the God feeling. The Jesus Christ feeling."

"What are the flumes for? Are they natural or man-made?"

"Olden days, sugarcane shoot through the flumes to the mills. I think they lava tubes and underground rivers. Mebbe some parts man-made."

"You like go shoot the flumes? You dare? We take you."

"Carry rice ball with umé for lunch, and come go flumes."

"Da kine ultimate solid tube."

"Indescribable. Da kine."

The tripped-out haoles could see into and under the Ko'olaus. "There are cities of treasure inside." "Ancient people are still living in there." "In white cities." "They have decoy funerals to fool us away from the entrances." The treasures were not diamonds and gold but hair, bones, teeth, dogs' teeth, sharks' teeth, feathers, and rocks. Are we being taken into the 'āina, or taken in?

The haoles had their big-gun scientist, Britt; the locals also had an important person, Big Eustace, who had come back alive from Viet Nam. He had an open maile lei hanging to his knees. It lay over his medals. Maile is expensive, or his people know where it grows. He sat in the seat of honor, the red leather car chair. Wittman filled and refilled

Eustace's plate, keeping the vet's mouth full, keeping his war stories stuffed up. So he wouldn't say "hootch" and "gook," and have to be argued against. So no fight between the hippie haole drug doves and the Hawaiian hawks.

Gia bragged for Eustace about his future, the benefits he would have as a war veteran. He would have extra points to get into Police Academy, and extra points for civil service. "Big Eustace gonna be one qualified police officer," said Cousin Gia. "Castle High grad, not even grad but dropout to Viet Nam, and he going to be a member of the Honolulu Police Department."

"HPD," said Big Eustace. "Centurion."

Brother Gabe said, "You won't be busting your old friends, will you?"

Bwana Boom said, "How about for public masturbation?"

Big Eustace said, "Things different nowadays. Everything went changed from before I gone Nam. Smallkidtime was more land and beach. No more Kāne'ohe Bay Clam Day, no more clams. Was horses up and down Kam Highway."

A kinsman tried to assure him, "Even yet now get horses. Get giant-lizard and wild-boar tracks."

"Get no mo' color. Everyt'ing get no mo' color." He got up and walked off, looking at this and that, saying, "Everyt'ing get no mo' color. No mo' not'ing."

No one understood him, that Hawai'i pales after you have been near the equator. The jungles in Viet Nam are greener than the jungles here, the sea bluer, the soil and the sun redder. Big Eustace came back from Viet Nam, and the beloved 'āina faded away.

At almost twilight, the number of people was at its height. Not a one of them came forth with a song or hula or chant to warm the *hale*. Before their company could disperse, Wittman's family summoned everybody, including those in the smoke room, to the word-adorned threshold. 'Ehukai spoke first; a kid can do corny, inauthentic ceremony, and it's okay. An innocent can break taboos. 'Ehukai thanked everyone. (His parents taught him that "Thank you" is all the language you need as you travel anywhere. You can even say it in your own one and only American language. Thank them for whatever they give you, and do for you. "Speak from the heart, dear.") "Thank you," he said. "Thank you for coming to our party. Thank you for being my friends. Thank you for the kind. Mahalo. *Con abrazo.*" He held out his arms. His parents each took a hand. In the days of old Hawaiʻi, they'd be thanking the kind people for a roofbeam and thatch, pigs, and a boat, and for the blowing of the sea conch. It had been a high, high civilization that gave its people all they needed.

Taña and ʻEhukai held a knotted vine across the open doorway. Some people were gathered inside and some outside. Wittman took up evergreens, bamboo, pine, ti, and palm, dipped the bouquet in a bucket of collected rainwater, and sprinkled the water in the six directions (east, west, north, south, up, and down), and upon the knot of the vine, the doorway, and the people. Wake up, skin. "*Me ke aloha pumehana*," he said phonetically from the dictionary. The family of three chanted the housewarming mele that Wittman had researched at the State Library downtown. They chanted English as melismatically as possible.

> O Kāne, O Kū, O Lono,
> I am cutting the omphalos of the house, O Gods,
> A house to make life strong,
> A hale to make life long.
> Give life to any wounded one who enters this House of Life,
> To any troubled one who enters this Hale Ola,
> To a person near death who enters this Hale Ola.
> Give life to me, your descendant in this world.
> Give life to my spouse.
> Give life to my children.
> Give life to my brothers and sisters.
> Give life to my parents.
> Give life to my whole family—the ʻohana.
> May there be well-being in this earthly life.
> Amama. Amen.
> The kapu of the prayer is accomplished.
> The kapu is freed.

Nobody joined in. Nobody sang along. The Hawaiians had been through lots of cultural revolutions, and gotten rid of this stuff.

The little family chanted, "O Kāne, O Kū, O Lono . . ." all the way through again. Repetition makes a custom. Doing things over and over establishes reality. Hearing the words more than once, the people will get it: We're claiming ourselves home. We *are* welcome. There *is* communitas. Scholarly Wittman finished by informing the guests that he found the hale-warming ceremony written out in English in *Na Hana a ka Po'e Kahiko, The Works of the People of Old*, by Kamakau. He'd changed the words to make sense to himself. He untied the vine rather than cut it.

Just as the sun began to set, a music, deep and basic, intoned under other noises. Once you heard it, it was loud, and sounded human, a thundering, belling chorus from warm throats and diaphragms. People who heard it asked, "Do you hear that? What is it?" "Where is it coming from?" "What are they saying? What language is that?" They followed the sound to the ocean side of Kam Highway. And there, in back of Bong's Grocery, were the Samoans, sitting square upon the ground, with mouths open, singing as if the music of the Earth were coming through and out of them. Their natural voices, not amplified through quadraphonic loudspeakers, filled and vibrated the resounding air. They sat shoulders and arms touching, making a rectangle, their backs to the picket fence that marked off their yard. They were a human church organ, and Godly music came from them. Church was all outdoors, and the sky was their cathedral ceiling. The doors to their apartment in back of the store were wide open; you could see inside, from one end to the other. They didn't have any furniture, no TV or musical instruments or decorations. Empty and bare, their house was a megaphone. They sang on and on, something epic without a break. We were returned to the time when language was one long word. They didn't invite the outsiders in, or chase them away. The non-Samoans sat on the outside of the pen, but enveloped in the all-holding music.

Impossible glory was coming from the Samoans, who have nothing. Lau-hala mats, which you hear are their treasures, covered grassless dirt. A few men wore formal pinstripe lavalavas; most were bare-chested. Junior, the kid of the host family, and other children were rolling about on the mats, surrounded by the adults, who were giants anyway. Usually Junior rolled about on the dirt, and the adults yelled at him. "Junyah! Gonna kill you, Junyah! I kill you!" Whenever you passed their vicinity, you'd hear, "I kill you, Junyah!" How odd to be raised like that—giants yelling to kill him, and then surrounding him with that music.

After finding out where the music was coming from, people left for other parties. Wittman got to the top of the hill just as Gia and Big

Eustace were uncovering the kalua pig. They shoveled off a layer of dirt, then unwrapped burlap sacking. Under that were ti leaves and banana leaves. Steam arose, and suddenly there was the pig—a thigh, an arm, an elbow, a knee. Like a cooked, disinterred human being. With Caucasian skin. A haole. Thank God, didn't see the face and eyes. People stood about giving advice. "Not ready yet." "*Imu* him longer." "Potatoes ready already." "What time you put him in?" "Dug the puka yesterday, heat up the rocks, put him in last night, early morning." Once in your life, at least, you get a party replete with the whole pig, very crucial and religious, just like Chinese.

Wittman looked down at his own house and the scene of his party. A trick that always makes him happy: Detach yourself and view things from overhead. Get an overview. See from this perspective, and be happy. The Samoan voices were booming all the way up here. The blue of the sea was deepening, holding the island, holding us to the island.

Below, people were in groups of two or three or more at the night fires, nobody alone. They were having discussions—"disgahssing," they say—talking and listening to one another—most wonderful human enjoyment. "Where do we come from?" "What are we?" "Where are we going?" He could make out individuals. Andrew was reaching up for fruit and looked like the Jesus man in the center of Gauguin's painting. That blue tree behind Andrew could be the idol with outreaching arms. The baby slept snuggled against the dog. Beautiful girls were petting a cat. Children and chickens and dogs were eating off the ground. The Black guys were on opposite sides of the party, integrating us; the *kuleana* for making racial peace is theirs.

Boys were leaping from the coconut trees to the greensward. Jumping quite a distance off the back of the house onto a slope, rolling down the slope, and climbing up the tree again. One boy was walking back and forth on the roof, back and forth, getting up the nerve. It was Li'l Eustace. I've been here long enough so that I can identify people by a silhouette far away, thinks Wittman. On the grass, big boys were swinging the little ones by the head. Where is my boy? I thought he was right behind me coming up the hill. I ought to care about all children the same as for my child. There he is—one of the littlest ones, being held under the chin, the back of his head against the big boy's stomach, face-up, and swung and whirled, his feet straight out, the big boy pulling backward, turning around and around. Oh, please, don't let go of him like a hammer throw. Don't break his neck. By the time Wittman ran down the hill, all the boys were gone, run off to another game. But for Li'l Eustace, still trying to get up the nerve to jump off the roof.

Wittman found Taña and 'Ehukai at the church supper at Landlord Tong's house. They were amongst people dressed in church clothes except for shoes, sitting at dining tables and card tables. Most of them looked like prosperous Chinese Americans. Landlord Tong was trying to convert Taña. "Five dollars off your rent if church member." His tenants were his souls. Mrs. Tong, leading Wittman to the buffet, explained why they were having church supper this day rather than Sunday, and that they were eating *jai*. Their *jai* looked like chicken croquettes, veal cutlets, hamburgers, and hot dogs but were really molded soybeans. Beckoned, Wittman sat next to Armando Del Real, who was engaged to the oldest Tong daughter. He was on R&R from Viet Nam. You could tell he was military, he was dressed so neat, in military-pressed aloha shirt and jeans, shirt tucked into jeans, belted. Scrupulous Wittman let on that he himself was a war resister.

Armando said, "I'm a Conscientious Objector. *And* I'm in Viet Nam. Some church members who will not fight man's war are in jail. I'm a medic. I'm keeping the Sixth Commandment. Inside the army and in-country Viet Nam, you still have choices. I chose to carry a sidearm. God wills that we use free will. I'm a good compromiser. I render unto Caesar." Armando had the same hyper, nervous intensity as Big Eustace; both of them seemed permanently startled. That energy that comes off of them must be the energy of Viet Nam. He jumped up from the table. "Want to come to Kāne'ohe? I need to pick up something. Anybody need anything from Kāne'ohe?" Good neighbor Taña said she could bring whatever from her house—Malolo syrup, salad, ice cream? "No, something I need to do right away." Caught up in his excitement, Wittman and Taña and 'Ehukai got in the Tong van and sped off with him. Wittman in the suicide seat, his family in the back. Armando drove and talked fast. In the middle of telling about growing up in New York, he said, "Don't tell Janie. My brother was killed in action in Viet Nam." His passengers could not think of what to say. Did he mean his sibling, or a "brother" like a Black or a Hawaiian? Or as in the Bible, where all men are brothers? He's Puerto Rican; he could mean a brother Puerto Rican.

Armando was laughing. He was going crazy at the wheel. "I'm only kidding," he said. "I'm kidding. You guys should see the look on your faces."

He sped on to another subject. "The Menehunes were from Puerto Rico. Did you know that? Menehunes are Puerto Ricans." He said "Pwerrrto Rrrrico," and made them laugh every time he said it.

'Ehukai said, "Pwerrrto Rrrrico. Menehunes are Pwerrrto Rrrrican, Mom."

They should have asked for news of Viet Nam, and steeled themselves to hear it.

Armando talked story, turning around often to look at every member of his audience. "Puerto Ricans came to Hawai'i a long time ago. They were so short, the Hawaiians thought they were elf people." He took his hands off the wheel, indicating the shortness of Menehunes and the shortness of Puerto Ricans. You know the war between the Menehunes and the owls? We shot Pueo with blowguns. Menehunes—Puerto Ricans!" He himself was quite short; why hadn't the army given him a height exemption? "You want to know how I got into the army? I stretched myself. I stood up tall, and my hair stood up tall. They couldn't push down my hair. Feel how thick it is." He was wired, like his hair.

"When I got here from Viet Nam, the day before yesterday, I took a walk downtown. I was waiting for the light to change on the corner of Bishop and Hotel Street. I saw an old Chinese man across the street step off the curb just ahead of the light. Cars stopped for him; somebody screeched his brakes. Suddenly, in the middle of the intersection—I had my eyes on him—he vanished. I'm not the only one who saw it. People got out of their cars, and people around me were asking, 'Did you see what I saw?' 'An old Pākē man disappeared right here on this spot.' 'He didn't get across the street.' Some people exchanged names, like at an accident. You know what I think? I think there's a hole to another world on the corner of Bishop and Hotel Street. That old man went back to China. And you know who traveled here through that same hole? Pwerrrto Rrrricans!"

In Kāne'ohe Town, he parked the van on the main drag, said he'd be right back, and ran off. He was gone for so long that Taña lit a joint, and Wittman took a hit too. He snooped in the black bag that was sitting under 'Ehukai's feet. It was Armando's medic kit. The druggies would give their right arm for this—hypodermic needles and vials of what was probably morphine. And what have we here in this bulging pocket? A gun! "It's a gun!" "A gun?!" "It's a gun, Mommy!" Wittman shut the bag, reopened it, wiped the gun with the heel of his hand for fingerprints, shut the bag, just as Armando showed up. He didn't have any object in his hands to show what his errand was. He made a U-turn and headed back for Kahaluʻu. Maybe he just wanted to get away from the churchiness and the in-laws-to-be.

Wittman, full of candor, said, "Is this the medical kit you carry in Viet Nam?"

Armando said that it was.

"Aren't you afraid that a druggie would steal the morphine? You must have a fortune in valuable drugs in there."

"We better get it home, then," said Armando, and stepped on the gas, zoomed through a red light. Neither Wittman nor Taña saw it soon enough to tell him to stop. Probably not inadvertently, he went through a second red light. They suspected him of purposely bad-tripping them. He's picked up on our being stoned and not offering him any. And he knows we know about the gun. Maybe he drove an ambulance in Viet Nam, and is having an ambulance-driving flashback. He's showing us how it feels in Viet Nam, that you could get killed any moment. He's addicted to adrenaline rushes, and passing it on. Grabbing him would be like grabbing a Menehune. Lightning would shoot through you; you would die of fright. Before the third light, Taña said, "Red light," but he kept driving fast. He didn't look for cars from the side streets. By the fourth red light, they surrendered to his driving. No more lights anyway to Kahaluʻu. He drove and speed-talked. "Puerto Ricans are island people; we like islands. We discovered Hawaiʻi. Have you looked at a good map? Hawaiʻi is exactly to the left of Central America, and Puerto Rico to the right, both a little bit south of the Tropic of Cancer. Columbus came to us four times. He was on the right track. There is a Southwest Passage. It's *through* the continent. You can shoot from Puerto Rico to California to Hawaiʻi. East-west, the Tropic of Cancer, twentieth parallel, Puerto Ricans went *through* Mexico, *through* America, *through* the Pacific Ocean, straight to the puka at Bishop and Hotel Street." When he said "*through,*" he went through another red light that they'd forgotten about. "We went *through* the passage hole that connects the oceans. *Under* Tenochtitlán—Mexico City. We popped out here in Hawaiʻi, and the Hawaiians said, 'Look! Menehunes!' Menehunes are Puerto Ricans!

We came popping out of the ʻāina, and they called us Menehunes. And do you know what country is directly west of here on the twentieth parallel? Viet Nam!"

After every crossroad, Wittman was extra glad to be alive. Time was falling apart on Armando. He was driving fast to catch up. The day before yesterday, he was in Viet Nam. The bombs had knocked him out of time, and he was jumpy to get back in sync. (Of course, he might have always been frantic, coming from New York; they didn't know him from before.) He was jumping about in the mythic time of the Menehunes, and in the historical past of the Puerto Rican diaspora, and in the Armageddon of the future, when the cosmic Hand comes out of the sky. And he'll be returning to Viet Nam again in a few weeks.

They arrived safely back in Kahaluʻu, and so the Day and Night of Many Parties continued on toward ten o'clock. The people along Kam Highway always knew when it was that time, because the tour buses came through, returning to Honolulu from the show at the Polynesian Cultural Center.

A barrage of noises and lights shot out from the part of the highway that was the center of Kahaluʻu. The Samoan singing stopped. People ran toward the commotion from all the many parties, out of Tong's Village, down from the hill, out of the Shooting Gallery. Trucks and cars going either way also stopped, converging at a lit-up place. The raying, glaring lights were coming from a tour bus. Its inside lights were on, and it looked immense, taking up half the highway. The scenic windows were each a superreal framed picture of haole tourists, mostly old people, some with hands shielding their eyes to try to see out into the dark. The driver was running around from one side of the bus to the other. "What happened?" "Accident?" "They got the bus." "They should turn off the lights." "Sitting ducks." "Duck soup." "Haole lady bleeding." "Where's the telephone? I want a telephone." "They stoned the bus." "Look there—a puka in the glass." "Smash 'em." "The Revolution has begun." "It's not an accident." "Not accidental. Attack on purpose." "They went stoned the bus with beer bottle." "No, Coke bottle." "Call the police." A couple of windows were cracked. A woman pressed a bloody handkerchief to her cheek. It looked like locals had ambushed the ten o'clock bus. The nastiest thing they'd done before to tourists was hold still for their cameras, then move at the click. They had forbearance, really; the air-conditioned tour buses went by every day, while there was no public transportation to get to jobs. "This is a political demonstration." "It's just kids."

Some of the Hawaiians on the hill were looking at the scene from up there. Had it been them, attacking the tour bus and then slipping away? Under cover of the commotion around the bus—voices, running footsteps, sounds of metal against metal, and rock against metal—a dark wall was growing, being built. A looming barricade—a stake truck and old cars—blocked the highway, both lanes. Black figures were pushing another car into the roadblock. The ends of the barricade were the broken-down crawler crane and the locked and thorny kiawe bushes. People were running about along the sides of the pile, and on top of it. People hid in the bamboo. "They're stopping a big load of dope coming through tonight." "Stop da kine drug traffic in Kahalu'u." "They like steal the dope." "Drug war." "They making one demonstration for to get buses for locals." "Da kine da tourists!" "Fuck the tourists." "Stone the tourists." "Kill the tourists." "Quiet. They be coming." "Fight. Don't let them through." "Don't let them make one puka," one hole in the barricade. Silhouetted men on top of the truck were looking toward Waiāhole-Waikāne, waiting for something to come from that direction, which was the way the tour bus had come. Some people had baseball bats. Flashlights went on and off. Up on the hill, tiki torches were burning.

Soon, a caravan of tour buses were stopped in a line. A honking, braking, skidding car almost hit the barricade and the people in the bamboo. From the Kāne'ohe side came the sounds of sirens. Swirling red and blue lights were coming. The Shooting Gallery turned off its lights.

"Let's go. Let's get out of here," said Wittman to the group around him. "Come on. Let's go home." His wife and son went with him. They met people still coming to the excitement. Figures were running in the dark through one another's yards.

The Ah Sings ran inside their own house, bright with all its lights on, now empty of guests. They shut the door, and held one another in a family hug.

Crashing and thrashing came through the bushes, and thudding footsteps up the stairs and across the boards of the porch. Wittman stepped quickly over to the side of the front door, and grabbed a rifle that someone had left standing in the corner. He held it against his shoulder the way he had seen the man at Kaena Point hold the rifle, and stood in front of his wife and child, and pointed it at the door. The doorknob shook and turned; the door swung open—it was only Bwana Boom come back for his rifle.

"Don't shoot."

"Britt. I might have killed you."

"He might have shot you."

"Is it loaded?"

"Yeah, of course, she's loaded. I'm taking her down to the road to do a show of force. I'm walking through Kahalu'u along the highway. Let everyone see that we're armed. Don't fuck with us." A show of haole force. What do you mean "we," White Man?

"Take care," said Taña. "Don't get hurt; don't hurt anybody."

"Don't shoot anybody," said Wittman.

"I'm just doing a show of force," said Britt. This extraordinarily blond and white-skinned haole with his rifle against his chest walked straight from the banana stand to Hygenic Store and back, patrolling both sides of Kamehameha Highway.

The little family was left horrified and scared. Wittman had automatically and instinctively picked up the rifle. He had meant to pull the trigger and shoot whoever came through the door. The heavy rifle had fit his arms and body and hands; his trigger finger naturally fit on the trigger. He had never held a rifle before, but there's nothing to it. It would have been easy to use. He could still feel its weight against him. To not shoot, to not kill, he would have to rehearse, rehearse against instinct.

He knelt down and took 'Ehukai in his lap. "I shouldn't have done that. I did the wrong thing. Mistake. I got carried away. I lost it. I snapped. I should have asked, 'Who's there?!' I'm glad I didn't shoot. I hope even if he were an enemy I wouldn't shoot. If I shot Britt—or anyone—the consequence would be that I would ruin my life, and our lives."

Taña repeated things she often said, raising a boy: "The reason we don't give you war toys is so that you won't use real weapons when you grow up. You're practicing nonviolence. You have to experiment with ways of making friends. In danger, take one deep breath. An idea will come to you what to say and what to do."

Most of the night, there was running about outside, sudden shouts, hushing. No gunshots. More sirens. Bus engines throbbing. An unnatural electric light glowing. Wittman and Tañan put food the cockroaches would eat into the fridge, turned off the lights on the mess of the party, and went to bed. They looked at the moon, where people were walking now. Armstrong and Aldrin were in the right eye of the Man in the Moon, in the cauldron of the Healing Rabbit. The Sea of Tranquillity.

Someone knocked on the door. All of them got up to answer it. It was Andrew, wanting to talk. He told terrible things in his quiet Kam School–educated voice; you had to listen hard to get the horror. He was on the run from Johnny Jesús and Big Eustace. They were after him. Johnny Jesús already got him, had beaten him up, the fucker. He folded his arms over his stomach, bent over, straightened up. He did not look beaten up, no cuts or bruises on his bare torso and thighs. A young body can take beatings and drugs without showing. You had to take his word for it, it hurt.

"Johnny said he heard that I was sitting on the steps of Bong's Grocery waving a gun and threatening to get him. He worked me over, the fucker. Johnny Jesús and his goon took me for a ride, and worked me over. Shit, it hurts. Fuckers." He made a laughing sound. And he was in trouble with Big Eustace, too, and running from him. "Big Eustace tried to hang himself on the shower-curtain rod. He's gone psychotic on LSD, or from Viet Nam. I walked in on him, and saw the rod bend slowly until he was sitting on the edge of the tub. He said he was a loser, couldn't even commit suicide. People, women, came in, took a leak, took a dump, sitting next to him with the rope around his neck. Actually, it was my fault. I put acid in his beer. He reared up, and chased me—out of the house, around the hill, back into the house. I locked myself in the bathroom. He was kicking in the door, so I removed a louver, and squeezed out."

"Did you say you went through the window? You took out just one louver?"

"Yeah. If you can get your head through, you can get the rest of yourself through." He must have turned into a snake. "I got away. He couldn't catch me. What a jerk."

Andrew crashed on the floor, and his enemies didn't find him during the night.

The next day, the people of Kahaluʻu talked story about the parties. You heard about parts of the parties where you hadn't been.

Britt had made a legend. He was reported as walking barefoot, a haole who did not have tender haole feet but spadelike feet with fat pink toes. His towhead had shone bright. "He did show of force. Don't nobody fuck with the haoles." The locals had gotten the message, using his very words. He carried the rifle right down the middle of Kahalu'u, didn't shoot it or speak, just walked barefoot on the highway. "Don't nobody fuck with the haoles. They armed."

Something bad had happened to Sheraton and Clifton. "Disappeared." "Gone." Lynched. Wittman looked for them, asking their whereabouts, and kept hearing, "They gone." "Run out of town." "Those Popolos run fast, you know." "Rough 'em up, and kick 'em out of Kahalu'u. Don't come back." "So scared, so black, da Popolos." "Show those Popolos. Good for them." "Black haoles. Bad enough White haoles—we get Black haoles." "Fuckeeng black, those Popolos." "Out of town on a *rail*." "Lucky for them, not get killed." "Good for them." Wittman pictured a mob shoving the masturbation pole between Clift's and Sheraton's legs, and riding them, bucking them along the highway, flinging them into the jungle or ocean. "You should see their Popolo eyes—so big and round and sked." Scared. "Pop eyes like Rochester and Buckwheat." "They get white eyes shine in the dark." "They fuzzy-wuzzy hair stand up in air. No more Popolo in Kahalu'u forevah now." "Popolos go stay back to Main Land." "Gooood for Popolos, give us Welfare, give us poverty program." "Who they think they are?" "Fuckeeng Popolos, Welfaring us." "Good for you" means "You deserve what you got coming to you." "Serve them right." Many people sounded like eyewitnesses, but you couldn't tell by the complex verbs whether they'd been there, participated or not, only wished they had. "Rid of them." "Good riddance." Even the art girls: "They beat and punch 'em up, you know." "No mo' da kine black Popolo haoles in Kahalu'u." "Da *black*, da buggahs." Nobody spoke about anyone coming forth to try helping the domestic Peace Corps workers. Had the Drop-In boys also cornered them, kicked and beaten them? Clifton's and Sheraton's hearts must be broken. Wittman never saw them or heard of them again. Never could thank them, and apologize. Whenever the subject of the VISTA workers came up, people looked at one another and wagged their eyebrows. Hawai'i people are often wagging their eyebrows. What are they signaling? They have secrets, and they are not talking.

Cleaning up after the party, Taña opened a cupboard and found a good-luck gecko squashed, caught between the door and the edge of a shelf. Hung there splayed and squashed. She screamed and ran out of the house. The faithful art girls cleaned up the splat gecko for her. She sat on the porch floor and cried, which started Wittman crying. He put his hands in his pockets and walked in circles. She got up and put her arms around him, and they cried, then laughed to be crying amidst the spilled beer and wine and leftover cheese. Asian and Pacific Islander people don't like cheese.

Somebody had dumped hot coals at the base of a coconut tree, and burned the bark, surface roots, and the grass and earth. Surely they weren't torturing our tree on purpose? They merely put the coals where bare feet wouldn't be stepping. You could read motivations—well-meaning or hurtful—everywhere.

By day, not a trace of the barricading of Kam Highway remained. And no one knew or would say what eventuated. There was no evidence that anything at all had happened.

It is constantly rain-and-wind season on the Windward Side. The wind is time blowing by. Ko'olau is the name of the wind; and the Ko'olaus are also the mountain range. The city people had never seen such dark nights. They could swear that the day went out jerkily from window to window, as if they lived in a stage set, and a light at each window went out, east to west, snap, snap, snap. Māui was yanking on the sun. The dot of land was dissolving into rain and ocean and sky and dark. Wittman ESP'ed Taña and 'Ehukai a ball of sunshine, and it burst warm in their heads, behind the eyes. "Wow!" "Waa!"

There were sudden moments of sun. Light through leaves made green circles on ground and floor. When the storm that was giants stomping down from the mountains stopped, the silence slammed you. Your body stretched out thin, and your limbs reached to some far-off place.

Wittman wanted the city—TV, movies, telephones, radios. Theater is a city phenomenon. Kahalu'u was not a theater town. It's not a town. It's not country, with barns and harvests, either. The cops, ambulances, and firefighters have to come from Kāne'ohe. Kahalu'u doesn't have a government. What is Kahalu'u? A name from the olden days? The people here don't call themselves Kahaluuans. They call themselves locals. Waiāhole and Waikāne don't seem to be anything either. Areas remain unclassified, ungoverned, nowhere. Nor is there any such thing as the Hawaiian Tribe, for people to sign up as Hawaiian.

To give memorable shape to time passing, Wittman and Taña named the days. To slow the rush of them. To live them. One sureness: at the first working day of the month, throughout the islands, the tsunami sirens sound. Early in the morning, time straightens into a minute-long tocsin. Keep deliberate track. Name the days; otherwise, they speed past, and the nights become one darkness. Stop generalized time. They had these peculiar days, and named them:

The Day We Came to the Island
Bufo Season
The Day Wittman Circumnavigated O'ahu
The Day Wittman Circumnavigated Chinaman's Hat
'Ehukai's Naming Day
The Day the Children Drew Taña
The Day the Ant Walked Off with Sunburn Skin Peel
Menehune Morning
The Day of the Shed Fairy Wings
The Sunday the Husband Called for a Gun
The Day the Giant Bird Bobbed in the Bay (Was it hurt? Why didn't
    it fly?)
The Night the Windows Went Out
The Night the Princess Ghost Went Riding All Night
Our Housewarming
The Night the Samoans Sang / The Night of the Stoning of the
    Tourist Bus
The Night of the Drug War
The Night the Volunteers in Service to America Were Driven Out
The Ghost Princess Went Riding at Dawn
The Night of Fire on the Hill
The Night the Horse Hung Itself (falling off the hill)
The Stolen Stereo
The Shoot-Out with Pellet Guns and Air Rifles

The Day Johnny Jesús Hung Himself in Jail

The Day 'Ehukai Hitchhiked to the Cockfights ("Have you seen 'Ehukai? Our son is lost.")

The Day They Burned the Cat (set fire to it and swung it, but it did not die)

The Funeral of the Run-Over Cat

The Digging Up of the Cat

The Day Vilma Got Hit by a Car

The Day 'Ehukai Got Bitten by a Poi Dog (Hawaiian dogs don't have rabies)

The Day of 'Ehukai's Rant ("I'm going to tell Wittman on you. I'm gonna chop off your head, and throw you in the rivah, and stomp on your stomach, and kick you in the *okole*. Fut-fut yo' eyeball. I'm gonna tell. I'm going to sink your raft. I'm gonna hit your baby bradah.")

The bad days and nights outnumbered the good days and nights, but not badly enough for them to leave Kahalu'u, nor was there a place to go.

Wittman began to hitch rides with Big Eustace, going into Honolulu for Police Academy, with Mr. Tong and Mr. Bong, with truckdrivers that supplied the Hygenic Store, with Britt, going to the university. He had to get out of the mud, organize himself, define things, read at the State Library, walk on proper sidewalks, and be cool inside air-conditioned buildings. The ex–city person was heading back to town.

He chose one of the courtyards at the Honolulu Art Academy, and sat like an old China Man at leisure waiting for a poem to come. This place had been carefully thought out, the pandanus and black bamboo trimmed and contained. The blue tile roofs framed a square of sky. Most times, he had the courtyard all to himself. He sat on a stone bench under the eaves, got up, and walked on rocks across the pond to a pair of Chinese rosewood chairs in the corner. He sat in one, facing the empty one. Behind him, through the open glass doors, was a roomful of Buddhas.

One day, a flower appeared in the pond, as if a pink cup had been set on a saucer of green leaves. A guard walking through the courtyard said, "That's a lotus, and it blooms one time in ten years. I was here when it bloomed once before." Wittman squatted on the rock in the middle of the pond to get a good look at it; he'd never seen a lotus before. Delicate, sturdy, translucent petals shone in a ray of the sun. No smell that he could catch. Lotus flowers had also been wrought in bronze and gold and stone; the Buddha statues were holding or sitting on them. A tourist lady came into the courtyard. Wittman told her that that lotus flower was blooming today for the first time in ten years, and would not flower again for ten years.

"No," she said. "I don't believe you. How do you know that?"

"The guard told me. He saw it ten years ago."

"He said that to make you feel good," she said.

Wittman wandered amongst the Buddha statues—*fut* in China-town dialect. (The locals call old guys "the old futs.") He was determined to learn something. The ancestors made these images out of stone to last for thousands of years. Try to read them; there must be a message. He got down on the floor in front of the gold reclining Buddha, and imitated him/her. He held his hands and fingers in mudras. Examining more Buddhas, he copied each one's teaching mudra or blessing mudra. He sat with legs in lotus position, and half-lotus. He aped their smiles, returned their smiles. A smile spread from his mouth and face to the rest of his body. Try to hold it; be strong as a rock fut, who is stone but somehow soft. He smiled with this one and that one, and each fut gave him back its individual smile. He felt his attitude changing.

Mesmerized by names, Wittman entered the Waikīkī Jungle. A banana tree with bananas grew out of an open spot in the concrete. A palm tree reached a balcony, and shaded it. Doors were open to make room, and people sat in doorways and on windowsills. You could see inside their lives, which were mostly the television, always on. They had a short-walk access to the ocean. Trade winds carried the smell of marijuana. There were sudden outbursts of kids. Gypsies and Pilipinos and bad-looking Whites raised kids in the Waikīkī Jungle. Wittman, a father now, had an interest in and noticed kids. These children were probably supporting their parents by bringing in Aid to Dependent Children. The Gypsies could very well be the same ones he'd seen in California; they gypsy by plane and ship.

He went through alleys and passageways, and came out into the back of the International Market Place. He passed the Restaurant for

Two in the banyan tree, which was closed. The Waikīkī Jungle is in back of the Strip, which is many strips—the Jungle, then Kuhio Avenue, more hotels and shops, sidewalk, a strip of lawn, then a strip of beach, man-made; the sand, shipped from the Mainland, covered marsh. Waikīkī. LBJ was saying, Win in Viet Nam, or else fight on the beaches of Waikīkī. Sunburned haole tourists wandered culture-shocked, suffering from the heat and humidity, confused as to whether they were having fun. Women pushed men in wheelchairs. One long-lived man escorted many widows and wives whose husbands didn't travel anymore. Couples and entire families were dressed all alike, in the same pattern aloha shirts and muumuus. Hoboes or hippies—"transients"—wore blankets, hot coats that were also their sleeping bags. The sand-sweeping machine made comb patterns as it went around rolls of sleeping people like the dead in body bags. (Above them was the Gold Coast, where rich people live.)

Wittman got obsessed by beachcombing. Treasure hunters swept the beaches, swinging metal detectors, looking for lost jewelry and coins. They'd stoop and pick up something, save it or toss it. The world was going through a craze for puka shells, and he did see quite a lot of those tiny cups with a natural hole for stringing. And specks of pale-green glass, olivine, Pele's green jewels. And sea ants or fleas or spiders. Keep finding what you have never seen before—you change; the world changes.

Middays, huge old men, like whales, all in a row, steadily swam straight across the sea, paralleling the shore and the horizon. They were enormous people. Their brown arms moved evenly, fluently, arm over arm.

Wittman often went to the front of Fort DeRussy, where the peace march had stood, but did not find the pacifists and the Communists again.

Then, one fine day, Sunday, August 10, the first weekend after Hiroshima Day and Nagasaki Day, a huge peace parade came toward him. Fun-in-crowds attracted him into its midst. They were doing things right, as at the beginning of the peace movement, when all was non-violent. Nonviolence was all. The parade was official—city- and county-permitted. A police escort cordoned off half the street for at least a hundred people—and some of them were servicemen in uniform. Amid the aloha wear and hippie wear were military uniforms—navy whites, army olive drab, marine red, white, and blue, and air-force blues. At least one person from each branch of the service was against the War in Viet Nam. They were marching with a banner of the map of Viet Nam, long and jagged like a dragon rampant. And a huge vertical poster with a mushroom cloud. Remember Hiroshima and Nagasaki. We dropped the bomb *twice*.

U.S.

ANZUS

JAPAN

STOP BOMBING KAHOʻOLAWE

We were bombing the only island named for a god, bombing the god, Kanaloa, the island's other name. We invited Australia, New Zealand, and Japan to use it for target practice. (A bomb fell in the mayor of Māui's backyard by accident.)

18

OLD ENOUGH TO FIGHT

OLD ENOUGH TO VOTE

The all-red Commie flag and a National Liberation Front flag were toward the back. Wittman saw the familiar faces of the people he had stood with. A couple of civilian men with bullhorns were the only ones yelling, and yelling different yells. Hawaiʻi people are shy.

Soldiers and sailors and airmen walking for peace in uniform! It had to be against the rules. They were risking arrest, time in the stockade and brig. The military people were not walking as a group but mixed among the civilians. Each one had made the decision on his own to be a peace demonstrator. Wittman kept track of them, watched a soldier intently watching the parade, then suddenly step off the curb, and become part of the peace movement. The soldier worked his way to the front, and met and talked with an air-force officer who was at the head of the parade. The officer gave him leaflets, which he handed to fellow marchers as well as people on the sidelines. Wittman took a leaflet, and read that the Walk for Peace was sponsored by Hawaiʻi Resistance, and was on its way to Sanctuary at the Church of the Crossroads. Sanctuary had begun four days ago, August 6, Hiroshima Day. Louis D. "Buffy" Perry, the air-force lieutenant, had left the protection of the church today to invite his fellow military to go AWOL and join him in Sanctuary.

The Walk for Peace went down Kalākaua, King, Beretania—streets that Prewitt had traveled. They walked toward a rainbow in Mānoa Valley. Buffy shone. He was tall, blond, a leader, an officer. Wittman followed his whereabouts as Buffy moved through the parade, now in the middle, now the sides, and the end, and to the head again. Answering arguers, Buffy kept walking, and as they walked and talked, they became part of the parade. He accepted a lei, and wore it over his uniform, probably against the rules. He did not have the frantic air of those who'd been to Viet Nam. Speaking calmly, he explained Sanctuary to his fellows one by one. "This isn't the kind of AWOL where you get stoned and miss the ship, and miss roll call. I'm taking careful responsibility, and deliberately not showing up at the base. I'm taking political action in Sanctuary." He said outright to a HASP (Hawaii Armed Services Police) on the sidewalk, "I'm AWOL, but I'm not hiding. Taking Sanctuary is not hiding. I am making an honest, open declaration against the war. You can arrest me. Or you can come with me and be in Sanctuary. We'll walk to Sanctuary together." The listening HASP man walked along with him. "Sanctuary is a place of safety in the midst of a society at war. I am building peace during war. The Church of the Crossroads is giving refuge and haven—Sanctuary. Sanctuary is sacred ground that upholds our highest ideals."

Wittman eavesdropped on Buffy talking to GIs on R&R: "You don't have to go back to Viet Nam. Come join me in Sanctuary." This parade was delivering him to Sanctuary. He was building the Sanctuary as he walked.

Buffy Perry was our Billy Budd, the handsome sailor, who was said to be "the center of a company of his shipmates . . . made up of such an assortment of tribes and complexions . . . of the Human Race." "A sweet and pleasant fellow," he could "strike peace" on a "quarrelsome ship." "But they all love him." "Blessed are the peacemakers, especially the fighting peacemakers."

Ben, a sailor carrying a duffel bag, said to Buffy, "I've made up my mind. I'm going to do it. I've been thinking about doing this since Wednesday. I heard about you on the Hiroshima Day march. I was on that march too, jumped base to be in it. Someone asked me to carry a sign, and I figured, What the hell, I'll carry a sign. But when I got to the park in Ala Moana, I sat down and really thought hard. As soon as I heard about you on the march, I started thinking. . . . Well, here it is: I got three ways I can do something against the war if I mean it. I can get out of the service and go into politics—but I don't have any education. I can stay in the service and organize—but I've already made the move to get out and I can't take that back. And I thought, Well, that's it, man; you've got one possibility left. . . . And I thought, Is it worth it to you to do it? And I thought, If it would save one guy, even one guy's life is worth five years of mine. It's a fair trade. So I decided to do it." The courts in Hawaii were sentencing deserters to five years in prison.

Ben helped hand out leaflets. Hippie girls took turns carrying his duffel bag. Buffy and Ben walked up and down and back and forth across the parade, keeping everyone interested, paying attention to everybody, coming back to check on this one and that one.

Buffy went over to an MP on the curb. The man had football shoulders, head thrust forward, a hand on his weapon. Wittman, witnessing, said to himself, If that MP tries to arrest Buffy, I'm going to aid and abet resisting arrest. As a civilian in this democracy, I'll order the MP: Let this citizen, who is serving our country, have his right to assemble, and speak, and leaflet. Buffy informed the MP, "I'm AWOL, on my way to Sanctuary." The MP accepted a leaflet. Discussing it, Buffy continued walking, and the MP talked and walked too. The next thing you know, the both of them are walking in the Walk for Peace all the way to the Church of the Crossroads.

The Walk for Peace went up University Avenue and arrived at the Church of the Crossroads, next to the Varsity Theater, which was having a Jack Lemmon double bill: *The April Fools* and *The Odd Couple*. Entering the church grounds between the red columns into the courtyard was like arriving at Shangri-la. People poured into the church through its open sides. They sat and lay down on the grass and in the shade of the palms and under the eaves of the breezeways.

On the steps, which were like the platform in front of a Japanese castle, the AWOLs spoke to the crowd. Buffy Perry read his Statement of Conscience, which was printed on the leaflet: "Above all laws, above all patriotic or nationalistic duties, is the duty to stop or destroy any force which interferes with positive human life forces. . . . Are people going to wait until the whole earth is contaminated before they do something about it? By then it will be too late. We could work within the system to stop the annihilation of all humanity. But is there time? I think not. Thus, I've chosen to begin a lifestyle of non-cooperation on any level with the military establishment. I urge all my brothers and sisters to do the same."

Reverend Mitsuo Aoki welcomed the men to the Church of the Crossroads and into Sanctuary. Oh, proud, proud was Wittman — a person of one's own Asian ancestry declares Peace, declares Sanctuary. By his perfection of appearance, manner, diction, you could tell the Reverend Aoki was of that Nisei generation who were American patriots in World War II. He caught his newcomers up: A year ago, the fifteen hundred men in the 29th Brigade petitioned the Hawaii National Guard for de-activation of their unit, and asked that they not be sent to Viet Nam. Anticipating those men coming to the churches for help, the Church of the Crossroads, the First Unitarian Church of Honolulu, the Quakers, and the university Wesley Foundation started developing the idea of Sanctuary. In the autumn, two marines, Gary Gay and Tom Met, came to Crossroads in chains, sitting-in in the front row at a meeting on non-violence. It was a demonstration to awaken the conscience of the churches. They also went to the university YMCA and the First Unitarian Church, which offered them Sanctuary. They refused, and continued their demonstration at the Kaneohe Marine Corps Air Station. They then turned themselves in, and are serving prison sentences at the naval prison in Portsmouth, New Hampshire. The church members struggled over the spiritual basis and the ethics and morality of Sanctuary, and ended up voting for it. The Reverend Aoki finished by saying formally, "We grant you Sanctuary."

Gene Bridges, a lawyer and minister from Berkeley's Unitarian Universalist Association, Social Responsibility Division, read out the ideals and rights of Sanctuary: "In its broadest contemporary meaning, Sanctuary refers to community solidarity with one of its members' confrontation with the illegitimate authority of the state. Sanctuary breaks down the tremendous feeling of isolation that young men in our society feel when they contemplate alternatives to . . . submitting to dehumanization, and to committing murder in an illegal and immoral war. Sanctuary gives meaning to their acts, offers the hope that by their stand, they might effect some change, and provides them the opportunity to raise the issue of conscience in their own words. For the individual concerned, Sanctuary provides physical sustenance, but more importantly, moral support of a community of like-minded people. Sanctuary for the first time provides a forum for GIs who oppose the war to plead their cases before the public. If they oppose the war, they no longer have to think distantly about Sweden (or Canada). They look to their local church. Moreover, the solidarity established between soldiers and draft resisters and the civilian public (i.e., church members) convincingly breaks down the popular image that the peace movement opposes individual GIs as well as the military system. It is consistent with the theology of a church for others to stand with men who, because of conscience, find that they cannot obey the law."

Wittman sat on the grass at these men's feet, and felt a joy-in-human-beings coming back to him.

One by one, GIs stood, walked to the front of the crowd, and committed themselves to Sanctuary. They would stay, keep Sanctuary until no more war. Jerry, a man in an aloha shirt, identified himself as a soldier, and orated: "I should start by saying this is a statement of my own. I have not been influenced or led by anyone. I started out by leaving Camp Smith with the intention of making it to Canada. I spent a couple of days trying to find a reason for all of the feelings in my head . . . . I inquired about the Sanctuary at the church and decided to come down and find out what was happening. After an evening of inquiries, I decided to sacrifice my hopes of freedom and join the cause. Here I am and here I will stay until we are bodily removed by the authorities. We have all taken a stand against the undeclared War in Viet Nam."

Ben, the sailor with the duffel bag, had applied for CO, but it was denied him. He would create another way, then, to peace. He paused often as if he were through speaking, but his listeners waited for him, and he went on: "I joined the Sanctuary both out of conscience and the belief that the only way to put an end to the atrocities occurring so frequently, both in Vietnam and within the military structure of our country, would be through actions such as mine. . . . I began to realize that I was, in fact, being trained to do violence and killing for the government. This was the first great moral crisis in my life and after deep consideration, I resolved that I could not do killing for any purpose. This was two years ago. At that time, I lacked the confidence necessary to take a firm stand and say No to the military."

Some of the GIs were giving the first public speeches of their lives. Wittman and the crowd applauded and loved them, and went silent over them.

The AWOL GIs understood that the Church of the Crossroads was a base from which to reveal themselves as being for peace in Viet Nam. They were not hiding out. They would make this act and deed of Sanctuary public. Eight of the GIs on the Walk for Peace decided to stay — one air-force airman, a marine private, one navy airman, three seamen, an army private, and an army spec 4. Nine, counting Buffy, a lieutenant in the air force. They got on the phones, called their commanding officers, and announced that they'd gone AWOL.

Awaiting their turn on the phones, the AWOL GIs sat at desks, or on the lawn, or against a red column of the courtyard, and wrote their Statement of Conscience. Their heads were bowed in concentration over their papers. One GI, who called himself "Charley," tapped letter by letter with his index fingers. "Excuse the typing," he wrote, "but its kind of a trip also excuse my grammer and spelling but its my best." They formally put their ideals, commitments, and moral values down in so many words, in their own words. Each of these mostly uneducated men, high-school dropouts, wrote his conscience down, so in a sense grew and built a conscience, firmed it up. They spoke their conscience, wrote it, read it. The Statement of Conscience was the first essay that most of them had ever written, and they marveled over it with the community. Educated people, students and teachers, psychologists and sociologists, political scientists from the University of Hawai'i across the street, studied and discussed the statements, and over the coming days pushed the GIs to deepen and refine them. Writing Statements of Conscience would be the daily work of the men in Sanctuary. It honored Wittman to be consulted for a word or a spelling.

The GIs read the first drafts of their statements over the phone to their commanding officers at Schofield or Pearl Harbor or Hickam or Kaneohe, and announced that, because of their thinking, they were absent without leave, in Sanctuary at the Church of the Crossroads, at 1212 University Avenue in Mānoa, Honolulu. The sergeant at the other end must have said, "You're *what*?! You're going to *what*?!" They had to keep repeating themselves: I'm taking a stand against the war. I'm not going to go to Viet Nam. I'm not going back to Viet Nam. I'm not reporting for duty Monday morning. I'm putting you on notice of my action.

Sanctuary is my moral and ethical stand against the war, that is, the police action, the undeclared, unofficial, illegal, and immoral war in Viet Nam. I am committing civil disobedience. I am following my conscience.

The men called their mothers or fathers, usually their mothers. In most cases the parents hadn't heard from their rebellious son since he ran off and enlisted. In Southern and Midwestern voices, GIs confessed that they'd run away from the military. Cy Johnston, a marine who'd been wounded (the wounds didn't show), said to his mother, "I would rather go to jail than go back to Viet Nam." Parents hung up on sons, disowned them, called them cowards, advised them to finish what they started, not to be a quitter and a coward. Fathers said, "Be a man." Mothers said, "I'm going to kill myself if you don't get back to your base immediately. Or come back here. Come home." Vince's parents said that they were flying right over to Hawai'i. After speaking to his mother, Cy phoned his father collect, and heard his father's voice refusing the call. "I don't know anyone named Cyrus Johnston. I used to have a son by that name, but he died a week ago." Cy was trying for a medical discharge—his wound certified him unfit for combat—but he had orders to return to Viet Nam duty.

The atmosphere was so high that the non-GIs wanted to stay, to live with the GIs in Sanctuary. Wittman Ah Sing, free to come and go, left the church grounds and crossed the parking lot to a pay phone outside the Varsity Theater. He called Mr. Tong to get Taña. He was just that much older than the Sanctuary GIs that he had a wife to call, and he had an education. He told Taña about Sanctuary, and invited her to join him there. Bring food, clothes, sleeping bags, toothbrushes, supplies for ourselves, and extras for the AWOL GIs. And bring 'Ehukai. She immediately understood Sanctuary. He saw again why he'd married her. She said she'd be over right away.

Then he called his mother. His father, who was camping on the river, did not have a phone. The moment she picked up, he said, "Hi, Ma. I'm all right. I'm in Sanctuary."

"You're *what?!* You joined a church? What for?"

"I'm protesting the war, Ma. I'm in Sanctuary with soldiers and sailors dropping out of the war. But don't worry. I'm safe. Sanctuary means safe."

"They got guns, Witt Man. I don't like you being around guns."

"No, no. They're pacifists. Pacifists don't believe in guns."

"What about the police?" Mothers are prescient. He'd had to make his way through the parking lot, which was full of cops, MPs, HASP men, Secret Service undercover agents, FBI, and people looking for a fight.

"Yeah, but they can't come inside Sanctuary. That's the point of Sanctuary, Ma. No authorities with guns can come in."

"What good you doing? Come home. Go to Canada."

"I'll do the same thing you did in your war—help them put on a show."

"You got money, Witt Man?" There was a static, as if Comsat weren't up yet, and their voices were going through the old undersea cables. "Plane ticket for Mario at least. How long you say your honeymoon vacation lasting? You coming back? You need help?"

"An antiwar show, Ma. A peace show."

"I want to help out. You want me to come on out there? I'll come down to Hawai'i."

Ghost cables seemed to swing in the ocean, touched, crackled. You could get a lightning bolt in the brain. "Huh? What you say, Ma? Bye, Ma. Can't hear you so good. Gotta go. Aloha."

So Wittman, Taña, 'Ehukai, and about two hundred other supporters joined the AWOL GIs in Sanctuary. They were the Sanctuary Community. Every day, new GIs went AWOL and joined Sanctuary. A dozen men by August 12. On a cardboard sign in front of the chapel was the roll of honor. By the end of the first week, these were the names which were written upon it:

Louis D. "Buffy" Perry
Dan Overstreet
Eric Harms
John Veal
Robert Shultz
Howard Pollaske
Bob Matheson
"Charley"
Mike Waters

Greg Laxer
John Bolm
Albert "Duffy" King
Oscar Kelley

"Charley" signed his name just like that—"Charley" with quotation marks or rays of light. For whatever (maybe personal) reasons, some men—Ben, Cy, Vince, Jerry—procrastinated setting down their names. There were eighteen men on August 17. By the end of the month, there were thirty-four. Many more GIs, non-AWOL, hung out at the Church of the Crossroads, in the American Servicemen's Union Coffeehouse, in the courtyard, and at meetings. (The ASU button was black and white, a white hand shaking a black hand.)

The layout of the church was a rectangle of low one-story build-ings with tile roofs in a Mediterranean Japanesey style. Diamond Head side was the chapel; *mauka* side was the multipurpose hall, classrooms, and the Coffeehouse. The University Avenue side had more classrooms and offices, and *makai* side was the parking lot for the Varsity and the bank. The center was a grass-covered courtyard, a plaza, surrounded by rows of Chinese-red columns, red for luck and blessing. Anywhere in the courtyard, everyone could see everyone else, and the dogs, on the bright-green grass. The palm trees in the corners and along the parking lot nodded their big heads down; they were curious about human activities. The community was in a box, a frame, open to the sky and sun. It seemed that God looked in. God could see one and all, and was interested in what each was doing—napping, eating, giving or getting a massage, tossing a ball, reading, writing, talking with new friends. Everyone in Sanctuary felt it—everything he or she does is important.

Sanctuary was a separate world, yet open to the street and city. Any-one could walk into Sanctuary from any angle or side, go right in between the red columns. No one was shut out. The authorities could walk onto the church grounds too, bust up Sanctuary, arrest everybody, take the AWOLs away, close it down. But the MPs, HASP men, the FBI, and the cops stayed in the parking lot, standing about, sitting in their cars and on their motorcycles. The only thing stopping them was the idea of Sanctuary. They all respected where the invisible borders were, and stayed on their side of them. Thus they consented that there is such a thing as Sanctuary. The space here is sacred. Kapu.

The chaplain from Schofield patrolled Sanctuary's University Avenue boundary. He yelled into his electronic bullhorn, and threatened the GIs to come out or else. He said to give themselves up, as if they were criminals. "You boys are breaking the law. You're going to the stockade. You're damned to Hell." He was a Black man, and his bullhorn-amplified basso-profundo voice preached damnation. "Surrender and be saved. . . . I'm telling you, for your own good. I'm responsible for you, for your soul and your career in the service. Get yourself outta here." He yelled at all his boys, did not single out any Black. He did not know that Walter was Black, he was so White-looking. And Cy Johnston identified with and attached himself to Blacks; his Black sergeant had risked his own life to save Cy's in Viet Nam. All day and into the night, the chaplain nagged and worried, threatened and cursed. He harangued his boys like gangsters under siege. "Give yourselves up or else. You're damned. Come on out. Come on out. You boys are in big trouble. Surrender peaceably. The goddamned Commie traitors are duping you. Don't be a dupe. Don't aid and comfort the enemy. Come out. Don't make the army come in after you." Damned from here to eternity.

One day his loud, hectoring voice blasted through the Sanctuary with new information. "It's not too late. You have a chance. Turn yourself in now. You are not a deserter. A deserter is AWOL thirty-one days. The law is: thirty-one days, *then* you are charged with desertion. Go three days AWOL, go four days AWOL, go five days, go a week, go two weeks AWOL, you can still be forgiven. Only come out now." Every day the chaplain roared the count. "Is it worth it? Thirty-one days AWOL— five years federal penitentiary. Come out now—to clemency. To mercy." That he used a bullhorn shows how thick he imagined the Sanctuary walls.

In the second week, a very unhappy man, Harvey, asked for Sanctuary. He said that he would kill himself rather than turn into a violent, raging beast. He'd gone AWOL from his submarine, where he hallucinated and attempted suicide. Whenever he saw a sharp object, he wanted to use it on himself. The church asked at the University of Hawai'i, up the street, for psychotherapists, and Linda Meyerson

Tillich, Ph.D. candidate, and her husband, René Tillich, came to treat Harvey for "battle fatigue" and "burnout." Harvey wrote in his Statement of Conscience, "Now I feel that I am making a real stand for the first time in my life. I feel at peace."

Though healthy-looking, Linda Tillich was dying young of a degenerative illness, yet she camped in Sanctuary and helped people like Harvey, who could not stop trembling. She tried to talk him into presenting himself to the military hospital—she assured him he could get a medical discharge. But Harvey said he was better off in Sanctuary than at any time in his life. "I am not turning into a violent, raging beast," he repeated.

The Tillichs organized twenty-one AWOL GIs in *ho'oponopono*, which means "to put to rights." To this day, people in Hawai'i have ho'oponopono, a conference where they talk and listen, explain, pray, confess, apologize, and at last understand and forgive and reconcile everything and everyone. Ho'oponopono makes aloha possible. The men would speak their minds. They would sit together, everybody confronting everybody face to face, and mouth to ear. They would speak and listen to one another all through the night, until each understood his own feelings and thoughts, and the feelings and thoughts of the forming community. They would labor to grow identity, one in relation to the others. The image of ho'oponopono is canoemen preparing to catch a wave; and *ho'oponopono* also means "to edit." During the emergency of war, in one marathon night, the AWOL GIs would make a new society.

Left out of ho'oponopono, which was for AWOL GIs only, Wittman thought, I'll put on a show. The play's the thing for the forming community to say its new heart.

At the State Library, he browsed for a play against war. He read in the beautiful courtyard, where stacks were open to the weather. Books were shelved outdoors, under the eaves, just out of the rain. There were six free typewriters under another eave. He considered *Henry V*, which is in the public domain. Westmoreland had been in that war too. We could hoot the St. Crispian's Day speech; the common people would not "concent" war.

The play he decided on was *Viet Rock (A Folk War Movie)* by Megan Terry, a blueprint outline, or "pretext," for actors to improv. Surely, thought Wittman, she wouldn't mind AWOL GIs' not getting copyright permission. Admission: $1.50 free-will donation, $1.00 for students. The money goes to the Sanctuary. She'll never find out about us doing the play in far-off Hawai'i, and sue for royalties. We'll be making up the play anyway, just use her structure and title. You can't copyright a title.

Wittman announced a casting call, and twenty people showed up. He didn't turn any of them away. Use whoever shows up, was his policy. Each could play multiple parts—primordial flower, fish, dinosaur, infant, mother, inductee, army doctor, bird, airplane, Custer, Apache, American, Vietnamese, ARVN, and Viet Cong.

"Charley" and John Norris volunteered music. "Charley" played piano in New Orleans, and now he played in Waikīkī clubs. He'd go AWOL from Sanctuary and from *Viet Rock* to play Waikīkī. The same cast never gathered twice; free spirits don't stay put. John Norris, a church member and World War II vet, played the ukulele, bass, and banjo when his church duties allowed. The actors sang, with or without accompaniment. The music of the times was rock and Dylan dirge; the words mattered, and you heard them over the music.

> When the bombs fall
> The Viets will rock and rock.
> When the napalm bursts
> Then the Viets roll.

However sad the words, rock'n'roll music is happy. The audience who watched rehearsals cheered and whistled, danced and let it all hang out. People came to see what was going on, and joined in. Rebels against private space and furniture make every ground and floor they sit or lie upon public property.

Weaver Hall, the multipurpose room with the platform, was already stage-set with a forest of antiwar picket signs. Wittman added to a sign that said "Non-White": "Non-Black Non-Red Non-Yellow Non-Brown." The play opens with people lying on the floor. Sit down, and you are already in character, a ground-sitting hippie. Standing in the doorway, you are a soldier about to enter sacred space, deciding to leave the war world for the peace world. On or off whatever drug, you get in sync with whatever's happening in the play. Uniforms are costumes. Every night, even opening night, was the first rehearsal for somebody, never the same show twice. Down came the wall between actors and audience.

One night was advertised as the gala opening night. A standing-room-only audience came to the Church of the Crossroads expressly to see Wittman Ah Sing's *Viet Rock*. Oh, joy. The stage once again.

As promised, Wittman's mother, Ruby, flew over. "To help out, Witt Man." And flying in with her came Wittman's ex-girlfriend Nanci Lee—always ready to put on a show. Nanci was a graduate of Disney University, a classmate of Ron Ziegler, Nixon's press secretary. She'd been a mermaid and a hula girl, and Ron a swashbuckler on a jungle ride. Ruby and Nanci played the two mothers, Mrs. Sherman and Mrs. Cole, who follow their sons as far as the Induction Center. But they can't go inside, so helplessly fight with each other. They speak from their individual tables at a coffee shop. "God didn't designate my Laird to be a fighter." "You do it for him, eh?" (The play foresees: Russian mothers will take their sons—officers—out of the barracks and home from Chechnya. And Israeli parents join their sons and daughters at army camp. And Singaporean and Japanese parents pass home-cooked meals through the fence to their soldier boys. Poor, clumsy, dying Mrs. Prewitt had said to her son, "Promise me you won't never hurt nobody unless it's absolutely a must, unless you jist have to do it.")

In a scene about congressional hearings, ". . . several Vietnamese women, crying softly, kneel before the Senators. They plead and cry. Their hands flutter in bewilderment." The Vietnamese women have no lines; they are mute Oriental stereotypes. Fortunately, PoPo also flew in to help. She looked like a Vietnamese granny, and improvised talkstory: "Once upon a time, there was a beautiful daughter named Q. War came to her village. Her brothers and her betrothed were drafted away. To feed the old people and the children, Q became a prostitute. She sacrificed her engagement to her beloved. She sacrificed her marriageability. She left her village. Then she became a second wife, the pretty wife, then a nun, then the wife of a military general, then . . ." PoPo crammed an epic that ought to have gone on for days into ten minutes; it might have been all the story she knew. Too bad—the telling and hearing of the full myth might have ended the war. (The Vietnamese who are amongst us now say, "If the Americans had known the story of Kieu, they would not have warred with Viet Nam.") Nanci Lee, wearing a golden crown and golden wings, mimed PoPo's story; she danced with a crossbow and arrows. She chanted, "We will win. We will win," and jetéd off into the wings.

Some nights *Viet Rock* did not get to Act II. Entr'acte, people took the stage; they ranted; they talked story.

One intermission, Wittman, high on actor's energy, strolled across the courtyard with eyes for Nanci of the dark tresses. He hardly noticed the two blondes, Linda and Taña, whose long golden hair wafted in the trade winds. His wife is as ordinary as himself. He sat with Nanci on the steps of their theater. Never before had he said "I love you" in Chinese to a fellow Chinese-speaker. The kissing breeze was playing on skin and skin. Chance 'em. She was in costume, an ao dai, the same as a cheongsam but with slits up to the waist and dancer's tights underneath. The ao dai is why Vietnamese women are the most beautiful in the world.

Wittman spoke to her as director to actress. Also as ex-boyfriend to old flame. His brown eyes looking into her brown eyes, he said, "*Nan Ci, ngo oy nay.*" There. Said. "I love you" in the primal, root language of his id self, to one who could hear it.

"I love you too," she said in English. Nothing special. Normal hippie flower-child etiquette in the Age of Aquarius.

Some nights, Wittman and his feckful friend and enemy, Lance Kamiyama, who had been partners putting on college plays and two-man shows, got to do Bones and Jones. (Lance, hearing that Wittman was putting on a show, had also flown over.) In four-legged pants, they were Chang and Eng, the Chinese American Siamese twins, the Union-Confederacy joined twins. They pushed and pulled each other, hit, ran, tripped, fell, tried to coordinate, tripped, and fell again.

Bones: Here we are come go stay again, Mr. Jones. Stuck and enmired forever a long long time.

Jones: *You* the one stuck and enmired, Mr. Bones. I'm for withdrawal.

Bones: I'm *having* withdrawals. I'm getting that pulled-apart feeling, from you, Mr. Jones.

Jones: Pull yourself together, Mr. Bones. Heart and mind. (They bump, chest to chest.) Heart and mind. (They bump, head to head.) Come stay go AWOL with me from the war.

Bones: It is my fate and doom to be stuck to an unmanly man. (He shoves his brother, and they tumble into a heap.)

Jones: Refusing involuntary servitude, I am no less a man. We be twice the man, Mr. Bones. (They hug, trying to move in unison.)

Bones: This war, Mr. Jones, you come over to my side. Be on the same side as me, for a change. We would not have such a coordination problem. Shoulder to shoulder, bolder and bolder.

Jones: *You* the problem.

Bones: *You!* You the problem. (They jab each other with their fingers.)

Jones: *You!* I am perfectly well integrated. (He swivels, and they are back to back. The ligament connecting them is pretty flexible.)

Bones: Which side are you on, boy? Which side are you on? (They chase each other in a tight circle.)

Jones: I am on the side of the North *and* the South. (They hide and seek, looking for each other between these two legs and *these* two legs. Oh, here you are.) I tell you, I am an integrated man. I am a true American human being.

Bones: Mr. Jones, do you know the karma and *kuleana* of the American human being?

Jones: What *is* the karma and *kuleana* of the American human being, Mr. Bones?

Bones: Mr. Jones, it is this: Whoever we war upon, any nation or half-ass nation in the world, we have blood relatives over there. We nuke and napalm our own brothers and sisters and cousins and uncles and aunts, and twin.

Jones: I admit, Mr. Bones, Americans are internationally related and connected to every da kine person. You would think we'd think twice before hitting them. (He pats the shoulder that he himself has hit.)

Bones: I apologize to you, Mr. Jones, for putting a perfectly good American such as yourself into Relocation Camp. (He extends his right, inward hand.)

Jones: It's okay. I apologize for bombing North Viet Nam and Cambodia. (He extends his right, outward hand, and they shake.)

Bones: Wait a minute, Mr. Jones. Can you apologize for what you haven't stopped doing? Stop the warring. Then you get the comfort of apologizing.

Jones: I'm apologizing, Mr. Bones, as a Frenchman, who withdrew already.

Bones: You withdrew because you lost la guerre, Monsieur Jones. The Vietnamese kicked your derrière out. (He kicks backward, and hits a butt.) Quit bombing Tahiti, then you get to apologize.

Jones: Trade, Mr. Bones! You quit bombing Kahoʻolawe, we quit bombing Tahiti.

The Asian American brothers buffaloed off to a clapping, whistling, stomping ovation. God, we're good. It's all coming together—theater and the right political cause. Lucky to be relevant in interesting times.

Viet Rock climaxes at Saigon Sally's bar, where the dancers are mixed-race couples—White American soldiers and oriental women. Wittman and Lance cut in on the couples, and try to retake their/our women. A character called SERGEANT, played by an actual sergeant, goes bananas, tries to talk to people flashing by him. He is invisible and castrated. "Right now we're in the grips of the most prejudiced war we've ever fought. . . . This here minority ain't Western European; they's our little yellow-skinned brothers with slant eyes and too small to tote our guns. They think it's more important that that guy in the White House learn to eat lung under glass. I say warm yer spareribs! Get on with the war! Get on with this war—and—win it!"

"*Giant explosion.*" Saigon Sally's bar is blown to bits. "*A clustered death. The bodies are massed together center stage, tangled and flailing in slow motion. They stab one another, shoot one another, and choke one another as they fall in a heap to the floor.*" They mutter common sayings of the age. Then they arise as fragile angels, enter the audience, touch them, look into their eyes, and leave, singing "Viet Rock."

Actors and audience clapped and whistled, stomped and cheered bravo and brava, as if the play had ended in triumphant victory.

Leaving the multipurpose hall, Wittman entered a miraculously lit mise-en-scène: the Crossroads Sanctuary. It shone in the black night, light coming from the hibachis and candles, and from the moon and stars. And the people shone. The fires made faces and hands golden, and threw shadows of giants onto the red columns and the courtyard walls. Each dear person was a star of resplendent Sanctuary, and God was audience, looking down from the open sky. This one, that one would rise from a cooking fire, and walk to the next fire, carrying a joint, popcorn, hot dogs, an idea, a story. Too ecstatic to go to sleep, many people stayed up through the night talking, marveling at one another and this Sanctuary they'd made out of nothing. In the whole dark universe, I've met you at this bit of fire, and we speak with each other, and listen to each other. All of life and the war led up to this present time of being here with you.

. . .

Sanctuary was not just theater—it was school. Its inhabitants went to every level of school. The GIs taught and played in the experimental preschool and the alternative free school. Hale Mohala had a Summerhill philosophy, that children are basically good; leave them alone and they'll be all right, they'll learn to read. Mario 'Ehukai enrolled without a birth certificate; he wouldn't be traced for the draft of the future. His peace-loving teachers would raise him to be free. He'd get over the tantrums, and the nightmares that he'd been having, even in Sanctuary, sleeping on a church pew. Most of the free children were haoles. No Kill Haole Day. One Latino kid and two or three hapas. One Korean American, Sam Kim, whose father, Sam Kim, was in a MASH unit during Korea. The children formed a club, Kids Against the War. They voted unanimously against war, and wrote down their decision, and signed their names. The parents kept a copy of that paper, starting their sons' documentation, resisting the draft a dozen years from now. On the blue cover of the notebook of minutes, the children wrote in block letters: VIET NAM WILL WIN.

One day, Wittman, looking for his son—'Ehukai was off the church grounds, at the Charlie Chaplin festival at the Varsity—came across the VIET NAM WILL WIN notebook in the schoolyard. He opened it. The pages throughout were blank. Children are primitive. Their furthest thinking is VIET NAM WILL WIN. Their thinking is dualistic: win or lose, good or bad. How afraid they must be. The enemy are coming, and will hurt and kill us. Our parents and the soldiers won't protect us. The grown-ups are sacrificing us. And it's okay. We can't like it, but we'll like it.

The parents and the GIs built a play area under the Lunalilo Freeway. They tied ropes and nets in the tree whose top branches stuck up between the ramps, built a tree hootch, and started a vegetable garden and a flower garden. The children played marbles, which they shot into pukas in the ground, laid out like a baseball diamond. "Take the base." "Two handspans." "I put my kapu here." "Poison!" "I kapu. No can shoot me." The kids drove Linda's go-cart wheelchair around and around the parking lots.

At least two of the paid teaching staff were Revolutionary Communists. One was the girl, Melanie Toy, from the demonstration in

Waikīkī. The other was a haole woman whose own kids were in the school. (Her parents reported her to the FBI.) The Red teachers did not, within the hearing of parents anyway, teach the children about violent overthrow of the system. The GIs did not tell kids about tiger cages and fire cages. The Marxist women gave a class in Communism for the GIs, who made fun of them, Hanoi Hannahs. Linda held ho'oponopono group therapy for the Marxist women and the hippie women.

The parents and teachers worked on democratically loving all the children the same amount. Treat every child as if he or she were your own only child. No kid gets singled out for extra loving; everybody gets extra loving. Work against the motherly instinct to favor your own kid. Always give somebody else's kid the biggest cookie. All the women, Marxist and hippie, agreed to teach the children and the GIs: Stop crying "Ma." Cry for your father instead. "Don't automatically call for Mommy. Practice calling Daddy."

During war, mothers dream this dream: she—mother—is winged, and flies, swooping down upon the son, the brother, soldier, criminal in danger, and picks him up by the straps of his overalls or by his belt, or catches him up in her arms, and flies him high and away. Unable to fly, she would go to the war in her son's place. She would go ahead of him, walk point herself.

It was better that GIs rather than parents and women tell the boys, "You don't have to join the army when you grow up. You can be a man without joining the army. You don't need war to be a man." In Sanctuary, men were helping to raise and teach the children. The children had men with them day and night. And the men told them that they must not hit, or fight, or go to war.

The church preached the history of Sanctuary, divine protection for those who broke society's laws. Sanctuaries had existed at times in Greece, India, China, New Guinea, Samoa, Tahiti, North America, Morocco, Arabia, Europe. Moses built three cities of refuge on either side of the Jordan. All six cities were accessible by good roads, and harbored those who'd killed purposely or accidentally until they could have a trial.

People who knew the Big Island (where the Peace Corps trains) pooled their knowledge about the sanctuary there. To this day, you can visit Kulanakauhale Pu'uhonua, the City of Refuge, on the Big Island, Hawai'i. During wars, it offered noncombatants, the too-young and the too-old, even the enemy, a safe place of retreat. Defeated warriors could live in safety. The fugitive would speak loudly to Keave, whose tall black lava-rock tikis still stand—two at the land entrance and two at the sea entrance—and give thanks, obliging himself or herself to that deity. The priests put to death anyone who would harm the fugitive under *pahu kapu*. After two or three days, refugees were free to return home, divine protection abiding wherever they went.

Wittman, listening, flashed on his high-school Latin—*fugere*, "to flee." He saw black feet on the black sand beach running, the enemy warriors behind gaining on the fugitive, breathless, trying to reach the City of Refuge, the images intercut with the slow march to Sanctuary.

The book of the Sanctuary was *The Velveteen Rabbit, or How Toys Become Real* by Margery Williams, published in England in 1922. GIs who were in Viet Nam but hours ago held our children in their laps and read to them, and listened to the children read. 'Ehukai sat in Harvey's lap and arms, and Harvey, who was afraid that he was about to turn into a violent, raging beast, read him *The Velveteen Rabbit* again and again. 'Ehukai learned the lessons of the lonely rabbit, who, stuck on a cupboard shelf, is befriended by the Skin Horse. The Skin Horse has been through a lot; he is a veteran of war, and it is he who teaches the rabbit what it means to be REAL: "Real isn't how you are made," says the Skin Horse. "It's a thing that happens to you. When a child loves you for a long, long time, not just to play with, but REALLY loves you, then you become Real."

It hurts to become real. All feelings—even good feelings—shake the body. The children and the soljers learned: becoming real takes a long time. It's okay to take a long time coming alive. It's okay to almost break. It's okay to be soft like velveteen. "Generally by the time you are Real, most of your hair has been loved off, and your eyes drop out and you get loose in the joints and very shabby. But these things don't matter at all, because once you are Real you can't be ugly, except to people who don't understand." Get yourself amongst people who understand and honestly see you as beautiful. Amongst understanders, you can let it all hang out, and be yourself. "Once you are Real you can't become unreal again. It lasts for always."

In *Gandhi's Truth*, which was the AWOL GIs' other favorite book, Gandhi wrote, "This is the real me." The Velveteen Rabbit was utterly nonviolent. You can't be any more passive than a stuffed animal, and he turned out all right.

Harvey and 'Ehukai would be all right too. Only keep reading to one another. But Harvey disappeared. He had suddenly taken Linda's advice and committed himself to the military hospital. Wittman brought 'Ehukai and *The Velveteen Rabbit* to Tripler, but Harvey was in restraints and not allowed to have visitors.

'Ehukai will be all right, Wittman thinks. His grandfather is here. The rumor around Sanctuary was that an Indian or hapa Indian had come amongst us. Zeppelin Ah Sing looked like Mesquilito and Don Juan. He was often hunkered down in the courtyard, in his element, talking to young-men-who-listen. He taught me how to make something out of nothing.

The book that Zeppelin brought was *Timothy Mouse's House*, Wittman's smallkidtime storybook. 'Ehukai and the other free-school children, following the illustrations, built mouse houses out of take-out cartons. The flaps were the peaked roof. They cut out windows and made shutters and awnings. They turned matchboxes and matches into four-poster beds, and small spools into chairs, and larger spools into tables.

Zeppelin was the Sanctuary handyman, keeping the plumbing going, repairing dry rot. He made spotlights out of tin cans for *Viet Rock*. He and GI assistants installed showers. There would never be an Ah Sing and Son Hardware, but maybe Ah Sing and Grandson.

Wittman had spent his life rebelling against his father's answers for living. All his old man cared about was money, property, the material things. In the grove of palms, Zep was getting some kind of motor to run. 'Ehukai was assisting, using tools from his own little tool chest. Wittman hunkered down with them.

"Dad," he said.

"Yeah?" said Zeppelin.

"Thank you for always supporting me. You're a good father."

After a silence, his father said, "You're welcome. You're a good son."

When 'Ehukai is grown, maybe he'll remember this thanksgiving, and say Thank you to *his* father.

.   .   .

The night of the Marathon, ho'oponopono, Wittman got out of the boatlike bed that he and Taña had made out of two pews. He left the church full of sleeping civilians, and walked outside amidst the civilians sleeping on the grass. The lights were on in the classroom that had a rug. Through the windows, he could see men and one woman sitting or lying or crouching in a circle. Linda Tillich and René Tillich were opposite each other. The AWOLs were staying up all night. The least Wittman could do was sit up all night with them. Leaning with his back against the door, he could hear this voice, then that one. All was silent but for one voice at a time telling a life.

He heard Cy Johnston ask, "Do you know what it does to a person to have to kill another human being?"

Someone answered: "You don't have to tell me, man! I went with a couple of guys on a patrol. We went inside of a village. And there was this family harboring VC, and we got out this mama-san and her help-less son, and we set up a machine gun, and we told her, 'Start runnin'!' and she was pregnant, but we hit her in the back with fifty-caliber, shot that baby fifty feet away from her stomach, and just ripped her in half! Now do you know what war is?!" Wittman refrained from peeking at who the speaker was. Let the man have his privacy. "Can you imagine what that's like? Can you imagine what it's like when we have to come down there to a village lookin' for somebody, and can see this, can you see a *six-year-old* kid walkin' into an ammo bunker with a hand grenade and pullin' the pin on it, blowin' the whole place to smithereens, and the little kid don't even know what the hell he's doin'! He thinks it's a damn toy! . . . The people just want to, they want to go out, they want to work in their fields, they want to cultivate their rice, they want to make their little humble livin', they want to have love, they don't want nobody comin' in there. We come in there, we go, 'You got to have it our way, you got to do it the way we want it, or else you ain't goin' to do it no way at all.' "

All went quiet. Guys were probably patting the speaker on his back, or hugging him.

Art spoke. He had been wounded on his second—voluntary—tour of duty in Viet Nam and was in line for a Purple Heart. He said, "I was in the infantry in Viet Nam and I walked point all the time. I got suck-ered into walking point. They built up my head. They said, 'Wow, you're really good at it!' . . . And I got shot in the leg, got a piece of shrapnel in my stomach, and got hit in the elbow." He had an older brother, who had gotten shot in the head, and died at home.

Linda asked, "What's walking point?"

"That's walking in the front, always stepping on all the booby traps. I seen myself and other people kill civilians for no avail, just so you wouldn't have to wonder if they were VC, and I seen the American machine, if you can call it that, tear up a whole half of a city, Saigon, looking for VC. And when I came back to the States, I was on funeral details, honor-guard details. And I was good at it. Did about eighty-some, I think it was. Eighty-some funerals. All these people were saying, 'Why?' Every one of them. I never heard one of them say, 'Oh, I'm so glad my son died.' They always said, 'Why? What did he die for?' "

"Charley," who played the piano for *Viet Rock*, said, "I very often went to Saigon, to some of the orphanages. And from what I was told, we . . . we're supposed to be helping in Vietnam, but when you go to an orphanage and see the kids there without their parents . . . and you know they was murdered, and you just can't help. And I was stationed at the hospital after I came back from Viet Nam, and I seen so many guys coming in that was all shot up. . . . It has been said that when a man enters the military he loses a majority of his rights as an American citizen. I have been called a machine, but I say that I am not a machine. I am a human being who is made of the same flesh and blood as other men, and I also have the same domestic habits. So I ask why shouldn't I and other American servicemen be given the same rights?" "Charley" 's parents had seen him on the TV news, and called the Church of the Crossroads. They disowned him.

René pushed the men to articulate — to build — their values. Having and holding values, morals, a code of ethics will save your life.

Ben, whom Wittman befriended as fellow Monkey, claimed that he learned discipline and morals from the navy, not his parents. "It was in boot camp that I learned to control my temper and got a little more self-discipline that I needed. I learned what authority was and made the distinction between moral and immoral authority, sane and insane authority." He had appealed to enlisted men and officers on his ship to try for peace. "Talking to them was like talking to a blank wall. A couple of them started thinking about things a little heavier, but in general I didn't do much good." In Naval Electronics School, he leafleted "for a radical organization and did some organizing." He had followed his best friend into the NES ballistic-missiles maintenance program. But when he realized he was to use his training to bomb and kill people, he refused a promotion and announced that, if and when the ship sailed for Viet Nam, he would not be on it. "And it didn't look like they were going to do anything about that except give me more menial jobs to do. Instead of working on the gear, I was working chipping paint and swabbing things and cleaning things. About a month later, they reduced me to a seaman. And the same day, they told me I was getting transferred to a ship in Hawai'i which didn't go to a combat zone. They were appeasing me in that way. When I got to Hawai'i, they told me, 'Oh, boy, you can go back and get your third-class status back and everything will be okay and you don't have to go over and fight the war. You can just sit on the ship.' " He could have sat out the war, but "that was a cop-out, that would not have been meaningful. . . . I told them, If I take anything from you, it's like being bought off, and I'd have to pay you back for it."

In the secret-keeping night, men told one another about their sex troubles. Ben said, "I had a girlfriend. She gave me VD, and I was in sick bay, and I made out a report giving the name of a guy as the person I'd gotten the VD from. I was trying to get them to give me an administrative discharge for being homosexual. I started thinking, Hey, I'm miserable in the navy, and I'm not doing much good on this ship, so why don't I just get out? So I walked down to sick bay. He wanted my life story, so, just to be funny, I told him I'd been to bed with eight hundred and sixty-three guys. He wrote it down and typed it all out. And they were going to do an investigation and let me out. And then I thought, Wait, now, that's not very meaningful . . . copping out this way, getting out so easy." The very next day, Monkey Ben tried to undo his plot, but the report had already been filed. "I'm not queer," he insisted. The GIs were so young, they were still figuring out categories of persons to love and to befriend and to reject.

Wittman listened to the AWOL GIs go back over their lives, figuring out how they got to be who they were and how they came to be here, in this present place. Reviewing their paths, they saw where they'd lost their way.

George told about his life of but a month ago. He was becoming a derelict, AWOL for a month in the Waikīkī jungle. He had the longest hair of the soldiers. (The new army did allow mustaches; soldiers grew their hair to the limit, neat brush of mustache across their upper lip, and sideburns shaved at earlobe level.) "We just slept where we could find a place, like the beach and a park and a house that was being torn down the next day because it was condemned. And I lost my pride, and I started panhandling for food, because I was hungry. . . . In hopes that it would pick me up some, I dropped acid three or four times in about one month, and I dropped mescaline . . . and I smoked a considerable amount of marijuana. . . . That's one thing that made me lose my pride, because I got to the point where I thought, If I keep this up, I would become one of the freaks down in Waikīkī, and I didn't want that, yet I was so far down in my mood that I didn't know what to do. One reason why I came up here to the Sanctuary is to get away from drugs and try to get some of my pride back." The very air and ground of this place were giving him health.

Someone was confessing that he had helped set up an ambush. He killed two enemy, and two got away. Wittman peered in a window and saw Don talking while modeling a Play-Doh lion. "We left a bloody mess lying on a trail somewhere. Well, when we got back to the base camp, I felt pretty bad. It was the first time I had done something like that. . . . Ever since I was a kid, I guess I found that I couldn't go along with whatever the social demands were. I caused all kinds of problems in the home and in school. Like, I just decided I didn't want to go to school, man, and I didn't go. . . . I just couldn't stay within the boundaries."

Nobody replied to him or argued with him. They all only listened, allowing him to have his say.

Mel, who had a speech defect, like Billy Budd, spoke clearly at the Marathon and to Linda. Looking at her, he told about his boyhood. "I can always remember Mom and Dad saying we were poor people, and I'd say No, we're not poor people. We've got a television set and a car. And I couldn't understand what they were talking about." He confided a humiliating childhood incident: He bought too-expensive meat at the butcher's, and refused his father's order to return it for cheap meat. The shamed father beat the shamed son with a belt.

Many men talked about their fathers. They had run away from Father; Father had chased them out of the house; Father himself had left home. "Charley" said, "When I was in Viet Nam I wrote him about six letters and only got one back the whole year that I was over there. And he gave me the big line that he was working too hard. This is another point—my mother don't write. My sister writes for her, but the letters are short and it says the same damn thing every time. 'Such-and-such is taking a bath,' and all this other bullshit. So it kinda gets me. I sent my mom a thing about the complete Sanctuary, the way everybody feels, and I told her, I says, 'If you can't understand it, get somebody that does, and get them to explain it to you, and write me a letter. Tell me how you feel. I know that I'm right by doing what I'm doing. . . . It's what I believe in, what should change. I've got to live with myself, and if I ever decide to get married, I've got to bring up my children to do what they believe in.' "

Mid-Marathon, the group ganged up on Buffy. Men stood and paced; their shadows and silhouettes moved about. This impromptu community—"sudden Sanctuary," Buffy called it—was not living up to American ideals of democracy and fairness. They had left the military because of officers bossing them around. So, they asked, how come we have to have bosses and leaders now? And why should they be certain people—that is, Buffy and Cy?

Mac said, "When I do something that I feel is sort of important, I guess I'm looking for some sort of . . . approval, and I find Buffy somewhat noncommittal. Also, I try to meet him on a . . . personal scale, and again he seems aloof and standoffish."

Everyone wanted Buffy's personal love and attention. You throw in your lot with him, he ought to love you in return. Buffy tried explaining his leadership to his "GI confrères." "I think the aloofness comes from a belief I have about interpersonal relationships. I feel that, if I develop this type of relationship with you, then I should do it with everybody here. I've assumed a position of leadership, probably because I was the first person here. . . . I did it out of necessity."

Buffy and Cy sat still, taking the onslaught from young men who couldn't abide leaders, fathers, teachers, officers, and the government and country who had led them off in the wrong direction, and gotten them lost.

Someone announced, "I'm going to desert to Sweden before the Bust."

René Tillich asked, "How many of you can tolerate the thought that some amongst you are frightened of the Bust?"

Everyone talked at once about the Bust. The Bust was coming. It was to happen in two weeks. The Sanctuary was two weeks old, and in two more weeks, the Bust would come down. The authorities are counting thirty-one days from Hiroshima Day. The forces of the U.S. government will invade the Sanctuary, and bust it up. We should plan together tonight what to do. Or every man for himself? No, no, either all of us abandon Sanctuary, or all of us stay for the Bust. I'm not going to be here greeting the MPs and the FBI all by myself. They'll be bashing heads. Are we prepared to be nonviolent?

Wittman thought the Bust would make terrific propaganda — soldiers kicking down church doors, FBI agents dragging idealistic resisters from the pulpit.

Somebody said, and somebody else repeated, "The Bust is our opportunity to put the war on trial."

But the Church of the Crossroads is wide open. They won't have to kick down doors. We can meet them in the courtyard. So — do we walk docilely into the paddy wagon? We walk with dignity into the paddy wagon. Or are we going to go limp and make them drag us? We don't want to bring out their violence.

"I don't know that if an MP starts beating on me I can totally hold on to my nonviolence."

"I might snap."

"My natural reflexes are to hit back when I'm hit."

"Somebody hits me, he started it. I've got a right."

"How do you — I — control natural human reflexes?"

"If you see me lose it, give me a touch right here, like a wrestler. Remind me not to snap."

"Okay, but you have to be responsible for yourself. You can't just depend on me tapping you. You've got to get your attitude straight."

"Yeah, no matter what, don't hit back."

"You hit back, they'll add on charges — resisting arrest, attacking an MP. You don't want to get charged with penny-ante charges. You want a big charge — court-martial for trying to stop the war. We don't want a trial about resisting arrest or trespassing. We want a trial about the Viet Nam War."

"Ain't nothin' that says you can't yell and shout at them. Free speech. You get scared or hurt or mad, put it in so many words."

"No. Better to speak quietly, and without anger. Say your prepared statement. That we're not going to war. And why we're not going to war. We're for peace."

"Remember the film on sit-in training? We have to keep practicing taking taunts and curses, staying calm, sitting."

"We need to get arrested ceremoniously. Think of a ceremony. How about we stand at attention, in uniform."

"I'm gonna have to wear civvies. I tossed my uniform."

"We have to practice going limp. Roll into a ball. We have to collect football helmets. We should rehearse what to say at the arrest—a clear statement against the war."

"A group statement, or individual statements?"

"A group statement."

"Individual statements."

"Individual statements."

"Five years in prison."

"Five years—I'll be almost a quarter of a century old."

"They'll send us in shackles to Viet Nam."

"The church says we're only 'symbolic Sanctuary.' We've made our point. Let's get outta here."

"Are you staying? Are *you*? How about *you*? I'll stay if a lot of you—it doesn't have to be everybody—stays. I don't want to be the only one left here all by myself when the Bust comes."

"Nobody should pressure anybody to stay or to go. Nobody's thinking less of anybody else for leaving."

"We could be singing a peace song. 'Gonna lay down my sword and shield down by the riverside. Down by the riverside. Down by the riverside. Gonna study war no more.' "

They veered off into dreams about someday, when the Bust was over, when the war was over.

"You guys are my chosen family."

"We'll buy land on the Big Island, and grow vegetables, buy a cow. We can have kids. We'll raise them together."

"Yeah, make a commune. Let's do it. We'll share expenses and share labor."

"Buy a ship, and be a commune on the high seas. We'll go out beyond the jurisdiction of coastal waters."

It was like giving and getting marriage proposals, choosing and being chosen for a life in utopia.

They got back down to reality. What to do when the soon-to-actually-happen Bust comes. At the Bust, would the MPs shoot us? "They wouldn't shoot unarmed men, would they? And unarmed civilians, and women and children."

In the morning, Wittman got to join the Marathon. He went inside with members of the church and Hawai'i Resistance. The tired GIs had to watch their supporters hold a meeting. The Resistance urged the Church of the Crossroads to take more radical stances. The church reminded everyone that it ran other programs besides Sanctuary— Sunday services, the preschool, the alternative school. Everything would be shut down if the GIs kept flouting health and fire regulations. The Department of Health and the Fire Department had served Crossroads with notices of violation. They had to build more showers; they had to turn people away from camping overnight.

John Witeck of the Resistance argued: the more people who stayed on the grounds, the more protection they gave the AWOL GIs. He accused the church of "martyrizing" the GIs. A church member said that it was the Resistance using and "martyrizing" them, and that the Resistance was wildly recruiting AWOLs; improper screening was resulting in GIs' going AWOL and crowding in here for no moral purpose.

GIs stood and started to leave the Marathon. René asked them to wait, to speak. David said, "Hey, we're being filibustered. I watched it go back and forth and back and forth, and I just felt for all the GIs sitting in the middle. Why didn't you guys do this before we came? Why didn't you hash this out before we came? Why did you lay us out such a hassle when we came?"

Monkey Ben yelled at a church lady, "People are coming here, they're risking five years in prison! D'you think they're just doing it off the top of their heads? 'Okay, well, my boat's leavin', I guess I'll stay here—' My boat's in dry dock in Pearl Harbor. Everybody here has got five years laying on the line! I don't think they're just flipped out! That's five years, lady! What's that mean to you?"

René asked people, "Can you say specifically what you want from the church and what you want from the Resistance?"

One GI replied, "Well, the Resistance has the machinery and the people and the knowledge to help us reach the public. The church has the Sanctuary, and I don't think we need to have a party here every night; that's not what I'm here for."

The Marathon ended, but its idealism heartened those who heard of it. Talkstory of what the heroes said passed from listener to listener.

And the Sanctuary thrived because the larger community, Honolulu, O'ahu, was avidly interested in it, and fascinated with the AWOL GIs. The *Star Bulletin* and the *Advertiser* editorialized daily about the "flawed Sanctuary," the "hippie lark," the "malcontents," "troubled young men who really belong in the office of a psychiatrist," marijuana and LSD, and having sex "under the altar." (The papers did announce *Viet Rock* nicely, and reviewed it.)

To write and send out press releases giving the Sanctuary's point of view, Barrie Anthony "Buc" Buxton took upon himself the job of Sanctuary Press Officer. He organized the deluge of reporters and film crews from the national and international press—the BBC, Japanese television. He worked out a system for counting the number of AWOL GIs in Sanctuary, and kept the Hawai'i Sanctuary in touch with support from the mainland: The Orange Grove Friends Meeting of Pasadena was holding Sanctuary with fifteen persons, including five AWOL servicemen. (It lasted three and a half months, and "was never entered by military or civilian authorities.") The Minneapolis Friends Meeting offered Sanctuary to "any young men who are moved to reaffirm their commitment to God and their fellow men and their resistance to the draft. . . . we are willing to take over some of the burden of resistance which now falls so heavily on their shoulders." There was a GI–Civilian March for Peace in San Francisco, and 20,000 people walked nonviolently through the city. Our Sanctuary was in action on the world stage.

Maybe because Wittman was Chinese American, Buc chose him to tell his war to. He was Wittman's age and out of the service already, a veteran, not an AWOL soldier. He had flown dozens of air force missions in North Viet Nam (where we were not supposed to be). "I prevented war with China," he said, "because of my ability to speak Chinese." He and Wittman had different dialects, so spoke English. Buc intercepted a message in Chinese, warning our U.S. planes to get out of their airspace. The Chinese shot down a USAF jet. "I was able to verify that it was an accident, a mistake, they were not attacking. Two MiGs were scrambling to check on the intruders. One of the pilots sighted our aircraft and began to run through his standard sequence of arming missiles, locking on target, et cetera. The ground controller was telling him to just follow and observe, then screamed at him to break *off*. The pilot totally ignores his controller and shoots the plane down. It was obviously the act of an overtrained, highly zealous—deranged?—individual pilot in defiance of highest authority. The powers-that-be decided China had not committed an act of war."

What? We're at war with China? How widespread *is* this neverending war? It's World War III, but no one knows it? Wittman had trouble keeping track of the pilots—their side? our side?

Out of the Marathon, the GIs brought a game—Trust Ball. The Trust Ball, a beach ball, flew across the greensward from this one to that one. Wake up. Someone throws the ball at you—chooses you for truth—and you tell your feelings and thoughts about him or her. You throw it to another, and get truth about how someone thinks and feels about you. You might hear "I love you" and just exactly why—what it is about you that rouses such affection. The web of Sanctuary was woven strong by each talking with each. The citizens of Sanctuary talked about the Sanctuary, and one's place in it. They regarded and beheld themselves and their environment. They were conscious that they were conscious. Which is the highest high. Everyone kept marveling, "I am my real self here." Everyone was luminously beautiful. "Beautiful!" was an interjection of the era. Sanctuary was the ultimate love-in.

George threw the ball to Taña, and hugged and kissed her. He said to her, "I like the idea of walking up to a girl and hugging her and kissing her and saying Hi, and if she's married or not, it still gives you a good feeling, because you know you can do it, and nobody thinks anything about it. Like with Barbara and Bob, I'm sure they love each other, but Barb can go around and hug who she wants to. If you were out in public, you would be accused of being immoral, being indecent, by narrow-minded people. Like Walter, I can walk up to Walter, and he and I can put our arms around each other and say, 'Hi, what's happening,' and it gives you a good feeling that you can do that with another man without being called a homosexual. It gives a man a good feeling that he can hug who he wants to."

And Jeff said to Linda, "I met this one girl who's really out of sight, man. I rap with her for hours and hours, and that's all I've done is rap with her, you know. And before, man, I was, like, physical things first and then get to know them. . . . Sometimes I got pretty lonely."

Taña threw the ball to Wittman. He said, "I love *you*." She laughed, and said, "I love you too."

Time stilled, and the courtyard was a living tableau of Gauguin's last painting, *Who Are We? Where Do We Come From? Where Are We Going?* Men, women, children, an elder, animals, dogs, cats, birds, lizards sit, walk, sleep on the emerald-green ground. A peripatetic couple in robes lean toward each other, heads tilted, ear touching ear, one's arm about the other's shoulders. A young man scratches his head with his long arm, and looks like a monkey. The person trying to climb a palm tree could be a monkey too. The nearly naked young man reaching upward was Christ, and a beautiful woman holding her hands in gestures of blessing was becoming a goddess. The world was at a moment of perfection.

Vince disappeared. His parents phoned; they were in Waikīkī. Vince left the church grounds to meet them for dinner. They were waiting for him in their hotel room with the FBI, who took him away. The Sanctuary community never saw him again.

Walter, the Sanctuary's only known-to-be-Black AWOL GI, saw his mother and father on television. He wept hearing them tell the nation, "He's a good boy. We trust his judgment." Parents don't need to understand Viet Nam. Just say to the son, "What makes you happy makes us happy." The supporters of Sanctuary were proud; Walter chose the "white Sanctuary" over the demonstrations the Blacks were holding at the military bases.

In the courtyard, the sun especially lit upon the long blonde hair of two beautiful married ladies, Taña and Linda. Linda listened to the troubled young men speaking from the heart, and Taña drew them. Taña appreciated the way they appeared, and Linda appreciated the way they were. Linda listened to the soldiers for hours at a time. She asked them, "What are your hopes and dreams?" They created hopes and dreams for her. They were eager to have her study them, and took batteries of tests—the Raven Progressive Matrices intelligence test, the MMPI, Heinz Werner's test on their abilities to differentiate and integrate. She gave them scores on Erik Erikson's Identity Crisis Rating Scale, Personal

Alienation Rating Scale, and Social Alienation Rating Scale. She quantified their Moral Development and Ethical Clarity with Kohlberg's tests. They talked story about the pictures on the Thematic Apperception Test. Meanwhile, Taña drew and caught the qualities of eyes and mouth of this rebel, that peace activist, this and that soldier who had seen war. She captured the enlightenment in men's faces. She showed the men their portraits: You are this beautiful.

Out of a tree jumped crazy Harvey. He landed at Linda's feet. He had escaped from Tripler, wandered the Ko'olaus, and returned to Sanctuary. He asked Linda, "Is it bad if you feel like you'd like to be an ape? I was climbing a tree and began to feel just like an ape. Does that mean I'm becoming primitive and losing control?"

"What does an ape feel like?"

"Very free!" He laughed. "I guess exercise feels good."

Linda assured him that his new exhilarating feelings were okay. Playfulness is a sign of health. She sat back and enjoyed viewing the community. "Look at them. Before our eyes: losers to rebels, and rebels with a cause—to save us all. Making meaning in the face of absurdity."

Wittman asked Taña to be with him on Wedding Day, the thirty-first day of Sanctuary, when the Bust should have happened, but did not. There were four marriage ceremonies, weddings all Sunday long. John Witeck of the Resistance married Lucy Hashizumi, a Sanctuary supporter, and all the AWOL GIs present were best men. That included four new AWOLs: medics from the 9th Division—Daryl W. Benson, David Kisman, and Timothy Montagne—and Robert Long, a marine. They were all veterans of Viet Nam, and were taken into Sanctuary at the weddings. The grooms and grooms' men were bedighted with maile, long open strands of it from neck to knees. Some brides and bridesmaids wore muumuus with trains, and some wore miniskirts. Haku leis haloed brides and grooms. "Here comes the bride . . ." "I wanna hold your ha-a-and . . ." ". . . I promise to be true . . ." "In my life, I love you more. In my-y life . . ." And the long, long melisma of the Hawaiian wedding song.

Wittman and Taña stood in the back of the crowded church. Mario 'Ehukai DeWeese Ah Sing sat on his father's shoulders, so he could see and hear everything. They listened to four sets of self-written vows. It was like being married again and again and again and again. The whole community was vowing to support these marriages, and all marriages.

All were marrying all. We were now the married Sanctuary, and would stay wedded till death do us part.

Thomas Merton and the Dalai Lama discussed the timing of vows. Thomas Merton said that first we take the vow, then set out to live it. The Dalai Lama said that it is all right to live without vows, and after we fulfill them, then say vows.

To comply with the health and fire regulations, Wittman, Taña, and 'Ehukai left the church, and returned to Kahalu'u before the Bust.

The Sanctuary's leaders, its charter members Buffy and Cy, were not present on the day of the Bust, which came on September 12, in the early morning, about 5:50 a.m. Forty MPs swarmed over the grounds. They kicked in the locked doors, including the big church door, though the caretaker offered keys. Eight men, who were sleeping in the Coffeehouse, were apprehended; one of them was on legitimate leave. That night at 7:30 p.m., the MPs returned, again without a search warrant. They apprehended one GI who was on R&R from Viet Nam; he was a Canadian looking for information on how to apply for American citizenship. Sanctuary men already in the stockade were: Walter (he had tried to leave the country, and was caught in the airport), and Arthur Parket, Roger Edens, and Dan Overstreet, who had turned themselves in.

George returned from his speaking tour on the Mainland to find that the Sanctuary had vanished. He hid in the homes of antiwar strangers. His flight embarrassed the Resistance, who had announced that he would surrender at a demonstration. Five months after the Bust, he wrote a letter to Linda expressing his "loneliness, depression and guilt about betraying my commitment."

Don, who modeled the lion during the Marathon, had also left Sanctuary before the Bust, and was living in the mountains. Linda saw him on TV at a peace march. A wanted deserter, he clowned for the camera. About a year and a half after Sanctuary, he was arrested for smoking marijuana on Waikīkī Beach, tried as a deserter, and put into solitary confinement. (He later escaped, and no one could find his whereabouts, or how he was doing.)

From Canada, "Charley" wrote to the Church of the Crossroads, which he had formally joined. He confessed that he had avoided the

Bust "probably to avoid going to jail." For two weeks he was underground, moving from home to home, which drove him stir-crazy. "I stayed slightly drunk on beer pretty much all the time." One of his "captors," a speech professor, helped him write and rehearse a Moratorium Day speech. He was smuggled to the Mainland, where he gave his speech, and then went to Canada. He had a job and was doing okay. A year after Sanctuary, he crossed the border to visit his family, and was caught and court-martialed.

David, a veteran of Hamburger Hill, one of three survivors of a thirteen-man combat team, returned to his base, where he received psychiatric treatment and a slap-on-the-wrist sentence.

Harvey returned to the hospital, and got a medical discharge. Two years later, he wrote Linda that he was in college, active in the antiwar movement, doing draft counseling. Linda told Taña that his letter was full of rage but showed no signs of the illnesses she'd been called in to treat.

Jerry stayed for the Bust, as he had vowed from the start; he took his "stand until bodily removed." He was put in the brig, where he continued writing his diary and poems and parables. Reverend Larry Jones of the First Unitarian Church was his role model; he would be a prophet and teacher too.

The Sanctuary had lasted thirty-seven days. John Norris made this note in his log: "What became apparent to some of us church members who got to know the GIs as persons was that most of the men *became* conscientious objectors *BECAUSE* of their military experience. It was being *in* the military and for many of them being *in* Vietnam that brought them face to face with this conflict between their military duty and their consciences."

Linda wrote in her Ph.D. dissertation: "Vietnam duty provided the most unambiguous source of antiwar sentiment."

War causes peace.

Back in Kahaluʻu, ʻEhukai did not seem traumatized. He said, "I am a little guy, but I am not panicked."

Though the Ah Sings had not locked up their house, nothing was missing.

They took back with them an AWOL GI. They would set up Sanctuary at home. Theirs would have to be a secret, a secret safe house. The fugitive they aided and abetted was Eddie, a helicopter door-gunner in Viet Nam, who got to Hawai'i on R&R.

"Where you from, Eddie?"

"Oklahoma."

Eddie was jumpy and hyper, and seemed too short and too young to be in the service, stunted or not yet full-grown. His skin was too red, sunburned haole skin, and he had that blue-eyed stare that haoles get who've been too long in the tropics. He was to stay put in the back bedroom.

In the rush leaving the Church of the Crossroads, Eddie had not been formally received into Sanctuary. He had not called his commanding officer and declared himself AWOL against the war. Wittman, who had to protect everyone—home, family, everyone—would never consider telling him to inform the army about his whereabouts. The war was getting worse. Across the Bay, at the Kaneohe Marine Corps Air Station, battles were going on between Blacks and Whites. At the least, save this one person from getting killed, or killing any others. Give Eddie haven until the war's over. Think long-term.

Wittman and Taña discussed what they should do.

"This is not proper Sanctuary," said Taña. "Sanctuary is over. It's against the law to hide AWOLs. There is no sacred or legal tradition of a home Sanctuary. We can be arrested and go to jail for hiding a lawbreaker, just as if we were aiding and abetting any criminal, a bank robber or a murderer."

"We're all in danger, Taña. We're already in danger. But it's not too late. We could ask Eddie to leave. Should I ask him to leave?"

"We have to think out our values, Wittman. What do we value? I would risk our immediate safety for a safer world in the long run. I would want some good family to hide our own son from war."

"And we'd be setting him an example. He'll learn that war is not the only action that makes a boy a man. Nonviolent peaceful action also tests bravery. Okay, I'm for making a home Sanctuary."

So they called 'Ehukai in from play, and explained that Eddie was an escaped soldier. And they were hiding him and breaking the law.

"I understand," said 'Ehukai. "Eddie is a secret, and I will not tell on him. He is our secret."

Eddie hadn't heard of a Statement of Conscience. He had yet to be taught the principles of Sanctuary. Taña told him the family rule from before their kid was born: Every evening, no matter what, everyone sits down for a sit-down dinner, and we converse. Eddie had the discipline of Basic Training: chow down—five minutes flat. He ate in the cave of his bent head, hunched shoulders, and arms. Drawing him out, 'Ehukai said, "Talk story to me about Viet Nam, Eddie."

Eddie stood up. "I stood in the door of the gunship, like this." He held an imaginary machine gun against his chest, jerking. "And I hosed 'em like hosin' with water, hundreds of rounds, like water pourin' out. I felt high. I was high. The highest feelin' in the world. We're flyin'. The door gun pushes against me like this, and I lean into it, and push, push against it. I can't fall out. The chopper flies low and sideways, and I'm hosin' 'em. I shake all over. It's jerkin' my guts. Three hundred rounds per second stream out of my gun. Nothin' like it." He did not say what or whom he was shooting, whether he had hit them or not.

On only the third night of hiding out, the door-gunner left his room, left the house, went out. You would think he understood, you didn't want the neighbors to know that a fugitive was hiding out. You didn't want Landlord Tong to think Wittman and Taña were trying to sneak in an extra occupant. He was jeopardizing them, home and Sanctuary.

Eddie's hosts found themselves waiting up for him, as if they were his parents and he was out late after curfew. They stayed awake worrying over him, talking about him. There was banging on the door in the dark of night. It was Mr. Bong of Bong's Grocery with a phone message from the Police Department in Kailua. Wittman had better come right over and take responsibility for Eddie. Mr. Bong let Wittman borrow the Bong's Grocery van. At the police station, Wittman vouched for Eddie's good character. Wittman looked local, and Eddie looked like a boy. (He *was* a boy, too young to vote, too young to drink, too young to rent a car—you had to be twenty-three to rent a car in Hawai'i. Wittman suddenly wondered, did young men need a driver's license to drive a jeep or a tank?) Eddie had borrowed somebody's motorcycle and run a stop sign, and the motorcycle died in the middle of the intersection. He couldn't kick-start it up again, kept jumping on the kick-start until the police came and got him. They let him go in Wittman's custody, in loco parentis. Wittman paid the fine or bail or bribe.

"Hey, thanks, man," Eddie said. "I'll pay you back. I'll square it with you." He had the good manners to say Thanks.

"It's okay," said Wittman. "You're welcome." That thank-you would have to do for the meals, for taking his laundry to the Laundromat, for the room and board. They had to entertain their unlimited houseguest, and entertain him well, so he wouldn't go out. "The way to really thank us, someday, if need be, you hold Sanctuary for somebody."

Eddie stayed home for the next couple of days and nights. He made model cars on the kitchen table. The Hygenic Store and Bong's Grocery had stocks of model cars. He sneaked to the stores in roundabout ways through the bamboo and cane. 'Ehukai helped assemble and glue. They did not read the directions, and glued wrong parts to wrong parts, and had pieces left over. Maybe Eddie couldn't read. Are illiterates allowed into the army, and given remedial reading classes?

One day, when Taña was not in her studio, Eddie and 'Ehukai lined the cars all the way around the porch railing. Eddie hurried back and forth along the row and set the cars on fire. Torched them. They exploded in chemical-color flames. Popped and sizzled. This one caught fire from that one, poof, poof, poof. 'Ehukai jumped and leapt, ran up and down the stairs, rushed toward and away from the flaming cars. The alcohol, glue, and plastic left patches of car colors and black on the railing. Eddie said that when he was a kid he'd made and burned five hundred model cars. He couldn't have been poor. A poor kid would've treasured his one model car. And Viet Nam hadn't turned him into a firebug; before Viet Nam he'd been destroying his creations.

Eddie could not stay hidden. He had to go out. He didn't come home nights; he slept days. Taña explained the risks, and the consequences of getting caught—their cover would be blown for any other AWOL or refugee from this war and next wars. "Also, you have to stay hidden from Big Eustace and the locals. They will beat you up for being haole, let alone a deserter. The Hawaiians are super-patriotic." "Yeah," he said, hanging his head. "Yeah. Yeah. I know. I know." He must have been no different with his nagging mother, always telling him what to do.

Then, one day, the knock on the door was another AWOL GI asking for Sanctuary. "Sanctuary," he said, like a secret password. His name was Sam, a tall athletic-looking all-American type person. He brought a duffel bag full of possessions; he'd packed for a long trip, and had a note-book. Eddie owned hardly anything, and had had to be outfitted with a toothbrush. Good. Two of them—they could keep each other company. Sam ought to be a good influence on Eddie. His square, tan-covered notebook was entitled "Statement of Consciousness." It was subtitled "Journal." He'd written his name, rank, and serial number on the title page, and "United States Army." His handwriting was like a kid's, some lettering, some script. "I cannot bear the military INjustice. I did not join the U.S Army to be under The Military Code of INjustice. It is everywhere throughout the Service. Whereas, I resign. The INjustice would shock you. Hypercritical perverts took over The Army, including the officers, many whom are homosexuals." He wrote a page of slogans: "Make love, not war." "Love is all you need." The rest of the notebook was empty. Well, Sam was capable of writing. Maybe he could develop his Statement of Consciousness, and influence Eddie to write a state-ment. Maybe not—he'd signed his name as if to say, The End. The notebook was supposedly a journal, but he'd only written in it that one day.

Taña gave Eddie a sketchbook. He copied Sam's slogans, and signed his name.

Like everybody in America, Sam kept speaking about being free. "I joined the service to defend our freedom. I should be free in the army. But in the army, I'm not free. I have a right to go AWOL. It's a free country. We're going to Viet Nam to bring them freedom, but *we* don't have freedom. The military mentality is not free." He hadn't been to Viet Nam.

Eddie did not mind Sam's talking about Viet Nam without having been there. And Sam liked having the little guy along, looking up to him. Eddie listened to Sam in admiration, such a verbal, smart sidekick he'd teamed up with. The small soldier and the tall soldier walked the same way; they made their shoulders big, and moved shoulders and feet in rhythm. They wore aloha shirts from the PX. Their haole skin was parboiled by the Viet Nam sun and the Hawai'i sun.

The literature of this home Sanctuary was comic books. Their favorite was *X-Men*, and their favorite power was invisibility. Sue Storm, the Invisible Girl. To be able to disappear at will was 'Ehukai's favorite power too.

So here they were, two haole deserters living in the back room, on futons on the bare floor, like Japanese. They came and went, treated the place like a hotel with maid service. A crash pad for AWOLs. They were not picking up on the culture of the household: Tell your family where you're going, and when you'll be back. Greet one another good morning, even if you get up in the afternoon. Bid farewell, even if you're just going through the bamboo and cane to the store.

Now two AWOLs were calling for help any hour of the day or night. They ran out of gas; they're in Pearl City. They got into a fight with some sailors. They're almost drowned in the Toilet Bowl. Some local haole girls had told them that the Toilet Bowl was a good, safe diving spot. Their borrowed car was chased by a car full of marines. They got away, and drove about the island until they met up with those same marines. The branches of the service fight one another. The island is full of boy gangs, including cops, who cruise around until they run into the enemy. You would think that those who'd made it back from Viet Nam would be extra careful. But they're excited, speedy, off guard now that they're home.

Wittman and Taña trapped their AWOLs in a calm moment, and asked them about the future; they ought to be formulating one. There has got to be an end to this host-and-hostessing of houseguests. They asked, "What are your plans?"

"I don't know."

"What will you be doing next? What's your next step?"

"I don't know."

"Where will you go when you leave us?"

"Switzerland, I guess."

"Sweden. You mean Sweden. What about Canada?" The one-way plane ticket to Canada would be cheaper than to Sweden.

"Is Sweden in Switzerland? Is Canada next to Sweden?"

Taña drew a map of the world, and informed the men and her son, "Here's Hawai'i, and here's the Mainland—the Beeeg Island—South America and North America—the U.S., Canada, and Mexico. We're parallel to Mexico, and almost Viet Nam. And on the other side of the Atlantic Ocean is Europe, and up north in Europe is Scandinavia. Sweden is right here. Switzerland is down there. It's Sweden that has been harboring evaders of the war. They're the country that gives the Nobel Peace Prize." It was hard for any of them to plan the future.

What's the use? All endeavor—education, work, thought, even art—has led to war. The AWOLs can't take care of themselves here, let alone in a foreign country. No fair just shipping them off. They'd be international fugitives wanted for desertion in wartime, never mind that it's not a war, it's a police action.

Eddie went over to the sink and downed painkillers with a handful of water, his back to everybody, wolfing the pills. His bruises from auto and bike accidents and fights were turning yellow and purple, healthier colors than black and blue. "My head hurts from thinking," he said.

The two younger people looked with anger at the two older people. These established adults were not providing enough. They were taking away freedom, threatening the youths with exile, putting on the pressure for money and goals. AWOL Eddie and AWOL Sam went out, and stayed out missing for four nights in a row.

Sam came back by himself to report that Eddie was in the neurosurgical ward at Tripler Hospital. Wittman told Sam to stay hidden, and hitchhiked to that pink hospital on the hill overlooking Pearl Harbor. To the southeast was Punch Bowl, the extinct volcano where servicemen are buried. Wittman walked past kapu signs and uniformed officers, and through the swinging doors to Neurosurgical Post Op. There was a ward full of young men who had been wounded in the head and/or spine. A totally paralyzed man, quadriplegic, lay on his stomach, his head out over the foot of his bed, his face toward the floor. He was looking down at the bare floor, no book or magazine beneath his eyes. He could be asleep or unconscious or dead. Like in a war-movie ward, two rows of beds were lined against the walls with an aisle down the middle, and in each bed was a grotesquely wounded soldier. An unwatched, unheard television set stuck out from each wall.

Wittman walked between the rows, looking for his AWOL soldier. He had to look hard at each one to try to identify Eddie. Skulls were bandaged, faces wrapped; eye slits and nose and mouth holes, like the Invisible Man. People hung in hoists and harnesses. Each one was in a different position in casts and amid equipment.

In the far corner, Eddie was sitting on the edge of his high bed, legs dangling. He was smoking a cigarette. He looked like a raccoon, peeping out of swollen black-and-blue circles. A bandage went around his face as if to keep his jaw from falling open. Wittman sat next to him on the bed and took a cigarette. The two of them sat there, slump-shouldered, smoking.

Wittman said, "You should take care of yourself. You look awful. What happened?"

"I don't remember everything. I was on the bike. Then I was in the air over the street. I hit my head on a pole. I shoulda worn a helmet."

"Take better care of yourself. Are you hurting? Pain?"

"Nah. I'm on painkillers. Nothing broken. They put me in here for observation. If I pass out, they have to wake me up. I haven't passed out."

Eddie was the only patient awake. Wittman asked after the most spectacularly wounded. Eddie pointed them out one by one. "That poor guy over there—that White one"—you could tell by the skin of his upper arms, which weren't bandaged, that he was White—"he's the sergeant who shot up Kaneohe Marine Corps Air Station. He shot that guy over there for fucking his wife. And him too, and him. He's famous, in the news, on TV—the sergeant who shot up his barracks. Some men took his side. If I was him, I wouldn't come to. Come to, he'll face murder charges. *His* friends ganged up on *him*. And the MPs shot *them*—that one and that one. That paralyzed one over there shot himself after shooting *him*. The nurses will come in pretty soon and turn him over. *He* shot *him*, and the MPs took him down." Quite a few had unbandaged black skin. "He shot him and him. That one over there didn't shoot nobody, just himself. These are the lucky guys, got shot and lived." So there were people here from two riots—a race riot and a romance riot. "And that guy in the coma—the vegetable—they found him in the Witch's Brew." A siren girl had told him to swim in the Witch's Brew. Not a one had been flown here from the fighting in Viet Nam. They wouldn't be counted as Viet Nam casualties, but Wittman thought they should have been.

Wittman's namesake had spent the Civil War in hospitals, reading to the wounded, giving them nickels to buy milk, writing to their mothers, holding the dying in his arms, and kissing them goodbye.

Wittman asked, *sotto voce*, "Are you under arrest?"

"Nah. Nobody mentioned AWOL to me." Eddie talked loud, not worried about being overheard, everybody passed out. Maybe men in his unit were covering up for his absences at roll call, as they did for Prewitt.

"I don't need any more hospital," said Eddie. "Let's get outta here."

He put on his aloha shirt on top of the hospital gown, which he tucked into his blue jeans. He didn't check out, skipped the paperwork, went AWOL from Tripler. From a laundry bin in a hallway, Wittman nicked an outfit for himself, a worn green hospital gown that had a tiny spot of blood and "Government Issue" on its front, or back. He wore it like a coat, flapping open. It was fashionable to dress as if you were a patient in a psycho ward.

He escorted Eddie hitchhiking back to Kahalu'u, kept a watch over him in case he passed out from concussion. Shook him awake when he nodded off.

About ten o'clock one evening, Eddie and Sam drove up in a car, had a snack, and announced that they were turning themselves in. "I'm turning myself in." "We're turning ourselves in. Drive us to Schofield. Turn us in."

They packed their few possessions. Eddie said for 'Ehukai, who was asleep, to finish the model cars. Sam gave Taña his journal. "Hang on to it for me."

Wittman driving, both men got in the back seat and dropped acid, swallowed every cap they'd been holding. "Wow." "Wow." Neither of them talkers, they made noises at the hallucinations that came on and whizzed by and through them.

Wittman asked, "Are you sure you want to do this?"

The sounds and images of his voice hung in space. This? You sure? You want? You do? You? This? Pictures and feelings ballooned large and ballooned small. "Wow!" "Wow!"

"You don't want to change your minds?" asked Wittman.

"Oh, wow!" they said as they changed minds.

Wittman tried not to think about five to fifteen years in prison, so they wouldn't pick up on that bad trip and flip out. Don't bring them down. How to stuff them with resources? Tripmaster Wittman tried to imprint his charges with all the wisdom he could think of. "There's only a few life tasks you, we have to do," he said. "Create one good human being—yourself. And you don't have to love everybody. Just love one other human being." Too bad they were so against homosexuals. "And stop the War in Viet Nam." Working against war would give them a politics, a way to connect up with the whole real world. "Look. The moon is out. You can see the Rabbit in the Moon. The Man in the Moon's right eye—that's the Rabbit's head. Her ears are where the left eye is. The

Rabbit is stirring a pot of medicine food for you. You will be all right. See her? The Medicine Rabbit. All of existence is working to benefit you."

"Wow!" said Sam.

"Wow!" said Eddie.

No one thought about the astronauts who'd gone to the moon and back.

Giving the nonreaders words-to-live-by, Wittman quoted the healing poet of the American Civil War: "This is what you shall do: Love the earth and sun and the animals, despise riches, give alms to every one that asks, stand up for the stupid and crazy, devote your income and labor to others, hate tyrants, argue not concerning God, have patience and indulgence toward the people, take off your hat to nothing known or unknown." Taking off one's hat is like saluting.

Wittman drove toward a guard station at the entrance to Schofield. The kiosk was lit up in the black night. The two guards with guns and helmets stood out starkly. The barricade was at its lowered position.

"Stop," said Sam. "You can drop us off here." Wittman parked in the main driveway of Schofield Army Base. Sam and Eddie, stoned out of their minds, got out of the car, and walked extra straight toward the gate. Eddie turned around, and called out to Wittman, "You get fifty dollars apiece for us. Don't forget, collect your money." He took a step toward the car. "Tell them you captured us. Fifty dollars apiece reward. You got a hundred dollars coming to you."

Wittman watched Sam and Eddie approach the gate, which opened for them. The MPs were in a jeep facing the AWOLs. Suddenly, its high beams flashed on and lit up the two men, who walked into the lights with their hands up over their heads.

Wittman hoped that this sight of his soldier friends would not be his last. He resolved he must find ways to bring them safely back home. He drove back to the Windward Side, and abandoned the car on a shoulder of Kam Highway. He walked to Kahalu'u, which is not a town, or any kind of official place. It's nowhere, a place for fugitives and refugees to keep coming.

Wittman and Taña stayed in Hawai'i until 'Ehukai graduated from the free school at the Church of the Crossroads, then Stevenson Junior High, then Roosevelt High School. All summer after graduation, beautiful girls from his class phoned asking for Mario. They talked with him about the future. "Remember me? I've been thinking about you. I'm so concerned for you, Mario. What are you going to do with yourself? Aren't you scared about what to do with your life?"

"Yes, I'm concerned about what to do," he answered. "No, I don't have a job yet. No, I don't have plans for college."

"Want to hear what I'm doing? I'm supporting myself, and getting an education, and I'm being of service to my country. I'm being all I can be. You can be all you can be too."

Those girls had become military recruiters! Girl graduates were talking the guys into joining them in the new volunteer Army / Navy / Air Force / Marines.

"No, thank you," said Mario. "I'm not interested in joining the military. Please don't call me anymore."

Wittman and Taña hugged each other for joy.

EARTH

There! That's what I wrote during two years of living at friends' houses after the fire—Bessie's back bedroom, Danny and Hillary's cottage. I wrote past the place where the burned book left off. But found no happy ending. The War in Viet Nam won't come to a happy ending. Fiction won't tell me what's happened to "Eddie" and "Sam" and "Sheraton" and "Clift," people Earll and I knew in our real Hawai'i years, whose actual names I can't remember. I lost the "Statement of Consciousness" journal in the fire; I should have sent it to the parents, whose address in the Midwest was on the last page. I should have written more letters to my brothers Joe and Norman in Da Nang and Korea. I shouldn't've left their APO and ranks off their mail, which probably never reached them; I was refusing to go along with any military system. I should have better counseled my sister Carmen, who married a soldier; he walked point on jungle patrol. The wedding was in the chapel at Schofield; I was matron of honor, and the minister—Wes Geary—was the one who bullhorned the Sanctuary. I should have demanded that Earll not ship out with the Merchant Marine for Viet Nam. Our son, Joseph, and I went aboard the ship, the Sea Train *Carolina*, to say goodbye, and saw the torpedoes and rockets roped to the deck.

But it can't be too late. Things that fiction can't solve must be worked out in life.

My mother comes to me in dreams. She is at her largest and most powerful, midlife, my age now. She says, "What have you been doing to educate America? What have you done to educate the world? Have you taught everybody yet?" The Chinese idiom for "everybody" is "big family." "Have you taught the big family yet? You go teach the big family. Teach the nation family." Waking up, I am imbued with the urgency to get to school, gather classes, invent workshops, start new schools. Educate everybody. That is my charge from my mother. My calling and vocation. My mother has always busied herself with telling me my life's task: the education of America and the entire world. In China, I saw an enormous temple with gold-and-red columns and a sweeping roof, many rooms, bells, gongs, no statues. At its center was a high altar honoring this four-word poem: EDUCATION HAS NO CLASS. Meaning that education is classless; anyone can learn. A magnificent temple had been built to that idea. My mother passes on to me orders from the eternal ancestors. "Educate everyone. You do it."

Men in war and men in prison hear their mothers talking to them. MaMa had the ability to talk all the way to Viet Nam to Joe. He heard her on the aircraft carrier, heard her voice over the sounds of the rocket launchers and the planes taking off and landing. She scolded him not to get hurt. Don't you get killed in Da Nang Harbor. Don't you get killed anywhere. You better come home alive and well.

Because I asked everywhere for Books of Peace, and I told everyone that I had lost the one I was writing, veterans of war began sending me their stories. Bob Golling, whom I met during a visit to San José State, writes me this letter: "Dear Lady, I can talk-sea-story and war-story to you. I was USN from 65 to 69; many strange* and wonderful stories I hope to write in the new year 92. . . ." (Asterisk his, for itself, doesn't refer to anything else.)

He encloses a story, "On the Gun Line, 12May69." A ship is rocking in the river current. "The Captain wanted to have ready steam in case we had to kick it in the ass and get the hell out of there. . . . Maybe he didn't like the tradition of the Captain going down with his ship. . . . The afternoon had been hot and yellow, muggy, summer temperatures growing rice in thousands of fields." They couldn't see the fields through the trees; the yellow was from the sun and the firing. "One round every 15–20 minutes . . . We were shooting at what? We didn't know. The enemy, of course. The Viet Cong, whoever that was. Boooommmm! We didn't want to be there; we wanted to be back at Subic Bay, P.I., going on 'liberty.' Booomm! The 5" gun would punctuate any day dream. Day dream, night dream, who could tell what was real?"

Another Viet Nam veteran I met at San José had a name like my husband's, Errol. He gave me his service pin. "I carried this for twenty years." It was the black eagle-anchor-globe insignia of the marines. "You take it. I want you to have it." I thanked him for the pin, and for all he gave in the war. But now I'm the one carrying the pin. . . .

Local veterans I don't know are writing me letters of sympathy and apology. They are sorry that they did not come to my rescue during the fire. "I thought about breaking into your house, and saving your writing."

They also send me fuzzy mimeographs and burry tapes about a religion that they discovered in Viet Nam. Caodaism. Caodai temples have an eye above the main door, like the one eye on the dollar bill. Those temples were not fired upon. Maybe they were VC; maybe they were CIA. This present era we're living through is named the "Third Amnesty of God in the Orient." The First Amnesty and the Second Amnesty were when other religions began. Several veterans sent me "The Outline of Caodaism":

> Humanity lives in sufferings.
> We suffer as a result of heart breaking ideological conflict; cruel wars, effete ethics. We suffer a terrible form of anguish with a mixture of inferiority complexes, moral sterility, and spiritual void. It is our duty, to seek, by all means, if not to end those sufferings, at last, to relieve them.

The paper explained "GOD'S MESSAGE." God speaks in the first person: "I founded at different epochs, five branches of the Great Way." The world's religions were "each based on the customs of the race particularly to apply them. Nowadays, all parts of the world are explored: people knowing each other better, aspire to a real peace."

The Viet Nam veterans had saved this material for twenty years. It came with maps of North and South Viet Nam, and a map of the whole country in relation to China and Thailand. The Holy See of Caodaism is northeast of the Mekong River and halfway between Bien Hoa and Phnom Penh, Cambodia. At the "Holy Mother Temple," rituals, incense, prayers, hymns are offered four times a day, and "high masses celebrated at Temple at Midnight on the 14th and 30th of each month (lunar month)." "Adherents' Duties" are: "Not to kill living beings . . . Not to covet in order to avoid the fall into materialism through the needs of possession and domination . . . Not to practice high living . . . Not to be tempted by luxury which attracts a cruel Karma . . . Not to sin by word." I am fascinated to know that islands of peace existed in war, and that American soldiers found them in Viet Nam.

Fires, past and current, set the veterans to writing me. They have flashbacks, and they recall bombings, but also moments and islands of peace. Paul Woodruff, who was at the dream symposium, writes on my birthday. He came back from Viet Nam feeling "like a fire had burned my past life. I had my things and my family and girlfriend, and other friends too but none of these meant what they should have meant to me." He went alone to a cabin in the woods where he had gone as a child with his family. "There I got to know books and writing again, and began to feel a bit more like myself." When he saw a picture of young men on the way to the Persian Gulf, an image came to him: his brother's harmonica sent back from Marine Boot Camp. "Trainees are forbidden to have anything with them that is a reminder of their former lives. . . . My brother came home from Vietnam as I did; and although he had a rough landing, he is doing well. He is a school psychologist, and played the harmonica to his own sons every night at bedtime when they were young. . . . I also remembered a silly thing I had done, which I had forgotten the day after: halting, during an operation, near a tall half-built pagoda—not a sanctuary. We were under fire and for some crazy reason I took shelter in the mud and bamboo huts at the base of the pagoda, where the workmen lived, though the thin walls offered no protection at all. The one-eyed Hoa Hao warlord, whose adviser I was supposed to be, had to send his servant to call me out to the safety of a ditch. I knew better than to hide behind bamboo, but for some reason I thought I would be safe there. This was somewhere in Tinh Bien District of Chau Doc Province. That was my false sanctuary. (A few weeks later the warlord, who had come over with his men to our side, was shot through the one eye by a sniper. Everyone knew that was the only way he could be killed, because his skin was protected by a charm. Has any veteran told you how much magic there was in Vietnam?)"

Yes, veterans of Viet Nam keep telling me about the magic that once surrounded them, and refugees also tell of having left a place where laws of nature were different—were magic. The very air had been enchanted. You had to roll up the windows of your truck against the highland air. Breathing the spirit-filled air caused a rock to grow inside your stomach, like cancer. The rice was magic too. A Viet Cong could live on one bowl of rice a day, and run as fast as a car all day long. And he wore shower shoes. A Montagnard tribesman found a white elephant near Pleiku, and brought it to the Saigon Zoo. In wartime, a child poet always comes. One was born in 1958 near Hanoi, in the Red River Delta; his name is Tran Dang Khoa. Soldiers would take shelter with him, and hear him. He sang of white storks, black rain, the rice.

A white elephant was born when the Buddha was born. A white buffalo calf will be born in America; peace will come with the return of White Buffalo Woman.

I have been given directions on how to get to lands of peace. There are routes along the Mekong River, and in the Mekong Delta all the way to and from Cambodia. (They were traveled in safety by both VC and locals, until those who didn't understand about sanctuary areas tried to find and destroy the "Ho Chi Minh Trail.") From the three-story medicine-manufacturing drugstore in Cholon (the Chinatown of Saigon), I'm to drive Highway 4 past the Taoist pagoda Phu Lam, past the Buddhist cemetery–refugee camp. (You used to have to go through the 9th Division's first and second checkpoints.) Then go over a single-lane bridge to My Tho, a village of houses with holes from shelling. At the docks on the Mekong River, I'll find a boat flying a brownish-lavender flag with a reverse swastika; a wooden cross is nailed to the bridge. Take the boat downriver for about two miles, maneuvering amongst motor launches, gunboats, sampans, rowboats, hydrofoils. On the banks are fishing huts, microwave-relay transmitters, the hulk of a downed helicopter, cranes that are always dredging up something, even wrecks from World War II. Around a bend, on your right, Phuong Island—sanctuary—will appear. You can't miss it. A temple nine stories high rises up on pylons over the water; and beside it, a pagoda with two tall green freestanding columns holds up an arch with the name of the island across it—Con Phuong. A globe made of metal tubing, the continents of twisted iron, hangs suspended from the arch. On top of the pagoda is a metal cutout about twenty-five feet high of Jesus and a disciple, maybe Peter, in saffron robes. On the other side of the cutout is Buddha, sitting on the world. The yellow dragon of Viet Nam coils around nine blue-and-red columns, atop which are yellow artichokes and pink artichokes. An eighty-foot map of Viet Nam, north and south, stands on a platform; plastic soldiers and tanks mark the highways and hills. If you arrive at night, four long neon lights in the four directions will guide your way.

The islanders will rush to greet you; they'll press close to look at you and welcome you. They'll take you by the hand, and lead you up four cement ramps to the "prayer platform," a circle one hundred feet in diameter. Always the people are praying. They pray in even ranks behind a row of monks. A deep gong sounds from afar, and then each monk rings the bell on the palm of his hand. Now and again, everyone makes the Catholic sign of the cross, and kneel-bows three times in the *lai*. (*Lai* may be the same as the *lai* in Chinese which means "tradition" and "manners.") The islanders will ask, "Do you want me to teach you how to pray?"

They'll take you to the ceremonial hall, which has no glass in the windows; the smell of gasoline blows through everywhere. You meet the elders, and Dao Dua, the Coconut Monk. He may not speak with you if he's under a vow of silence. He'll smile at you with his whole head, though. "His whole head smiled," someone wrote. For years, he held the vow that he would not talk until the war was over. But at the Tet Offensive, he decided that he must not deny himself speech as a way to peace. Some of the veterans who wrote to me were there when Dao Dua spoke. He was directing the making of an octagonal table and the two-story building that would house the table and a peace conference. He said, "Thieu would sit here. Ky would sit here." Dao Dua is a hunchback, only four and a half feet tall, and hasn't lain down since the 1930s. But others describe him as a thin Taoist with long hair, not hunched over at all; and he was not living on the island but in prison, fasting with three hundred draft resisters. And he has a cat and two mice for pets. Maybe there are many monks known as the Coconut Monk. And Taoists are said to have the ability to appear in many places at once. Some say that Dao Dua was a Frenchman with an M.S. in chemical engineering, who came to Indochina as a colonial administrator. The French injected him with "a poison that made him crazy." He left his wife and child, and lived in a coconut tree. He got the name Coconut Monk because he and John Steinbeck IV brought two coconuts to U.S. ambassador Ellsworth Bunker; one was carved with Bunker's name and the other with "Kennedy SOS," which is what John Kennedy carved on a coconut after PT 109 sank.

If you're lucky, Dao Dua himself will invite you—"We go NOW!"— on a tour of Con Phuong. To reach the village proper, you always have to go through an immense cement building on pylons; it's a home and a shop and a meeting place and a market. You follow Dao Dua, wending through alleys, and arrive inside houses of woven grasses and thatch. At the Teacher's Chamber, there are cardboard walls with differential equations and English words on them. The windows are in the shapes of crescent moons, triangles, and stars, lit by green, pink, and blue neon. People come forward to try out their English. And the children, who are everywhere, want you to learn how to pray.

There's a house that's like a musical society of old ladies; they sing, and play guitar and "bloot," which is how they say "flute." From the opposite shores of the river would come bursts of machine-gun fire and blurping and thwomping mortar rounds. (In 1970, the Coconut Monk held off a flotilla of the Vietnamese navy, and magically saved the island from obliteration.)

If you go there, see whether you can find the albino teen-ager, a man by now, with blond hair and light eyes. And the holy man who speaks French; he wore a gold turban, and lived in a room with a balcony that floats on the water. They'd sat evenly so that the house wouldn't tip over. And there's a tailor who sews Tao suits for the American visitors, and would not take payment. "You Tao man now." And what happened to the purple-robed blind man with a bump where his third eye would be? They'll all invite you to come stay live with them.

There was only one part of the island, I'm told, that was somewhat off-limits. Refugees from the Tet Offensive, maybe VC, not part of the community, were living on the other end of Con Phuong. If you wanted to go to the perimeters anyway, the unarmed Tao patrols would walk with you. The Tao patrols are not a police force; they're omnipresent in case some citizen needs assistance, medical help, or spiritual help, or even help building or moving something. At the time of the Tet Offensive, six thousand people lived on the island, which is a sandbar only one mile long.

As you leave, everyone urges you not to go, and please come back soon. Dao Dua will give you farewell gifts — incense from the wood of a rare tree, bloots, pipes for smoking, a bell made of brass shell casings and shrapnel. Whoever hears that bell becomes enlightened.

Among the letters, one Anonymous Veteran wrote explaining to me why veterans need to report to women. Yes, women are sanctuary; women bring soldiers home. But also women need to hear the war stories. "Native Americans consider war an altered state for which warriors were prepared with ceremony, and from which warriors were welcomed back with ceremony. In this way the entire community (women, children, old people, the ill and handicapped) participated in the war. They shared the risk and responsibility, the suffering and loss, the victory or defeat, and then went 'home' together. I have met many men for whom women were the way home."

How should I reply to all these people? In person. I have to look in their eyes and faces, and tell them, You are home. Thank you. I have to give them something, reciprocate gifts. And happy-end the wars.

I'm asking the Community of Mindful Living, Buddhists, to help me organize a workshop. Sherdyl (Charlie) Motz, six years U.S. Navy, one year on River Patrol Force in Viet Nam, Sufi, volunteers there, and will seek out his every veteran contact. He's sending and handing out invitations to come gather for "Reflective Writing, Mindfulness, and the War: A Day for Veterans and Their Families."

A veteran of the Korean War wants his name taken off our mailing list. "The Viet Nam vets are getting all the attention." But we're inviting veterans of every war, and their families. Everyone hears only "Viet Nam." Viet Nam is the war on the American conscience. "Korean Vet" warns, Don't trust veterans to know about war and peace: ". . . a young scholar, such as a grad student at Berkeley could have a greater knowledge and a more accurate perspective on a war than any veteran of that war who might brag that he knows the war because he was there— something I often argued with returning servicemen who visited the Berkeley Campus during the Vietnam war. . . . Emperor Liu Ch'i said, 'Piss in the hats of intellectuals and generals.' Liu Ch'i, I believe was onto something in his not giving special respect to the competence of veterans of war.' " Korean Vet read about my fire losses. "I still regret not having rescued your manuscript and other goods from your home when I was so near there during the fire." But I am not to feel guilty. "In war what conjures up guilt more than killing is letting one's friends down, one's failure to act and to brave adversity. I can imagine the conditions being tough enough that you should have turned back. I would not want you to feel remorse for not having braved impossible circumstances. . . . Take care, dear stranger!"

My life rushes toward the day of the workshop, June 19, 1993. It's the

Fifth Month, Fifteenth Day on the lunar calendar, the holiday for Chu Ping, whose name means "peace." He immolated himself in water. The dragon boats race—even in the U.S., in Oakland, on Lake Merritt—to honor his martyrdom for peace.

Oh, no. Three days before the workshop, my mother wants to come make *joong chay* with me. She wants to stay a couple of weeks, maybe forever, and live with us in the temporary house we just bought. I always fall in with her time and her uproar. She wants to be taken to a big Chinatown to buy leaves. She's gotten harder of hearing and seeing; I have to interpret shadows and lights and shapes. She doesn't much care about sounds. She never listens; she's the one does the talking. "All I have left is my mouth," she says. "I am nothing but a mouth." She still gets angry seeing and hearing repercussions from to-do in China. I yell benign realities at her. I have to learn to yell without getting mad.

We go to Oakland Chinatown, Asiatown now—less hassle than Big City San Francisco. Oakland Asiatown is a recombinant Cambodia and Laos and Viet Nam and Thailand and the Philippines and Korea and China, but my mother is seeing the Stockton Chinatown of long ago. "There they are!" she shouts. "Joong leaves!" But they aren't there; she's hallucinating them. They aren't anywhere that I can see in the piles and aisles. "No, MaMa. I'll ask for them." But I can't leave her while I run around the market. She'd get lost; she'd get knocked over in the crowd. "And green beans!" she shouts. "Take me to the green beans." I pick one of the narrow, dark aisles, and guide her by the arm into it, and—lucky—we come upon shelves and bins of green beans and peas. Some were marked in English, "Beans," "Peas." I recognize the Chinese for "green" and "bean" or "pea" (they don't distinguish). But which of these green beans/peas of myriad shapes and sizes does my mother want? She sees something red, and hollers, "Swan-brand flour! Buy lots of boxes." I yell, "This is Swan brand for baking cakes. They don't make Swan-brand flour anymore." I mean, that's Swans Down Cake Mix, no more Swans Down All Purpose Flour. ("Goose"/"swan" the same.) She yells, "It *is* Swan brand, and I do want to make cakes and chay." I say, "I don't think it would be good for making chay. Too sweet. It's got sugar and powdered eggs and powdered milk in it." Everybody must be looking at us, two white-haired ladies from the country talking too loud. I've regressed to adolescence, minding what people think. We stand out; we look and act like nobody else. She hollers, "Buy the Swan flour! Buy

green beans! Buy joong leaves! Buy yellow sugar! Buy *nahw mai fun!*"
Nahw mai fun is a kind of rice flour. I say, "Let's decide on the green
beans, MaMa. Do you mean small round ones like these? Or these flat
ones? What green beans do you mean?" I press beans and peas into her
hand. I would've known which peas/beans if I'd paid attention; I've had
half a century to watch her cook. She yells that even a stupid person
would know. I choose a sack of any-old green beans, small and round
like peas, and holler, "Here they are! Green beans!" At the bins of flour,
I yell, "Here's the nahw mai fun!" I can read the word for *mai,* "rice,"
but not for *nahw,* and don't know what *nahw* means. Glutinous rice?
"MaMa, is nahw mai sticky and sweet?" "Of course it's sweet. All rice is
sweet. Know nothing." I pick up a big bag of fine flour, and my arms are
full and cannot hold on to her. I tell her to hang on to me. "Hold on to
my arm, MaMa. I've got the nahw mai fun. I've got the green beans.
Here's the yellow sugar." I grab two kinds of brown sugar—the kind in
sticks and a box of C&H—one in each hand. "The leaves. Where are
the leaves?!" I stop a young man in an apron, and ask in English,
"Please, where are the joong-chay leaves?" He says, "Over this way," and
turns around, rushing off for them. I push and pull MaMa along to keep
up with him. And there they are—long plastic packs of leaves, marked
"Bamboo Leaves" in English and in Chinese. Oh. I thought we used ti
leaves, like Hawaiians. I had harvested ti leaves from the garden in
Hawai'i endless summers ago, and mailed them to her. She scolded me
for spending too much on postage ($4.00), but hadn't said they were
the wrong kind of leaves. These are only $1.25 a bundle. "How many
bundles do you want, MaMa?" "How much are they?" No matter what
number I say, she'll say it's too much. To get her to splurge, I should say
less than a dollar. "One twenty-five," I say. She says, "We've got plenty at
home." Yes, but tattered and split, dried out, and resoaked in the washtubs and bathtub year after year. "Buy some new leaves, MaMa!" She
says, *"Ho la!* Buy two bundles." Then, all this stuff in my arms and
hands, and pressing my mother's hand under my arm, I steer for the
counter. We pass the clerk who showed us the bamboo leaves. He says,
"Gwoa joong chay, la." Amazing—a young person of a new generation
knows the ancient words; he's using the special verb *gwoa* for "to make,"
as in creating, fashioning joong, filling and folding and tying joong. The
holiday has not been lost through the many cultural revolutions.

We are in the middle of a long line when I remember the red wood for dyeing the inside of the gelatinous type of joong. You slice that joong like a jelly roll. I've forgotten what the red wood is called. It's poisonous; you soak it in lye. But MaMa doesn't remind me of it; I won't have to get out of line and find it. The woman at the counter says, "*Gwoa chay, ma?*" Wonderful—twice—people know that we're preparing for the holiday. I want my mother to have the joy of hearing Chinese voices singing the old words. I shout, "She said, '*Gwoa chay, ma?*'!" "Of course I am," says MaMa. "It's the solstice."

I am about to herd her into the car when I notice that Earll found a parking space right in front of an herb shop. MaMa would enjoy the herbalist's. The door is wide open, and just inside are boxes and a counter piled high with tree bark, $35 a pound. "Look, MaMa! They're selling tree bark for thirty-five dollars a pound." "Thirty-five dollars a pound?!" yells MaMa. "Cheap! To buy it from China, it's a hundred dollars a pound. Thirty-five dollars a pound! Buy it! A bargain! Buy lots." You cook the tree bark with buckwheat; it's good for hypertension. As the herbalist bags the tree bark, I ask if she sells the red wood for lyeing and dyeing joong. She does! Rich with purchases, we go home to celebrate further the holiday for the peace martyr.

The night before the meeting with the veterans, for which I ought to be getting calm and peaceful, I have a dream that might as well have been my awake life. I am helping MaMa gwoa joong chay. We're standing at the kitchen table in Stockton; it is covered with layers of plastic table-cloths, the thick red one, and a translucent one on top to protect it, and orange placemats to protect *it*. Everywhere are the ingredients for mak-ing joong. The tub of water full of soaking leaves is on the stool. There's a bucket of yellow beans—their green skins have been soaked off. Brave Orchid is ordering me about. Get this, do that, don't do that, don't know anything. You're forgetting ingredients. She corrects me; I correct her. She's dropping peas and beans and string onto the table, chairs, floor, the filling falling through cracks in the recycled leaves and between the new leaves. You take two leaves and fold them like a boat with one end open; you hold this holder in one hand, and fill it with so much rice, so many beans—I think the kind I bought are mung beans—not that much, too much, too little—a strip of the saltiest fattiest pork, lop-cheung sausage, and a hundred-year-old egg yolk. She's cheap—half an egg yolk. Then fold the sides and tops of the leaves down, and tie the fat bundle with string of a certain color to mark what's inside. The red and white strings and pink plastic string are unspooled and tangling and dangling in the food and on the chairs and floor. You tie X's, crisscrossing the joong or parallels encircling it; here's the kind with shrimp, here's the kind with meat, and the jelly kind with the red splinter, tied with X's *and* circles. I keep an eye on my mother so that she doesn't drop the little scissors or pieces of string or hulls or any other debris into the chay. I try setting up an assembly line, and confuse her. She's having a hard time gwoaing the joong because her hands have been turned/ burned into hooves, and each hoof is inside a net. She can't make an intricate book of leaves. The old dying woman, the netted cow, is about to return to the electric spangling grid and web, into and out of which all life jumps. Hooved to travel hard and far, she is yelling last-minute instructions at me: "Hold the ends of the leaves toward you! Whoever holds the leaves away from herself!?!" I *am* holding them that way, but she can't see me, and assumes that I am doing it wrong.

I gwoa joong all by myself, and think a thought I often think: I am in America, a lonely place. I am lonely. Gone are the days when clans of women ground corn together, and slapped tortillas, and patched a quilt, and danced the hula. They washed clothes together in the river; now one waits alone at the Laundromat. Alone, I make one joong after another.

When I look up for my mother, she has become Elephant Mother standing on her hind legs. She picks me up in her enfolding arms. I look into her eyes; she is beholding me with deep, large brown eyes, warm and soft with elephant-size love. I am bathed, imbued, pervaded by love. Mother Elephant World is joyful because of having me, and I am happy through and through. Then I am a standing-up adult, watching Mother's immense back as she goes out the door—the back door, which leads to the porch and outside. The door is closing on her. Oh, don't leave me; let us be together awhile longer if not always. But we have had our lifetime.

Not in dream, I clean the kitchen of my new place. The air smells of joong being boiled for hours. I continue cleaning the other rooms, caring for the just-bought house as if it were to be our permanent house. We're on Claremont Avenue, the second house on the Berkeley side of the Berkeley-Oakland border. Over the sidewalk is a green sign with an oak tree, "Welcome to Oakland." The firefighters had decided on College Avenue as the firebreak. This boundary is a safe place to buy a house.

Dawn of the day of meeting the veterans, I paint some more of the entryway to the basement. I dig peelings and bamboo leaves and coffee grounds and ashes into my new compost; I'm making earth. This house from 1916 has two fireplaces, one in the room I'm using to write in. I plant geraniums cut from Stockton into the strip of city land in back of the house, Alcatraz Avenue, and cactus ears, also from Stockton, and rocks from everywhere into the city strip in front of the house. I'm making a desert of California natives. I strew grass seed, and think about Walt Whitman's grass, which grows from the dead. A family of blue jays—parents and two big babies—peck and eat seed all the while I'm sowing. One of the twins tries jumping into the lemon tree, not flying but jumping again and again into the trunk, and bouncing off.

I have gotten rid of my bothersome family. We have been a household of four—MaMa, Earll, and niece Cher Nicolas, who's finishing her graduate program at Cal. Suddenly, they're all gone, and I can concentrate to make order. They took away most of their stuff, clutter and impedimenta. MaMa claimed my garden tools that felt comfortable in her hand and many hydrangea heads. She lifted up a hat that she had crocheted with multicolor yarn, and I stood under it for her to put it on my head. The pompoms touched my forehead. MaMa was looking up at the hat, admiring her creation, not at me in the hat. I felt the beam of her joy shoot over my head; I felt it touch my hair, glance my scalp. While getting into Cher's car, she yelled, "I want that big flowerpot. White pompom flowers! I want the white pompom flowers." The hydrangeas, which are in the green-blue-purple spectrum, must look white to her. Cher said, "I want a week at a spa." They drove off for Stockton. I am free of them. Earll left to perform his John Wesley Powell play at the Grand Canyon. Our son, Joseph, is playing music and singing in Micronesia.

To prepare myself, I read some James Jones. In his *Viet Journal*, he described Quang Tri as he saw it from a helicopter: "It was sort of stunning. Mind-numbing. The first thing you noticed was the color. There wasn't any. It was a black-and-white movie. Everything was gray. Covered with coat after coat of the dust. Dust from the enormous artillery barrages both sides had poured into it day after day, and from the U.S. aerial bombardment. A good-sized town, but in the heart of the city not a single building was left standing. The streets themselves were obliterated. Even the thick walls of the old Citadel had been smashed down to their foundations. Here and there part of a wall or a bent girder or a spaghetti twist of steel reinforcing stuck up out of the rubble, becoming a landmark by its height."

I also read some of *From Here to Eternity.* Prewitt spends most of his AWOL time reading, and making lists of books to read. He is interrupted, and doesn't find out what happened to the kid who wanted to be a great writer in *Look Homeward, Angel.* In the stockade, Prewitt meets The Malloy, who teaches the men to take beatings without fighting back. I can teach better than that.

The phone is ringing. A woman says she's not a Viet Nam veteran or a relative of a Viet Nam veteran. But she's friends with a "Chinese" Viet Nam vet, who won't come meet me without her. I think, He should be bringing her, rather than her bringing him. I say, Have him call me. He does not call.

I shower; and sprinkle my wet hair on the dress I'm ironing. I decided against the too delicate pink dress or the too army-green dress. I'm wearing the green-and-silver-gray blouse and culottes that my friend Patricia Gillespie brought back from Indonesia, where she'd been in the Peace Corps. Almost all my clothes, including underwear and socks, have been donated by friends, relatives, and strangers. I bought these cheap jelly shoes. All the clothes I buy myself are green.

It takes an hour to do the ordinary things one ought to do every morning. I make and eat breakfast, pita bread with egg and cabbage and zucchini, which I grew in this backyard. I wash the dishes, always many dishes to wash, and pots and pans and utensils, no matter how many or few people are eating.

I arrange my hair out of the way with my Navajo silver-and-turquoise hairclip. I put the Marine Corps insignia the vet Errol gave me in a buttonhole. I hope that no one will challenge my wearing of it. In my backpack, I put comb, brush, and makeup, though I'll probably not have time to use them. I check again and again on my notebook and reading glasses. I'm bringing my wallet and money; if the College Avenue bus comes along, I'll get on it if I feel like it. I might walk all the way, only one mile. I know exactly where everything is, keys in the zippered pocket, glasses with my notebook. A small packet of tissue paper, the accessory the elegant woman can't do without. I'll carry the multicolor pens in my sister's pencil box. I took it from our parents' house; her second-grade teacher gave the box to her, resplendently filled with World War II medals.

I pet the hydrangea heads goodbye, and marvel that flowers on the same plant can be different colors and sizes, some with blue buttons or lavender or green buttons in their centers. I count them. Fifty-two. Sometimes all you can do about myriad beautiful things is to count each one, give each one a different number, for want of coming up with fifty-two individual, unique descriptions. The impulse to do something about or to living creatures is the motive for shooting them—to get them to hold still, to get a better look. I try to remember the hydrangea's feel on my fingers and hands, try to get my skin to remember. Fifty-two, even after my mother took so many.

I leave the house at about 8 a.m. Our flyers said we are to start at 9 a.m., with registration. I don't have to get there until 9:30. Let the veterans reconnoiter and reconnaissance for half an hour. It's the last of the spring, a warm morning; I choose the shadow side of the street. Let the buses go by; try not to be in a hurry. Nobody I know stops to linger and chat. This and that occurs to me to say to the vets, but I don't jot it down. If it's important and vital, I couldn't forget.

I see my reflection and photo in the window of Avenue Books, a poster of me and Maya Angelou and Margaret Sanger. The bookseller is saving the poster for me; she jotted my name and number on the back of it. All along the way, I pass places where people have helped my life. I pass St. John's Presbyterian, venue for the Antiquarian Book Fair; first editions of my books at high prices. A girlhood friend of a girlhood friend was selling a first-edition *Woman Warrior*; I autographed it to make it worth more. At Derby and Benvenue is the studio where the men let me use the telephone during the fire.

I pass the apartment of an old boyfriend, from before Earll. (He's an Israeli citizen now.) The homeless guy who looks like Santa Claus says "Hi," though I don't give him any money today. His bedroll and things are on the other side of the street. I pass the Newman Club, which donated a hall for my final exam during the graduate students' strike; we didn't cross the picket line. Instead of stopping at the outdoor Café

Strada, I sit for a while on the bench in front of the Lowie, now the Phoebe Hearst Museum of Anthropology.

At the back of the Faculty Club, Therese Fitzgerald of the Community of Mindful Living comes up the path with a heavy cardboard box in her arms. She's tied her long, curly hair away from her pretty face; she's ready for work. She says she's worried that people won't be able to find the Faculty Club; she herself hadn't known which building it was, or where the entrance is. She's a Cal alumna too; in our years, the Men's Faculty Club had men members only. Crash it at last. (I'd gone inside it during senior year; Earll worked behind the counter. He met Herman Kahn; he let Mario Savio use the office typewriter. Earll wrote love letters to sorority girls for the waiters, Greeks from Greece; in return, they gave him food and wine left over from banquets. My mother, walking right here under the oaks, said, "Is this the dangerous wild?" My father answered, "Yes. Tigers, lions, bears—*chai long, wah.*")

Then Carole Melkonian, True Grace (her dharma name), comes; we hug. She'd been watching me. Having tea at Café Strada, she saw me walk by. "You were striding like a warrior." "Oh, no, I'm not a warrior. I don't want to walk like a warrior." I thought I was walking meditatively. "I mean," says Carole, "you have a strong, purposeful walk." I lead the way down the path to the front of the Faculty Club. The ground is wet; it rained last night, or the sprinklers were on for a long time. Therese says it will be a hot day; the ground will dry. I ask her to teach "walking meditation" to the vets.

We go looking for the O'Neill Room, where the Friends of the Bancroft Library held a luncheon for me and my parents on the occasion of their displaying my papers. My mother kept her table mesmerized with talkstory. You could hear her all over the room; she held the center of interest, though few understood her Chinese. She never stops for translation. I gave my father a surprise: in a glass case for containing treasures were the Chinese editions of my books with his calligraphy in the wide margins. He'd written commentary and poems in answer to me, and they will be kept forever in the university library. He said in English to the crowd, "My writing."

We go through the front door, past the front desk, through the Great Hall, with the moosehead and the fireplace you can stand up in, through the Clark Kerr Dining Room. I'd checked out the Faculty Club when I rented it, and again when I ordered the food. Michael Gardner, another CML worker, Therese, and Carole make signs—"Vets Workshop" and arrows—and leave to put them up about the building and campus. Out on the veranda, outside the O'Neill Room, where we're going to gather, I meet Sherdyl, who looks like Mr. Worf of the Klingons, except clean-shaven and light-skinned. He has the shoulder-length hair, and the scored lines, like a carapace, on his forehead and nose, probably scars. From his voice on the phone, I pictured a thin, ethereal man.

Therese piles a table high with the Buddhist teacher Thich Nhat Hanh's books—Free. Help yourself. Parallax Press is an affiliate of the Community of Mindful Living. Faculty Club employees set up a table with bottled water, iced tea and hot tea, hot water with many choices of teabags. It must be nine o'clock, time to begin. We'd decided against coffee, can't meditate on coffee. Therese says that fixing tea for themselves will give people something to do, to familiarize themselves with being here. A good hostess, I welcome gladly a man sitting by himself on the veranda. But he isn't a veteran, and isn't there for the workshop, he's just sitting. A woman comes along, looking for "the conference." "The veterans' workshop?" "No, the hypnotism workshop."

Bob Golling, the first veteran who'd written to me, who wants to talk sea story and peace story, arrives. Alongside him is a hearty man with skulls all over his pants. They are both stocky blond men, and remind me of the friend being rocketed to Venus. Then comes a vet all the way from Stockton; Abe Smith is tall and dark-haired, like the young Abe Lincoln. He seems too young to be a veteran of Viet Nam. Time has stayed unmoving for him. Abe and I hug upon meeting. Homeboy.

Howard Henton rushes in. "I saw your announcement in the *Express*, and here I am." He's tall and thin with a dark beard, another Abe Lincoln, a Berkeley type. And standing behind him is a quiet, shy man; he has clumsy timing, or I do. We stick out our hands at the wrong moments. I hold my hand out for too long without saying anything, can't think up a question for him to answer and be put at ease. I say my too-long name, and ask his name. I think he says, "Dave." We do not catch each other's eye. He's too red; his skin looks parboiled. Vets' faces sometimes seem tenderized, as if with meat tenderizer. Soul wounds show on the skin. I escort Dave over to the tea table in the foyer between the veranda and the O'Neill Room, and pour him a cup of tea. Every-body is immensely tall, not just in comparison with me, but objectively so.

I go up to a hapa-looking woman, and ask if she's Claire Hsu Accomado. "No, no," she says, "I am Lily Adams." Lily has brought three or four people from the Veterans Center in San José. "I was a nurse in Viet Nam. I got back and retrained in psychology." She has devoted all her adult life to helping soldiers.

My friends Jeannie Houston and George Ow come; they drove together from Santa Cruz. I feel happy and relieved seeing their familiar faces, and hugging and being hugged. George is elegant in pleated linen pants and white Pontiac Grill sweatshirt; he is the owner of the Pontiac Grill. My red Pontiac Grill T-shirt burned in the fire. George, a businessman from a family who has lived for generations in the Monterey Bay area, was a medic in Viet Nam. Now he works as a philan-thropist, and is a patron of writers, historians, and filmmakers.

So many people crowding inside the foyer, I edge into the O'Neill Room. Carroll Blue introduces herself. She is a producer of *Nova*, and flew in from San Diego. Carroll and Jeannie hug. They know each other, and each of us knows Al Young. Al and Jim Houston send their aloha via Jeannie and Carroll and George. It's all us. All of it is us. I called for those in war, and got my own friends, here all along. It's always but ourselves, making the world, making war, making peace. George wants ideas as a Viet Nam vet, and all he gets is me, Max, same old friend, already known.

Therese leads people, rearranging the half-dozen dining tables. They recall the argument about the conference table—round or rectan-gular, what dimensions?—at the Paris peace talks. They carry the tables this way and that way, try configuring them into a horseshoe, but there are too many remainder tables. "Remember those puzzles where you move the little squares to form words?" "I had one with numbers that had to add up." "Remember Rubik's cube?"

George Ow is sitting by himself on the veranda, which is sometimes an outdoor restaurant. I go to sit with him. He says, "I'll let the others handle the tables." I say, "It would have been good to have given the dele-gates in Paris actual tables to bodily move, or reconstruct, or build." We watch the group solve the table puzzle, which started out in an E shape. They take apart the E, and make and dismantle the horseshoe, U shape, and settle on a big square, the horseshoe filled in, and push the one left-over table to the side.

I choose my chair and place, the side of the room with the long casement windows behind me. I open two windows, then decide to shut one so that my voice will not dissipate to the outdoors. The people can be looking toward me, toward the Bay, and have the glade and Campanile to see.

Jeannie asks if there's a special place I want her to sit. I seat her opposite me, across the square; I'll have my dear good friend to look at. Lily Adams has already seated herself on the northern side of the table and room. In back of her are windows lush with oaks, pines, redwoods. I like this room because three sides are open to nature.

Carroll Blue is across from Lily. Instinctively, without having to discuss and plan, we four women of color anchor the room, one of us in each of the directions. Like Native American and Taoist shaman women. Altogether, half a dozen women upholding the Yin amidst about twenty men. And there are four Asian Americans—Jeannie, Lily, George, and me. I ask after Paul Fujinaga, a vet who sent me a poem called "Fucking Gooks."

> John Wayne I was, in fatigues and boots,
> here to kill those fucking gooks
> . . . They'd touch my hair and say, same-same Vietnamese.

Paul isn't coming, but Lily carries that poem in her purse. "To show to Asian American vets."

I welcome the veterans by thanking them—for being here today, for coming from so far—the Peninsula, Marin County, the San Joaquin Valley, and even San Diego. "I am gratified and honored to be here with war veterans and families and friends of war veterans. You have lived, witnessed, and suffered terrible events, wars. You veterans of the Viet Nam War have been home for almost two decades. Twenty years, you've been home from war." (I say, "Viet Nam War." I got what to call it from librarians, such as Bessie, who named it and catalogued books under "Viet Nam War," though it was not officially a war.) "Korean War veterans have been home for almost forty years. And for the World War II veteran, it has been half a century that you are home." Howard Lapin, World War II veteran, gives a nod and a smile.

I am trying to gather us in time, to bring us from out of the past into the now. If they could hear my voice repeating "home . . . home . . . home," they might follow it and return home. Home free. Odysseus took twenty years to get to and from the Trojan War. "Twenty years after Viet Nam, right now, you are returned to America, and picturing, remembering, thinking about what happened. Twenty years ago, explosions blew up and entered and resounded inside of us; we carried the effects and consequences in our very bodies. The body's knowing, that raw energy, rises up from here"—I put my hands on my stomach and my chest— "up to the aware mind." (Surely, men have these sensations too, not peculiar to me and other women who've had babies.) "That journey from the traumatic thing to the transforming words takes twenty years. The conscious mind is waking up! You are now ready to gather the smithereens, and narrate them into story. We'll put that war into words, and through language make sense, meaning, art of it, make something beautiful, something good."

I'd planned to keep my crazier ideas to myself, such as big-bang explosions knocking the frighted soul out of the body. But the veterans are so quiet, listening for me to tell them something vital. I blurt out that my mother was at the bombing of Kwangtung. At big bangs, souls jumped out of bodies. Jumped out of skins. She was a doctor, and ran a hospital in a cave. Only those who would get well were allowed into the cave. I asked her, What was the worst suffering? She said that people went crazy, lost their minds. Even men who were not physically wounded cried and rolled on the ground. My mother to this day has repercussions from the war. (And I am affected. Generations are affected.) Once, we were driving on the freeway above a dense grove of beautiful trees. She said, "The people of Stockton planted those trees to hide their houses from bombing." I tell about my friend Basil Kirtley, who was at the Battle of the Bulge. He played the bugle in the army band, and hoped being a musician would get him out of combat. As the explosions went off, his body bounced up and down, and slammed again and again on the ground. He's repeatedly told about having the stuffing knocked out of him by the earth itself.

In a war in Egypt three thousand years ago, Prince Hori of Western Thebes told about his feelings going into battle: "You determine to go forward. . . . Shuddering seizes you, the hair on your head stands on end, your soul lies in your hand."

I add, "There are antidotes to this violence to our bodies and souls." I picture but do not tell about my mother grasping and wiggling our ears, pulling our souls home by the ears. "Meditation and writing, and silence, are ways to gather the self together again." I invite each person to introduce himself or herself as a writer. I purposely ignore their identities as war veterans. I want them to redefine themselves. I do not want to hear ranks and serial numbers. Having no rank and serial number myself, I won't seem so different from them. As an example, I go first. "I talked story in Chinese; then, at about eight years old, I learned English and began writing. I wrote poems; I was a poet. I am over forty years old as a writer, and am probably the oldest of us here. For some of you, today may be your birthday as a writer. I have been writing almost continually, day by day, for more than forty years. I write every day. I make myself a writer daily."

Clarence Mitchell, the Black man next to Jeannie, brought here by Lily, says, "I'm older than you. I'm forty-eight." I say, "I mean your age as a writer. How long have you been writing?" He says, "Twenty years." I say, "You are a young man yet, only twenty years old."

The next person to introduce himself is the man one seat over to my left. (It happens in classes too, that nobody wants to sit directly next to me.) He is Marc Leggin. I am so excited—the meeting of veterans is beginning—that I don't hear him. I can't retain what he's saying. I am resolving to pay attention so hard that I can't listen. All I hear is the quality of his voice; he sounds Black American. He is one of those good-looking people, like my son, who can be any race depending on which feature you're focusing on. I feel all the people here are especially handsome and pretty.

Next to Marc is Bob Golling. He's got a sailor's tattoo, fading, on the lower part of his arm. He speaks of himself not as a writer but as a house-husband, father of six sons. "Boys are naturally violent. They need men to teach them about violence. Women can't do it. Boys have to be raised by men. There's a violence in boys that fathers understand. The father has to take on the responsibility to show sons how to handle their violence." He asks large questions, and has come here for answers. "Why war? . . . Where does violence come from?"

Around the corner of the table from him is Howard Henton, who says, "I reconnoitered you guys. I wasn't gonna hand over my ten dollars to some crooked outfit. Yeah. Yesterday, I went over to Albany, and reconnoitered you. I don't trust easy. I don't have a whole lot of trust. I cased the Community of Mindful Living, went all around your house, checked it out, and made sure you were legit." He says he has always wanted to be a writer, and is writing now.

Joe Lamb, who is gentle as a lamb, says that he had not been "in-country" but was stationed in Pennsylvania. He'd been a corpsman; now he's an arborist, a treeman. He works with the Berkeley-Borneo Big Home Project of the Earth Island Institute, and is always writing.

Between Bob Golling and Howard Henton is Tom Currie. Sherdyl forewarned me about Tom, that he is a talker who holds forth at coffee shops. Don't worry, Sherdyl promised; he would sit next to Tom and keep him under control. But he forgot, and is on the other side of the room. Tom greedily talks story; the sentences are so complex, poetic, trippy, I can't retain them. Sherdyl doesn't try to curb him, so I interrupt: Please give time to everybody else. We're just having introductions now; there'll be more time for stories. Tom blinks hard, and winds down.

The man in the skull pants is John Wike of Swords to Ploughshares and Stand Down. He says, "I remember—I was in an invasion and occupation. A scene just came to me from the Dominican Republic. You're right—almost thirty years go by, and it comes back. I'd forgotten all about it." They're impressionable. I have to be careful what I say. Quit suggesting sensational things—that it's possible to forget being in war, then wake up decades later.

Ted Sexauer, a tall, thin, intense man, sits up straight, and quietly says, "I went to Viet Nam to have something to write about." The kid writer went to war seeking his material, the core experience of his generation. He committed experience for the sake of art. I laugh, and other people make noises too. Honest Ted, who is a poet, has confessed the writer's secret—went to war to get stories. Values ass-backward. We benefited from Viet Nam. Viet Nam would make us writers. A writer's desire can fill the ranks of warriors.

Dave, the one I have clumsy timing with, has masses of black hair and beard on dark-red skin; he makes an area of darkness where he sits. As he speaks, rumbling from deep inside his large self, a plane goes overhead, too loud, too near. I think I hear him say that he wrote during the war—letters?—and that he is aware of himself changing as he writes. I ask, "Did you say that you can feel your writing changing you?" He says, "Yes, I can change myself, writing."

Lily Adams—her men sit on either side of her—identifies herself as a triage nurse in Viet Nam, now a readjustment counselor at the San Francisco Vet Center. "I treated civilians, POWs, and American GIs." She identifies as Asian American, her mother Italian, her father Chinese: "Maiden name Lee." People must often ask her what she is. Like most hapa people, she is a beauty, short curly black hair, big brown eyes, very dark hair, very light skin—Snow White looks. She doesn't seem old enough to have been in Viet Nam. "I'm here at your conference, 'Mind for Something,' as an experiment. I wrote journals as a kid, and I want to write some more. I'm conducting a lab experiment at the Vet Center too. I want to see if I can teach the veterans how to feel again." The veterans are not offended at her calling them her lab experiment. But she is a veteran herself, and has worked for them with her whole life. She and my brother Joe do the same kinds of work now that they did in Viet Nam. Joe worked communications on an aircraft carrier off Da Nang, dispatched planes, now dispatches the police cars to crime scenes all over Stockton. Once, he told me, "I'm still in Viet Nam. I've been in Viet Nam for twenty years. The war is not over. It's going on right now, every day." Neither one of my vet brothers, though invited, is here.

Sitting in the northwest corner is Richard Sterling, a student from the first class that I taught at Cal, 1989, "Nonfiction Prose." He told a love story about a Malay girl, and showed me a picture of her. I asked him to come assist me teaching vets. Richard came to the university on his GI Bill, and it was because of his faith and will that I had held classes during the strike. He'd said, "I paid for classes; I deserve classes." Thirty relatives flew in from Oklahoma for his commencement at the Greek Theater, the first college graduation in their family. Generations of Sterlings were in Viet Nam—his father, his uncle, himself. He had not identified himself to his fellow Cal students as a Viet Nam veteran. Today, he says, "I'm here to listen to your stories."

Across from me are two men who have the bearing of officers: Howard Lapin, veteran of World War II, and John Swensson, West Point graduate, Viet Nam vet, and instructor of a course on the Viet Nam conflict at DeAnza College.

My dear friend Jeannie tells the war veterans that, having been imprisoned in the internment/relocation camps, she is naturally a war veteran too. She didn't need to have been in uniform to be a veteran of World War II. She says, "I am Jeanne Wakatsuki Houston. I write." She wrote *Farewell to Manzanar* and *Don't Cry, It's Only Thunder,* one of the first books out of the Viet Nam War. She wrote it with Paul Hensler, who lived it, and told it to her. Their book came out so early that readers and critics did not trust that the occurrences in it—acts of generosity, such as the saving of children—happened in Viet Nam. Getting Paul to talk story, listening to him, helping him to remember, Jeannie brought one veteran home. She tells us how she became a reader, born into a house with no books. She was eight years old when trucks rolled into Manzanar, and poured mountains of books on the ground of the desert. The kids played with the books, climbed the mountains, made forts, threw the books at one another. "We didn't know what books were for," she says, laughing. "We were kids. One day, I opened a book, and read it. It was so wonderful, I read some more." She tells us she's writing a series of relocation-camp short stories, and a novel.

Clarence Mitchell is in a corner, moves his chair so that he's often hidden from my view. He'd hide, come bursting forth, and hide again. The few Black students in my classes act like that too, disappearing, then dramatically showing up. "I am an artist." Clarence is a painter, and hangs out at North Beach coffeehouses, where he sketches. He's made a bohemian life for himself.

Renny Christopher works with VFW Post 5888, Santa Cruz, which was kicked out of the Veterans of Foreign Wars for protesting the wars in Central America. The slogan "Wage Peace" on T-shirts and bumper stickers is theirs. She says, "All my life, my country has been at war. My first husband was a Viet Nam vet, a marine, and we lived in violence. My lover, also a Viet Nam vet, became my second husband—" George Ow says, "Hey, I want to read *your* book!" Everybody laughs, men and women.

Even sitting, Sherdyl seems to be carrying a too-painful body. His feet in sandals are red. I feel he got large to cushion shrapnel. The scars between his eyes look like staples. He gives both his names, Charlie Motz and Sherdyl. "Sherdyl" means "The Lionhearted." "In 1981, I took initiation in the Sufi order and stopped drinking and doing drugs." He explains, "I am journaling. Writing my pain, I am writing myself back to health. . . . Poetry writing and journal writing are instruments in my healing." *Healing*. I avoid that New Age word. It implies that something's wrong, that they're unwell, and need fixing.

Carole Melkonian is in the corner to my right, diagonally across from the other members of the Community of Mindful Living. Like Therese and Michael, she's positioned herself slightly away from the table, behind the veterans, as if holding them, backing them up. She speaks about the bell that she'll be ringing throughout this day. It is the Bell of Mindfulness, and she won't "hit" it or "strike" it. She'll "invite the bell." She holds it, a bronze cup in the palm of her open hand, the bell stick in her other hand, and breathes three breaths, establishing stillness. She "warms" the bell by touching the bell stick to it, then decisively rings it. The room listens to the rings of ringing reverberate and fade. The atmosphere clears.

The greetings over, I give instruction on how to meditate. I mustn't confuse it with praying or worshipping. And nobody's trying to convert or save anybody or any soul. The Community of Mindful Living is not a mind cult. "Meditation is simply sitting in silence. Most of this day, we'll be silent. Gather your attention. Finish your car trip driving here. Arrive in the O'Neill Room in the Faculty Club on the Berkeley campus on this beautiful spring day. Enjoy the present time and place. Be aware of your breathing. Meditation is simply conscious breathing. Breathe consciously. Be conscious of breathing in and breathing out. Being conscious of a natural biological function that is usually automatic brings mind and body together."

I suggest that they put down their pens and pencils, and whatever they may have clutched in their hands, and sit with a strong, relaxed, straight spine, eyes somewhat open and somewhat closed, so as not to get distracted by what's out there, or get lost within. "Thoughts and feelings will come and go; watch them come and go. Observe that they come and go. You can keep track of your breathing by counting your breaths from one to ten, then one to ten again, and again. One . . . one. Two . . . two. Three . . . three. Four . . . four. Five . . . five. Six . . . six. . . ." Now I understand why dharma teachers touch their chest, raising and lowering an arm at breathing pace. Can't count aloud and breathe at the same time. "You can use words or phrases instead of numbers; Thich Nhat Hanh says a short form of a gata: In . . . out . . . deep . . . slow . . .

calm . . . ease . . . smile . . . release . . . present moment . . . wonderful moment."

I stop talking. Let Carole mind the time and the bell. Quit worrying about how this is going, will it be successful? I frantically try not to waste, but am wasting, my meditation worrying about keeping up with my lesson plan. I peek at my watch, which I took off and put on the table, and at my schedule. I calculate how much time has been used up, and how much more to go. We are on time, but how to keep up? Everybody else also has a handout sheet with the schedule in front of him or her. But they aren't motivated to help move it along. I am crazy over time. Time drives me crazy. I can't wait until this day is done. Rush, get it over with, so I'll know how things turn out. I forgot to tell them to enjoy the peace and quiet we're making. What a relief when Carole rings the bell, and I can go on to the writing instruction.

"Writing is like meditation: you sit breathing in silence, only you add one thing—the writing. Instead of letting thoughts and pictures and feelings go by, you hold on to them. You slow them down. You find the words for them. . . . Writing, you shine light—the light of your intelligence—into a scene of the past, into the dark of forgotten things, fearful things. Dave said it: Writing, you change. And you change the world, even the past. You make history." I pick up a piece of blank typing paper. (I remember Thich Nhat Hanh picking up a sheet of white paper, tearing it in half, and tearing it again, showing that there is no such thing as duality: the left cannot be rid of the right, and the right cannot be rid of the left. In paper, a poet is able to see a tree, and a cloud, and water, earth, and the sun.) I hold up the paper and say, "Write things out, and you won't need to carry memories in your body as pain. The paper will carry your stories. We, your readers, will help you carry your stories. See how light paper is?"

I pause. Then: "A scene is an event, an action in continuous time. Write a scene of joy, a scene of sorrow that happened once. Once upon a time . . . One morning . . . One night, it happened that . . . Envision the scene, and don't look away. Tell us—the people here with you— what you see, and help us to see it. We want to see it. We want to hear you. Use the other senses too. Something happened—a tragedy, a joy. What was the smell and taste of it, the sound and touch of it?"

I add, "To come home, Odysseus, teller of many stories, told his wife of the war and homecoming from war, and he listened to Penelope tell all her life from when they parted.

> "Odysseus
> told of what hard blows he had dealt out to others
> and of what blows he had taken—all that story.
> She could not close her eyes till all was told."

Then the bell sends the veterans off to write. Looking out windows and over balconies and around corners, I watch them settle into the many nooks and crannies in and around this redwood Maybeck building. A few people take the Great Hall all to themselves. Most go out into the almost summer day, and write at a table on the veranda, or the back patio, under the trellis of bougainvillea, ablooming red. I stay in the O'Neill Room to make a stable center for anybody who wants to write with me.

The Campanile bongs eleven bongs.

I set out to write a scene of joy—I saw fireflies. It happened at Thich Nhat Hanh's retreat at Omega Institute at Rhinebeck, on the Hudson River. In 1991, before the big fire. I stayed on for two retreats in a row, one for veterans and the other for civilians. Earll and new friends I'd made, veterans, left after the first retreat. Suddenly, my serenity was set upon by four hundred people, too many people, four hundred strangers in crowded excitement. I'd made a mistake by staying. And the organizers set up a tent. Thich Nhat Hanh was staging a tent show just like any American born-again revival cult. And with the vets away, out came the statues, idols, graven images on altars that had been tables. The plain Quaker Zen look was gone. I had stayed too long at the fair. I didn't like the new crowd, individually or en masse. I especially disliked the Asian and Asian American girls. What were they doing among all these Caucasians? There was a flirty girl from Japan in a red, white, and blue sweater with AME on one sleeve and RICA on the other. We're euphoric; we've bombed Iraq. The mob was divided into groups of two hundred. The community did not meditate all together. Thich Nhat Hanh didn't sit with us, though he led walking meditation, holding children by the hand. A middle-aged woman whined that she'd like to have her hand held. Why couldn't Thây hold her hand? Just because she'd grown up, he wouldn't hold her hand. At the small-group discussion I attended, a paranoid psychologist called us "candyass Buddhists" and stomped out. His wife had dragged him there; it does no good to be brought. . . .

Abe Smith from Stockton stays writing just where he'd been sitting, near me. I feel like a mother hen or mother cat, some animal mother, and he's my chick or cub. About four people—not constantly the same four—stay with me in the O'Neill Room. The younger Howard goes out, maybe reconnoiters some more, comes back. It's fun to watch him write—he enjoys himself so much, writing and laughing, laughing and writing, so pleased at what he's coming up with. Therese sits in back of him, and when he laughs, she laughs.

At about twelve-thirty, we regather to learn walking meditation. Therese says that she's never taught walking meditation in a room like this; we should go out to the wide veranda. Some follow her outside. Some are chased out; the servers want to set up for lunch. Therese speaks in a soft musical voice that carries. (I think I hear Virginian tones. Though cute in appearance, Therese can suddenly get severe and intimidating.) She puts her hands behind her back and walks in an oval on the gray redwood. Shirley Temple is about to tap. "You can hold your hands like this, or here, or at your sides. Think a word with each breath. Build a road of words." She connects the walking to the writing! "There's no destination that we have to get to. We're walking to be walking." The writer doesn't have to know where the story leads or ends. Build the road as you go. "Step by step. You are mindful of every step and of inhaling and exhaling. In in in. Out out out out." Three steps per in-breath and four steps per out-breath. "In in in. Out out out out. Be mindful of each step as you place your foot on the earth." Then she tells us that her brother is in a coma—he'd been in an accident—and explains, "I made up a song/mantra as I walked for my brother." She sings in the stillness:

> "I didn't know how precious life is
> until I saw you lying there.
> I must have forgotten how precious life is,
> and then I saw you lying there.
> I couldn't believe how precious life is,
> as I watched you lying there.
> And then I practiced taking care,

taking care of you lying there.
And now I know how precious life is,
how very precious life is.

"Maxine can start our walk." I lead the way without looking back, hoping they're following. I breathe, paying attention to everything, and walk down the wood stairs, turn left under the oak trees toward the music building. I think, Here I am, leading a platoon of ex-soldiers in peace, in peace, in peace, walking home, walking home, walking home, walking home. I walk onto grass at the top of Faculty Glade, walk to the outside of a group of girls on and near the bench, down the paved path, and stop for awhile under the stand of redwood trees at the bottom of the hill, and look up and up.

Young men ought to have basic training in this walking meditation, not march left right left, imprinting the martial march into their bodies. We are changing our walk, so changing our bodies, so changing our minds, changing the world that we're stepping on lightly. Human beings are basically good. That's why it takes so much training to march march march kill kill kill kill. I hope they're not embarrassed doing this weird, slow, silent walk amid the public. No, they're tough veterans; they can take social embarrassment. But it's the Berkeley public they're walking through; many people fear and dislike Berkeley, hold things against Berkeley, formerly the other enemy.

I continue my worrying. Worrying is my basic state of mind. What if nobody is following me? I'm on my own trip. They've left, are taking a break, and won't come back. They won't know when and where to meet next. Next is lunch. It's long past noon; they're hungry. Maybe some people went off to buy coffee and a snack. I'd ordered a buffet; what if they grab their food and don't wait for everybody else? How to get them to bring their food back to the table, and not to their individual nook, so we can eat all together? And what if I didn't order enough, and these big men don't get enough to eat? It's going to be a vegetarian lunch. Most of them would want meat, especially having paid $10.

I continue the walk, walking to the bridge, and go on up to its center. I lean over one side, then the other, watch a twig and its shadow float under the bridge and on downstream. I listen to the run of the water around the rocks and plants. I planned *not* to lead them onto the bridge, which abruptly goes over to the busy thoroughfare beside the Campanile. But we gather there, looking down on one side or the other. I see the veteran writers all at once, together on a bridge. Being in front, I'd missed seeing the group. I'd rather be in the middle, surrounded, or at the tail end, keeping an eye on the whole bunch. There's joy in the overview.

Just as we return and turn toward the Faculty Club, the Campanile bongs one. One. Breathe one perfect breath.

So far, the timing of the day is right on. I can see, above the balustrade, Carole Melkonian supervising lunch preparations. As we walk into the foyer, there is our meal wonderfully set out, the most lavish buffet—the Mediterranean Luncheon, the costliest on the menu.

It looks expensive and plentiful, not skimpy, though vegetarian. Dolmas, couscous, and whirls of cheese and spinach that are called pinwheels Aram. The table that had the Parallax Press books on it has been moved diagonally across the foyer and covered with a lush white tablecloth. A vase of tall white flowers sprays above the spread. The hot tea is in shiny chrome pots, pitchers of iced tea and bottles of water in sparkling crushed ice, flatware wrapped in white cloth napkins. Huge bowls of two kinds of salad with green and purple lettuces. Many kinds of grain. Tabouli. Hummus. Pita bread in triangles. Spanakopita. Babaganoush. Therese sweeps her arm above the food, offering it to the veterans. Aloha. Partake. I am the first in the buffet line, breaking into the kaleidoscopic presentation. I'm hungry; they must be hungry too. Hemingway, who wrote in cafés, said you write well hungry; your senses are sharp.

In the O'Neill Room, a wall has been folded back; the space has grown. The servers separated the tables, covered each one with a thick white linen tablecloth, and rejoined them to make a huge square banquet table, so big that there are two centerpieces, potted geraniums. I know it costs a fortune to clean and press such immense tablecloths. The veterans can't miss that they are being elegantly honored.

And they do sit, waiting until everyone is seated with a plate of food. I say, "Now eating meditation, mindful eating." A few people laugh; they think I'm kidding. "For about fifteen minutes of eating, let's eat with no conversation, like turning off the TV at home for supper." I am trying to tell them of a profound Buddhist practice. They don't know how much planning went into deciding on those fifteen minutes of silent eating. The Community of Mindful Living and I considered how odd and unnatural it is for most people to dine together without speaking to one another. Where would they cast their eyes? Shouldn't there be a "break" for get-acquainted normal conversation? Therese suggested a "rest" after lunch. But isn't the whole time supposed to be a retreat, and restful? A "break" would break up the concentration, break the atmosphere, break the rare silence. Richard Sterling says, "We're grunts. We didn't talk at mess. We grunted." Tom Currie says, "I am a grunt in life. I have no guilt being a grunt." It's a compromise that we eat meditatively for fifteen minutes, then chitchat.

I explain the reasons for and benefits of silent eating. "Use your other senses to know the people around you." (Oh, to me, talking is a sense.) "Without talking, you can still communicate with your fellow diners. Look at them. Smile at them. Rest from your usual social personality. Without the distractions of conversation, *see* your food." Naked lunch. "Feel the energy and atmosphere of the room. Listen to the sounds"—birds are singing!—"and smell the food and the cut grass. Hear the noises of your chewing, and be aware of tastes and textures. Slow your eating, enjoy each bite." (I've heard Thich Nhat Hanh say, "Chew each mouthful fifty times," and he's said "forty times," and "thirty times," the numbers going down as he re-estimates our capabilities. We're not to get obsessed by numbers. My parents had also given us precise numbers of times to chew, according to a worldwide health fad popular between World War II and Korea.) "There are two kinds of rice on our plates. Viet Nam is a land of rice. Suffering went into the making of this food. Don't forget the truckers and the cooks. Eating, we connect ourselves to all life, people, earth."

I like the silence. Silence is easy for me. My shyness disappears in silence; I don't have to think of what to say. The silence contains us. Jeannie and I smile across the room at each other. She doesn't burst out giggling, as she has at other silent meals. I look at all the people—which always makes me happy when I remember to do it, to lift my view and behold everyone in sight. I look often at dark Dave, who seems hurt, who seems to be having a hard life. He looks back, but holds eye contact for barely a moment.

Carole rings the bell. Most people are already finished eating. The slowest meal takes no longer than fifteen minutes of actual eating time. We stay quiet. I begin a conversation with Marc, on my left, about how good the food was.

The waitperson is a Black woman my age. She serves dessert—ice cream—and places a cup of tea before each person. The meal ends with the veterans' being served tea. (The hostess would serve each samurai with both hands, kneel, and bow to the floor before him.) They kid around with the waitperson, who kids them back. Somebody says, "She's not suffering."

Howard, who laughed while writing, suddenly recognizes Dave opposite him at the big table. "I can't believe it. The Ninth Division. I've only met two other guys in the Ninth Division." I can't hear Dave's reply; he seems nervous and embarrassed being the point of loud attention. It's not everyone who likes being found from out of the past. Howard keeps marveling at finding a company mate. I ask how many people there are in a company. It varies—sometimes eighty. A squad has six or seven soldiers; a platoon equals four squads; a company is four or five platoons; a battalion is four or five companies; a brigade is four or five battalions; and a division is three or four brigades.

People get up out of their seats and visit with one another. Marc— who looks Middle Eastern, but I can't tell (maybe he's Black?)—is leading a discussion about the wrongness of again bombing Iraq. (I agree.) Bush said we won; Saddam Hussein said they won. One good thing that came out of the Viet Nam War is raised consciousness, the idea that war is bad and there is no winning. The world has begun to question war. And there ought to be truth in recruiting. Kids join up for an education and benefits. They ought to be told forthright: "The purpose of the army is to kill people." "Yeah, the purpose of the military is to kill." "To kill and to support killing." They laugh at the court-martial cases for refusing orders to go to Iraq. Hundreds of young women and young men are claiming they volunteered for the volunteer army, but not for war. "They're surprised, the military can send them to war." "They're suing to get out of Iraq on the grounds that they hadn't contracted for a war." "Women soldiers are arguing that they shouldn't be taken away from their kids." Marc does a falsetto: " 'You're sending me to *war*? You can't send me to war.' " "What did they think they were learning to shoot guns for?"

I get to speak tête-à-tête with Lily Adams. I am avidly curious about this sister. What did you do in Viet Nam? How did you stay safe? Where do you get the strength to care for the soldiers and the veterans for continuous decades? She was at Cu Chi, where the population lived underground. "I talked to them in the few Vietnamese words I'd learned. Prejudice against me never came from the Vietnamese. The Vietnamese *liked* Asian Americans—not just me because I was related to the Lees, but for what I was. We were long-distance cousins, connected, and recognition was fun, positive. But I didn't want such a scene in front of the GIs, who would question my loyalty. I didn't want to piss anyone off, end up dead or raped. I didn't have it as difficult as the men in Basic Training who had to play the gook. They'd get, 'This is what a gook looks like.' They had to shoot at targets with slant eyes. After training, they continue calling you a gook. In Viet Nam, you had to prove you're American. Racism constantly, all the time. When I wasn't in uniform, the majority of soldiers thought I was a Vietnamese whore, because whores were the only ones on base after five o'clock. I was the only woman in line for the PX, and an ARVN checked my ID. My greatest fear was getting killed and not making it home as an American." She means her body would have been left in Viet Nam, mistakenly buried as Vietnamese.

"I am so glad," I say, "you made it home. I get to know you. I am so honored. How did you take good care of yourself?" The only advice I gave my brothers was, Take care.

"You develop a sixth sense. The sound of the helicopter coming in is godawful. You know how bad it's going to be. The woman who cleaned my hootch was VC. She was playful; she warned me at night, 'No. No sweat. Quiet tonight.' Or 'Lieutenant, lot of noise. Careful.' When I came in soaked with blood, she didn't look at me. No eye contact. She had sympathy for me. The worst stress was when we weren't busy, didn't know what would come in that door."

Lily could appreciate the others' watching out for her, and also our army's kindnesses. "People connected to the Vietnamese gooks, quote unquote. Units adopted orphanages and villages and old people. They brought old people in to the medics. Many soldiers kept in touch with their humanity."

Again I ask, "Where do you get the strength to care for the soldiers and the veterans all these years?"

"I'm good at calming people down. I lost my mother when I was eight years old. I learned to mother. You have to acknowledge pain, feel the pain, which is like an infectious wound that needs to be dug out, the gunk and junk. At first, I didn't grieve. I had to learn to grieve, becoming close to people and leaving. The teamwork we had in Viet Nam can't be reproduced in civilian life. My PTSD—I shut down my feelings as a defense mechanism. I had ten years of denial. I'd hear a helicopter and run out to receive the wounded."

Today, for the first time, I think about PTSD—post-traumatic stress disorder.

Around two o'clock, Carole invites the bell. The timing is perfect, we're neither behind nor ahead. I should quit worrying.

I speak about listening. Listen to one another. Tune your ear. On the stage, great actors don't just act as if they're listening; they really are listening, and they do that by breathing in the speaker's voice. You breathe in, and take the speaker into your lungs, and ears, and heart. Listening, we draw people's stories out of them. "When and if you feel like reading, please read aloud what you wrote. We'll go in a natural order. Hearing someone else's story, you may feel moved to read in response." (Just a few hundred yards away and thirty years ago, I studied the *Canterbury Tales*.) I anticipate most people having to be coaxed to read. Who will be the first olive out of the bottle? (And how to limit Tom Currie?)

"Well, I might as well go first," says the younger Howard. He is very jumpy, wiry, Italian-looking. I can picture him tiptoeing the perimeters of Viet Nam and of the Community of Mindful Living. He reads about boys new to smoking buying mentholated candy-kind cigarettes, Kools, Salems. He does their voices in swinging, jazzy dialogue. Snot streamed from the smoking, laughing, crying boys. So snot was what he was laughing at while writing. He can hardly read for laughing at his own jokes, and making us laugh.

We barely return to silence—each reading should be framed in spacious silence—when Tom Currie begins. He's filled the yellow legal pad, a gift from the Community of Mindful Living that he was delighted to receive. "I want to say everything I know and see, all the forever-gone past and forever-going present, to catch up in the net of my flung words everything that is happening in this too-full moment, all my life, all at once. Too late, I regret the unsaid. The desire and impossibility to say all my life in one instantaneous word, a speed of words . . ." Me too. Me too, Tom. It's my life's desire too, to say everything, right now. You speak for me. But I have to interrupt this waterfall of consciousness. "Tom, it's time to give someone else a chance." Tom blinks, opens and shuts his mouth, and makes himself stop.

John Wike, Dominican Republic vet, reads, pushing back from the table, rocking on the back legs of his chair. The skulls on his pants remind me of Tommy Traddles in *David Copperfield*, who cut out paper skeletons; they flowed from his scissors. Wrathful Mother Kuan Yin dances on skulls.

John narrates a story he calls "The Kidnapping of the American *Teniente*." One night, in the Dominican war, he and a couple of friends, a local sugar-mill accountant and a squad leader, Sergeant Torres— "We were good friends"—walked to a club in a town near the army encampment. ". . . these times away from their unit let them be people and see and know the Dominicans that they had conquered and stayed to keep conquered." Eight or ten young rebels came into the bar. They were former residents of this town, and known to many in the bar. Because they were "visiting home," they had left their guns in the jungle at the edge of the town. The locals greeted them carefully. A slight hush fell. "Hostile and nervous glances were made towards the American teniente and sergeant sitting at a table in the back of the bar. After a few drinks, the rebels crowded around the back table, demanding of the bar, the accountant, and the Latino sergeant that they surrender the Gringo teniente to them, to be taken back to the mountains as a hostage. All the while I sat grinning foolishly as if I didn't know I was the stake in this, while under the table I held a pistol aimed at the most vocal of the rebels. The one whose eyes flashed hatred at me." John stops.

"Then what happened?" people ask.

"You have to buy the book to find out. I'd forgotten that incident until I began searching for a military experience to write about. This is the first time I've told anyone about it. I never mentioned it to anyone, ever, until today. The Dom. Rep. Nineteen sixty-five."

Joe Lamb, who was a corpsman stationed in Pennsylvania, reads a scene set in the Naval Hospital. A young soldier has had his legs amputated. He is growing an afro, and refuses orders to cut it. An officer, filling out forms for court-martial, asks for his vital statistics—height, weight, etc. He answers, "Will Counts, Private, L.A., Negro, four feet three inches, sir." The officer says, "I mean, your real height, before." Will screams, "Measure me! Measure me!" Joe's voice transfixes us. " 'Measure me!' " The strangeness of an adult body changing height.

Ted Sexauer reads a draft of a poem. He was a medic. A medic has to be cool. "We set a night ambush. We've done this a million times. Pacification. . . . I could say I'm not part of this. I am. I am one soldier, under orders, under arms. I can't stop it. I'm sanctioned to intercede in the lives only of those who've already been shot. . . . PURE HELL BREAKS LOOSE! ALL THE NOISE IN THE WORLD!" When the battle was over, one of his guys handed the medic a souvenir, a barber's scissors: "Long, tapered, thin, pointed, with an arm like the tail of a 'Q' trailing off one fingerhole to hold the second finger. . . . We killed a medic. . . . They're giving me one of the tools he carried. I keep it in the back of my drawer."

Nobody wanting to follow Ted, I say, "*I* want to read *my* piece now." I read to them about feeling bad among crowds of strangers at the retreat at Omega, Rhinebeck. The friends I'd made had left, and I didn't like the people I was meeting. We'd just bombed Iraq, and I was feeling prejudice against human beings. I tell how the psychotherapist sneered at us, "Candyass Buddhists." And about how the one vet who remained at this civilian retreat had scolded, "Officers!" On his first day in Viet Nam, under attack, this vet, Anthony, shot and killed a Vietnamese, probably VC, who turned out to be a sixteen-year-old girl. "You killed a girl." The officer called him a killer, a murderer. Anthony yelled at us, "What's this extra-special guilt for women and children? Like it's extra bad to kill women and children? What about men?! The goddamned men don't count?! 'Save the women and children.' 'Women and children first.' 'Shoot the men!' Men don't mean nothin'. Men should count too." He shook his head. "Officers."

And yet, one night, while I was sitting in meditation with two hundred people, a spark of joy flew into me. I thought a firefly had flown into the room from behind my head. It zipped around to my face, and entered my left eye. But it was not a bug; it was a spark of joy, which became all brightness. I and all existence were entirely happy, though bombings, though wars, though lonely in the universe. This pure happiness was mine for about a week, in retreat, continued on the airplane home, lasted through traffic, lasted in the city, amongst strangers and my daily people. I want everyone to have this happiness, at least once in his or her life.

When it's his turn, Howard Lapin, the World War II vet, reads about flying a plane, a bomber, over beautiful Africa. The morning sun warmed him, and warmed the green earth and the water. Shadow and brightness crossed Africa. All seemed hallucination, but real. He had to concentrate on his instruments, and not keep gazing out at the miraculous land. "Remember World War II? Africa, the North Pole, the Pacific Islands."

Marc reads about a bunch of grunts, each one well characterized by voice and antics. The main guy was Fubar. The listening vets laugh, and explain his name, "Fucked up beyond any remedy." Marc uses the word "pacification" too. U.S. policy in Viet Nam wasn't war; it was pacification. It wasn't peace either; it was pacification. "I applied for CO status, and got out. I wrote myself out of the military."

Lily Adams is the only writer who tries a scene of joy—her daughter's graduation. Oh, the beloved young woman in academic regalia. The satisfaction of being her mother. The band playing "Pomp and Circumstance." The slow ceremony made time for relishing each moment of this day of culmination. She concludes, "I want to find the happiness in my life, the rest, the fun. It is not all Viet Nam."

John Swensson stops the readings, courteously asking after my burned book and house. How was I doing? I'm okay. This is their time; I've got to let everybody read. I don't want to digress. But John thinks I too need my losses listened to. I ought not to be above it all. I should be as generous as everyone else, reveal my life too. Yes, we're going to rebuild. But it isn't *rebuilding*. Nothing can be made the same as before. House and book will be made from new, different materials and the accumulating mana of new present moments. My brother Norman, who was in the air force engineers during Viet Nam, is the architect. If not for him, I wouldn't want to build at all. He's designing a house that befits the Oakland hills, not a French-English cottage like the burned house. He says, "Building in those hills took fifty years to evolve. Everyone's trying to fix it overnight." We're still drawing; we're taking our time.

The elder Howard tries to console me with a story about Thomas Carlyle's losing his book. His illiterate maid burned the manuscript for kindling. In another version, the cat ate it. I have a catalog of writers who lost their work in fires: T. E. Lawrence, Aldous Huxley (a California fire), Hemingway (a fictional fire), Ken Kesey, Gogol, Kafka, Goethe, Lao She, Gerard Manley Hopkins, St.-John Perse, Louisa May Alcott (maybe fictional), William Carlos Williams, Ralph Ellison, Bharati

Mukherjee and Clark Blaise, Al Young, Toni Morrison, Rita Dove, Robert Nichols. Josephine Miles told about a Berkeley fire in which every poet in town claimed to have lost a masterpiece. Five years later— ta-da—the Berkeley Renaissance. Making good their brag, the poets did the best work of their lives. Malcolm Margolin told me about a publisher who lost a writer's only copy of a book. The writer wrote it again. The publisher found the first book under a pile of stuff, and—*mirabile dictu*— the two books matched, almost word for word. The Universal Mind remembers perfectly. Books and poems exist elsewhere than on paper.

Avoiding more talk about me, I call upon Abe to read. He is no longer sitting next to me; he moved next to John with the skull pants. The sun coming directly into his chair was too hot. Now I am all by myself on my side of the table. I like the sun shining on me. You would think a fellow Stocktonian would also enjoy the hot sun. Abe asks for the poem he'd mailed me. I get it out of my backpack. It's a "concrete poem," orange paper rolled and glued into a cylinder. He could read forever; the poem has no beginning and no end, taped together at its title, "THE FIRE." Fire is start and end and start. The poet turns the tumbler in his hands, and reads impressions of fire. Shy or sly, he doesn't read aloud the many lines and rows of circles, so I don't know whether they're zeros or "Oh"s, like the sound of moaning, like the sound of the wind. They remind me of when I was a kid writing around a lampshade a "1" and as many zeros as possible, for the years I wished my parents would live. A circle contains everything and nothing.

Abe then reads the scene he wrote today: American soldiers rolled by on the big trucks, passing hungry children along the road. Abe threw a candy bar, and hit a kid in the chest. He breaks off reading, crying. We are silent, then applaud.

George Ow passes.

Renny Christopher, a pale, dark Caucasian woman with black eyebrows that make intense expressions, writes from the point of view of the woman who listens to the men who went to Viet Nam:

> He told me about one of his men,
> shrapnel across the belly,
> guts spilling out, red-black snakes writhing,
> he pushed them back into the wound,

and safety-pinned it shut
to wait for the dust-off.

On my map
the two coastlines—
California's
Viet Nam's—
look like they should fit as jigsaw pieces if only I
could bring them together at just the right angle.

Everybody who wants to read has read. We sit in silence. Ted and
Tom, who are both hungry for listeners, say, "Well, if nobody else is
going . . ." "I might as well go again." Tom reads some more about the
earth and the cosmos, space and the stars. Ted reads a poem about a
standoff at the village well. He watched a papa-san bow and grin, shuffle
and scrape, being nice to the Americans, so they won't pour soap into the
water. The listeners give Ted silence, then applause. Ted says, "I wonder
what our counterparts, the writer veterans in Viet Nam, are thinking?"

Clarence jumps down his throat. "What do you *think* they think?
Invaders out of nowhere bombing them, tearing their country apart,
killing their family and friends and neighbors. What do you *think* they
think? How would *you* feel? Strangers invading your country and your
village, and wrecking it, and wrecking your life." He rants, "How would
you feel? What would *you* think?"

The Campanile bongs four o'clock. Jeannie and George stand up;
they have to start the long drive back to Santa Cruz. Jeannie says
farewell with loving aloha.

George says something like, "I really wanted to come here to be with
Maxine—but Viet Nam vets?! Jesus. Jeez." Elegant George has his
shades on, and is crying, tears running down his apple cheeks. "Thank
you guys for your stories. I liked hearing your stories. I guess I haven't
finished my reconciling yet." He turns to go.

I say, "George." He looks up, expectant. But I don't have a wise
enough thing to say to him. "You say you haven't reconciled yet. Reconciliation isn't something you do once and for all. You have a lifetime to
do it in." Then I think, What a dumb thing to say. That he has to strug-
gle forever. I feel bad, putting George through meeting Viet Nam vets,

who must have been young brutes to him, gooked by White GIs and Black GIs.

Sherdyl stands and walks over to George, shakes his hand, holds his shoulder, and says, "Take care, brother."

After they're gone—George will spend the next two hours in the car with Jeannie; they can talk—I say, again inadequately, "Asian Americans have special pain over Viet Nam, Asians against Asians." The playwright Reuben Tam said it better: "Gooks killing gooks. I was a gook killing gooks." A kid I knew from grammar school, Ted Lee, got back from Viet Nam and killed himself. He left a note for the police, telling them to take care of his mother and father. Lily passes me her card to give to George.

I say to the group: "We have lived with one another's stories for a short while. Do you want to reply to the writers?"

People talk at once about the boy getting hit with the well-meant candy bar. "War against children. War by children." "We were children, and we fought children, even smaller and younger than ourselves."

And "We had superior weapons, and real medical equipment. They had barber's scissors."

Many people repeat, " 'Measure me!' "

Abe Smith thanks Lily for her story. "I liked hearing that your daughter went to school and graduated. She could be in a war." He himself was in the stockade at her age. A couple of other people mention that they'd been in military prison too.

The younger Howard says that his favorite stories were the ones that made him laugh—Marc's Fubar and mine. "I've been there." I made this vet who laughs while he writes laugh. I tell him I had fun watching him write, chuckling when he wrote "snot."

We praise the elder Howard's flight over Africa. "We were at war in Africa?!" "Morocco." "Tripoli." Nobody is left out of the praising.

We end the day in meditation, and a last invitation of the Bell of Mindfulness.

The man with the skull pants—John—asks a favor, that we perform a goodbye ritual which veterans do. We stand and hold hands in a circle. I feel the strong squeeze of a hand, and pass it along with my other hand. John says prayerfully, "Welcome home." We say, "Welcome home." "Home." "About time." "Yes, home." "Amen." "I don't want to let go."

A few people put their hands together and bow, the way Buddhists bow, the way Vietnamese bow.

Michael and Therese and I walk across campus toward Bancroft. We marvel; we did arrive at communication. Therese—her dharma name is True Light—says, "I feel elated and also relieved." Me too. I'm glad it's over. I don't like excitement. Explosions went off as this one and that one spoke out. She adds, "That guy Clarence was out of control and angry."

I walk home, having many thoughts and relivings along the way. I let the buses pass; I can't bear the crowd. When I get inside the house, I have an outburst of feelings. I want to be asleep and unconscious, but have turned into a frantic baby, too tired to rest. This is post-performance energy, but there's no cast party for the too-wired to unwind. I turn on the TV, and eat ice cream for dinner. I wander about, pace from window to window, don't do anything useful. The sun is going down. I phone Jeannie. They did have a good drive back. "No, George never talks about being a vet. He's all right, but I think Clarence is not. He's very unhappy, Maxine." Now two people, Jeannie and Therese, are worried about Clarence. I say he seems healthy and normal to me; he enjoys food—three or four helpings. He has his art, and North Beach, his bohemia of friends; he can express loudly and colorfully his thoughts and feelings; he has Lily Adams watching over him. Jeannie says that John Swensson has an officer's bearing but was shaking when he spoke. Next time—we have another workshop planned for August—she will drive in with John.

Hanging up, I do not feel debriefed. It isn't only George who should call Lily Adams. I phone the number on her card. The Vet Center is closed for the day. "If this is an emergency, the number to call for the Suicide Prevention Hot Line is . . ." I shouldn't be asking Lily for help anyway. In a triage situation, she should tend to me last. Or first—I am the least wounded.

My mother, who ran a hospital in a cave at the bombing of Kwangtung, taught me about triage. She said, "I refused to doctor anybody who was going to die anyway. I refused to take care of the dying. None of my patients died."

But what about the Buddhist idea: "However numerous the sentient beings, I vow to save them all"?

Earll phones around nine from the Grand Canyon, where he's working. I tell him about Tom, Sherdyl, George. I can't tell the whole thing; he wants his turn to be asked after, to be listened to. I want the unreasonable, that he'd been there with the veterans, and that he'd been there at the fire. I need to look up the sutra, "Knowing the Better Way to Live Alone."

When I finally sleep, I have this nightmare: A big black—burned but alive—charred pig would not die. The dark-red wound along one haunch is like volcano earth cracking open. A brown-and-white dog comes by. (Earll is a reincarnated dog.) Please, graft skin off the dog's leg to the pig's. A man's voice narrates: "The worst psychic and spiritual punishment: look on while another is undergoing torture." Mine is the plight of women and most people during war. I should have warned the veterans that it would hurt to hear and carry stories. I led them into additional pain on top of the PTSD they already have. Pig's leg, dog's leg, man's leg. "Measure me!" The black pig is also Blues Berry, the soldier in *From Here to Eternity* who was beaten black and blue, to death. Blue Shiva dances a whirling dance on one foot, transmuting the poison he drank.

In the morning, Carroll Blue calls to talk about a film she wants to make about the spiritual—a film that could make the invisible visible, which is one reason she's interested in the vets. I suggest she film Mayumi Oda, painter of goddesses, gatherer of women. Mayumi has painted Christ on the cross as a brown woman. On a Girls' Day before the fire, women made dolls in her studio. Most of us had never had a doll; we'd been little girls during wars by our various countries. From the pile of fabrics on the studio floor, I chose a piece of peach-coral silk with summer flowers. It was from Mayumi's mother's last kimono, one she had not traded for food during the war in Japan. I gave my doll gray yarn for hair, and with sumi ink, Mayumi drew for her an Asian face. The scarf around her neck would protect her voice. I carried her with me on many travels but forgot her the day of my father's funeral ceremony, and she vanished in the fire.

I ask Carroll about Clarence—anything wrong with him that she could see? She says, "I've got a take on everybody there. Clarence is a Black man. He was *being* Black." I ask, "Is Marc a Black man?" She couldn't tell; he could be Black or Middle Eastern or South Asian, a kind of Indian. So—a Black woman's ability to discern who's Black is no better than mine. I say, "I'm glad you were there. The Black men appreciated a Black woman listening to them." Carroll says she had difficulty with the silence. She didn't love it, as I do. Her parents had forced silence on her: "A quiet girl is a good girl."

Sherdyl sends a note. "You put heart and soul into the workshop. The shared writings were very deep and wonderful for me to hear. . . . I myself had two nightmares the next two nights."

I call my psychotherapist, Rhoda Feinberg, in Hawai'i. I tell her I've induced nightmares in the veterans. I made them worse. I should have warned them. They opened their consciousnesses, and terrible things went in. As usual, she says, "You aren't that powerful. . . . And one can set up nightmares by warning about nightmares. Next time, try having an end-of-the-day ceremony. How about writing down things you want to be free of, and burning the pieces of paper?" I picture a hibachi on top of the white tablecloth. Or walking in procession into the Great Hall, and burning our woes in the fireplace. She and I say in unison, "Burning is too violent." How about a bowl? Everybody could write something, and leave it behind in my koa-wood bowl.

A white cat drags its burned, bandaged leg through another night's nightmare. In real life, Mother is saying, "Two people in the village had to have their legs amputated." She herself did the amputating. "Your Sung Chew ancestress split her little toe fleeing from the soldiers. . . . And that is why you girls have a cleft toenail."

Carmen takes MaMa to the podiatrist, who cuts her toenails. "I was so embarrassed," says Carmen. "Her socks were filthy; she'd been gardening in them. She said to the doctor, 'It's such a hot day, I changed my socks five times.' She must not have changed them in five *days*."

"MaMa exaggerates," I say.

"Like you. Five times. She has such high standards." The podiatrist, Carmen says, offers three alternatives for what to do about a wart: cutting away, burning, and—. My ears shut against hearing one more awfulness. How about leaving well enough alone?

For years, MaMa wore the Day-Glo green T-shirt that my brother Joe had worn on the flight deck. She wore it until it became shreds; then she used it to bandage her legs.

The next day, I go to join Earll at the Grand Canyon. As a U.S. Park Service and Grand Canyon Association interpreter, Earll is doing his one-man, one-armed John Wesley Powell show, *Down the Great Unknown* by Lee Stetson. Usually the show is on the rim, but we and the mules have carried the props down for shows at the bottom. Supporting my husband, I put his black tie and his spirit gum and fake beard in my backpack, and follow him, walking down the trail. We will spend eight summers living at the Canyon; they feel like one long summer, and we have been here forever. The Canyon is time solid. Two billion years of time as rock. After we blow ourselves up, and human beings are extinct, the earth will still be like this. Here is stability. I look hard now at the Canyon, for the future, when there will be no one to look at it. I will be dead, and it will not be different. I am standing on the ground that I could have been on a thousand years ago and could be a thousand years hence. Here is silence. I am alive, seeing the past and the future. There are places of the Canyon that human hands and feet have not touched, and never will touch. Here is emptiness. We can do nothing with all this space and land. It's not useful. You can't ski it, can't farm it, can't mine it. No water; no gold. No City of Gold. Not enough uranium. Boulders as big as cars drive into the dams. The rangers predict that in a hundred years the dams will be no more.

I can see the Grand Canyon being used for ceremony: Half the world's people kneel on the North Rim, and the other half on the South Rim. They bow toward one another and the abyss, and renounce their thousands of years of war, past wars and future wars.

I've flown backward in time—Mountain Standard Time; the day is shorter, and night comes fast. Everybody sleeping on the rim or inside the Canyon dreams epic dreams. Visions, like the clouds, rise out of the Canyon and into our sleep. It's easy to sleep here; you stay asleep all night for the completion of the big dreams. Dreams, clouds, tribes and generations of people may be coming out of the sípapu, the hole from the third or fifth world. The Place of Emergence. The Navajo and Hopi are said to avoid the Canyon, except for the Hopi on salt quest. The Havasupai live at its bottom, where they grow peaches.

The Grand Canyon and Oʻahu both have a rim where the people live, edging the uninhabitable. Now and again, I have the feeling that the expanse always nearby is the ocean. The Canyon fills with clouds and haze. (Some of it is pollution from Las Vegas and Los Angeles.) The river-hewn rocks are embedded with seashells and barnacles. Here, I know that Earll and I have been married for many lifetimes, and will be together always. In infinities of time and space, we are lucky to be able to find each other, in reality and in dreams. Sometimes we lose each other, but we're together again. One of the houses on the rim faithfully flies the black-and-white MIA flag.

Walk a ways below the rim, and there will be no other people. I am alone in the natural quiet. The noise, the ongoing arguing, is in my head. And the loud crunching is the sound of my own footsteps. The roaring is the wind in my ears. The poets do not have words for this place. Phyllis Hoge, who said, "If a woman is going to write a Book of Peace . . . ," lives near, and hasn't written a Grand Canyon poem. Larry Smith, poet and painter, says he hears the Canyon *basso profundo* but without words. "Ooh-la-la," says a French tourist. Wordless before the Canyon, I sketch it, draw it in miniature on postcards. (Europeans want to look at my drawing, and talk to me about what I'm doing, even offer a critique. Japanese are themselves sketching. Americans, ignoring me, point their videocam at the section of the Canyon I'm looking at.) No matter how large the canvas, a picture of the Canyon is miniature.

Geologists name and time the strata of river-cut rocks, and read the earth. Powell, himself named after John Wesley, named the pinnacles temples in honor of Zoroaster, Shiva, Vishnu, Rama, Confucius, Mencius, Buddha. At the Great Unconformity, where Tapeats sandstone touches Vishnu schist, my hand spans one billion years.

As Powell, the Civil War vet who lost his right arm at Shiloh, Earll gives voice to the ideas about peace formulated more than a hundred years ago: "If the War took something from me, it gave me much else, foremost of which, I suppose, was the opportunity of learning to command men in difficult circumstances. And it provided me with men for the Canyon expedition—Jack Sumner, my brother Walter, the cook, Billy Hawkins had all been soldiers in the War Between the States. And Bradley I found in an army outpost in Wyoming shortly before our departure. He thought the adventure foolhardy, but said, 'If it will let me out of the army, I'd agree to explore the River Styx.'

"And in truth to us veterans, even the unknown perils of the Colorado could never match the hell and horror of that War. . . .

"War. The nightmare relic of our animal condition. Many of our modern thinkers have found in war the evolutionary law of natural selection, 'the survival of the fittest.' But while injustice and cruelty stain the path of our history, I believe that man has risen in culture not by reason of his brutal nature; but because he has been emancipated from such cruelty. . . . I believe that human evolution is the result of the exercise of human faculties—evolution by endeavor. By the establishment of institutions, the evolution of reason, and the application of science, we are evolving—away from savagery, barbarism, and war, and toward civilization."

Three men left the expedition, and disappeared, maybe killed by Indians, maybe by Mormons. Years later, on a language-gathering expedition for the U.S. Geological Survey, Major Powell was a guest of Indians who admitted to killing three White men. The chief orates: "Last year we killed three white men. Bad men said they were our enemies. They told great lies. We thought them true. We were mad; it made us fools. When white men kill our people, we kill them. Then they kill us. We hear that the white men are a great number. When they stop killing us, there will be no Indian left to bury the dead. . . . Your talk is good; you are very wise; you have a good heart; we believe what you say. When you are hungry, you may have our game, gather our sweet fruits. We will show you the springs and you may drink. We will be friends."

Powell does not seek revenge for the death of his men. "That night I slept in peace, though these murderers of my men were sleeping not five hundred yards away. No good purpose would have been achieved by pursuing the white man's sense of justice, for our justice simply does not treat them with any understanding. They were simply defending their culture, and their land."

The veterans have got to see this play, and know this American history.

The second summer after our fire, we arrived at the Grand Canyon and saw that its little library had burned down the previous night but hours before we got there. For years, burned pages blew about and landed in the forests of the high desert. I identified charred paragraphs from *The Mill and the Floss*. The lost books included: Willa Cather's novels covered in flocked wallpaper; I read *One of Ours* at the Canyon. A set of four slender dove-gray books by Edith Wharton. *The Autobiography of Alice B. Toklas. Jacob's Room.* Women—Cather, Wharton, Stein, Woolf—wrote about "solemn doughboys" and "farmboys" who went to war. Women's war stories are not heroic; war is a pathetic waste. The Grand Canyon Library also had, and I read, Hemingway's posthumously published *Islands in the Stream* and Galway Kinnell's *Book of*

Nightmares and *Walking Down the Stairs*. Hemingway's Hudson and his friends play war amidst the islands between Florida and Cuba, and pass a burning village. His last remaining son is shot down in a warplane. The boy's mother asks, His parachute didn't burn, did it? Hudson lies, No. Galway Kinnell wrote about poetry in war: "The person who says 'Lieutenant! This corpse will not stop burning!' is just some soldier on some battlefield somewhere—presumably Vietnam, since death by burning characterized that war."

We go again and again by ourselves and with guests to the Hopi mesas. (To get there, you drive through three kinds of time—from Mountain Standard Time to the Navajo Nation, which is in the Mountain Daylight Zone, then to Hopi Land, Mountain Standard again.) I am curious about their reputation as pacifists. *Hopi* means "peace." I've read that six "Quaker Hopis" were in jail during World War II; they refused the draft because they had to be on the mesas for the ceremonies that keep this fourth world alive. I ask Dina, the docent for our tour group, about a rumor that the Dalai Lama left seven monks to live with the Hopis. They're to learn how to keep the old ways in America. The docent shakes her head No. "I don't know about that." Indians don't talk to outsiders about sacred things. They'll talk about "kachina dolls," toys for children and sculpture for tourists, but not much about the actual kachinas, spirits or deities or ancestors.

My friend from home, Deedee Ching (of a Chinese American warrior family), speaks up: "In our old village, we have kachinas too. Ours are on top of the roof." She points along the roofs of the pueblo that encloses us.

Dina asks, "Is your village still there? Are people living in that village?" She must be thinking that Deedee and I are from some faraway tribe of Indians.

I say, "Oh, yes. Our village is in China. It looks like yours—adobe, common walls, a pueblo too, except that our roofs curve."

Deedee adds, "And the kachinas are in rows in the curl."

Dina stands silent, then tells us, "A long time ago, six visitors, high priests, came here from China. They told my grandfather that they knew a rain ceremony. My grandfather's clan invited them to join ceremonies. That was the Flute Society. The Flute Society and the Chinese priests made rain ceremony together. And it did rain."

Deedee and I hold on to each other in elation. We have made connection with the Hopi. "It did rain," we repeat. I want to know more. "What did they do at the ceremony?"

Dina says, "I have never seen it. It's a private ceremony. I think it was a dog kachina the Chinese brought. The Flute clan still use it for rain ceremony." I figure it's probably a lion dog with a pearl in his mouth, or under her paw.

I believe the talkstory to be true, that the Hopi came from China, over five (or seven) rocks to Central America, then followed geomantic dreams north to the mesas. Hopi and Navajo babies are born with a spot on their lower backs or behinds, and Asian babies have that Mongolian spot too. It is the mark and proof that this child is one of our kind.

An unpresentable man staggers about, trying to sell a plastic bag of kachina dolls. Another strange man, at the top of some stairs, yells at us. Dina ignores them, as if they weren't there. The Hopi American Legion post newsletter has a column about the overwhelming problem of PTSD, and the need for services. I see: since they are not a warrior society, the Hopi must not have ceremonies that effectively bring people back from war. They do have many warrior kachinas, including a Woman Warrior or Hero Mama, but her legend is about attacking and defending, not about homecoming, as far as I know.

I am working hard to see this land for itself, and not in comparison with northern California. Scrub oaks are not less beautiful than black oaks and live oaks. These grasses and thistles around our apartment are not weeds. Plants coming up at all is miraculous. Don't water them to keep them green; they'll grow into yellow wands with seedheads nodding and waving. Gravity, wind, and time push things into a certain order. Everything falls into pattern. Two billion years of wind streaked the Canyon walls; I am seeing a picture of the wind. I am seeing the long-ago ocean's deposits. One June, I saw it snow. Why is it that the snow seems at perfection with no prints in it, and still at perfection with the footprints of deer and rabbit? But ruined when a human being walks through it, and marks it with shoe prints? The monsoon blows down the grass, and I see the weave of grasses and water, perfectly beautiful.

In August, at the start of the Perseid meteor showers, I fly back—the tiny plane to Phoenix, the jet to San Francisco, the door-to-door van to

Berkeley—for the next veterans' writing workshop. It will last two days; I'm determined that we deal with nightmares. I get home just before Larry and Edie Heinemann—Larry wrote *Paco's Story* and *Close Quarters*—arrive from Chicago; they'll be my houseguests tonight, then move to the Faculty Club.

I have a worrisome night, trying to sleep on the floor in the living room, which has only a wall and windows between me and the street. I hear footsteps and voices on the sidewalk right next to my head. The house echoes because it is still hollow of furniture. I have no will to shop for things, and have lost any desire for stuff. It's not fair. I've filled out more pages of insurance forms than written pages of book. To get insurance money, you have to list all your things, their original cost, their estimated value at the time of loss, and their replacement cost. You have to go to stores for these prices, and get the suspicious clerks to attest to them. Enough shopping. Once I write down the description of a thing, I'm satisfied. The words are sufficient; I don't need the thing. I list things, I as good as own them. I found an exact duplicate of my mother's bracelet, but didn't want it. It did not have the mana, because it did not have the history, of the burned bracelet. I move to the three-tatami room, which is quieter, and lie on the tatami until morning. I don't think I slept.

We get to the workshop early, this time the Louis Latimer Room—a long, narrow room toward the back of the Faculty Club. A narrow conference table fits nicely in it. I look for and don't see Clarence or any of the Black people, or Howard, who laughed while writing. There are three redwood walls with no windows, and a fourth wall of glass doors that open out onto a patio with trees. It is a beautiful summer day. I sit at the end of the conference table with the outdoors behind me again. Larry sits on the left of me, and Edie on the right. I wait for those I'm missing. The group falls into a silence. "Americans are afraid of silence." That's what Asians say. There they sit, all embarrassed, having already fixed their tea. Larry Heinemann goes scouting for coffee. I'd given him coffee at home, but he wants more. I'd forewarned him, we're going to meditate, which is hard to do on coffee. He brings back an industrial-size tank of coffee. He's arranged for the Faculty Club to refill the tank throughout the day. People help themselves, and are fast becoming speedy. I've also told him that these two days will be mostly silent, meditation being a practice of silence. He said, "I can't do that." I don't want to begin until nine-thirty, as per the schedule printed out for each person. I sit without saying anything. A scary silence. Larry and Edie, I know, are feeling the silence as weird. At exactly nine-thirty, I welcome everybody, and ask them all to introduce themselves. Doing things the same way for the second time makes for stability. People who were here last time will have to be the experienced supporters of the new people. No George Ow, and no brothers. But Wittman Ah Sing has arrived. I made him up, and he exists. He appears for real as Michael L. Wong.

Larry Heinemann, hero writer, Viet Nam veteran, sixth cousin of Abe Lincoln, is here to speak on writing the Viet Nam truth. So he tells them: Be honest. Tell the truth. Write it all. Don't spare your reader. He quotes Cochise, Chiricahua Apache: "You must speak straight, so your words may go like sunlight to our hearts." He himself speaks direct and sure. "Everything has texture, the air of this room, the air outside. Even what we can't see has texture. What is its feel on your skin, inside of your body? Get physicality—your physicality, its physicality, Viet Nam's physicality—on the page. Use your body's senses—write the truth. The worst day of my life . . . we killed five hundred people . . . nothing left of them but human meat. Human meat all over the goddamned place. We brought in a bulldozer." His arms thrust out and scoop out a huge field. "We dug a trench forty or fifty feet wide, and head deep, five, six feet deep"—his hands on his head—"and shoveled the meat into it, and then a layer of quicklime, then another layer of meat. We made a human-meat lasagna." I am so horrified, my ears keep shutting. "We weren't burying the bodies because they were soldiers to be honored. It was for sanitation. We lived next to the human-meat lasagna. The smell was in our hair, in our eyes, in the food we ate.

"Tell the truth. Tell the truth with your whole body. Don't spare the reader. You tell it. We killed plenty of people. I mean me. Me. Me. Tell the terror and horror of it. The total waste of it. Put the truth in your reader's hands. Write a letter. Write *her* a letter. Write *him* a letter. Write to me. Tell the truth to a real person here in front of you. She wants to hear your story. Tell it to her. I want to hear your story. Tell it to me."

He warns, "When you write the pain of war, you will relive it. You're going to live through the pain again. You *do* relive the war, the emotions, the smells. But this time, you have a method for handling it— writing. You can control it, put it down, pick it up. Writing is a craft of the hand."

I'd invited Larry Heinemann to help me teach because he had talked to my son and other sons about war. We were on a boat on the Yangtze, the closest he'd been to Viet Nam in twenty years. The weather was hot like Viet Nam, and the trees and flowers were the same. Chinese passengers pressed against the windows, and watched us eat. Earll and I and three draft-age young men were listening to Larry Heinemann talk story. Larry has three brothers. He and his younger brother were drafted at the same time. He tried to talk their youngest brother into not enlisting, even asked their family lawyer to keep him out. That brother has not forgiven him for interfering. Their mother pushed all of her sons to join the military. She *wanted* them to go to Viet Nam. Youngest Brother finished his tour of duty, and re-enlisted, a "two-time marine." He was sent home wounded. Larry doesn't know how he's doing now. Youngest Brother doesn't talk to or write to him.

As he told this, he looked at each of the quiet, listening boys, pinned them with the blue eyes with the black dot in the center. Husky dogs have eyes like that. People with dog eyes can see ghosts. Larry said to my son, and to the other sons, "Guys, no way is war good for you. It's harmful—to *you*. It's stupid. We were a bunch of dumb kids. The Vietnamese too, a bunch of dumb kids. Don't you be dumb kids." Larry, a veteran of Viet Nam, can say such things, which I want to say but do not have the authority to say.

Ted Sexauer tells Larry he re-upped in Viet Nam to save his younger brother from having to go. "I did the paperwork, took advantage of a little-known loophole, a legacy after the death of the five Sullivan brothers."

Edie Heinemann—"the real writer in the family," Larry says— speaks about writing letters to her husband every day when he was in Viet Nam. She is a red presence beside me, red hair, red cheeks. She wrote him the details of life back home, the daily events, the ordinary activities of family and friends, school. "Nothing important, not about the war." She wrote him safe; she wrote him home.

Addressing us women, Edie says, "It's easy for the support person to lose herself. You have to care for yourself, and not expend all your strength on someone else. Don't forget yourself." Edie met Larry at a mixer that her school gave for the servicemen stationed nearby. From there, he went to Viet Nam, and he returned there. ("I came back, I wasn't good for anything. The nuns at this weird Kentucky girls' school took me in. They saved my life.") Edie has spent two decades as support person for her husband, and for the kids, daughter and son. "I saved boxes and boxes of his letters, and he saved my letters. I'm thinking of bringing them out, reading them, and making a book. I'm getting ready to do my own writing."

Edie has visited Viet Nam. "I want to give you one important image from Viet Nam. The traffic is very fast, very busy with cars and bicycles and motorscooters. Our guide showed us how to cross the street. 'Don't look back.' Just scan one hundred and eighty degrees ahead of you, and don't stop moving." The way the Vietnamese cross the street is to pick out a goal—the place where they want to get to—and look only at it, not at the traffic. They walk steadily toward their spot, letting the cars and trucks and cyclos and bikes flow around them.

Larry says, "The news from Viet Nam is: The war is over over there. They went home, went to bed, and had lots of babies, who are playing all over the streets. They have wonderful trains. There's no sign of the war except for a little plaque in an out-of-the-way corner of Saigon. Now we need to get rid of the war here, and in here—in ourselves and in our memories."

I need Edie and Larry to be an example to us, show that it is possible for a veteran to come home and be married, and stay married. I wonder, but can't ask, How can you read Larry on being "fucking horny" on R&R? How can you bear to know that? That men go to war to fuck the enemy girls and women. American boys went to Viet Nam to lose their virginity. Earll was in Viet Nam—twice. Go ahead—kill, get killed, but don't be sexually unfaithful. But Larry writes fiction. He calls fiction "bullshit." "Bullshitting fiction." "You need to tell it. Tell it all. Tell it whether it happened or not. Don't leave anything out."

My turn, I tell about my brothers. I'm eldest sister to three of them. (I have the nerve to teach veterans because of being eldest sister to brothers.) Two of my brothers were in the Viet Nam War, one of them in-country. I admit that one motive for starting these workshops is, I want to give my brothers some ways to get over Viet Nam. "I sent them invitations the same as you." Neither one of them answered, and they aren't here. "Thank you for being my brothers."

Larry says, "Now I understand why you're having these get-togethers."

The Bell of Mindfulness sends all those who hear it off to write. The rings reverberate outward and define the silence, encircled momentarily by sounds. In the universe, there is much more silence than there are voices. Being quiet, we become like the great silence, and unite with it. Actually, the most that happens at these workshops is silence.

Loving to watch writers in the act of creation, I snoop out their writing places—a window seat, a winged armchair, an inglenook, a landing. I check Edie and Larry into their room upstairs; they can retire anytime. But they stay amidst everyone, write with everyone. We write all day, outside too, in the summer sun and in the shade under the redwoods beside the stream.

In the late afternoon, we bid one another good night. I suggest that tonight they have lucid dreams. "And remember what you dream, to tell us in the morning. Write those dreams down. We'll influence one another's dreaming."

The next morning, Hiroshima Day, I am rushing across Faculty Glade when the Campanile rings nine o'clock. I slow to walking-meditation pace, and spy Tom Currie on a bench next to the sculpture *The Last Dryad*. "Hi, Tom!" "Hi, Maxine!" Ever afterward, Tom marvels that I recognized and remembered him.

Sherdyl brings muffins he made from one bi-i-i-ig zucchini.

Eager Tom reads first. It's a letter to me. "Dear Maxine, I'm a blue shirt, a fireman, dreaming in my rack. The ship sails north into the beautiful Arctic Circle on top of the world." He trips out again into the cosmos. Time zooms, waves, turns, stops at the present moment. On a bench in Faculty Glade, a young man and a young woman are talking about *Star Trek*. Tom records their dialogue verbatim, then flies back to the Arctic Circle. A plane zooms out, then in; the tailhook catches it. A torpedo comes in, goes off, exploding colors, noise, death. "My first confrontation with death. Only death is damn final and certain. Death. Death. Death."

I want to reel Tom in. I'd rather hear about his down-to-earthly life in the streets. Is it true that he has a camp in the hills, and crashes receptions at Berkeley and Stanford for food? Long ago? Still? He grabs listeners, and tells whatever. The Ancient Mariner. He halts his reading at "Death," and says, "I don't know how to make sense of it."

Howard Lapin, our World War II elder, writes a letter to Captain Willie, "a fuck-up, who because of macho daring-do crashed his plane with twenty people aboard." "Out of false bravery, you gave orders that caused an accident that killed our own men." (Larry says, "Captain

THE FIFTH BOOK OF PEACE

Willie is the kind they fragged.") "Fuck you, Willie, and your stupid ground-pounder ways." World War II, the good war, language same-same Viet Nam. Good that Howard's here. The Viet Nam vets can get straight with Father and with that generation's war. Someone uses the term "World War II mentality," meaning jingoism. Howard goes quiet, and shakes his head. "No, that's not right. It wasn't like that." He asks the professional writers at the table, "Is it right to speak ill of the dead?"

Ted Sexauer has rewritten and continued the poem that began with the medic having to be cool, to keep down the "panic factor," and not "fail in the eyes of his unit." "I feared failing at my job more than my own death." He has lost his feelings, and can't make decisions. Ted *is* cool; he has the style that everyone wants. The others admire it, and seek his opinion of them and their writing. The instant he says the title, "Ambush of the Silver Cross," I see the Vietnamese medic's scissors open into a crucifix. (My mother's sewing scissors burned in the fire; she'd brought them from China, and must have used them for surgery in war.) The medic poet thinks about the enemy medic who was killed. "Today, peacetime more or less, 1993, holding the scissors, I can, at least, begin to wonder who he was."

Sherdyl continues a story about watching a "floating tree" on the infrared nightseeing scope. "It's moving straight across the river against an eleven-knot monsoon current. . . . Porpoise twenty-four, this is Porpoise twenty-six. Follow us! Flank speed! That goddamn tree is crossing at Point Yale Alfa. . . . We got to within two hundred meters of the tree and all of a sudden the damn thing opened fire at us! . . . VC palm trees. . . . Outsmarted by a fucking palm tree . . . After that, every tree we encountered in the river was treated to a liberal dose of grenades and small-arms fire." A tree flies by and explodes. "A tree sprouted arms and rifles, and shot at us. Suspicious palm trees. It took a long time for me to trust trees."

Then Sherdyl reads another scene, the Black River Rats on night patrol at Yale Bravo on the Soirop River in the Mekong Delta. A SEAL team, "real bad hombres," slid into the water to lay tricks and traps for VC. Sudden screams out of the dark. "There in the middle of the little river mouth was a large cypress tree, and both big, bad SEALs were up in the tree, yelling and waving frantically for us to come and get them. Our patrol boat bumped up against the cypress tree, and they both dropped down onto the deck with a sprawling thump. 'What the hell happened?' 'Crocogators!' " "Crocogators!" makes Larry Heinemann laugh his unstoppable laugh. All day, he'll think "Crocogators!" and start up again.

John Swensson, graduate of West Point, officer, writes about his last moments in Viet Nam, whose coordinates are: "East of Eden. Dau Tieng. Cu Chi." He caught the chopper, and took off amid ground-fire shelling. "Outta here! Goodbye, Dau Tieng! Goodbye, Viet Nam!" ("Outta here!" still current slang; Americans want out of wherever.) He reached down for the November *Playboy* on the floor of the chopper. Slithering out from under his seat—a cobra. He couldn't shoot it; he couldn't run out the door. Cobra wanted outta here too:

> "Snake! Snake!"
> I look down to my left and here's a cobra, head down, trying to crawl out. I look to my right and here's the middle of the same cobra coming out from between the seats. I hadn't noticed her 'cause I was scrunched down; the vibrations from the rotor must have waked her up and now I am sitting on top of her as she heads back for the Garden.

So—they fought crocogators, cobras, trees, elephants. Vietnamese soldiers rode elephants; rifles stuck out on all four sides of the howdah. Our city boys were in the wilderness. Viet Nam was alive with jungle and animals. Even the woods moved, and were the enemy.

Joe Lamb, who wrote the "Measure me!" story, reads to us about ourselves right here and now. "This weekend, here where Turtle Island opens to the Pacific, here where a little stream winds beneath Live Oaks, in a place where, only three grandmothers ago, the Ohlone fished for salmon and steelhead, where they gathered acorns for meal, here with twenty-five veterans, with twenty-five souls from twenty-five wars, with one soul from one war, we gather to talk about war and about healing. In this gathering, at this place, many answers have been taken from me, and many questions have been given back. Does the species itself wage war with itself? Where are wars fought? On the earth? In the mind? In the consciousness of the culture? In the collective soul? In the theater of the revolving soul? How long does each war last? Does a war end when individuals heal? When the culture heals?"

Joe's fiction is about some people at a Cheyenne grocery store, part of Elmer's place, a pool hall. Boys are playing pool, men playing dominoes, squaws shopping. Two Indian men come in and ask for "green." The grocer says, "No money, no green." The men lift up a ceremonial headdress. "Ray Blackhorse's war bonnet. Very old." The grocer takes a cold bottle of "green" out of the refrigerator. Boys climbing the water tower watch the Indians drinking the green. It's aftershave. "It makes them go blind," says a boy.

Somebody says, "Love stories. Where are the love stories?"

Robert Landman, one of the new people, a combat vet, says he has a dream love scene. He met a woman at the singles bar with a dance floor. She looked at him with utterly unconditional love in her eyes, which were green like Mother Nature. Her amazing green gaze enveloped him, and he felt good and loved. She held him and loved him with those eyes. He shipped out before he spoke to her. Robert himself has thick, dark eyelashes curling over eyes the colors of the sea. His mother must have green eyes. In his dream, the woman with the greenest green eyes asks him, "Did anyone tell you, you look like Robin Williams?" As a matter of fact, many people have. In his second dream last night, he's in Viet Nam again, walking with his M-16, finger on the trigger. This dream comes to him, even though he never used his gun in war. Though a trained rifleman, he carried his rifle upside down on his back. "I was signaling peace. Snipers understood my signal, and did not aim at me. My fellow soldiers did not razz me."

Dan Fahey lives right here, College Avenue, Berkeley. Billy Budd has come to be with me again. He looks like Custer too, tall and golden. Dan graduated from Notre Dame ROTC, then trained for and worked on the Tomahawk Cruise Missile. His ship was in the Strait of Hormuz and the Persian Gulf. He resigned, and as of today owes the government $39,000 in scholarship money. He is young enough to be the son of the Viet Nam veterans, they can father him. Dan writes his dream to Larry, "Dear Paco . . ." He is walking in shade alone. In the air are a white bird and a mushroom cloud. There are no living large creatures. Lucky ants crawl about. He meets a man about his own age, a Russian, seventeen, eighteen years old, carrying a gun in his arms and a knife on his hip. They look at each other, and put down their guns. The Russian, Petrov, has a ration of food; he opens the can and offers it. Dan and Petrov fling their weapons down the mountain. They eat together.

Larry congratulates Dan for quitting his military career. "You ain't gonna be a brain-dead lifer."

Mike Wong same-same Wittman Ah Sing. I made him up, and he's appeared. He's real, only Mike went to Canada, not Hawai'i. He has hardly aged, hair yet black, thin black mustache, tall and skinny in jeans and plaid shirt. I can feel him listen to me. He looks to me for cues on what to do next. May he still be idealistic. Last night, he dreamed a dream with three acts, set in Canada. A "European war" is going on. A table is laden with weapons, including an old rifle. The sergeant yells for Mike to carry the BAR. The skinniest guy in the company is to carry the heaviest weapon. Then he orders the soldiers to jump off a cliff into the river, and cross it. A man jumps in, and dies. The next man who jumps also dies. Then it's Mike's turn. "Jump, Wong!" He does not jump. "You a wimp, Wong?" He will not jump. "Wimp, Wong?! Jump, Wong!" The sergeant's yelling has the shock of the racial, but it's just Mike's name. Mike shouts out his own name—"Wimp, Wong?! Jump, Wong!"—until everybody is laughing. They crack up at each yell. Larry is in tears of laughter. Chinese American brother writer, the loudest, liveliest voice in the room. Loud and proud, a man on the margin functions in many countries at once, soldier *and* hippie.

I have to recognize all over again the man with the skull pants. He's in different clothes, and has a happy, upturned mustache; and he's changed his name to John Barron-Wike. ("One name is for my stepfather, the other is for my father. Both loved.") The Dom. Rep. vet now writes about Johnny coming home. "He-e-ere's Johnny!" TV voices come out of us; we're ventriloquized. He reads:

> My wife set up a "rehabilitative" picnic, since she was concerned about how I had been behaving since my return. I had probably been back about six weeks or so when this occurred. We went for that picnic to the banks of the Chickahominy River in Virginia with a newly graduated chopper pilot lieutenant friend and his brand-new wife, he on his way to Vietnam in a few weeks. It was a picnic to celebrate my return: home from tents to houses, from outdoor latrines to plumbed bathrooms, home from a hard green masculine world to one with the softnesses of beds and pillows and white wifely thighs welcome-home spread.
>
> We sat on the banks of the Chickahominy and sipped cham-

pagne and felt the sunny Saturday afternoon warmth and that of
the wine. Below us a ski boat started up with a backfire bang. I
found myself lying on the ground looking up at the three of them
looking down on me, faces of incomprehension and concern.
They are wondering what I am doing down there. I am wondering
why they are not down here with me. They look so young. My
friend Norm says, "Jesus Christ, I never saw anyone move that
fast," shaking his head. My wife is shaking her head too. The day
is not going well. . . .

I stood up shamefacedly, brushing the dirt from my clothes.
They begin talking much too loudly about other things. I turned
away from them and looked over the river, trying to calm my
pounding heart. When I looked back at them, Norm's usually ani-
mated face was curiously blank and shiny, while in his wife's I saw
his chopper tumbling in flames into a rice paddy four months in
the future, and in my own wife's face I saw the sad demise of our
marriage years in the future; and angry when I couldn't bear to
look any longer, I turned back to the river where the clouds had
lowered darkling while upriver the sound of cannon and musket
fire came to me and I saw that once again the Chickahominy
River ran red.

Abe Smith keeps clearing his throat, flipping pages, sitting forward,
sitting back. I look at him; Therese looks at him. He won't make eye
contact. I call on him. "Abe, would you like to read?" Larry says, "Read.
Take the pressure off, man." Abe writes about the flight out of Ben Hua
for home. He rushed for an empty seat amid the cargo. The pilot shared
cookies and smokes. It was a cargo of caskets, and they were filled. He
had arrived in Viet Nam with empty body bags, and was leaving with
full caskets. The government *planned* on our getting killed.

Richard Sterling names us: we were Dealers of Death. We were the
Gray Ghost of the Nam Coast—shot Haiphong to pieces. We had good
names. Not LBJ names but linebacker names, Nixon names. Rolling
Thunder. Shot the gooks to pieces. An orgy of gook-killing. We were
good at it. We had good names; we did a good job.

Our Captain was so cool he had two nicknames. His real
name was William A. Kanakanui, and everybody said he was a

direct descendant of the warrior king Kamehameha of Hawai'i.
I don't know whether it was true or not, but it wouldn't have
mattered; because we'd have said it anyway. When we spoke
of him respectfully he was Kanak, as in Kanak kicks ass. When
we spoke of him affectionately, he was The Pineapple, as in The
Pineapple gave us extra liberty because we did good. We had
such good names.

The only name the Vietnamese had was "gook." I count fourteen
"gook"s in his story.

Today, I read about my mother: She told me what to do after the big
fire. "Don't *hun* anything," she said. "You have hands, make more."

During walking meditation, Larry strolls fast, zigzagging across the
paths and grass. He passes Therese and Edie, the leaders, holding hands.
I'm walking holding hands with Jeannie, who's just arrived. Larry walks
back to the group, passes and repasses us. Edie says, "He's having a hard
time walking slow. He can't help speeding ahead." A mother pushing
her baby in a stroller passes us. A couple pulling their dog on a leash pass
us. Under the redwoods, beside the stream, Larry says, "This looks like
the spot where we blew away babies and a dog." John Barron-Wike says,
"I saw a mother blue jay feed a baby blue jay." We return from the walking to find a group of veterans smoking cigarettes on the patio. Richard
Sterling and Larry loudly relish memories of food they'd eaten in Viet
Nam.

In an amazing feat of teaching, Larry Heinemann replies to all the
stories. He calls the writers brave, for looking at things attentively, for
knowing things in detail. He remembers what each person wrote. "You.
You wrote . . ." He finds what we have in common. "You explained the
war as work. We're grunts. Grunts work. Work is a fact of men's lives.
War is a job. Everybody has an experience of a really shitty job. *Moby-
Dick* is about a lot of things, but it's really about the fact that Melville at
one time in his life, for a couple of months, had this really shitty job.
There's a lot of literature that comes out of that. Good jobs too, but lots
of shitty jobs. Explaining the war as work will start with that—the gig—
and the story will build on that experience. We had to do our job well.
Lives depended on us getting things right, the details right. We were
good at details, observing any change in the ground, the field, how to
take apart and put together machinery, all the parts. That skill, that

observation, that attention—you bring that to the writing. I'll describe what a track is, and how to do an ambush, and how firefights work, and how to set up a fragging. There are rules of fragging. I can tell you step by step how to make a booby trap out of a C-ration can. Booby traps are against the Geneva Convention. The army—what a gig. What a gag."

I ding him with the bell. I mean: Hear. Listen. Listen to him. He is so idealistic, to care about rules and ethics. He dearly values the Geneva Convention. But Larry regards the bell like a prizefighting bell ending a round. He puts his watch on the table and says, "Ten minutes." He praises Ted's description of the scissors, a tool of the medic's job. And Sherdyl for the stories about "river browning." And John Barron-Wike for information on how to flush a toilet during drought. Abe, how bodies are bagged and transported. Larry appreciates the writing-with-the-senses that produced Joe's hot-cool green drink of aftershave, John Swensson's cobra, Tom's Arctic Circle. He doesn't overlook anyone. "You told the truth, and you told it in detail, its specific, physical, real thingness." We love him. He listened to us. We feel understood.

My koa-wood bowl from Hawai'i sat in the middle of the table throughout the weekend. Quite a few people leave something in it to be rid of. Edie says, "Take it to the Chinese Cemetery." Someone says, "Monkey off my back."

Again, John Barron-Wike, "Peace Warrior," leads a holding of hands in a circle, and chanting. "Welcome home. Welcome home. Welcome home." Some veterans pound their hearts with their fists. "Peace. Peace. Peace." We hold hands again, and hold on for a long time; we do not want to let one another go.

I take the koa bowl home, and light a fire in the fireplace in my writing room. Sitting on the hearth, I decide not to burn the papers. I'll take them with me to the Grand Canyon, but won't bury them in the red dirt or under a rock. I'll keep them until it comes to me what to do. On *my* paper: I want to rid myself of desiring the impossible—that I control time.

At summer's end, Earll and I go to the East Coast. I'm giving the writing workshop for veterans at the other end of the country. Every other year, Thich Nhat Hanh gives a retreat at the Omega Institute, a beautiful campus on the lordly Hudson. Meeting rarely, the veterans he gathers save up their feelings, and explode. It may be that East Coast people are more dramatic than West Coast people. And these veterans lead with their military credentials, telling their years of service, branch of service, and where they served. They identify themselves as "combat vet" and "one hundred percent Viet Nam vet." None of them are Black. No Asian Americans. All Whites. No women. And all the same age, veterans of Viet Nam. They must feel safe being among Buddhists, and so are able to express themselves. They readily admit to killing, and they are in horrendous pain. The more killings done, or witnessed, the more PTSD.

I missed the very first retreat that Thich Nhat Hanh gave for war veterans. I heard that they stood in a circle, and a Vietnamese veteran and an American veteran stepped forward, walked toward each other, bowed, hugged, and apologized, and accepted each other's apologies, forgave each other. I wish I could've been there. The American veteran bowed? American bodies don't bow. And Asians don't do public hugging. Exactly what words and sentence structure did they use for the apologies? Active, not passive, voice? "I am sorry that [not "if"] I hurt you, that I wronged you." "I am sorry that I bombed you and napalmed you." "I am sorry that I warred against you." No excuses. On the other hand, why should there have been any apology at all? The Vietnamese among us were on *our* side; they weren't the enemy.

I heard that Thich Nhat Hanh told the veterans to use the sound of helicopters as if it were the Mindfulness Bell.

Veterans show me photos of themselves when they were teenagers—their high-school graduation picture, their first driver's license, the snapshot at the picnic before leaving for the war. The young man would look entirely different from the man before me. It would not seem that this boy could naturally grow to become this man. The body type, the hair color, the face—all changed. The man would cry showing me the picture of the lost boy.

People write and talk and weep and scream. Bill Turtle Warrior Ledger, U.S.N., 1968–70, writes a poem to nine people we killed in friendly fire.

> Killed 9 in friendly fire. You weren't friends of mine. I didn't feel friendly or sad. Those 9 guys were not my friends. Friends are people whose names you know, whom you care to hang out with, having good times. Friends aren't people you're pissed at for get-

ting themselves killed. Friends aren't people you kill, schlepping around in the mud and fear.

Bill is going to Bosnia, armed with a camera and a bell.

Supporting Bill, John Dancing Bear Everhart tells of the bravery and sacrifice of men killed in friendly fire. The men themselves had radioed, "Bring it in." "Cougar 6—they're over-running us. jesus christ—they're over-running us—bring it in—bring it in—bring it in." Self-immolation on the run. John himself had given the order, "Bring it down on top of them." He fire-bombed enemy and friends, wiped them all out. "the day i killed five americans was the day i wanted out of the war/out of vietnam—off planet earth. . . . no longer did i love my country/nothing made sense to me anymore."

A frequent refrain among soldiers: "It don't mean nothin'." Art James, who was wounded in Cambodia, where Americans were not supposed to be, explains the phrase "It don't mean nothin'." "We had our own language, which was understood more in the gut than in the head. We used the expression 'It don't mean nothin' ' for a lot of things. You said it after squirting bug repellent on a leech attached to your ankle in an effort to remove the leech. You said it when the monsoon rain drenched and chilled you but cleansed your foul-smelling fatigues. You said it when a very likable buddy nicknamed Cranky lost both of his legs. . . . Those who have participated in war and witnessed it know that it is not noble in any sense. . . . If it didn't teach us not to repeat it, then it still 'don't mean nothin'.' "

An *if* and four negatives in one sentence. Ends up positive.

When Art lay wounded on a medevac cot, some army personnel ordered him not to tell anybody about his top-secret mission. At the explosion, a pinkness had misted the air. It was his blood. The medic said, *"You will be okay. Everything will be all right."* Art rants, "Okay?! I'm covered with blood. My blood. I look down, all I see is blood. And that's my blood in the air. I'm a pink mist. And he says, 'Okay.' Do these legs look okay to you? Is this okay?"

Bathed in my warm blood on this occasion, I knew it was *The Lie*. The Medic, who we had assumed should exercise the healing powers of a god, succumbed to The Lie. The twenty-year-old "medicine man," so to speak, fresh and graduate green from Fort

Hood Texas Medical School, could dispense malaria pills or lance a pimple fairly skillfully on a fellow soldier's shoulder. (I had observed medics squeeze the poisonous effect of dioxin that defoliated lush jungles but dioxin also blemished the skin of soldiers; many of these sores made the burden of lugging a 50 lb. rucksack most unbearable. Blisters were misdiagnosed as "jungle rot," puberty, etc.) I learned quickly Medics were astounded and lacked the supernatural powers to reassemble the cranial skull when a small metal fragment entering the forehead, burst wide with impact, blowing forth the back side portion of the head. Medics did not know how to stop arterial blood flows, repack intestinal bowels or reattach sinewy dangling severed limbs.

. . . Medics were those soldiers who walked circumspectly hoping they would not be called upon to patch-up another soldier after some swirl of lethal metal ripped through the air. . . . **Medic!** was a dreadful wailing noise and often when such events happened, we would kneel together or stand over the wounded victim and plead with the medic, "*save him doc, save him, please save him, save him doc, save him.*"

Art raves. It's later, when I am reading him on the page, that he makes sense to me. "Medic! *The Lie! Save him!*" He looks at me, the teacher from Berkeley, "one who wasn't there," and says, "Medics. Medics are complex people."

Then Art turns on a priest. Father Phil, who has a pained face, keeps silent. Big Bob Weller, sitting beside him on the floor, touches his arm, puts a hand on his shoulder as Art goes at him: "What are you—chaplains, *officers*—doing in the military anyway? . . . Commissioned officers that we were ordered to salute: the quack priest, the false prophet, the endorsers of war . . . the Political Priest . . . the evil embodiment and incarnation of the memorable lie . . . the Nation's Lies . . . the Military Chaplain . . . military career person who makes a living sanctioning death . . . legitimizing and sanctioning *murder* . . . I point you out! I point you out!"

Art gets to his feet and dances a Shiva peace dance with bare, scarred legs; he talks and talks, going past the time limits and two-sentence limits I keep setting. I'm in charge of the bell, but can't establish silence. "Bell him," says one. "Let him speak," says another. "I should scream," says Art; "I could start screaming and never stop. I wanted to scream when I was over there, and I didn't. Now I can if I want to. It wouldn't be inappropriate for me to break out screaming." "Let it out." "Go ahead. Go for it." "Ring the bell." "No, don't stop him." We are out of control. I know they wouldn't behave like this if Thich Nhat Hanh were here. I ring the bell, and Art calms down.

Sister Chân Không, Sister True Emptiness, the head nun, leads the veterans in walking to the lake and chanting to the goddess of mercy. The veterans carry a long sheet of white paper covered with flowers and the names of their dead. Cole Morton, infantry officer, U.S. Marine Corps, 1967–68, honored: "All the people who died under my weapons." He did not have their names. The monks and Sister wear red-and-gold sashes over their brown robes. One of the monks has pinned on his back a scroll with the phonetic sounds for us to chant: "Kwoon Yum Po Saht kwanti om." Same-same my village language. My mother in prayer. "Kwoon Yum Po Saht" same-same "Kuan Yin Bodhisattva," who is compassionate listener, goddess of mercy.

Back East is filled with so many sounds. In the evenings, Cole Morton sings all the verses of "Aileen Aroon," overhead light haloing his silver mane:

> Castles are sacked in war,
> Chieftains scattered far.
> Truth is a fix-ed star,
> Ai–leen a–roon.

In our sessions here, I am hearing a lot of woman-warrior stories. Is it me evoking them? Jerry Crawford, who looks and weeps like the lion in *The Wizard of Oz*, reads about a Vietnamese guerrilla woman. He stalks her through the jungle, wanting her, addressing her in his mind. "You, the one I want to kill. . . . The sun spangles the killing field . . . the noises of the jungle. . . . Not one single word passes, the F.N.G. not getting it. . . . Tried touching you, Woman Warrior. Is the shimmering of the water your voice?" He catches and kills the woman, who had killed his friend. She sits up. Her spirit flies at and enters him. He carries her to this day. Jerry says, "I am myself a woman warrior."

An FNG is a Fuckin' New Guy, a Fuckin' New Gal.

Dan Möen Thompson, a descendant of someone on the *Arabella*, the next ship after the *Mayflower*, speaks in the careful voice of a Southern gentleman and Special Forces Green Beret officer. He reads about a Marine LuRP who captures a wounded VC woman and carries her on his back under fire through jungle and rivers. There's a bounty on all slant-eye weasels. His reward for bringing her in would be extra R&R.

There must have been many women in battle. A winged goddess appears at Vietnamese festivals; she flies and dances at Tet and on the Night of Wandering Souls in October. Her shadow flows in the moonlight. She was not killed; the veterans carry her alive within their own bodies. They captured her, but felt as if she'd been the one doing the capturing.

Dan then tells about a monk, or monks, that he fired upon. "He or they disappeared behind the big bell. I don't know if I hit him. I ran around to the other side of the bell, but nobody was there. Maybe another monk took him away. I'm going back to Marble Mountain to find out what really happened. I just phoned my daughter, and told her I'm going to Viet Nam again. I want to visit my old haunts inland, and see Da Nang again, and memorize Marble Mountain for my book, *Marble Mountain*. I want to know for certain. They couldn't have had rifles. They were monks."

I remind him that in China armies of monks went to war. They used kung fu and weapons, archery, swords, throwing stars. And Zen samurai monks trained with rifles. He mustn't think that all monks are pacifists like Thich Nhat Hanh.

Jerry says, "Maybe they were VC disguised as monks."

Amongst this small group, Earll can read his writing. He's here because I am here. He does not identify as a "veteran." The government hadn't designated him a "veteran" but an "ex-serviceman," though he was in Viet Nam—twice. Once before the fighting started—that is, before the Americans were fighting; the U.S. was not officially there— he sailed into Saigon Harbor on a seaplane tender. Diem came aboard; the sailors were lined up to salute him. About a dozen of Diem's soldiers, in camouflage uniforms and black berets, held automatic weapons at port arms. Earll remembers Saigon as an elegant old city, ironwork balconies overhanging the streets; it was like New Orleans. Rich people were honored to invite American sailors to formal parties. He met a little girl, and bought her a pigeon for a pet. Civilization on the ship was rude—the hot engine room, the grease, the Pall Malls, the voices coming over the bitch box, nights in the rack. Ten years later, he shipped out voluntarily with the Merchant Marine, and saw that Saigon had changed. He sailed from Honolulu. "I was sort of a spy for peace," he says.

But his ship, the Sea Train *Carolina*, was delivering weapons, missiles and rockets. I was aboard saying Aloha, and saw for myself torpedoes, bombs, locked in tiers onto the deck. Earll showed me the marks on the floor where bolts went in to make a brig cage. I think he went to Viet Nam for the adventure; he didn't want to be left out. His peace values were not firm. At the time, I felt betrayed. I was left behind in Hawai'i.

While waiting for him to come home, I caught a tiny item in the newspaper that the ship that I had seen docked alongside, to the left of his, the *Kitty Hawk*, was on fire in Manila. Eleven of her sailors had been busted for pot.

Earll still dreams navy dreams.

Earll and I go home for a few days, then drive to Malibu, where we join Thich Nhat Hanh on the western part of his American teaching tour. We're at Camp Hess Kramer, near Pacific Palisades. The veterans here would "retreat within the retreat." Claude Thomas, a vet from Back East, would speak to them veteran-to-veteran; Sister Chân Không would give Buddhist instruction; I would only need to teach writing. Thich Nhat Hanh's presence should pervade and back up everything. Jim Janko, Ted Sexauer, and Robert Landman come from the workshop I began up north. The vets are a group of only ten, counting me and Earll.

We meet sitting on cushions on the floor in a room with a pool table. Jeff Barber, a large, black-bearded man, sits on the floor with his prosthetic leg sticking out in the middle of the group. Ted sits in a chair. Sister Phuong—that's what Sister Chân Không is also called—says that she realizes that veterans have difficulties with walking meditation because it reminds them of walking patrol, having to be wary of land mines and booby traps. So let's try "ze skippeeng and ze jumpeeng and ze hoppeeng." The tiny bald woman, in brown robe and white socks, walks, walks, walks, tiptoes, tiptoes, runs, runs, runs, skips, shuffles, sashays, hop-hops around the half of the room that is not the pool table. Cooperating, Jeff with his plastic leg, Ted with his bad hip, Earll with his back going out, all of us prance after her, seriously a-hopping and a-skipping around the candle on the floor while the sun rises into the cañoncita.

Sister Phuong says, "This group of veterans, you suffer less than other veterans." She says such a thing with Jeff Barber's artificial leg sticking out before her. Where does she get the notion that these people have less suffering? Is it that they look so good? I am nonplussed. Maybe she means to say, "Please suffer less." There's a suffering contest? No one argues with her. We are naturally quiet people, except for Claude. We're writers, quiet because we can always express ourselves on paper. I figure she's comparing our group of Californians to the explosive veterans Back East. She's too impressed by drama. She's a Buddhist, she's Sister True Emptiness, yet doesn't feel the drama in our silence.

Claude An Shin Thomas, a compact, charismatic man, is still running on Viet Nam energy. He urges us to join him in Bosnia. We could stand on street corners in East Mostar and in West Mostar, and ring the Bell of Mindfulness for nonviolence. "We'll sweeten the air with the bell. I'm clear, go to East Mostar, bear witness, BE PEACE! Move toward the war zone, touch the people, and bear witness. If many of us, or even a few, went there, unarmed, we could stop the war, even for a moment. No one fighting admits really wanting to, but somehow haven't yet figured out how to stop." Then on to Viet Nam. "For a month, let's walk from Saigon (Ho Chi Minh City) to the Ben Hai River (once the line of demarcation between North and South), and on to Hanoi. I believe we will be the first group of veterans to move through Viet Nam without any government sponsorship or restrictions. The first group (to my knowledge) whose sole purpose will be 'Peace.' " And Europe, through the lands of the old wars and death camps. And Iraq. "I'm walking to as many sites of suffering as I can possibly visit, and in each of these places do service. Everybody, let's go to Viet Nam. Don't worry about money. We'll come up with money. And let's invite Thây, take him with us back to Viet Nam."

Behind his back, people are saying they don't trust Claude. He's a mythomaniac. His numbers don't jibe. His geography is off. He says he killed three hundred; he says he killed five hundred. He was seventeen years old, and crew chief of a helicopter gunship? Impossible. And now he's got a new name, An Shin, and turned into some kind of a Zen holy man. Claude says, "I always have been a Zen holy man."

But *I* trust him. Claude reads to us about speaking last month at the

Church of the Crossroads in Hawai'i. He met Hawaiians getting ready to join the service, and warned them about war, as no one had warned him. "Those going to and those coming from Viet Nam passed one another on gangplanks and at airports without talking." But the young Hawaiians just stood there rubbing their bare stomachs. One of them said, "The war's over, man." They turned away from the out-of-it ancient old vet. I trust Claude for the accuracy of his seeing; he noticed the mokes and bradahs rubbing their opu.

At the plenary meeting, Thich Nhat Hanh is explicating one by one "Fifty Verses on the Manifestation of Consciousness." He writes on the board the Sanskrit and Chinese and English, and sometimes the Vietnamese and French, for states of mind. He gives extra lectures at night, lectures for two hours twice a day. I remember listening to a liberation theologist in Ann Arbor; the auditorium was emptier each evening of the series as he went on and on, offering theories, scholarship, analyses. The Dalai Lama also gives lectures that are like philosophy classes. What the crowds want is a village priest giving homey sermons. But wise men, when they are old, have to burst forth with all they know at the height of their languages.

It's up to me to teach the veterans practically.

Ten people working for four days, everyone is able to write a complete story or poem, and read the entire work to everyone else. We discuss them to our hearts' content. I love Jim Janko's narrating voice—steady, urgent sounds from Illinois, the heartland. He is small and quick, a baseball player, a tap dancer. His thick hair stands up; every bit of him is alert to everything and everyone. In his story, on "a day of water and sun," he and a friend are walking ten klicks away for water. The narrator trips a mine next to the well. His friend is killed. "He's dead. But he wanted to play for the Cubs. We were going to play for the Cubs when we got home. He was gonna play first base and be called Bobby. We'd have ballplayer names, Jimmy and Bobby. He's dead." He adds, "For the Vietnamese who set the trap—May they heal. May we heal." (Home, Jimmy played on a vets' team, the Flashbacks. They ran around all the bases—home run—no matter what.)

Ted reads two poems, and makes an announcement. The serious poem is about a general giving out medals for outstanding work at "pacification." The joke poem is about a guy who ate, without sharing, all the antipasto his mother sent, and got constipated. ". . . the Mediterranean hors d'oeuvres / have stoppered his ass to a standstill." The poet hadn't learned to give enemas in medics' school. His experiments didn't work, and the guy had to be medevacked out. The listeners laugh like toilet trainees.

Ted's personal news: "I won the VA." The Veterans Administration has recognized his disabilities as service-related. "Now I've got new worries—a rich person's problems. I've always been poor. Now I have a deal with the VA. I'm ambivalent, getting labeled by the government one hundred percent disabled." We applaud and congratulate him. "I want to learn to be generous."

Robert Landman talks from notes about serving with a "mechanized unit." The outnumbering, us versus them, was fifty to one. His friend Raoul got killed, sniped, right next to him. "The person next to you getting killed is how they motivate soldiers to use their guns." The mechanized unit captured a VC soldier. "The CO was hard and unrelenting in his style of interrogation, and when he seemed satisfied with his harsh performance, he nonchalantly walked away." He hadn't asked the questions that Robert would've asked: "How have you come to be here? What was life like for you before the war? When the war ends, what will you do?" Robert made friends with the South Vietnamese Army interpreter:

I asked him if I could talk to the NVA soldier. The interpreter said, "Sure. What do you want to talk to him about?" When we approached, the soldier appeared apprehensive. I asked him his name. I told him mine. I asked him how he came to be here. He was drafted out of school into the army. I said, "Me too" and "How old are you?" "Nineteen." "I'm nineteen also." "Do you have a girl friend or a wife?" He said, "Yes." He showed me her picture. He asked me if I had someone special in my life. I didn't, but I think the interpreter said, "Yes," as he was nodding in amusement as to how the conversation was going. The interpreter asked me for my wallet, which he opened to the pictures inside, one an attractive woman and another of a happy family scene . . . pictures that come with a new wallet that for some reason I hadn't taken out yet. With a big grin the interpreter pointed to the picture of the woman saying, "She's number one!" The NVA soldier was nodding in agreement, and I didn't have the heart to tell him that she wasn't my number one, and felt I did not want to rob him of enjoying the moment and my good fortune. . . .

In that moment, everyone and everything became silent on that side of the mountain. There are many different kinds of silences. . . . This was a peaceful silence . . . beyond all understanding . . . lasting only a moment as the silence was intruded upon by the noisy approach of the helicopter and those in charge in the company coming back for him. The activity of the war was closing in on this little island to assault this moment of peace. The helicopter arrived and was hovering above the trees. I wanted to say something else but did not know what to say or how to say it. I had a black scarf around my neck. I took it off and gave it to him. He put it around his neck, and we looked at each other and I wished him well. He smiled back at me. Within a few minutes, he was gone, but something remained, something unexplainable and transformational. . . .

I realized that he was not the enemy. I could no longer be a soldier. The war was over. From that moment on, I did not want to be in a position to bring harm to anyone. When I told the CO and top sergeant, I was threatened with a court martial and being sent to Leavenworth, and in that profound moment of peace, I was not afraid or intimidated, and responded, "What's the worst that can happen . . . send me to Viet Nam?"

Now I know why, for the rest of his tour of duty, Robert carried his rifle upside down on his back. I picture the stock as one of his wings.

Jeff Barber is at a crisis point in every part of his life. He's splitting from his wife. He's moving his rock shop from southern California up north. He's gone without a cigarette since June 23. And today is his birthday. (The retreatants are surprising him with a birthday cake at dinner, his first ever birthday party.) His sense of smell coming back, Jeff remembers the scent of wet land and water buffalo. "I went to Viet Nam to lose my virginity." The girl next door is impossible, so you fuck someone on the other side of the planet. "John Wayne!" He uses "John Wayne" as an ironic expletive. "Glad to get in that shit." His jobs were loading dead bodies and mine sweeping. The fighting was with fellow marines. There was a suicide: "He got to leave."

Ted says, "It was macho to be shot, to take a bullet, to be carrying shrapnel."

Claude says, "And the most macho—top macho—is: getting killed!"

Jimmy says, "No bigger macho than that."

Big macho roars of laughter. I wish Sister Chân Không could understand their jokes.

Claude has promised the veterans that Thich Nhat Hanh will speak personally with them. But Thây is busy; he's way behind on transmitting the fifty verses about consciousness. Claude says, "I know where his room is. Let's go knock on his door. Let's drop in on him." Thây likes and favors Claude, who treats him like a regular person. Jimmy Janko says, "Maybe we better not." I say that in ancient times you quietly sat at the teacher's door day and night, to prove earnestness and patience.

On the fifth and last morning of the retreat, Thây finishes explicating all fifty verses, summarizing the last thirty in a triumphant finale. He segues into an invitation to the veterans to come sit by him. A to-do and stir as people pass chairs up for Jeff and Ted. Thich Nhat Hanh turns his head, watching this veteran and that veteran make their way through the crowd, to be seated on the floor before him. He too is sitting on the floor, but on a platform. His expression is at once benign and severe, patient and impatient. He is a small man, a humble monk in a brown habit, big ears, a real person—and he is Buddha. He speaks to the vets as one of them: "We try to learn from our experience in Viet Nam. Out of our sufferings, we should learn something. Veterans have something to tell their nation. Veterans have experience that makes them the light at the tip of the candle, illuminating the roots of war and the way to peace." And soldiers do not wage war by themselves; they are the hands of the entire body of the nation. "When you touch fire and your hand gets burned, it is not the responsibility of the hand alone. It is the responsibility of the whole person. We cannot just shout at you and say, 'You did that!' We all did it collectively."

He calls out the veterans' names, and presents each with a book of his poems, *Call Me by My True Names*. "Maxine and Earll Kingston." I am standing at the edge of the crowd, next to a side door. He calls me and Earll again. I step through the crowd, accept the gift, and sit down with the veterans. Somebody behind me gives me his or her cushion. Earll stays in the larger congregation. The book is inscribed, and has a pretty bookmark tied with raffia. I feel honored, and thanked. But I know that some of the vets don't like being singled out, and find it shameful to be looked at by the crowd. Others feel that the community is holding them in its embrace.

Our small group goes back to the pool-table room, where Claude begins a ceremony of goodbye. He says, "I wasn't able to say goodbye to anybody in Viet Nam. I want to say a mindful goodbye to each of you." A short guy in baggy pants, Claude has to reach up high to hug the tall vets.

A knock on the door. A woman peers in and says that she found a veteran who has just arrived. Of course, invite him to join us. We go on with our fare-thee-wells. The door opens again; the woman announces, "This is Gail De La Fuente." A woman veteran. She is like a blonde doe, stepping carefully, large eyes looking at each and all of us. She sits in a chair, at the edge of her seat. She is dressed in a lightweight suit and high heels. I've been wearing the same clothes all week. She was a triage nurse; she must have seemed like a golden angel in Viet Nam. And she must have looked exactly as she does now, not aged at all. Jimmy says that Fuente means Fountain. She speaks the names of places in Viet Nam where she served. Ted asks if she could tell him something that he was always wondering about; he'd patched up the wounded and medevacked them out, but never knew what became of them. Does Gail know where they went? Ted and Gail recall places and routes in Viet Nam, and match them up. She says, Yes, they came to her hands after leaving his. She is planning to go to Washington, D.C., in the fall, to the dedication of the memorial to women veterans of Viet Nam. She has visited the Wall before. "I wanted to look for people I met in Viet Nam, wounded people, and the ones that died. I stood at the Wall, but I didn't know their names. I never knew their names." She is crying. Tears fall over her round pink cheeks. "I didn't know their names. I don't know their names." We sit there quiet, some people crying with her. Jimmy reaches over, and says with a laugh, "My name's Jim Janko." She turns and looks at him, her blonde bob shimmering like a halo, and takes his hand. They shake hands, laughing.

It is never too late. People disappear; then we meet new, familiar people, and with them continue our journeys.

We breathe together in meditation. At the bell, Gail De La Fuente says, "I remember part of a poem," and starts saying a poem. "Neruda," says Earll, and recites some lines. "Keeping Quiet" by Pablo Neruda. Jimmy knows some lines too, and can say them in Spanish.

> Now we will count to twelve
> and we will all keep still.
>
> For once on the face of the earth,
> let's not speak in any language;
> let's stop for one second,
> and not move our arms so much.
>
> It would be an exotic moment
> without rush, without engines;
>
> we would all be together
> in a sudden strangeness.
> . . .
>
> Now I'll count up to twelve
> and you keep quiet and I will go.
>
> Ahora contaré hasta doce
> y tú te callas y me voy.

Gail De La Fuente was real. Her entrance seemed like theater; it seemed like a miracle. Miraculous and real. We were not expecting her. We were about to call it a day. At the last moment, the heavens open, the Angel descends. Everyone is bathed in light and magic. A new character shows up, and suddenly everything makes sense, and is redeemed.

We get out of Malibu one day ahead of a firestorm that is rushing through canyons next to the one we were in. It's fire season again. Fire is not apocalyptic. Los Angeles is burning, but the fire is not the Fire Next Time. It's not the Day of the Locust. Earthquake, fire—it's just weather. Continental drift is not a moral force.

Okay. So what else have I learned from these disruptions to my life? I don't trust born-again changes. The elation won't last. Character has to be existentially formed over a long time. There are people who have lost everything—health, friends, feelings, hope. Most of the veterans have no spouse, and they do not want a career. Some are homeless. Now that I have entered their lives with promises, I better stay. I can't be another one who abandons them. I feel a vow coming on—that I will be the writing teacher of the veterans for my whole life. I will help them write until the stories full of explosions become quiet.

The Sunday before Thanksgiving, the leaves on the oak trees around the Faculty Club have changed to yellow and brown; the redwoods are the same as always. Tom Currie, waiting for me, is again sitting by *The Last Dryad*. I decorate the O'Neill Room with bus posters, the Streetfare Journal series, which are on twelve thousand buses in fifteen American cities. The poetry you see on city buses was put there by George Evans, who left home at fourteen and lived in the streets, alone and in gangs. He enlisted in the air force at eighteen, and was a medical corpsman in Libya. In Viet Nam in 1969, he was night-crew chief of an emergency triage unit. He studied for and got his GED while in Viet Nam. Protesting the war, he was court-martialed for disobeying orders, and was honorably discharged. He graduated from Carnegie Mellon in English, and from Johns Hopkins with an M.A. in writing seminars/English. He is a poet, and has come to read to us, and to listen to us read. (George has Chinese eyes. I asked, "Are you hapa Chinese?" He said, "It's possible. I could be Chinese. I was adopted.")

We hold the writing silence all morning and into the autumn afternoon. Oh, it's good to be with the veteran writers in my own workshop again. Like being back in my own classroom. No excitement but in the writing. So we continue. . . .

The newcomer today is Pauline Laurent. She's so pretty but so sad, a Viet Nam widow. She was seven months pregnant when her husband was killed. Two men came to her door. One of them said, "I regret to inform you that your husband has been fatally wounded." She yelled at him, "What do you mean, 'fatally wounded'? Is he dead? Dead?! He's dead. Say it. 'Dead!' Goddamn it, say it. 'Dead!' "

Bob Golling tells a story from the point of view of the body escort:

In September 1966 I volunteered to be a "body escort." A "body escort" is an official military escort that makes sure the deceased/remains gets home to his family. He makes sure that if the family wants one, there is a military funeral. He assists and consoles the family any way he can. He is usually a friend of the deceased. Actually I think I was conned into volunteering. I was about the same age, same religion, same race, and same color. Why not go? . . . it's easy duty. . . .

The boy's father answered the door. He was thin and shorter than I, old too, like he should have been a grandfather.

"You'll stay the night with us, Bob, please stay," Mrs. Doherty asked.

. . . Upstairs they showed me his room. It was a room like I had always wanted, only large enough for one single bed, a dresser, a desk and a chair. His things were still there. I wondered how long they would be.

That night I did stay with the Dohertys. I was careful not to disturb the comb, the hairbrush, the razor used so few times. I was careful not to move the drawers hiding secrets of a boyhood now ended. I was ever so careful, too, when I slid between the cold, cold sheets of his bed and turned out the light of my own boyhood.

As I'd hoped, George Evans replies to the veterans with his life and his poetry. He talks story, then reads the prose poem about the thousand and one gold bodhisattvas at Sanjusangendo in Kyoto.

. . . row upon row of a thousand standing figures, carved, painted, and gold leafed with a calm but stunned look of enlightenment, five hundred on each side of a larger, seated figure of their kind, miniature heads knotted to their scalps representing the fragments of a time when their heads exploded in dismay at the evil in this world, the way our heads exploded in the war, though we don't wear our histories where they can be seen.

Each statue has twenty pairs of arms to symbolize their actual 1,000 arms. . . .

But each hand holds twenty-five worlds it saves, and because each figure can multiply into thirty-three different figures, imagine the thirty-three thousand worlds they hold, how much distress there really is, then multiply that by a thousand and one and think of what it's like to stand in an ancient wooden temple with all that sparkling compassion, even for those of us who believe in almost nothing.

George asks us, "How many heads do we have and how many arms and how many worlds do we hold, and just how far will we go to end our war?"

On walking meditation, at the ring of the bell, everyone stands still, and sometimes, when I remember to look at them, I see the ordinary people standing there shining and golden. Each one is a spike of light. A community standing straight with palms together or hands at their sides look like the 1,001 bodhisattvas.

To get to Green Gulch Farm, you cross Golden Gate Bridge and take Highway 1, switchbacking and hairpinning over the mountains above the sea. Definitely leave the city, and enter nature. Green Gulch is a working farm and meditation center. We meet there in the new year, in the yurt, which was just built. Light fills the round space through the circle of windows and the skylight. We are at the center of the universe; we are the most important people in existence.

I sit in the chair closest to the potbelly stove, fired up behind me. I announce the loss of our World War II vet, Howard Lapin. He died of a heart attack before Christmas. Remember his beautiful bass voice reading about flying over Africa? He was a recipient of the Distinguished Flying Cross. He lived and worked in Africa, and Asia, and Latin America, nineteen developing nations, and eight states of the United States. His disciplines—he was actually *Dr.* Howard Lapin—were transportation engineering and urban planning. "My finest deed was vetoing a plan to flood the rain forest in Brazil," he'd said. He was stationed near Chungking, the wartime capital of China, "a haven for many people from farther east." He was aware of being near the Hunza people and Shangri-la. "The Cheng Du Valley, where our four B-24 airbases were, was also the location of a great university," he'd written. "Other than the disturbance made by our aircraft, with its remote location and scholarly tradition, the Cheng Du area was sort of a haven of peace, I think." Howard was a member of the Unitarian church, and also the Buddhist Peace Fellowship, which he had joined last year. Our group has lost its elder, but today another veteran of World War II has come—Melis Van der Eijk of the Royal Netherlands Navy. Like Rimbaud, enlisting in the Dutch army.

And something unprecedented happens: a large group of women enter the yurt together. There is an immensity about them, individually and en masse. A vastness. Heat. They are not angelic. One of them is another one's mother. I fear them. I have fear-of-women. Woman warriors. They speak like my mother. "I'm going to tell you my big secret. Don't you ever tell it. Don't you dare betray me." The women have come, and I have to heed them. "You didn't know, did you," they ask, "that sixty-three women were killed in the line of duty in Viet Nam? And their names are not on the Wall. The Doughnut Dolly who was killed holding a baby—her name is not on the Wall. The Doughnut Dolly raped almost to death by a GI—she killed herself—*her* name is not on the Wall. Eight nurses killed in action—we planted eight trees in their honor."

The clear center of the group, Woman Vet—she doesn't want me to disclose her name—tells us what not to call her. Tells us who she is not. We are not to ask, "Were you a nurse? Were you a Doughnut Dolly?" (Behind her back, the other vets are saying, "What did she *do* in Viet Nam?" "She was a spy or something, wasn't she?") She scolds, "Is there something wrong with your hearing? I said ARMY SPECIAL SER-VICES! I was a Department of the Army Civilian with Army Special Services."

She writes, then reads: "Please don't misunderstand, there's nothing wrong with being called a Doughnut Dolly if you were one. But just as all women in Viet Nam were not army nurses, all civilian women in-country were not Red Cross Doughnut Dollies. . . . The feeling I get when someone says, 'Oh, you were a Doughnut Dolly,' is that a value judgment has somehow instantly been made. It feels like a put-down, as though our efforts, our contributions, our sacrifices as civilian women don't count. That we might have been there, in Saigon or Long Binh maybe, but we're not to be taken seriously. After all, we didn't have real jobs, and were never under stress or in mortal danger. . . . 'Oh, *you* were a Doughnut Dolly?!' . . . the not so subtle implication sometimes being 'Then we *know* what you did in 'Nam!'

"Do you??

"I recently read a poem written by a Pulitzer Prize–winning poet entitled 'Doughnut Dollies.' I read it and was insulted. Insulted and dismayed—that age-old slander about women and the military was being perpetuated by such a well-known author . . . 'war cheerleaders,' 'officer's material,' 'camp followers' . . . We must have gone there to get rich quick, or to find a husband!

"We women went to Viet Nam for many of the same reasons you men did—out of a sense of duty, loyalty, adventure, or patriotism. Our President had said, ask not what our country could do for us, but what we could do for our country, and many of us took his words to heart. We went to Viet Nam because our brothers were there in need of support and comfort. And in supporting you, we served our country."

Woman Vet shows us a picture in the latest issue of *California Zephyr*, the Vietnam Veterans of America newspaper. It's herself twenty years ago, a thin young woman, a beautiful madonna with enormous dark eyes and thick black hair. She held two toddlers, a boy in her right arm, and a girl in her left. The jumpsuited girl seems to be Amer-Asian, a dust-of-the-earth child. Woman Vet was looking at the boy, and cooing at him, or about to kiss him. Both children made worried eyebrows at the camera. She had done all she could to lift and fly the babies out of Viet Nam.

The veterans hear Woman Vet out. No one argues with her. They receive all she says with silence.

One evening, I lead the veterans, unrehearsed, to read in public. At A Clean Well-Lighted Place for Books, at Larkspur Landing, a good-size audience fills all the folding chairs amidst the bookshelves. Tom says, "They came to hear Maxine. And they're getting us." Bait-and-switch. But I mean to give the veterans my readers. My readers should love them.

For the audience, as for the veterans, I ring the Bell of Mindfulness, and invoke Avalokiteshvara, the bodhisattva of compassionate listening. "We invoke your name, Avalokiteshvara. We aspire to learn your way of listening in order to help relieve the suffering in the world. You know how to listen in order to understand. We invoke your name in order to practice listening with all our attention and openheartedness. . . ." Ring. Ring. Ring.

The veterans, who are sitting amongst the audience, walk to the microphone one by one:

". . . Say it. 'Dead!' Goddam it, say it. 'Dead!' . . . My husband is dead. I know it."

". . . I volunteered to be a 'body escort.' "

". . . 'Measure me!' . . ."

". . . Vietnamese teachers taught me their language. How can a human being learn to love a people, then kill them?"

"Snake! Snake!"

> ". . . My dead friends are worthless.
> I love them and they're worthless.
> I can't trust them to be what I've made of them
> in my mind. And where are they, anyhow?
> My fellow survivors from that time —
> it would break my heart too much
> to find out they'd become
> ordinary or crackpots,
> jerks like the rest of you."

"I learned to meditate during my year in Viet Nam. Often I hummed the tune 'Old Man River' to myself. The sky was deep, beautiful black. There were torrential rains during the monsoon season. And sometimes the lights of Saigon, twenty-one klicks away, lit up the sky, but mostly there was only starlight, moonlight, and the velvety, black, caressing sky. . . ."

The new guy, Scott Morrison, sings, accompanying himself on guitar, and jazzes up the audience:

> "I'm gonna be an Airborne Ranger
> I'm gonna go to Viet Nam
> I'm gonna be an Airborne Ranger
> I'm gonna kill the Charlie Cong"

A man standing at the back of the room, near the dark doorway, says, "Open mike. Is this an open mike? I want to read." He has a lot of pages in his raised hand. Oh, no, a crasher from off the street. I can't turn away a Viet Nam vet, but once he gets on platform, I'll never get him off. And audience members, one after another, will pop up to the mike, rapping and improvising. I would dishonor the veteran writers who have been working all year. From across the bookstore, publicly, in front of everybody, I say to this veteran seeking an audience, "The evening's late. We've been reading for two hours. No, this is not an open mike. I invite you to come to the workshop." The man lowers his hand.

When it's over, the crowd surrounds the readers. They love the veterans. Each vet has a circle of interlocutors. Women apologize for spitting at them when they came home. The people do not want to let them go. I leave, hoping that the whole audience of forty souls won't regard themselves as invited to the workshop.

Our next gathering is in a bunker, the basement of the Cal Alumni House, the Presidents' Room. Portraits of the presidents of the University of California hang on every wall. Gary Gach, veteran, Buddhist and Chinese scholar, makes up a poem on the spot:

> Sages from frames
> beholding
> looking at flowers.

The sages are the university presidents, and we are the flowers.

Woman Vet has returned, and with her more women—Kate Beckwith, a second-generation Doughnut Dolly; she and her mother were in Viet Nam at the same time. Bonnie Humble, U.S.A.F. Nurse Corps, Viet Nam, 1970–1971. Joan Prager, civilian with Army Special Services in Viet Nam, and Service Club Director in Korea and Germany. Maureen "Mo" Nerli, U.S.O. in Nam. Maryanne Teng, a student of Thich Nhat Hanh at Plum Village. Sara Haines, American Red Cross, Supplemental Recreational Activities Overseas/Da Nang—Phu Loi—Qui Nhon, '67. Her sister vets call Sara "Poet." And Dan Fahey brought a girlfriend, who sits lotus-position on the floor.

Kate gives us the motto given to her by old Mrs. Dowling, leader of the Doughnut Dollies: "We are NOT entertainers! We are RECREATORS!"

Ted Sexauer passes me a note: "I would like to read today—have a writing problem I need the group's help on." He tries out on us the speech that he will deliver at a black-tie reunion of the 173rd Airborne

Brigade. They will be honoring the women veterans, and his words have to be sufficient and appropriate. "As a medic, I identify with the life-sustaining roles women had in Viet Nam." He would include the women in "the embrace of our camaraderie." "We have invited twenty-five women to join us tonight, to act as representatives for the approximately thirty-one thousand, five hundred women who served in-country. The exact number of women who served in Vietnam is not known; for some reason, the Department of Defense did not keep those statistics — the best estimate I'm aware of is that approximately eleven thousand, five hundred military women were there, about ninety percent of whom were nurses, and approximately twenty thousand civilian women were there. As I speak of our guests, I will refer to all of them as veterans; the civilian women obviously are not veterans of military service, but they are veterans of the Viet Nam War — they were there, they had an important job to do, and they did it well. . . . Ladies, we know that none of you were drafted. None of you had to be in Viet Nam. We know that no one is truly selfless; we know that you had your own lives to live and your own reasons for being in Viet Nam, but we also know that, at the heart of it, you were there because you cared about us. And that is why we care so much about you. . . ."

The women love the speech. Kindness, gratitude, awe flow from the men toward the women. The women beam, and snuggle into their seats. This bunker is a men's club that at last welcomes women; and the women are letting men into their sorority. (My secret wish for the vets: that these many single men and single women find mates from amongst our community.)

Woman Vet tells/reads about starting A Circle of Sisters . . . A Circle of Friends. "A lot of women volunteered for Viet Nam through churches and relief groups, and the U.S.O. and the Red Cross, which are not military services. These sisters do not get benefits such as VA hospitals and vet centers. And now the new statue beside the Wall would honor women veterans, but not civilians. The Circle of Sisters recognizes civilian women who served in Viet Nam as Viet Nam vets. We wanted a place at the dedication for our own small ceremony. So we organized A Circle of Sisters . . . A Circle of Friends, and with no money, contacts, very little time, and a lot of determination, we were able to convince the powers-that-be in D.C. that we weren't just two crazy women from the West; that we really had been in Viet Nam; that fifty-five additional

American women—not just the eight nurses—had also died in Viet Nam, and that they deserved to be remembered too."

Six months ago, at the capital, Woman Vet was running across the lawn toward the Viet Nam memorials, late for the dedication ceremony. She carried a wreath of anthuriums. A cop stopped her. This cop, this kid, wanted to see her permit for the roped-off area. She had left it in the car. "And from a distance," she tells us, "as far away as Viet Nam perhaps—I watched 'her' as she lifted the floral wreath, and, using it as her battering ram, knocked that unsuspecting officer of the law out of her way."

We laugh and interrupt her story with applause.

She explains, "It was an out-of-body experience. I felt myself shoot out of my body—a flaming angry spirit took over, and hit him. I watched from afar as a woman thwarted struck out in anger. Her act of violence *shocked me*! I was appalled, embarrassed. That woman whose roiling rage I witnessed was me." Woman Vet works as a cop. She pictured her supervisor at the PD shocked.

"You hit a fellow peace officer," says Bob Golling.

Severe Ted says to the group, "If I don't say it, I won't be able to sleep. You people laughed at the violence. Why? I'm questioning laughter at violence."

"But it was just flowers. She hit him with flowers."

"Anthuriums."

"It was a heavy wreath."

"It was an act of violence. Why did we laugh? Why did it make us laugh? Why does violence make us laugh?"

"It was funny. It's funny whacking a cop with a floral wreath."

"Cop whacking cop."

"We were on the woman's side. We wanted her to get to the ceremony."

"Violence makes a good story. It's dramatic. We get off on it. That's the way our species is."

"We are a culture addicted to excitement. Have you noticed? Everybody is always saying, 'Wasn't it exciting?' 'Weren't you excited?' 'I'm so excited.' 'It was so exciting.' "

"They say, 'the theater of war.' They mean, it's not war. It's theater. It's a play."

"Desert Storm. It's a film title. It's not a war. It's the weather. It's nature."

"We're veterans of language. We're responsible for naming."

Shining Bob Golling defends our laughter. "We were laughing because laughter is almost crying."

Woman Vet isn't saying anything. She is listening to criticism without speaking. I'd instructed writers not to defend their stories. If you must speak, say Thank you. She is a large woman. She has grown a large body to be able to contain all she has experienced, and to be heeded, to be seen. She hit that Washington cop to be *felt*. I've noticed that people after the fire are building huge houses, bigger than the ones they lost.

Another woman vet, Jean Watson, a nurse then and a nurse now, tells about her last moments in Viet Nam. Her hair is gray like mine and frazzly; wrinkles ray her sad, kind eyes. She says, "War is a consciousness. The Vietnamese have a word for 'sorrow of war'—'bao nishron.' " She reads, "The savage breeze was coming in from the South China Sea. I was leaving Viet Nam at Quen Yan, leaving for home, leaving the madness. 'Lady! Lady, take him. Take my number-one son with you.' Out of the Guernica-like scene, a madonna holding up her son came at me, crying, 'Lady, take him.' Her son was crying too. Flies were taking refreshment in their tears. It would have been a selfless act of love to save his life." Jean stops reading. Tearful listeners ask, "Did you take him?" "How old was he?" She shakes her head No. "One year old." She turned away, hearing "La-a-ady . . . La-a-ady."

Jean also lived and worked in Afghanistan. She met many widows, and broke bread with Afghanis, with men too. "They are generous and kind. They are my brothers. I guess I am their sister."

The last reader of this day is John Mulligan from Scotland. (Jean, a Scottish American, was his nurse, and calls him the Mad Scotsman.) He immigrated to America at age seventeen, and at eighteen was drafted into the U.S. Air Force to Viet Nam. "Can they do that?" people asked. "You don't have to be an American?" "Aye, they'll take anybody." He's haunted by "mean ghosts," and reads to us from a piece called "Shopping Cart Soldiers," in which there was also a good ghost, a white fox. Insects and the dead tortured Finn the Albanach. The gunship, playing matador, buzzed a white bull. "Romeo Robinson put a bullet into his balls and everybody laughed." The bull jumped into the air. "Pain can move mountains." The White One ran into barbed wire, which entangled it. Its soul streamed out of its neck. In another scene, after mercy-killing his wounded friend, Finn's soul leaves him. His soul is an Asian woman. When "Shopping Cart Soldiers" becomes a stage play, John plans to cast an Asian actress as the soul, Madman. Now he reads her speech in his own Albanachian voice. "I felt in that instant a terrific force pushing me out of his body, out of the whirling, vibrating aircraft, out into the cold, rushing air. . . . I couldn't leave him completely. Like the head of the bull I too seemed to be attached by a sliver of skin and ligament." The soul remains connected to Finn by a thread, and trails after him everywhere: Viet Nam, Scotland, and San Francisco, Telegraph Hill and Washington Square Park, where homeless vets sleep. She says, "Some men aren't meant for war; their souls are far too old. They've seen it all before. The Albanach is just such a man. I knew it and he knew it the very first moment we stepped onto the red soil of Vietnam. I can say this with some certainty, with some impunity, for I am his soul, his spirit. I do know that much at least, though I don't know everything!"

John says, "One, one, one, one by one, one hundred and fifty thousand Viet Nam veterans have died by their own hand since the war ended. Three hundred and thirty-three thousand homeless vets pushing shopping carts through American streets every day — just like us!"

The listeners catch their breath; they say: "Soul. I hardly ever hear or use the word 'soul.' " "Souls are going to appear onstage?" "I'm marveling, you all believe in souls too." "So many people believing we have souls." "We do have souls. We do."

John looks around at us, smiling, everyone smiling. "I've got me smile back," he says. "I lost me smile, and today you gae it me back. I was going to end the book with Finn committing suicide. Today I mean to have him live on."

We saved Finn's life.

I note to myself that there are many Asian women among the veterans. Jeannie, Lily, Maryanne Teng, Kim Redemer, Jade Lee, me. Why? Maybe John Mulligan imagined us here, pulled us in on a silver thread. And we have our own motives. America's wars with Asian countries. Our wanting the people of our several nations to love one another. They can start by learning to love us. We're here to be loved. White people would come up to Jeannie and speak in anger and confusion about Japan and relocation camps, and she'd answer, "That's okay. I forgive you." She laughed, telling me her reply, which was what they need to hear. We're here to give them mercy. We look like the goddess Kuan Yin, and provide images of her. Veterans who've been to Asia recognize her. Sherdyl, Bob, Richard, navy men, know Avalokiteshvara, Kuan Yin, Kannon, as goddess of the sea; her shrines are in ports on the South China Sea and East China Sea and the Sea of Japan. We're reminders of her. She is everywhere, and all will be well.

June 12, 1994, is the first anniversary of our meetings. Sunday at Spirit Rock in Geronimo Valley. Michael Gardner drives, Therese and I riding, Highway 101 West toward Point Reyes National Seashore. Point Reyes has ghosts, a lighthouse, seabirds, the redwoods. A great rock sits in a field. Thich Nhat Hanh tried teaching meditation to Gorbachev and George H. W. Bush at Spirit Rock.

Answering the question, "What good things have I done for myself this year?," the veterans give troves of happy-birthday answers. "I am writing." "I am writing poems." "I am writing stories." "It is my birthday as a novelist."

The dark giant, Rich Gilman, who keeps disappearing, writes about me. "I saw a frail-looking, very tiny Oriental woman with greying hair which seemed to be trying to reach the ground. She was sitting in the semi-circle, positioned right near a glowing wood fire, surrounded by quite an eclectic group of people. I was perspiring, scared, and uncomfortable. This tiny, frail-looking woman who seemed to be garnering strength from the people around her started to speak. It wasn't what *You* said that commanded my attention, so much as your voice and manner. 'Stay for a while, listen to us and be welcome here.' . . . Meeting Jim Janko was the most powerful, intoxicating, and bonding experience of my life. How did this person know my fears, trepidations, and issues — even better than I, and in only a couple of minutes? The one strong thread of info I kept hearing from Jim: Maxine was a way show–er. 'Like when you were scared shitless in 'Nam,' Jim said, 'and there was something pulling at you to go down a certain path. And that by listening and following that voice, you'd get out of it okay. That is what Maxine is bringing to us Vets.' I immediately connected with Jim, but the ease with which that happened scared me. . . ."

I *am* a way show–er. It's always been true. One summer day at Chi-

nese school (a one-room school, kids seated by age), a boy did something bad, and Teacher hit him with a ruler. It was one of those rulers
with a metal strip. (MaMa and BaBa never hit us with rulers; being hit
with a ruler makes a person stupid.) The teacher made the boy walk up
and down the rows of desks. She followed him with the ruler, which she
put into each student's hand. Everybody was to hit him hard—three
times? five times? He was crying, curling his hand up, and the teacher
was making him open it for more hits. The teacher handed me the ruler.
I did not take it. I shook my head No. She went on to the next kid. When
Teacher and Bad Boy stood in front of them, one by one, my sister and
brothers and other sister refused to hit him. Corrinne, the youngest,
says, "The Hong children were the only family who did not hit him.
You set the example. We copied you." I hardly remember this event; it
was so natural. I can lead because I am Elder Sister. I am a leader of
men because they are my younger brothers.

But they don't know, I make up the way as I go. And I get scared.

It takes a year; at last we have a proper eating meditation. Michael
organized and arranged box lunches on a table under an oak, the name
of the kind of sandwich written on each white box. Cookies, bottled
water, juices. Therese, Michael, and I round up everybody. We sit in the
grass in a circle, and are quiet. The circle is perfectly round. Therese sits
across from me, the two of us wearing straw hats. I can see everyone.
Everyone can look at everyone else. The redwood trees stand tall and
old to the north; the blue sky stands forever high above them. The Bell
of Mindfulness sounds and re-sounds clear, circling peals. We breathe,
and the wind is breath, moving the redwoods and the clouds. All is
quiet. All is peaceful. Now and again, we loft all together into the sky,
and land solid upon the earth. It takes a year to create twenty minutes of
peace. It feels as if, for those twenty minutes, all wars do cease.

In late summer, one cold summer's day, almost autumn, Therese, True
Light, takes us to a home, not a public institution but a home, a house
in the country, rural Sebastopol. It's good to move the workshop from
place to place—find more veterans, get the old veterans to leave their
apartments and the daily city rut, cross bridges, take a long drive on
country roads, on a Star Route, through apple orchards to a new home.
"Turn left when you see four mailboxes." The redwood farmhouse sur-

rounded by birch trees belongs to Marg Starbuck and Bill Boykin. He is a World War II veteran and worked for Shell Oil. They lived in Saudi Arabia for three years. Marg, whose hair is whiter than mine, befriended the veiled women. Images of people being taboo, she painted abstract impressions; the long streaks of black and red look like tall women draped in lengths of cloth or hair; they also look like the world as seen through a narrow opening. (Bill says, "The Vale of Kashmir was the most beautiful place on earth. It's probably gone now.")

Marg seats me in a little kid's school desk. Doris "Lucki" Allen, a newcomer, a Black woman with big-frame glasses who carries a cane, sits in the queen's chair, the wooden throne directly across from me. The atmosphere is hers. At the windows, birch leaves hang like yellow curtains, and dim the light. Some people sit on a built-in, padded bench along one wall, long, narrow windows above them. You can see the soaring and wheeling hawks and turkey buzzards. Everyone else is sitting in a squarish circle of settees and chairs about a round coffee table with rocks on top. It is day, and dusky; we seem at the bottom of a high-walled place, a well, a secret dark place. Illumination comes from faces. (Soldiers blacken their faces because human faces shine, even at night.) Words, stories are hovering at edges and around corners, to come out of mouths. Marg's white paintings, then her orange-and-blue paintings glimmer into sight. The lit potbelly stove stands at the far end of the room, away from the people. There are many people of color here, and dark Caucasians, and almost as many women as men.

For today's writing-in-community, I give a lesson on rewriting. Each time you rewrite, you're going back into the tunnel, and bringing more knowledge out. You can safely examine the explosion again and again. You will see it more clearly, see more details, and make better sense of it. You shine more light on some question, problem, hard time, suffering, memory, ignorance. You will return to the core event, and you will return home a different person. The story changes, and you change. And history changes too, Viet Nam changes.

Roman "Hopper" Martinez checks in. (The vets have named our salutations "checking in.") He says, "Today I haven't killed anyone for twenty-four years, four months, and twenty-three days. I started not-killing anymore on Father's Day, June 21, 1970. I know I stopped killing then because that was the DAY I was wounded." It's as if he's at AA; killing is an addiction that he's recovering from. "My name is Roman

Martinez, and I am a killer. I am a beast. I am still a trained killer, but luckily I have learned to write about it rather than act on it. I am a killer with an off-and-on switch." He looks like Santa Claus, like Jerry Garcia. He and I admire each other's long white hair. Roman has written a narrative about his PTSD for his claim against the VA. I made copies of it for the workshop. Our question is: how can Roman rewrite to turn this claim into a short story, from red tape to literature? Roman entrusts us with keeping "this incident" private until after the claim goes through. He composes by speaking to his wife, Miriam, and she types in all caps on his Purple Heart stationery:

> I AM V.N. VET. I SERVED WITH THE 1ST INFANTRY AND THE 101ST AIRBORNE DIVISIONS IN 1969/70. I TURNED 19 IN V.N. AND WAS WOUNDED WALKING POINT ON FATHERS DAY 1970 (JUST OVER A MONTH BEFORE TURNED 20). I HAVE BEEN WRITING ABOUT THE STRESSORS I EXPERIENCED FOR MY PTSD CLAIM. IF I PUT THESE MEMORIES TOGETHER MAYBE SOMEONE WOULD LIKE TO READ THEM BESIDES THE GOV'T CLAIM ADJUSTER.

He reads aloud, weeping, while we follow along, "HOPPER'S LAST B.B.Q." Hopper's crew found a downed helicopter:

> . . . I WAS OVERWHELMED TO FIND OUT THAT THE SMELLS THAT HAD ME SALIVATING WERE COMING FROM MY COOKED BUDDIES. THERE WAS A PILE OF ASHES WITH 3 LUMPS IN IT; THE LUMPS WERE THE AIR CREW. I HAD PARTIED WITH THE ENLISTED MEN JUST THE NIGHT BEFORE. OF THE 3 COM-RADES, 2 WERE MY FRIENDS; AND THEY WERE COOKED JUST RIGHT; ROASTED IN A MAGNESIUM FIRE. OF THE ENTIRE UNIT AT THE CRASH SITE, ONLY MYSELF AND A BLACK SGT. HAD THE INTESTINAL FORTITUDE TO PUT OUR BUDDIES INTO THE BODY BAGS FOR THE TRIP BACK HOME. WHILE THE REST OF MY SQUAD WAS PUKING-THEIR-GUTS-OUT ON PERIMETER SECURITY, THE SGT. & I BAGGED OUR AIR CREW. I HELD BACK MY TEARS EVEN WHILE I HAD BOOTS & OTHER BODY PARTS COME OFF IN MY HANDS; LIKE PULLING A DRUM-STICK OFF OF A ROASTED TURKEY. AFTER BAGGING THE MEN, I FELL

IN AS ONE OF THE PERIMETER GUARDS. WHILE LOOKING
THROUGH MY TEARS, I HAD A CHICKEN-SHIT SGT. ORDER ME
TO HELP CARRY THE BODY BAGS DOWN THE HILL. I TOLD HIM
THAT IF HE DIDN'T HAVE THE BALLS TO BAG OUR MEN, THEN
HE DIDN'T HAVE ENOUGH TO DO ANYTHING. HE TRIED TO
ORDER ME TO CARRY THEM, SO I FLIPPED MY "16" ON TO
AUTO AND INVITED HIM TO JOIN THE OTHERS IN THE BAGS.
LUCKYLY, OUR LIEUTENANT CAME UP TO US & TOLD THE SGT.
THAT HE SHOULD NOT PUSH HIS LUCK. THINKING BACK ON
THE EXPERIENCE, I HAD NO QUALMS ABOUT PERSONALLY
SENDING THAT SGT. TO GOD. IF HE HAD NOT BACKED-OFF, I
WOULD HAVE BLOWN HIM AWAY AND BAGGED HIS REMAINING
BODY PARTS.

THE REMEMBRANCE OF THIS OCCASION BRINGS ON A
DEPRESSION, AND SOMETIMES A RAGE. THE SMELL OF HOT
METAL (SUCH AS A HOT SKILLET) OR BURNED BARBEQUE
MEAT, BRINGS BACK ALL THE EMOTIONS OF DISGUST, SOR-
ROW, RAGE, AND I CAN BE TERRIFYING TO THOSE AROUND
ME; MAINLY MY FAMILY. "WHY IS DADDY SO MAD AND HOL-
LERING AT US & ACTING LIKE HE'S GOING TO KILL?"

The hearers stay silent. I should have reminded them to breathe, rung the bell. But I am speechless. We are all of us in horror, disgust, sorrow, rage. What to do? What to do in war's aftermath? Make a story. Tell the story until a happy ending. I ask for ways that Roman could rewrite. I prod, Would you say there's a full scene here? More silence. They dislike criticizing one another. Someone suggests writing about the party the night before. "We'd get to know the people who were killed. Their personalities." "Show them having a good time." "We would care about them as individuals." "So their death won't just be gross." I suggest using direct quotes when Hopper and the sergeant argue over carrying the body bags. "What exactly did you say? What exactly did he say?"

Vince Dijanich, an operations manager for Pacific Bell and an FNG here, says, "Roman has to develop the scene, tell who these guys are, use more dialogue. And what happens after he gets home, with the family at Thanksgiving? But, still, there'd be one thing missing: ideology. Vets are always telling this event, that event, this happened, that happened—but without an ideology. Vet writers should have an ideology. Your stories have no ideology. No political consciousness. No sense or vision of how or why we came to be there and whether our being there was right or wrong."

Nobody debates him. Nobody argues. In the silence, Vince repeats, "No ideology. Where's the ideology?" Nobody answers. We are not interested in ideology. It's okay with us that we don't have an ideology. Ideology is what got us into trouble in the first place. Communists have an ideology. Ideology is Marxist, and capitalist. We don't want ideology. Good for us, I think, we don't have ideology. Vince is disappointed in us; he'll leave us. But we aren't going to work up an ideology to keep his interest. That's the way silence works: a thought hangs out there in the air, and disappears.

Sometimes we come out of the dark well, and stand or sit on the wide balcony facing west, and look out at the hills and valleys, and Marg's barn studio. Marg and Bill pick lettuce, cook soup, slice bread and cheese. We have a picnic meditation on the yellow grass beside the vegetable garden trellised with raspberries.

Keith Mather, a deserter, among men and women who do not approve of deserters, tells about a walk to the courtroom. He gave the peace sign, and many people gave him the peace sign. His neighbor gave him a leather ring. (Officers beat him, and took the "personal civilian jewelry" off of him.) Be strong. The charges were: desertion and refusal of a direct order. "AWOL is such a weird charge—jail time for going home." Keith, who comes from generations of pacifists—his grandfather was proud of him—testified for seven hours, and was sentenced to four years of hard labor. A group of women who supported him sprayed the courtroom and the documents with red dye; they went to jail for six months each. "Maybe Leavenworth will be safer and easier than the Presidio." The ocean wind blows through the prison. He refused absolutely to wear the uniform, not even prison pajamas. The blanket was taken away during the day. Naked, he hid toilet paper in his armpits, and used it to cushion his sit bones. That happened not far from here—the Presidio Post Stockade on Custer Boulevard.

Keith seems to be telling about several trials and two or more jailings out of sequence. There were at least two trials, one for going AWOL when he was inducted, and the second when he refused to wear the uniform. For a year, he was moved from jail to jail. "One had been a ballroom during the Civil War. In Canada, they sent me to a g-a-o-l. A terrible thing—once you get in jail, they can keep piling up charges and jail time. This has been my nightmare." He escaped, walked from the toolshed and away. He spent twelve years in Canada. I won't urge chronological order on him; he should be free of time, not doing time anymore.

Keith looks and sounds tired. He is a muscular man who does physical labor, construction, and is tired out. On weekends, he lets his tiredness show. I talk with him alone; he reminds me of my great-uncle the riverboat pirate, but Great-Uncle was in his seventies. "The country is at it again," Keith says; "never learns." He means the bombing of Iraq. "There's a demonstration in San Francisco tomorrow. I'm going with my kids. I don't know if I have it in me."

I ask, "You don't have it in you to walk?" I myself am energized and uplifted in demonstrations, surrounded by hopeful people. When a war puts me in despair, and I want to give up and die, and let the stupid world die, I join a demonstration. I love being at the bottom of hills, looking up and seeing people filling the streets all the way up the hillsides behind me and before me. We make a dragon. A peace dragon.

"I don't have it in me to go to jail again."

Oh, no, Keith thinks that it is his responsibility to go to jail. That jail is all he can do, the ultimate that he can give for peace. "But you don't have to be arrested," I say. How to persuade him that walking, parading, is good enough? Writing letters, writing stories and poems, is good enough.

Let Mike Wong hearten him. Deserter Wong uses the government's Viet Nam statistics to show that the peace movement won over the war movement.

Deserters, draft offenders, COs, nonregistrants: 1,085,250.
KIA, severely wounded, slightly wounded: 150,375.

We won. Peace won over war.

Mike proudly calls himself a deserter. "I'm going to change 'deserter' from meaning 'coward' to meaning 'brave.' Remember the dolphins that were being trained to deliver explosives? Some of them escaped; they deserted from the military. Those dolphins were deserters. I'm a deserter too."

It's time to walk. Therese instructs: Mindful walking is the strongest carrying of body and spirit into the present reality. I add, Marching to cadence chants and stalking—"Sneaking," Mike Wong calls it—through the jungle took your walk away from you. You have to reclaim your walk. Enjoy this beautiful country, Sebastopol, where there are no mines and no booby traps.

Marg and Bill lead the way down the hill. In the distant meadows are big horses; little ponylike horses in the near meadow walk toward us. The nonwalkers, Lucki and Ted both with canes, are smoking and talking on the balcony. A great clear wind is blowing, and blows us down the hill. I stand amazed before a cathedral of giant old eucalyptus trees, then slowly fly between the two rows of them. All is movement, sunlight and wind flickering the blinking and winking crescent leaves; hundreds of arms are waving. The sky. Rushing clouds. Sounds and noise, soughing and sighing. All breathing and existing. Smell the air. Maryanne and Therese, elated, are flying too. I feel my hair lift and fall, and my light body lift and land. The trees point my awareness into the sky. The people who've been in war must be freaking out, but they trustingly walk. Leaves and twigs crack underfoot. Gunshots—hunters. Only hunters.

At the other end of the eucalyptus forest, the group stands together and looks out into valleys. Therese asks for a history of this place. Marg says that sheep farmers lived here, and names the former owners.

Roberto says, "People lived here before that. I can feel . . . there are many people who are dead on this land. Lost from here."

He's talking about the Indians. He's Indian. I say, "Oh, the people long ago."

He and Bob and Joe say, "It was not long ago." "No, not a long time ago." "The Ohlone."

The Ohlone had a thousand years of peace. People from every tribe walked to this coast from all over Turtle Island, and lived a thousand years of peace.

We walk back through the meadow along the outside of the forest. The little horses trot to the fence, and people pet them.

Later, Roberto carefully reads about being a child among the animals and creatures. He grew up hurting over the killing, the slaughter of the chickens, the butchering of farm animals, the hunting of other animals. At "a little war" between ants and a roach, he dropped water on them. He weeps over the endless suffering of innocent creatures.

Vince, who looks Indian like Roberto but larger, puts his arms around him, holds him. The two dark men huddle in the corner.

Roberto is again the boy who knew to be horrified by the violence of the natural world.

Our compassion has to include the animals too? How can we finish hurting?

Vince reads about soldiers on their time off. They got cash from the telemachine, smoked a coupla joints, played guitar, wrote, living one day at a time. Sudden switch to a sight of enemy Vietnamese on the ground. "The Americans took a prisoner, and pulled him along by the hair. The helicopter wind pulled on his hair too. . . . I dream this scene again and again. My wife has to change the sheets; they're soaked in terror sweat." Vince's writing doesn't seem to have any more ideology than anyone else's.

Doris "Lucki" Allen writes about today, about how she got lost on her way over here. She's a high-ranking officer, probably the highest rank among us; her job in Viet Nam had had to do with reconnaissance, and she's admitting to having gotten lost. Her gray curls spring out from under a military-looking hat with braid. "My friends in Forrestville charted a course to Sebastopol with their own hand-rendered map. I did get lost coming here this a.m." She goes on:

Maps were my tool in Vietnam. As an interrogator of Prisoners of War and as an intelligence analyst I had to know the locations, the terrain, etc. Only then could I extract in an intelligible way the response which would help me to produce and ultimately disseminate viable intelligence.

Before Vietnam one of my jobs as the Latin American Desk Officer at the Strategic Intelligence Center (CONTIC) at Fort Bragg was to keep track of all physical movement of both Fidel Castro and Che Guevara as they plotted to take over, and maintain their Communism in Cuba. Maps of all of Mexico, Central and South America were absolutely essential to produce strategic intelligence on any "target" in Latin America.

Dad made map reading a joyous past-time when I was a kid. My siblings and I left home at an early age to attend Southern colleges. Mom and Dad bought us a car and proceeded to prepare us both mentally and physically for our cross-country sojourns. It usually started, this orientation, three to four days before we were to take off. We'd all sit around the dining room table; maps from the U.S., Texas, Louisiana, Mississippi, and Alabama spread on the table and floor. During those times we had to "plot with a vengeance" since there were so many places where "Colored" folks couldn't go—but that's another story.

Lucki calls the Bell of Mindfulness "Hong's Gong." She says, "I feel there's something subliminal going on here." Miki Kashtan, who has come to us from Israel, agrees, "It's magic." I argue against the supernatural, and for the ordinary, the real. I want Lucki to tell me top secrets. I want the story about interrogating prisoners.

Jimmy Janko, medic who ran out of supplies in the Renegade Woods, so many wounded and dying, writes us "Prayer":

> Jaguar, night flesh of shamans
> Quick body of silence
> Yellow eyes of the night sun
> Dark paws of the earth
> Have mercy
>
> River, water blessed by sky
> Holy water of shamans
> Mover of earth
> Sculptor of valleys
> Shaper of shores
> Lover of fish
> Have mercy
>
> Corn, eating the sun all summer
> Sister alchemist, creating ancient food
> Gold kernels under silken hair
> Feast for insects, animals, humans, fungi
> First mother of the Hopi child
> Have mercy . . .

He calls also upon Flower, Earthworm, Stone, Egg, Eagle—Have mercy. In Viet Nam, he shouted power words to the wounded to keep them alive. Here, he taught us "the oldest prayer": "May all beings be happy."

President Clinton has announced that we will bomb Haiti on September 18, which is tomorrow, Sunday. Today is the day before we bomb Haiti. I've almost forgotten to bring it up, barely conscious of that war. My country is inured to bombings. The President and the newscasters spoke matter-of-factly; the war hardly registers. I am grateful to have this group to tell thoughts to.

"Oh, it's not going to happen," some vets assure me.

But last night, through the night, I heard again the roar of bombers in the sky. I heard engines, machines, planes go and go and go. I was not dreaming. I thought clearly, This is not a nightmare; this is actually happening. I am awake. I am hearing sounds of war. Warplanes are flying on and on and on, to kill on my behalf. I got out of bed, and looked out the window. I saw cloud covering; the planes must be up in the highest stratosphere. I timed it—half an hour of planes flying south. I fell asleep, awoke, and heard the roars continuing. Across a clearing between clouds, I think I saw darting a silver airplane, an equilateral triangle, like a spearhead shooting straight. As I was about to look away, I saw another such killer plane follow behind it; then the clouds closed. I wonder what a C-6 Transport looks like. Each is as big as a football field; they're like flying gasoline stations. After delivering tanks, when it flies home empty you can run laps and ride a bike for miles inside the C-6.

Also in the news: a female white buffalo has been born. She has soft white curls and a pink nose. Indians from all over America are making pilgrimages to see her. She is the fulfillment of a Native American prophecy. White Buffalo Woman is come. She heralds peace among nations. An Indian said, "This is as important as the birth of Christ." She is "the Princess of Peace."

We meet in December at Mills College in Oakland, the alma mater of quite a few of the women who are part of our group. All is elegance. Spread before us in the Alderwood Living Room is a buffet on white linen, silver urns and pitchers, arrays of pastries, Danishes, muffins, bagels. Roman is wearing a Santa hat, his long white beard and hair aflow. (He's a Mexican American Santa, and gives toys to kids via the Darwin project.) We sit in straight-back chairs and wing chairs at the magnificent conference table. Overhead, chandeliers bejewel the carved wood ceiling. Tall windows frame the tall evergreens, which are blowing in hard winds. Open stacks of leather-bound books surround us. Joe Lamb finds *War in the Balkans 1400–1950*, some such impossible numbers.

Each one of the veterans has had a moment when life blew apart. (HE = High Explosives. *Vin din no.* The twirling dust was a man, incinerated and evaporated.) If he or she could write the explosion, its every smithereen, and narrate what led to it and came from it, the self and the world would become whole. They only need an ethos, a simple set of positive ethics as ground and base.

Ellen Peskin of the Community of Mindful Living hands out copies of Thich Nhat Hanh's Five Wonderful Precepts, moral principles which articulate a stance against killing or causing other living beings to suffer; the importance of helping those in need and using speech and our powers of listening to be truthful and compassionate; the commitment to healthful living and consumption.

The Precepts are also five plots for stories. You will never run out of things to write about. Moral laws are as true as laws of physics. Break them, you hurt. I'm not trying to put anything religious over on anybody. The Precepts are not too different from the Bill of Rights. You could just as well put the First Amendment into practice. Speak. Write. Assemble. Practice a religion, or not.

Miki Kashtan, who was drafted into the Israeli Army in 1973 at age eighteen, says, "Do you realize how subversive the Precepts are? They're revolutionary. What if we *did* these things? 'Prevent others from profiting from human suffering. . . .' Messing with profit in America, taking a vow to be a moderate consumer, we'd turn into revolutionaries."

I say to choose one Precept, and write about struggling with that ideal. Maybe write how, once upon a time, you happily accomplished it. Most people pick the First Precept, Reverence for Life. Having a law against killing makes it possible to admit to and scrutinize killing.

Miki became head of her unit, and had to train the other women. "Insanity and futility. I didn't even believe in armies. . . . Voluntary? Try asking for a transfer. The woman with a thin mean mouth said, 'You only leave on a stretcher.' " The soldiers had to swear an oath that they would give their lives. But Miki didn't really vow the oath; she didn't say it aloud. "I thought I would lose my mind. I was constantly moving away from myself, from telling the truth. I felt a fundamental separate-ness. . . . I could not support that oath." She even had to participate in antipeace training. One girl would role-play the pacifist, and the others argue her down.

Miki wrote about the agony of shooting a target in the shape of a human being:

> . . . I take my rifle. I place it on the sand sack. I tuck it in its familiar place under my shoulder. I look at the dummy. Circular, with a silly little head and a target tacked on. I try to aim. I know how to do it so well. But I shake with every move as I try to con-centrate. I hear our officer give the command. I burst out crying, and put the rifle down. Everyone else has already shot the first bullet. They look at me nervously. I am unable to stop. I can't even touch the rifle any more. Someone approaches me, tries to calm me down. I keep on crying. Any time I look at the dummy or at the rifle, a new burst of sobbing seizes me. I will never again do this, I think as I cry. . . .

She adds, "One step at a time I arrive at a painful inner resolution to leave this country."

Martin Higgins' story is about a Black soldier he calls Brasso. Brasso served a long sentence at hard labor digging out the "grease pit." He killed himself by drinking Brasso metal cleaner. I'm reminded of the prison scenes in *From Here to Eternity*. I wonder, are those who die by suicide and in accidents honored on the Wall?

As for me, I talk story about meeting a Vietnamese boat girl, Twee Tranh; she was in one of the audiences of Earll's John Wesley Powell show. I asked Twee about her life in Viet Nam, and how she came to be here. She said, "I was lucky. I never experienced war." Her family was able to keep away from the bombs by obeying the leaflets that the Ameri-cans dropped, warning of the time and extent of the bombings. The family was never separated; she didn't consider what befell them as war. The safest place was out to sea. "Our family had a flotilla of eight boats. The eight boats always stuck together, and if one went to an island, they all went." They lived on fish; they bought rice and vegetables and water from the people on the little islands. I asked how they paid for these necessities and for the eight boats. "My grandfather was very rich. He was going to open another cannery. Anybody would give rice and water for gold bars." She made a circle of fingers; she might've said "gold *balls*."

I asked about the Vietnamese gangs torturing and robbing Vietnamese and Chinese Americans. She said that lately she herself had had the house broken into three times. I said that, if it were me, I would blab the hiding place of the gold; why do people take the torture? She said, "But they sweat to make the money. They pour blood into the fields to make things grow. They don't want to give away the money so easy." One of her cousins was in the hospital for a month after torture by a Vietnamese gang. I read in the paper that the gangs pour boiling-hot water on Grandma to get other family members to talk. Why do Vietnamese hurt one another like that? Twee answered, "People torture the people they know. They know them and know just the right torture to use. Grandmas are the most stubborn, and would never tell the secrets." We laughed.

I told her about the Chinese myth that 108 outlaws hid in a sanctuary, and after the sanctuary was broken up, they went to the southeast. Do you think we—Chinese and Vietnamese—could be related?

"We do have a myth," she said, "that the Vietnamese race began with one hundred children, fifty boys and fifty girls."

"Chinese are always painting and embroidering a hundred children!"

"Those ancient people had a toe that folded over the other toe."

I exclaimed that the women in *my* family have a split little toenail. I started to take off my shoes; does *she* have strange toes too? "No. After all the intermarrying, modern Vietnamese don't have that anymore. Those were the primitive ancestors." (She herself was in a mixed-race relationship. Her Japanese American boyfriend sat beside her, and listened to her, and gazed and smiled upon her. The flotilla of eight boats had been picked up by a Japanese ship, which took the family to a refugee center in Tokyo. They studied English there for two years, then lived in Texas, then California. Twee is working for a graduate degree in the humanities at San Francisco State. Her mother paints nails, and her father works in a grocery store.)

Twee told me some of her own "very old myth": "There was a beautiful daughter whose parents and family were caught up in a terrible war. To feed and care for her family, the girl became a prostitute. She had to sacrifice her engagement to her betrothed. He went to the war, and they were separated for many years. When he returned, he married somebody else, her sister. The first sister and her betrothed, now brother-in-law, met later in life, and became friends. Her name is Kieu. I feel that if the Americans had heard the story about Kieu they would not have come to fight the Vietnamese." Now she tells us. Too late.

I said, "Well, if we had known anything at all about you, your music, your language, we would not have gone to war that easily." I wonder aloud: "What is it in Americans that you think the story about Kieu would've appealed to? Our valuing of devotion? Our appreciation of sacrifice?"

"Yes," said Twee. "All that."

There is another Chinese *and* Vietnamese story that goes as follows: One thousand years ago, a Chinese general led his army across the border into Viet Nam. He espied an enemy soldier keeping watch in the moonlight. The soldier was reciting poetry. The general turned back, saying, "We don't fight with a people whose soldiers sing poems."

In January, on a warm winter's day, we return to the yurt at Green Gulch Farm. As we meditate, a pair of swallows fly in on the breeze through the open door, circle the dome, and fly out. We sit in a concentration of light from the skylight and windows all around. The swallows fly into the yurt again, and circle under the skylight and above heads, but no one looks up. Again that feeling of being in the center of the universe. We're it.

Green Gulch Farm is an idyll for writers. I sit with my notebook and pencils in its many writing places—awhile at the bench and table at the bend where farm meets wilderness and valley abuts hill, awhile in the garden, awhile in the forest shade of coyote bushes, eucalyptus, oaks, and pines. I write indoors beside the shrine to the anthropologist Gregory Bateson, who lived here his last days. I walk by myself the path between the vegetable and flower beds, harvested and fallow, down the middle of the small valley to the banks of the pond; a great bell hangs there. Scott Morrison, who has a ponytail like a Revolutionary War patriot's, is sitting in the shadow of the bell. He's writing a novel, and he's writing songs. Everywhere I look, someone is writing a poem or a story. And pairs of veterans are speaking with each other. Look at them. They are glad to see one another. They are talking about life, how good it is to be alive, to see you alive. Oh, I am so happy. I am happy watching over people in communication. I set this up—this communication. Oh, listen to them—high voices and low, feminine and masculine, many voices making human sounds, a song of overlapping, overlaying lyrics. I ring the bell, and they laugh, interrupted. They have more to say. They are happy. This communication is what I live for. I am accomplishing the purpose of my life: to get each to communicate with each, and all with all. If nothing more happens, today is culmination enough. I am happy. Oh, most wonderful world. For this day, I have made some of the world as I like it. May it last.

Writing on the deck of the yurt, I watch Larry Vaughn writing too. He stretches his hurting legs—one of them a phantom leg—out on the warm floorboards; his whitish hair, beard, and mustache shine in the sun, and his earring sparks. He is writing about the smell of Viet Nam, the smell of the Vietnamese, "my assigned enemy." He himself had smelled of fear. He reads to me: "Every M-60 round I pounded through the body of my assigned enemy passed through him and into the heart of his mother, his father, and his whole life history, their pain stains the lining of my soul." He makes a wish: "They're going to live; I'm going to live." Surely, the good as well as the bad reverberates backward and forward through generations, ancestors and descendants.

Inside the yurt, Dr. Doris "Lucki" Allen reads: "Bullets fly, people die. . . . Four small secondary explosions . . . dust off. . . . When I finally persuaded them to listen, the resultant action yielded one hundred and seventeen secondary explosions up to one hundred feet high. That made me feel good." She means that one of her intelligence reports got the Americans to bomb. Lucki calls herself a pacifist. Trained in languages and psychology, with experience as an interrogator, she taught a class in "the techniques of Interrogation of Prisoners of War." "Incidentally, no one ever knew during my entire career in the army that I am a pacifist. I often recall that during my days at Tuskegee I stood around and watched all of those beautiful Black men in various formations and activities—preparing themselves for war. I wondered—why are they here? Preparing for what? To fly off and die—for an integrated world— I was a pacifist then and I am a pacifist now. I wonder why 30 years later. . . . Could it have been that if they could do it—I too could do it."

My task is to get her and everyone to write what "it" is.

Lucki has yet to write the scene where she interrogates a Viet Cong prisoner of war. What methods she used, what she got out of him.

I see how Lucki can think of herself as a pacifist, despite her citations and silver stars. She and the person she's interrogating could save people from getting killed. It would be to everyone's benefit to reveal the plans for the upcoming attack, and so prevent it. There were battles that did not happen because of Lucki.

She was the Cassandra of the Tet Offensive. "The first time my credibility was tested and denied was when I furnished intelligence predicting the Viet Nam Tet Offensive. I made that report thirty days ahead of time—which I considered enough time to take defensive action and successfully foil that offensive. As you all know, many of those fifty-nine thousand–plus names on the Wall in Washington, D.C., didn't have to be there. If only they had listened and acted on just that one piece of intelligence!!!"

I want to know but don't dare ask what tactics she used to get top-secret stuff. If she were to narrate step by step *how* she spied out the "most tightly kept secret," she might be at peace. She could pick up the identity of pacifist that she lay aside.

Sherdyl writes, "I only personally killed one man." It happened when he was "river browning" in the Mekong. "Don't kill the prisoners," shouted the "Enswign." "But it was too late. I watched in slow motion as a line of M-16 slugs marched through the water up to the man I was covering. He grabbed his chest, and then his head jerked back and he sank into the wet abyss. Over and over I replayed the scene of the VC I had killed alongside our boat. He had been trying to surrender and was unarmed and helpless. He had been less than fifteen feet away when I opened fire. I envisioned the bullets splashing up to him, hitting his chest, and saw his head rocking back sharply. I had killed my first human being."

How few words it takes to say it, the fact—I killed a human being. One sentence gets it out. The telling is as short as the doing.

Yigal Ben-Haim, a member of the Israeli peace movement and Swords to Plowshares, is thinking about returning to Israel. He was wounded while fighting Egyptians in the Battle of the Virgins. "After years of silence, I have finally decided to write about the lost generation of the Yom Kippur War—my own generation. I know that during this difficult time when another war is still on with no clear end in sight, I could not write another Hannukah story of our victory and the enemy's defeat. The war I remember was fought by ordinary people who went to battle with great fear, little to say about it; and yet with deep belief that there was probably no other choice. Today I have a choice. I can sort through and reflect on those events as well as voice my opinion."

He visited the Wall in Washington, D.C.

As I pushed myself through hundreds of school children, I noticed how different they were from their Japanese counterparts. On a recent trip to Japan, I had observed hundreds of Japanese children visiting their holy shrines and temples. They were all in new school uniforms and tightly disciplined by their teachers. Here, in the name of American freedom, the children were everywhere, running up and down along the memorial as if to say, "Today, life prevails." . . . Perhaps at times tears speak better than words, but the kids were everywhere, running up and down. I felt the pain coming off the wall, blending with my own pain. But the children, like all children, were pumping their own life energy into the painful past of the memorial.

A boy of about 14 years old, noticing my crutches, asked me anxiously, "Were you there in the war?"

"Yes," I said, "I was there, but really in a different war."

When you get older, wars tend to blend into each other to all look the same. You come back from there a different person forever. Some of us can simply hide it better than others. The kid desperately wanted to know more about my war, but I ran out of words.

Our work is to keep coming up with the words.

It is almost spring, and our part of California is monsooning and flooding. We are meeting at Mills College again, and Grace Paley is coming to teach us. Bob Golling brings Cecil Brunner roses. A Cecil Brunner grew on either side of the front door of our burnt-away house; they climbed from door to roof. Bob presents a pink rose to each of us ladies; we wear one in our hair or on our breast or on our hat. Miniature full blooms and buds open through the day. The air smells of roses. Pauline, standing on the balcony with a rose behind her ear, looks pretty and happy, laughing in the wind and spatters of rain. All day, through the great arched windows, we watch the storm. The big trees swing, arch, and bend. Walking under them are neighborhood kids touring Mills with the Upward Bound project. This part of Oakland, where Earll was born and raised, is now a Black neighborhood.

Preparing for Grace Paley's visit—most people haven't heard of her—I read aloud her prose poem about a boy who shot off his trigger finger.

> . . . He had used it to point accusingly at guilty persons, for target shooting, for filing alphabetically. None of these actions concerned him anymore. To help him make general love, he still had his whole hand and for delicate love, his middle finger.
>
> Therefore he joyfully married and fathered several children. All of them had shot-off index fingers, as did their children. That family became a peaceful race apart. Sickness and famine didn't devastate them. Out of human curiosity they traveled and they were stubborn and tough like the feathery seeds of trees that float over mountain barriers and railroad valleys. In far places the children of the children of the man with the shot-off index finger gathered into settlements and cities and of course, they grew and multiplied.
>
> And that's how at last, if you can believe it, after the dead loss of a million dead generations, on the round, river-streaked face of the earth, war ended.

And I read the poem with the line, "It is the responsibility of the poet to be a woman." Woman Vet and all the women love it. Pauline borrows a photocopier and makes copies for one and all. Men ask, "What does this mean? 'It is the responsibility of the poet to be a woman'?"

I tell about Grace's being in-country during the war. She was inside the tunnels in Quanh Binh, the Land of Fire. The peace movement had negotiated the release of POWs, three bomber pilots, and Grace went to Hanoi to receive them and escort them home. One of the bomber pilots, mulling over what job he could get as a civilian, perplexed her. "To be truthful," he said, "I really liked bombing."

I also read poems that connected the unbelievable war she eyewitnessed in 1969 to familiar things back home. The city of Dong Hoi was gone, "as though Baltimore had disappeared into the grass." She used numbers to write the poem "Two Villages." Duc Ninh, once "a village of 1,654 households," is now "a bomb crater that measures 150 feet across / It is 50 feet deep."

> In Trung Trach
> a village of 850 households
> a chart is hung in the House of Tradition
>
> rockets 522
> attacks 1201
> big bombs 6998
> napalm 1383
> time bombs 267
> shells 12291
> pellet bombs 2213

Lee Swenson, friends with Grace since the nonviolent-resistance days, is driving her from San José. He made leaflets for us with quotes and pictures. There's a photo of Grace wearing a knit cap, a smile, and words on a pillowcase poncho over her down jacket —

> MONEY
> ARMS
> WAR
> PROFIT
> WALL ST.

She's so cute, she'll disarm the vets, surely. She'll love them, and call them dear, and they'll love her back. A myth about her is that she calmed a police horse and kept it from charging into the crowd. Lee said, "How could they not be won over by this small person with white hair — not older but old?" An elder is coming to teach us.

When Grace arrives, people are very eager to read, hands and faces and bodies tensely signaling to go next. I nod to Jean Watson. She reads about working as a nurse in burned-out villages. Some children remained alive. "Women pick up the pieces. Waist, hip in blood. It was our job to fix the wounded. Help them return to battle to kill again. Women follow the soldiers and the war. I was sisters with the Vietnamese women selling sex to the soldiers. . . . Now, working for peace is my obsession. . . . Women transmute war."

Ted Sexauer squares himself, ready to confront the peace activist, and reads: "Dear Ms. Paley, you might not remember me. We met before at the war memorial in San Francisco. This is the twenty-fifth year of my PTSD." He holds up a book, *Paradise of the Blind* by Duong Thu Huong. On the back is a blurb, "critical acclaim," by Grace Paley: "We have been hearing for many years from Americans who seemed to consider the Vietnamese experience — life and war — their own. At last a woman, a Vietnamese woman, tells us Vietnamese life."

Tough Teddy calls upon Grace to answer for her use of the adjective "Vietnamese." "To call the war 'the Vietnamese experience' is an error," he says. "We call it 'the Viet Nam experience.' Viet Nam was *our* experience too. I've just been back to Viet Nam, paid for by my hundred-percent disability money. I heard the Vietnamese call it 'the American War.' You don't sound very sympathetic to us. Are you tired of us?"

The room is tense, upset. Ted is angry at Grace. Who is she anyway? Is Maxine trying to foist Jane Fonda off on us? I say to Grace it's okay to wait until everyone has read, or she could answer now. She says, "I'm a teacher. I've taught school. Let's wait until I hear everybody." I've never seen her look so tired, maybe jet lag.

Woman Vet lets loose wrath at Grace and "hippies from Berserkeley, . . . cowardly stay-at-homes, . . . hypocrites, . . . partying while servicemen and servicewomen were risking their lives. . . . I was against the war, and I went to Viet Nam. Responsibility and patriotism moved me. Twenty-three years later, hippies are yuppies greedy for Gulf oil." When Woman Vet was in Viet Nam, her sister was in the demonstrations at Humboldt State. "We're friends now, as long as we don't talk about that Viet Nam time."

Rich Gilman sees Grace as I do. "You look like my mother," he says. Grace says, "You look like my son." He reads to her about enlisting. The recruiter came to his high school, and gave a high-making speech about being "one with God." Rich was fourteen years old, three and a half years away from graduation. "You couldn't even take the GED until nineteen. I aced the air force exam, got all the questions right. The recruiter wanted me so badly, he lied for me about my age."

Rich was a "rock ape" in a "weird little war." "We bombed the rice paddies of China. Our planes flew out from Taiwan six days a week." Under cover of the Viet Nam War, our country attacked and provoked China.

Reading to Grace, Pauline weeps. "I am a third-generation widow. . . . He didn't come home for dinner." The army trained the married man to leave the wife behind: "If the army wanted you to have a wife, they would've issued you one." Her listeners inhale audibly.

John Swensson, West Point graduate, officer, writes two letters to Grace. "1966. Dear Anti-war Bitch—" As if he has thrown a grenade into the middle of the table, the group shrinks back away from the bang. Oh, no. I brought Grace here to be adored—for the people I love to love one another. I've sandbagged her. John rants against "the cowards who stayed home." He calls names until he gets embarrassed, and stops. "And it goes on in that vein." His other letter, dated 1969, begins, "Dear Grace, We're making mistakes." Officers were admitting to friends, fellow trusted officers, their doubts about Viet Nam. "We're doing illegal things, committing crimes. Our pilots are breaking the law. They're ordered not to teach the Vietnamese to fly the planes, but disobey as soon as they get in-country. The laws and orders don't mean nothin'."

Jack Noble writes about the common soldiers trying to get out of the war: "My first exposure to peace came among the grunts. . . . The order 'Search and destroy' became 'Search and avoid.' A grunt went out in the jungle and stabbed himself with a pungi stick. Another grunt got his wife to file for divorce, so he could go home on emergency leave. Grunts said, When they got home, they were going to strangle the first longhair they came across, yet let their hair grow longer than the regulation half an inch. . . . I saw pictures in Stars and Stripes of the Democratic Party convention and riot in Chicago, and wanted to fight harder for my country."

On his way home from Nam, Jack called his parents, and his younger brother answered the phone. "What are you doing home?" asked Jack.

"I'm going over in seventeen days," his brother said. He was on his way to Viet Nam.

"It was a catharsis point for me. I can still hear it, my younger brother's voice, 'I'm going over in seventeen days.' That was when I knew something was not right. I had done all that was necessary, all that I could for my country, everything my country asked of me. My mother had a nervous breakdown with me gone, and now she has to send another one. And four brothers behind me. I had the concept that every family had an obligation, and I fulfilled it for my family. What's going on? War stunk. I was ready to tear people apart." When Jack came home, he joined the peace movement.

Eric Schwartz, who looks too grunge-hippie to be a computer worker at the Bank of America, riffs on "the stink of the Nam." "I had the stink of the Nam on my body. . . ." Grunts used to say, "Ah can smell a gooner a mile away." Eric sums up his life: "Viet Nam vet—a breed apart."

The people who were there say the smells of Viet Nam: piss tubes, shit burning in kerosene, diesel, aviation fuel, insect repellent, gunpowder, water buffalo, napalm, napalmed flesh, fear, oilskin body bags, the ARVN (who could turn out to be enemy), betel nut, sweat, terror, rat infestation, tobacco, marijuana, candles, foods, ngoc nam, nook nam, ngam dam, nuoc cham, whores, tigers, crocogators, incense, farts, feet, anger, the desire to kill. Agent Orange, which did not smell like oranges. It was a horrible, indescribable smell. "Your nose and lungs shrivel against taking it in." "Dead smell." "Metallic dead earth." There was a pollen that dusted everything, but it might not have been pollen; it might have been poison.

I ask, "So what is the smell of a Vietnamese person?"

Grace says, "Cilantro. They smell like cilantro."

Kim Redemer, Buddhist from Thailand, addresses me. She questions my incessant push for the happy ending. "Maxine, you've told the group that writers have a responsibility to inspire hope." In her soft, determined voice, she quotes me: " 'Too many veterans have killed themselves and too many have written suicide endings. Today, let's write a happy ending.' " She reads, "I received news from my friend Mary that our mutual friend Jean had committed suicide. 'No! that could not be true. Are you sure?' Fighting not to accept the terrible news, I hoped to hear something different, a mistaken identification by the police, Jean is safe and alive, a happy ending! . . . No one can rewrite the tragic ending of Jean's story. Jean is gone. She took a handful of her sleeping pills and then walked into the icy waters of the Bay. . . . How could a competent therapist, who was able to help her suicidal clients choose life, choose death? . . . The depths of our personal lives and psyches are very private: none of us has knowledge or power to alter another's life. No matter what we do or what we write, people who lose the will to live and want to kill themselves will succeed."

She concludes, "Maxine, I want to believe that happy endings will inspire our readers to see light at the end of the tunnel. Please tell me how I could write a happy ending for Jean's story. . . . 'Spring is here, that dead-looking cherry tree with a tiny white flower in January is now in full bloom. Every branch and limb is covered with white delicate cherry flowers. . . .' Is that the happy ending you want?"

I stay silent. Let her ask the Silence. Or maybe Grace will answer her.

Grace tells the group that she takes up her ordinary responsibilities as parent and citizen—you know, PTA meetings, neighborhood duties, school-board stuff. Her local womanly group holds ceremonies thanking the school board for various bonds and ordinances. Showing up for the Thetford town-council meetings—that *is* political activism, and naturally connects you up with the wider world, civil rights, war and peace. (I feel that in meeting here today talking about our common lives, we're like mothers in Grace's stories rocking baby carriages in the park.) "In 1961, very early on, people got wind of a war very far away. 'Oh, come on, that's not happening, can't be.' Our vigil added on wider concerns. We weren't against you. We were trying to bring you home." Grace was raised in army camps; her father was in World War II, as were both her husbands. "They came back damaged, crazy. My husband came home from Germany, fine for the first week, then lay down on the couch and turned his back on everything." (That's what my brother Joe did, for a year, on our parents' sofa.) "He wouldn't talk, and I thought, What's wrong with me, that he doesn't love me anymore? Wars are like that." She's addressing the Nam vet, a breed apart. She is saying, You are not different from the soldiers of the Good War. You are not a breed apart.

Outside, the storm is gusting; inside, there are outbursts of excitement and stillness. People make statements, then contradict their own statements; they argue in one direction, then the opposite. They are giving up their specialness, defending it hard, then letting it go, becoming ordinary. It is a Buddhist ideal to be ordinary. Mid-sentence, tones of voice change from cynical to idealistic. "No such thing as a good war." One can say a sentence, and repeat it with the opposite meaning. "We lost." "Good thing we lost. What kind of people would we have become if we'd won?" "We won."

It continues to rain until floods cover northern California.

Meanwhile, Brave Orchid has moved to a small house trailer, parked (illegally) in my sister Carmen's backyard. I would invite her to live at my new house, but it is taking forever to build. It was her idea to buy a house trailer, and learn its layout before she goes blind.

"I want walls on either side of me to hold on to. Buy me a car house! And make the good old house a *soo hong*." A *soo hong* is a home where sojourners can stay for free. You mean the homeless, MaMa? Let them in? "No, not the bum-how, not the drug dealers. It's for the village cousins. Whenever they are on the road and have no place to stay, they stay here. The house will always be open." Like World War II, when the soldier cousins came through, changed into and out of uniform, and traveled on to Asia and Europe, to and from Chicago and Boston and New York. "Name the *soo hong* for your father. Just call it Soo Hong; it would sound funny with two Hongs." Soo Hong Hong. Hong Soo Hong. Community Community.

The writer veterans continued to meet season after season, year after year.

We had a gathering to which I invited Vietnamese veterans, from the North, Hanoi, to join us. It happened in October, near my birthday, fire season, fire weather. In the Tenth Month in Viet Nam, the dead come to the market place; you can visit them in the banyan tree. Vietnamese have Días de los Muertos too.

Earll, Lee Swenson, and I were parking our car under the eucalyptus trees at Mills College when another car, carrying Ho Anh Thai and Nguyen Qui Duc, pulled in next to us. All of us piled out of our cars, and effused friendliness, shaking hands, looking into faces, smiling. Ho Anh Thai, North Vietnamese, a slight man in a dark suit with a buttoned-up dark shirt, no tie, said quietly in English, "It is an honor to meet you, Mrs. Hong." Nguyen Qui Duc—or "Duc Nguyen, which

Americans can remember better"—identified himself as translator, journalist, editor, writer, and Asian American. Thai and Duc could be from two different Asian races, Duc Nguyen a stolid young Chinese, and Ho Anh Thai Filipino. They're both very alert, listening hard. Lee and Earll walked with Thai between them to our plain classroom, where the tea and coffee and breakfast pastries were set up. I offered tea, the most polite thing to do in China. Maybe same-same Viet Nam. I made the tea for Ho Anh Thai, and served it to him with both hands. Some vets had gotten there even earlier than we had; they went up to each of the Vietnamese and introduced themselves. They must have felt relieved to speak American English fast with Duc, and to hear American naturally flow from his large square mouth.

George Evans and the writer and editor Wayne Karlin came in, escorting Le Minh Khue. She looked too young to have been in the U.S.–Viet Nam War. She does not speak English; she and I took each other's hands and held on. She smiled a slow, sweet smile but a sad smile, sad downturned eyes. I tried to say a lot with my eyes. I got her some tea.

I lined George's bus posters along the chalk trays—Dorothea Lange's photos, and poems by Wallace Stevens, Langston Hughes, Carl Sandburg, William Carlos Williams, Lorine Niedecker, Charles Rezni-koff. More veterans entered, saw the Vietnamese—Khue easily seen, large features, long curly brown hair—and went over to meet them. Ann Marks, a peace activist who had gone alone to Viet Nam during the war, rushed for and grabbed Khue's attention, which annoyed some of the vets, that the FNG was taking over. I mobilized the organizing of the school chairs in a circle. It was long past the starting time that I'd sched-uled. I kept walking to my place to sit down, but nobody followed my lead. I got up, tried again. I gestured with my hands and my whole body: welcome, sit. Wayne and George were unpacking and arranging books on the table. Most of our vets seated themselves, and still the guests were standing outside the circle. I wondered whether the Vietnamese felt as shy as they appeared. It must be scary to get into a ring of American veterans, the enemy who'd warred on them. I kept standing up, walking over to them and inviting them, gesturing, nodding, heading for the chairs; they nodded Yes-yes and smiled, and stayed standing there. For-got all about the bell.

At last, they walked with George and Wayne into the circle and took their seats. They sat all in a row, not interspersed, as I would've liked.

Ellen Peskin invited the bell. Its peals faded into silence. Everyone composed himself or herself in attitudes of meditation or prayer. They landed. They folded their wings. Silence settled upon us, gathered us, held us. Worries, unexpressed, stilled. It did not matter that we did not speak the same language. We are not arguing. We are not shooting, bombing, booby-trapping one another. We are alive, breathing together. Nothing else needs to be done. This is it. This is peace. *Now* the war is over.

I hoped that everyone else realized that we have arrived at peace. We are in peace. Every moment, we are making more peace. I peeked at Thai and Khue. He looked as if he were used to this sitting in silence, breathing the common air. Khue had not changed her erect, relaxed posture from when she first sat down; her hands were in her lap, not on the desk arm. Duc sat with athletic energy at rest, like any American young man, like Jeremiah. Jeremiah "Psycho Dog" Calvillo-Zua Zua is "Son and nephew of Vietnam Vets / survivor, street gangs / youngest member of Writing Group." He is the last surviving member of his Six Pack—"We wolves of the city / We pack animals." I hope the Vietnamese are impressed to have come upon this community of meditating Americans. But maybe they think we're meditating because *they're* Buddhists, and we're stereotyping them. Or they're thinking, So this is Viet Nam's influence on the U.S. The Bell of Mindfulness rang again.

I introduced Le Minh Khue as coeditor, with Wayne Karlin and Truong Vu, of *The Other Side of Heaven—Post-War Fiction by Vietnamese and American Writers*, published by Curbstone Press. Stacks of the book are on the table. At age fifteen, she joined the People's Army of Viet Nam and the Youth Volunteers Brigade, and worked for four years as a sapper on the Ho Chi Minh Trails, Routes 15 and 20. From 1969 to 1975, she was a war reporter on the radio. She's won a national award for best short stories; she also writes novels, and is an editor at the Writers' Association Publishing House in Hanoi.

Ho Anh Thai also lives in Hanoi. He was in the war against China in 1979. A short-story writer, novelist, and columnist, he won the Hanoi Writers' Association award for the best novel published in five years. He'd been a diplomat to India.

Some of the vets already know Duc Nguyen, a local writer, like you and me. Duc came to the U.S. in 1975. His father was an ARVN colonel captured during Tet and imprisoned. He is proud of being a Vietnamese *and* being an American. I've heard Duc read; his language is all-American. "She had feet to die for." "Just a dork, I guess." "I can't see shit." "Talking money." "Just to get laid." "A gig at six o'clock." "Lay off." His audience cheered, "Yo!" "Ho!"

I called on Bob Golling, who is most socially capable, to introduce himself. Bob said his name, and "I don't know what else to say." Keith Mather said his name, went silent, then added, "I was drafted, and jailed for resistance." The others said their names, and what relation they have to Viet Nam, where they were during the war, in-country or out. They said Vietnamese names of cities, hamlets, villes, villages, plains, rivers, deltas.

Wayne Karlin said that he was up in the air bombing the Ho Chi Minh Trail — the Song My — when Khue was on the ground. "If we had met two decades ago, we would have tried to kill each other."

George Evans said, "There was a time we would have killed each other."

Wayne read his writing about Khue: "I was a helicopter gunner, and she was clearing bombs on the Ho Chi Minh Trail, the Song My. She worked while under attack from our aircraft. I flew above the jungle canopy, transfixed with hate and fear and searching for her in order to shoot her, while she looked up, in hatred and fear also, searching for me. Friends now, we talk about how it would have been if I had found her then. To waste someone, we called killing in the war. I would have wasted her. I see her face, at last emerging from the jungle canopy. She looks at me and sees the same. Mutual *seeing* of the humanness we hold in common. Realization of how terrible it would have been if we'd succeeded in killing each other brought us to moments of what I can only describe as a grief so intense that it changed us so we could never again see each other — or ourselves — in the same way."

Such searching and finding, and recognition — like lovers. All the veterans were looking at Khue with love. She looked kindly back. Mutual seeing. Beholding. They were all in love with her. And loved her more deeply when they heard her read her story in Vietnamese. We got to hear that language like bells, like running water, ringing and dinging, and tick-tocking like time. We should have heard it before.

Duc read Khue's "Tony D" in its English translation. Father and son, both thieves, steal the bones of Tony D.

—Listen, these bones are more valuable than gold—they're American bones.

—Dao and I dug them up. They're a hundred percent American bones. Dao knows his stuff—he measured them. There was even a chain around the neck, hooked to a name tag. The last few letters had worn out; you could only see part of the name. Tony D. The name of the unit is also faded. Dao's got the tag— he's peddling it now.

The ghost of Tony D, who was a Black man, haunts whoever holds the money for his bones. The old father tries to exorcise him by lighting incense to him and praying to him. "You'll be returned to your father, your mother, your wife and children—it's better than being left in the jungle." The story is filled with nasty characters, greedy for the money the bones can bring. We haunt them; they haunt us.

(A refrain from George's poetry: "*We want the bones! We want all the bones!*")

Soft-voiced in what must be Vietnamese Indian English, Ho Anh Thai reads from "Fragment of a Man." Husbands are always leaving home, and wives searching and waiting. The women deny that the men are gone away to war forever. " 'Stop. Snuff out the incense and stop praying. The airplane flew to Thailand. They're having fun over there. Get ready for him to send some packages home.' " A widow sifts through "every pile of leaves, every rock, every clod of earth around the bases of the trees." She is trying to find "a small comb made from a piece of an American warplane," engraved with her and her husband's names.

Oh, I am so in awe of Khue and Thai. The woman writer wrote about men, and the man writer wrote about women. They could see and feel from the other gender's point of view.

After pointing out that GI dog tags don't have the name of the unit, Ted started off the discussion. He'd just made a trip to Viet Nam, and wanted to check out his observations. "I'm interested in the conditions for writers." He had carried books by Thich Nhat Hanh to supply his old monastery in Huế. Ted understood that those books were not freely available over there. On the day he went through customs—and he did get the books through—the people here got the news that two Buddhist monks had been arrested and jailed. He asked our visitors, "Can you read, write, and publish what you want?"

Thai and Khue said Yes, they're free to do that.

Barbara Sonneborn said that her husband was killed in Viet Nam, and she went there to learn more about what happened. She's taken out a loan on her home to make a film about war widows, Vietnamese and American. "In a village, I met a widow whose story I especially wanted. But in honor of my hosts, I refrained from asking questions. I know from personal experience that people are not free to speak." Barbara had seen for herself the lack of freedom in present-day Viet Nam.

Thai said, "Yes, now we can write and speak as we want."

Khue said, "Yes." She could have said, Didn't you hear what I just read to you? Our dark stories do not flatter Viet Nam, yet no one stops us from writing, translating, publishing them. We travel everywhere, telling terrible things.

And they could have said that just yesterday, at their very first reading in America, they were demonstrated against, and San José State canceled the program. The demonstrators were immigrants from South Viet Nam, American residents and citizens, and some ARVN vets. But Barnes & Noble gave the readers a venue; half of the listeners were Vietnamese.

George got impatient, raised his voice: "Fifty-eight thousand on the Wall! *They* lost two million! Four million! *One* death is terrible. One dies, the world dies. We need to see what we've done. They've been in war for generations. We can't imagine—we can't judge—their society. The miracle of how much they've gone through, and are alive. And we go there, we go to them asking for more. They are rebuilding a devastated country, and we criticize them for not being free like us. We can't expect them to be like us. Who are we to ask them to do things the way we do them?"

Barbara kept on pressing, "But I was just there, and I witnessed . . ." She was charged with the distress of the people she'd met—women who told her that family members had been separated and taken to different rooms and tortured.

Some of the vets asked, How free are *we* to tell *our* stories and truths? "Can we speak out and be heard in our own country?"

Wayne answered, "America does not want to hear from its veterans. The literary market does not want vet lit. That's what they call it—'vet lit.' And they don't want any. The level of denial in Americans—the publishers are not interested, the readers are not interested."

"Vet lit," the vets repeated. "Vet lit." We are writing vet lit, and nobody wants to read us.

Miki addressed Khue. "Please talk to us about women in war. How was it for you as a woman soldier?"

Khue said, "I was fifteen years old, and I went to save my country. Everything was wonderful. I was full of joy. It was the most wonderful time. I felt love. I felt romance."

Many people excitedly agreed with her. Yes, yes, it was a wonderful time, wasn't it? We were young. We had adventures. War was a great adventure. We had fun. We made tight friends. Mike Wong said, "Yes, in my life too, it was the best of times, it was the worst of times."

I was dismayed. The most peaceful ones here were looking back at war, and it was good times, good fun. Khue is not the woman warrior I wished for.

Miki jumped into the middle of the circle to keep order. "Wait. Wait for the translation before you talk." People were replying to questions or statements that they thought they heard. "Now your turn, the English translation. . . . Okay, now, the Vietnamese translation."

Jimmy said, "As a medic, I did not feel camaraderie. Medics were off to the side."

Earll said, as he often says, "It's the body. At seventeen, eighteen, the body feels high, quick, alive. Everything you do is full of energy. Nothing—the world, the body—can ever feel as good again."

I said, "This is one of our spousal disagreements. We've had it from the time I met him till now. He was twenty-three, and I was twenty-one. I can't stand it—that you feel that the teen-age years were the high point of your life. And they were over long before I met you. You had your high points, and I wasn't there. I have to insist, we existentially make life. At adolescence we have barely begun that work. We have quickness and strength in middle age that far surpass a teen-ager's."

"But the body."

"I mean the body too. We existentially grow even the body."

Duc said, "The isms in Viet Nam now aren't capitalism and Communism. They are Vietnamese romanticism and sentimentalism."

I said, "I want to talk about the Ho Chi Minh Trail. Song My. Today, for the first time in my life, I am believing there was and there is a Ho Chi Minh Trail. Ho Chi Minh Trails." Duc had to translate several times. He probably said, "She doesn't believe in the Ho Chi Minh

Trails. She thinks Song My is an illusion." Or "a delusion." I explained, "I've always heard that there was no such thing as the Ho Chi Minh Trail. It was something our government made up—the route by which the North was attacking the South—so that we'd have an excuse to bomb farther north. Everybody said, Ho Chi Minh Trail? No such thing. It's the other side's propaganda, a figment that the other side made up. Sometimes, even the government claimed it didn't exist; they wanted to deny that we had planes that far past the DMZ. 'What Ho Chi Minh Trail? We aren't bombing the Ho Chi Minh Trail; there isn't one.' And the left denied the existence of the Song My—I never heard those words before, and now I hear Route Fifteen, Route Twenty, it even has route numbers—to show that there was no justification for the bombing."

Earll was the only one who remembered with me that America had believed that the Ho Chi Minh Trail did not exist. Noam Chomsky, on the grass in front of Sproul Hall on Viet Nam Day, proved semiotically—no Ho Chi Minh Trail.

Khue said, "Yes, there was a Song My Trail. I helped build it. I remember the triple-canopy forest and the craters. It was my work to fill in the craters."

Rich Gilman said, "I was a flight engineer. We bombed the Ho Chi Minh Trail every day, a couple of times a day."

Rich kept looking at Le Minh Khue; his small eyes were wells of feelings. And next to him sat Sherdyl, also steadily looking at her. Khue returned the gazes of the giants, and held them. So—flying over the Ho Chi Minh Trail were Rich and Wayne, and on the ground was Khue. And now they meet and cannot get enough of one another.

Keith said, "I was AWOL in Canada, and met a Vietnamese who was also deserting the war. We stood in the snow and bowed to each other."

Keith and Mike were sitting together. I pictured Mike as the Vietnamese man bowing to Keith.

Duc said, ". . . irony . . ."

I asked, "What's the Vietnamese word for 'irony'?"

Dimples winking, he said, "There isn't any. Vietnamese don't have a word for 'irony.' "

"Really? Did you say the Vietnamese language has no word for 'irony'?"

"Nah. Not. There must be five or eight words for 'irony.' "

Everybody laughed. Duc, Khue, and Thai came up with one word after another, "irony" in Vietnamese, and we laughed at each one. Irony. Irony. Irony. Irony. Irony. Irony. Irony. We were laughing at jokes in Vietnamese. I couldn't even think of one synonym for "irony" in English.

Before our time was up, I asked Khue and Thai whether they had questions for us.

She spoke quietly, and he translated, speaking for himself too. "We have one question. Why didn't you know about the war?"

Many people tried to answer at once. No one disputed the question, the assumption: You were ignorant of the war. "I had to stop reading the newspapers. It was so depressing, and full of lies." "Our government lied to us, false body-counts, always lots of enemy dead, few dead on our side." "The media was into misinformation. They lied to us." "We were betrayed by our own government and the corporate capitalists and arms dealers. Our economy was based on war." "There was a tenet, 'The President knows more than we do. The President is acting on secret information.' " "Our foreign policy was the domino theory. That metaphor was irrefutable. Jeez, Henry Kissinger got a Nobel Prize for the domino theory."

Ann Marks said that we are now working to know our history. Finally, twenty years after the fall of Saigon, the Berkeley Historical Society is putting together an archive on the war; it will be on computer. And she's helping to plan a ceremony on Armistice Day/Veterans Day. At last, the Berkeley Viet Nam dead will be remembered. Without support from any organization or government, Ann had traveled alone to Viet Nam during the war. "I was saying to my brothers, the soldiers: 'Whither thou goest, there will I go.' "

Wayne said that they had to catch the plane: Khue and Thai were setting off to see the USA, many big cities, and one small town in America's heartland: Gambier, Ohio. The circle broke up, people stood, continued talking. Rich Gilman hugged Le Minh Khue, fellow kid soldier of the Ho Chi Minh Trail. He looked straight ahead and the tears were falling from his open eyes. Sherdyl hugged Khue. His eyes were shut; she held him and rocked him like a baby. Her head came up to the chest of these big men. They clasped her against their heart. O, precious being, alive, unharmed. You're all right. I almost killed you, and did not. Thank God. You're here, alive. I did not kill you. You are dear to me. Dearest. O, glad. Glad. They had not seen the enemy; the VC had been invisible, hidden in the dark, in the jungle. She had been the enemy — this lovely, lovely woman.

Khue walked over to me, and we hugged too. We hugged because unable to speak. She gave me a black lacquer vase with a pair of goldfish on it.

I shook Thai's hand many times. He asked me to send him my writing. "And I'll write about this day for the Vietnamese newspaper, and send it to you."

People brought out cameras; they took pictures of one another in various groupings. Bags and boxes had to be reloaded into the cars. George asked me how to get to the San Francisco airport; I got Earll to give him directions, and listened for a while to George repeating the norths, souths, lefts, rights funny. I tried to break up the goodbying. They'll miss their plane. The veterans could not part. They could not leave one another. I'd lure somebody, anybody, outside, and he'd go back in for more hugging, crying, picture-taking, exchanging of addresses and histories. I found Earll and George, and suggested that Earll drive to the airport. Great idea. More switching of luggage from car to car. The people inside were organizing themselves for a group photo. Get people outside to come back in. Standing in the doorway, I saw the picture that will develop: Mike Wong has one arm around Ted and the other around Lee. Khue's right hand is raised, waving playfully. Tall Woman Vet stands behind Khue and Ann, and has a great wide smile — I've never seen her smile. Barbara has her arm through Thai's arm. Keith is sitting on the floor, big smile, hands together leaning forward into the camera. Jimmy and George and Earll are kneeling on one knee, as if genuflecting, Jimmy's eyes closed; he's holding a dish of water like an offering. Sherdyl has his hands on Kim's and Kate's shoulders. Jeremiah "Psycho Dog" is laughing. Miki is laughing too. Tom's eyes are wide open. Everyone looks young and happy. "Come on. Come on," they called to me. I sat on the floor next to Keith. "Where's Rich?" "Disappeared again." Ellen took pictures with each of the cameras. Then everybody went out to see the travelers off. Goodbye. Goodbye. Earll drove away, the other car following.

Toward the end of eating meditation, Earll came back, and told us about the ride to the airport. "Happy," Thai kept saying. "Happy." George played navigator, but Earll drove directly to SFO. Thai and Khue said that last night George took them for a tour of the Bay Area and got lost. He'd kept saying, "I steer by the moon." Khue asked, "Do all Americans do that—navigate by the moon? That's why you lost the war."

The BBC called me. They wanted to make a documentary about writers and teachers journeying across national boundaries: *Stories My Country Told Me.* Desmond Tutu would travel from Capetown to Johannesburg, Eric Hobsbawm through sections of the former Yugoslavia, Eqbal Ahmad between Pakistan and India. And I would visit my ancestral villages in China. But I've been to my villages already. I suggested, how about taking me and a group of American Viet Nam veterans to Thich Nhat Hanh's community, Plum Village? We will find a great story in Plum Village. The producer, Anthony Wall, said, "Plum Village is where your heart is. We'll film where your heart is." *La querencia.* Unlike American foundations, the BBC would fund international travel, and a project with a religious theme. The budget would allow for me, Earll, and four veterans. I chose two from the East Coast, Dan Moen Thompson and Jerry Crawford, and two from the West, Ted Sexauer and Jimmy Janko. Each of them had previously on his own gone on retreat with Thich Nhat Hanh. Plum Village would not freak them out. I chose Ted for inventing one-breath one-word poetry that can save a life. I love his "Poem for Tết":

POEM FOR TẾT

Lăng Cô village, Việt Nam
lunar new year, 31/1/1995

This is the poem
that will save my life
this the line that will cure me
this word, this, the word 'word' the one
this   breath   the one I am

I chose Jimmy because he used power words—"Pretty." "Home." "Baby." "Girlfriend." "Darling." "Don't die on me, motherfucker!"—that kept the wounded alive. I wanted Dan to get to live among Vietnamese monks; he could come to terms with having shot at one (or two) of them. And I wanted to know what became of Jerry and the woman warrior who lived inside of him. The BBC got faxes through to and from Plum Village. There is such a place. It exists.

On a cold November Friday, Kate Meynell, producer and director, hired a fishing boat and took us—a film crew, and me and Earll—plunging and pitching into the Bay. The fog and the waves poured onto the boat, which was moving too fast into the whiteness. The captain showed me the sonar-radar computer—nothing on the screen but more fog. Suddenly—Alcatraz. (Jimmy spent thirteen years as nightwatchman of Alcatraz. He hadn't carried a gun; he howled to scare away trespassers.) And suddenly—The Island. Angel Island coalesced—dark cliffs above us, and dark trees on top and on the sides of the cliffs. The open ocean between me and China. I am my mother, arriving at North America, seeing no landing place, no shelters, no cultivated farmland, no civilization. "*Bwoy,*" she said. "The wild. The dangerous wild." This is not the Angel Island I know, so sylvan and islelike as viewed from the bridges. I will crash into land and drown. I shouldn't try to live what I want to write. I should've stayed at home, making up the story about veterans journeying to Plum Village and living with Vietnamese happily ever after.

The boat rocking, and the wind blowing, and the waves and fog wetting everything, I looked into the camera and told what my mother has been telling me since my father died. Now that he could not be deported, I told on international TV that he had been a stowaway on a ship from Cuba. Three times he stowed away in a crate, and twice was caught and jailed in New York Harbor. He was deported to Cuba, came back to the U.S., redeported, and came back again. It wasn't my father who came through Angel Island but my mother. At the edge of the village, named Accompany to the Last, she looked back and saw my father's father standing there weeping. She bribed her way onto a series of boats. A soldier pointed his gun at the passengers and ordered them to stop eating. My mother kept eating. "Shoot if you're going to shoot." In danger, Brave Orchid is afraid, and she is unafraid, but always daringly talks. On another boat, she hid under the oranges. In Canton, she ran from robbers—soldiers and police who'd seen her stash money—ran into a big hotel, then another big hotel. She bribed a sailor, paid again for a ticket onto the USS *President Taft*, and came here. She was locked up for three weeks in the wooden house, the immigration station, on the other, leeward side of The Island. She ate noodles with catsup, and gelatin on bread. She does not like spaghetti to this day. She could come to America because my father won a visa for her at the gambling table. Jack Hong lost $600 to my father, and didn't have the money, so BaBa asked to have the visa that was for Jack's wife. Now, despite my fears, our little boat sailed all the way around The Island, filmed it, and returned safely to land.

Filmmakers maneuver equipment, props, the light, people, time, and they are always late. At dawn we were in Oakland Chinatown, really Asiatown now—Vietnamese, Filipinos, Thai, Laotians, Cambodians, Burmese, Koreans. Hours of takes and retakes to make a point about national identities. We never got to the affirmative-action demonstration at Berkeley. I'd wanted to be filmed walking down the Mario Savio Steps, through Sproul Plaza to Sather Gate. Some days, each and every table and stand is manned and womaned by Asians—business clubs, professional clubs, social clubs, service clubs, political clubs, religious clubs—all Asian, many kinds of Asians, many kinds of Chinese. Asians have to form clubs, *huis*, associations, societies wherever we go. We have a genius for *communitas*.

I wanted the BBC to show the world a multicultural, multiracial America. Every time we go to war, we're in schizophrenic agony. Whoever the enemy is, they're related to us.

The director wanted a gourd, like the one the All-Seeing Immortal carries. Kate envisioned fancy shots of me looking into the magic water gourd, and witnessing faraway and long-ago events. Scenes would start framed in the mouth of the gourd, and shimmer into clarity. I spied a gourd in the window of a flower shop that was closed, and wasted time trying to get the bartender next door to find the owner. As the vans were leaving our house, my friend the librarian, Bessie, drove up with two gourds that were sitting in her recycling bin.

Our caravan—Ellen of the Community of Mindful Living, Earll and I, and the cameraman and the soundwoman and the director in one van, and the rest of the BBC crew in the other—drove to the vets' workshop in Sebastopol. We were late. Bad enough that I was bringing a crew

of strangers. Bad enough that I favored Ted and Jimmy. But I was stealing the veterans' time. Filming en route—the cameraman backward in
his seat next to the driver, Ellen, Kate and the soundwoman in back
uphoisting the furry microphone over our heads—Earll and I answered
the question: Why Viet Nam?

The film crew crowded themselves and their equipment into Marg
and Bill's house, and set up lights that glared into the eyes of the women
sitting on the wall bench. Lit up, the house no longer seemed to be the
well, the cave, the darkness of Creation. Woman Vet and Miki kept saying, "Don't shine that thing on me." The cameraman shut off the lights,
but the equipment stayed in position. Kate suggested that I announce,
Anybody who doesn't want to be filmed can sit out of camera range.

I introduced the crew. Kate Meynell, producer and director. Soundwoman Sara Chin. (Sara is a young woman with bone-white hair; her
ancestors, like mine, are from southern China. She is a writer.) Cameraman Allan Palmer. Camera assistant Hilary Morgan. All but Kate are
local people, like a pickup band. They greeted the veterans, and disappeared behind the equipment or to the kitchen or outdoors. I failed to
get everybody to sit together in meditation; filmmakers are observers,
not participants.

Trust Ball, the truth game Wittman and his contemporaries played
in Sanctuary, would be visually interesting on film. I brought a globe
balloon, Planet Earth with topographical features and clouds, no
national boundaries. But the lights did not go on, the camera did not roll
for Trust Ball. I was at once disappointed that Trust Ball would not be
filmed for history, and relieved—we could be ourselves.

While I gave instructions, Jeremiah "Psycho Dog," who was with us
when his oldest gang friend, Barbarian, was murdered in prison, inflated
the globe. He threw it to Earll. Earll said, "I knew you were going to
choose me. I know your ways, Jeremiah, because I was like you. I want
to warn you, my younger self, about the danger of being smart, being
smarter than others. Be patient with them. Be careful of them. You have
an amazing verbal talent that can turn into bullshitting, or it can turn
into poetry. . . ."

Thus went our game. Therese threw the ball to Richard Sterling,
who had upset her by writing the word "gook" so much. He hugged the
earth, rested his chin on top of it. "Therese. Ah, Therese. If you weren't

already married, I'd ask you to marry me." He threw the ball to Sherdyl. "Here, big guy."

Affection moved back and forth across the room. The world floated from person to person. Spider Grandmother was weaving her web, binding us each to each, each to all. Everybody embraced the earth, held it in wide arms with fingers entwined, as if the earth were one's own big belly.

Scott Morrison threw the ball to *both* Mike Wong and Jade Lee and asked, "What *is* your relationship? Lovers or what? Everybody's curious. Come on, let us in on it."

Jade said, "People don't understand true friendship between a man and a woman."

Mike and Jade said to each other, "You saved my life." "You mean so much to me. You saved my life."

Ted Sexauer and Barbara Sonneborn made connection. "I'm touched to think that you care what I think of you," she said. "I feel you don't like me. I'm not sure what went wrong between us. I feel your severity, your irritation directed at me." Ted assured her that he does like her, respects her, finds *her* intimidating.

Barbara threw the ball to me. I gave her a wish, that she finish her film, *Regret to Inform*. "You are dogged," I said, "doggedly making the film, and doggedly questioning our Vietnamese guests. I'd like to see you more graceful, taking it easier, not insist so hard. Maybe things get done anyway—even better—without constant worry." I wanted to go over to her and rub the frown lines between her eyes. I should have praised her more—she and Pauline Laurent—Viet Nam widows who came to the realization: They wanted their husbands neither to be killed nor to kill others.

Jack Noble told Pauline to lay Viet Nam to rest. "I respect and honor your loss of Howard," he said, "and your writing about him. I'm not criticizing the writing and all the hard work you've done. I don't mean to take anything away. But I'd like to read and hear what you have to say about other things that have nothing to do with Viet Nam. I'd like to see your description of some more of the world that's not Viet Nam. For example, an autumn day."

Other people chimed in. "Yes, trees." "The sunlight through the birches." "Butterflies." They were calling out the sights.

The ball went to Woman Vet, then to A Circle of Sisters . . . A Circle of Friends. We made circles within and around circles.

The BBC came back into the room. Allan squatted with his camera before me, filming me teaching the community about community. Sangha. The Buddhist word for the community that lives in peace and harmony is "sangha." To live happily, wholly, truly, each of us has to create sangha. The sangha is the place—the sangha is the people with whom you can exchange feelings and thoughts. The sangha inspires you, and keeps you thriving, and makes life worth living. Build the community with resources at hand, whatever's, whoever's here, whoever shows up, whoever happens by. Make community, *communitas*, sangha of those people in your apartment building, on your street, at your job, wherever you are.

I said, "We've all had experiences in communities already. The army is a community; the people on a ship, your Basic Training group, your platoon, your class in school, your therapy group, AA, your gang—all communities. Today, please write about yourself as a member of a community, a sangha."

Jeremiah "Psycho Dog" said, "Sang gha." Chinese intonations. He's saying, "Life family."

Director Kate invited people outside for interviews; one by one they left writing-in-community and eating meditation. Like an anthropologist of old, she chose people at the margin, FNGs, Ann Marks, Shepherd Bliss. Tom Currie shot back with his own camera. I could see him in the grass beside the path; he's gesticulating, telling the international audience about the cosmos. The BBC was getting some beautiful pictures of the fog-hazed groves. The fog was staying all day in the trees and on the yellow fields, valleys, and hills. Black buzzards and hawks flew in the white sky; and the wood-rail fence was a black line. The people, the crew surrounding Ann in her red sweater, were tiny, like bodhisattvas or fairies in a Chinese mist painting.

Kim read first today; she would have made a beautiful picture, classical Asian American Indian profile with Marg's orange-and-white oil painting behind her. I expected her to write a sangha story about her family in Thailand or a group she counseled. "Americans are lonely," she said. "There will always be war. You can't just have no-war." She explained nonduality. I can't like it. Asians often observe that Americans are lonely; it is lonely here. "You try to stop your pain by watching TV . . .

There are many reasons why we feel lonely and separate from others . . . the very basic values of our culture: independence, individuality, and privacy." She read:

> I used to give up my seat for children, elders and people with disabilities, or offer help to people who are blind to cross the street or get on public transportation. Often times, they declined my offer. Then I gradually became less sensitive to people around me and very hesitant to offer help. . . . One time during the rush hour on BART, an older female passenger held on to the pole by the train door, where the seats are assigned for the seniors and people with disabilities. A man and a woman in their early thirties sat there. He read a morning newspaper, and she was reviewing her papers. The train was crowded and this older passenger had a hard time holding on to the pole. After several stops, the train became even more crowded; she bent down and talked to the female passenger who sat next to where she stood. The woman looked up at her and with a surprised and disbelieving look on her face, she coldly said, "You want me to give up the seat for you." The older passenger calmly and confidently responded, "Yes," then pointed to the sign that said the seats are reserved for seniors and people with disability. The younger woman looked at the sign, and with a big sigh gathered her papers, put them in her handbag, got up, and let the older lady sit down. While the exchange was happening, the man who sat next to her did not take his eyes off the newspaper. The wall of independence, individuality, and privacy shielded him well.

Mike Wong wrote about himself as a member of a commune, Rochdale, in Canada. I pictured him, lanky hippie striding across borders, demarcating new countries, and being everywhere in the community, going about his responsibilities. He and Jade Lee and Jade's sister, whom he called "the warrior Cindy Lei," were the heart of a bohemia of friends. Everybody must have been in love with everybody else. I wished that I had found them, gone to Canada, and been young and Chinese American counterculture with them.

> We were a world unto ourselves, with our own government, a free medical clinic, a movie theater, a library, a health food restau-

rant, a store, a dance studio, and a host of other features of a community. We even had our own hippie "police force," Rochdale Security, and our own Mafia, the various drug dealer organizations. I joined Rochdale Security with the specific aim of field-testing nonviolence. We protected out turf from outside predators, confronted problems within Rochdale, and played security games with the police, sometimes working with them, sometimes against them, as the situation flowed. Through luck, determination, and the beginnings of skill, I survived a year on Rochdale Security without once harming anyone. . . .

Earll, my espoused one, wrote about the beginnings of the Hawai'i Performing Arts Company.

We fell apart eventually, but when we were good, God, we were good; we made them laugh, we made them cry, we made each other laugh and cry. We were on fire with the love of theatre, and we were going to last forever. We were young in the peak time of the century in the most beautiful place on the planet, young doing theatre. Up at six and into the car out to the pineapples, bringing *Peter and the Wolf* to O'ahu's plantation schools. I brush my wolf's tail poking through the hole in my Levis. I love my ears and whiskers, my red silk shirt, my black brocade vest. I'm a Mississippi riverboat gambler wolf. We drive the red dirt cane-haul roads between gigs and air dry our costumes out the car windows.
We travel Dickens' *Christmas Carol* to Moloka'i and Lana'i and the Big Island, and after three back-to-backs in Lana'i City, we lie in a circle on a flat-topped hill, our heads toward the middle, our bodies touching, breathing together and, humming into an open-voiced chant, bring the full moon up over Moloka'i. . . .

He compared the end of that time in Hawai'i to the last dance in high school: "And just when I was getting into it, it's over. Damn. And I still didn't ask Kathy Harris to dance."
Scott said, "But you get to go home with the queen of the prom." He meant me.
I had gone along on some shows, carried the props, remembered the

keys, led the applause. At the shows on the military bases, the army brats shouted, "Shoot the wolf!" then "Shoot Peter!"

Earll was the only writer who recognized our very own writing workshop as a living community, happening right now. "I ask everybody for a dance because everybody here is a great word dancer. You never ever—what a blessing—get it right because there is no right but only *more*. No better or worse story, no better or worse teller, only more. Tell me, show me *more*. And when you're done, may I have the next dance?"

Oh, such communities the veterans wrote: Barbara Sonneborn, a newly rebuilt village in Viet Nam. Yigal Ben-Haim, the children's house on a kibbutz near Haifa. Bonnie Humble, A Circle of Sisters . . . A Circle of Friends. Doug Howerton, MOVE in Philadelphia. Keith Mather, the Presidio 27. Kate Beckwith, the Doughnut Dollies, the RECRE-ATORS. Maryanne Teng, Plum Village. Sherdyl, the peace movement in Tucson: "Should we firebomb the ROTC? Or are the Druids going to levitate the building?" Scott Morrison, a group of Amish: "Seven families are a community." Lee Swenson, the Institute for the Study of Natural and Cultural Resources: "I want a community to grow old with."

Yigal gave a prayer in Hebrew, then English. " 'Life and grace and kindness and compassion be upon us.' " He kidded around. "Come on. It's okay to say 'compassion.' We're in California. We're allowed. We can say it. Come on. Compassion."

Laughing, we said a shameless litany of compassions. "Compassion." "Compassion." "Compassion."

I wished I could bring all of them with me to Plum Village.

The BBC crew dismantled the lights during walking meditation, and drove away in the middle of the readings. We sat the last meditation of the day, and lingered in the sunset, the twilight, and the night. Marg and Bill invited the stayers to help ourselves to the leftover bread and soup. Miki, wearing bedroom slippers, sat in my little school-chair. I sat on the floor. The darker the night, the closer the group sat together.

As if uttering a secret, Mike Wong said that he was feeling again a feeling that used to be everywhere when he was young. "I'm having it right now. That feeling is here again now. Do you know what I mean?"

"Yes, yes, a shiny, high, uplifted feeling." "It's the feeling of eternity—of being alive." "And knowing that we've always been alive, and will continue forever." "Yes, right now and forever are the same

THE FIFTH BOOK OF PEACE

thing. I know it. I feel it." "Usually we shut off from that life force. Our upbringing and experiences blur it." "I think I lost it because nobody else saw it, had it." "Don't outgrow this, Jeremiah." "It's getting stronger as we talk about it. I'm remembering it now. It's coming back." "It comes when you can get really quiet, calm, still. Then you notice it."

I said, "Write it down. Name it. Put it into words. When you read the words, maybe it will come back. Maybe it can be passed on to readers. At least, the words will remind you that once you had this knowledge."

"I'm naming it joyfulness-about-the-real-nature-of-existence," said Jeremiah.

I envisioned a line of light flowing out of me and curling around us, this one and that one, and all, and all, and flying here and there, enwrapping every being and thing I can imagine.

Maryanne said that she had such a moment seeing the moonlight on Plum Village. "I said out loud to myself, 'I will remember this.' And I do."

Many people repeated after her, "I will remember this."

We parted at midnight.

Jimmy, Ted, Jerry, Dan, Earll, and I rode in a van on our way to the Left Bank, to Montparnasse. The Eiffel Tower swung by—over there, between those buildings, those trees. There it is. There it is again. We're in Paris. The Eiffel Tower was shining in the sun. Its beauty is in its intricacy.

We rode through Paris catching up on past dissatisfactions, and anticipating the possible disappointment that Plum Village might turn out to be. In 1982, Thich Nhat Hanh led Vietnamese exiles and refugees to a land of flowers and fruit. They grow many plum trees and sell the fruit to feed the Hungry Children of Vietnam. But no way is Plum Village Shangri-la. Ted and Dan complained about Thich Nhat Hanh's retreat at Omega, where eight hundred people crowded into the leaky revival tent. Veterans camping in the rain and mud were flooded out, and slept on the auditorium floor. The sleeping bags wouldn't dry. The veterans' reading had been scheduled for midday among other activities; they could not read to the entire sangha, and they could not read as late as they wished into the night. Some vets left. "It was not well organized," said Dan. I felt guilty that I hadn't been there to organize it.

Dan, the Virginia gentleman, said, "I feel that Thây is uncomfortable with the West. He doesn't want closeness; his discomfort with Westerners would show." It's true that Thich Nhat Hanh teaches from afar. During Desert Storm, he threatened to cancel his trip to America. And when he got here—there—he scolded us for not being able to stop the war. Now we are chasing him to his home, trying to get him to give us personal attention, to make him speak to us tête-à-tête. Thây tells a story about himself as a boy searching for and missing a famous hermit. But near the hermit's hut, he found a well with the clearest, sweetest water, drank from it, and was satisfied. "I found my hermit." I get it: he's always trying to convince us not to bother him.

The next day, on the sunny train platform at Libourne, where we got off the fast train from Paris, we met pilgrims on their way to Plum Village, a monk from Japan and Patrick LaCoste, an Irishman/Frenchman. We're like Dead Heads, converging by plane, train, car, and van upon Jerry Garcia and the Grateful Dead. The little train came, and our group—the vets, the BBC—crowded into the last car, filled the seats and aisle with our stuff, sat on the equipment, and stood looking out the back window.

We arrived at Sainte-Foy-La-Grande on a clear, windy autumn afternoon. Extremely tall, leafless sycamores surrounded the train station. They were cobbed high up; thin arms of trees with separate trunks touched and connected at the top, making a frame for a canopy.

Sister Dong Yim and Brother Pop Thang, two bald people in brown robes, small as me, walked toward us, giving us constant smiles. Earll and I, smiling back, walked toward them, the vets behind us. When we got close, we stood still, put our hands together, and bowed. A lotus for you, Buddha-to-be. "Welcome home," said the nun and the monk.

And then—so embarrassing—Kate asked us to do the meeting again for the camera! I, the go-between, asked Sister and Brother, "May we please do that again—meet again—for the BBC TV?" Sister Dong Yim said, "I not used to movie star. You movie star. I not movie star." But she seemed to be having fun; they both looked like kids at play. All of us parted, and met again. The soundman caught the nun saying, "Welcome home," and "We go home now," as she led the way toward her car.

Sister Dong Yim drove Earll and me to the Lower Hamlet, which is in Meyrac. The handmade signs said: "Làng Hồng" and "Village des Pruniers" and "Vous êtes arrivé" and "Aller doucement respirer et sourire." The van went to the Upper Hamlet, which is in Loubès-Bernac. The community was divided into two hamlets; the monks live in the Upper Hamlet, and the nuns, women, and married couples in the Lower Hamlet. "Hamlet"—a word from the War in Viet Nam. I wonder why "hamlet" rather than *ville*, also a word from that war.

Steffie from Germany showed us to our room, which was a cell in a two-hundred-year-old structure. It might have once been a stall for cows. Asians enjoy subdividing great halls into many snug rooms, lowering ceilings, raising floors. We put our bags down beside the pallets, and followed Steffie to the dining commons. The cooking area was at one end of a roomful of plank tables. Over tea, she told us about mealtimes and the bell. I asked if she was studying to be a nun. She said in surprise, "No, no." She came here years ago, and decided to stay as a gardener. Felco clippers were sticking out of her back pocket.

Left to ourselves, Earll and I sat on our pallets, which were foam-rubber pads covered with a summer-weight sleeping bag. In my down coat, gloves, and cashmere hat I huddled against the tepid radiator. I planned to sleep with all my clothes and my new-age fabric luggage on top of me.

On the back of the door was a schedule with the times for Noble Silence, Lazy Day (Wednesdays), work, dharma talks, meals. We were to "refrain from sex to give full mindful attention to the retreat."

Meanwhile, at the Upper Hamlet, Sister Chân Không, whom all of us had met before, and Brother Sariputra were serving tea to the veterans. The BBC got some of the tea party on tape. Sister Chân Không—Sister True Emptiness—has deep dimples, big eyes, Frenchy voice, à-la-mode bald head—she might have been a chanteuse. Actually, she was originally a biologist. She warned the vets about having flashbacks while at Plum Village: "You may see faces that look like those you saw in Viet Nam." She gets her ideas about the nature of veterans from Claude AnShin Thomas, who led our workshops at Omega and Malibu. Claude had lived with the Vietnamese in the Lower Hamlet. She said he strung tin-can booby traps all around his tent. He thought that Thây had invited him to Plum Village to be tried for war crimes. "Every day he had told one story to me: 'That young girl is like the one I kill.' And then another tomorrow he said, 'That young man is look like the guerrilla we saw—he is shooting my friend.' He looked at any Vietnamese with the manifestation of his stored consciousness, souvenir of those he has killed during the war. And so it took him one month in order to get used to it. I say, 'Now look clearer, open your eyes. Here she is, born even in England, and she grow up in England. She has—she is of course a manifestation of her ancestor who have Vietnamese origin, but she's not the person you killed.' " Sister Chân Không laughed happily.

Near dinnertime, Earll and I and two British women looked for a ride to the Upper Hamlet. An Italian woman came along in a van and drove us. At the men's hamlet, on the main walkway, Carole Melkonian—our bell-minder from home—came a-striding, her dark hair blowing high. "My sangha," she said, hugging us.

In the kitchen, the community walked in procession around the stoves and tables, and filled plates and bowls from the pots and platters. I left my shoes among the shoes at the bottom of a flight of wooden stairs that were almost as steep as a ladder, and climbed into a loft area. Up out of the floor, I entered a mise-en-scène from *The Saragossa Manuscript*—a monastery of the Middle Ages. The setting sun slanted gold light through openings in the stone walls, and spotlighted people in brown robes like Franciscans. Monks and nuns have halos; their bald heads reflect the light. Every head without hair is a different shape. I found a seat in the middle of about fifty people at tables that were slabs of old wood. A row of people sat under the slope of the roof, which almost touched their heads. I recognized monks and nuns who'd been at Omega and in Taiwan. Oh, what a relief to be quiet; I don't have to think up conversation. We ate lily flowers, the "golden needles" Chinese have on New Year's Day. Rice. Tofu. Noodles. Vegetables grown in the gardens here, or given by the neighbors. And lots of desserts—boxes of chocolates—Godiva, sent to Plum Village by people from far countries. The monks and nuns are like kids, delighting in candy.

This is it already, all, truly. This sitting and eating in silence. Vietnamese and veterans are being at peace. Know it.

After we had been eating a long time, the bell rang. The silence-ending bell. A monk stood and introduced me to the community, and I introduced the veterans, who were sitting in different places, interspersed among the sangha. (The BBC crew were not there; they'd gone to the nearest town for dinner with meat and wine and coffee. Kate says that you have to keep the crew happy, at least feed them well.) I said each of the veterans' names one syllable at a time. Earll's name is impossible for an Asian to say in one syllable. My mother calls him Oy Low;

said with certain tones, it could mean Love Man or Love Guy. The Plum Villagers called him King. They called me Hong, same-same Vietnamese. Jimmy, who was sitting under the slope of the ceiling, stood, bowed, and bowed lower, a lotus-for-you-Buddha-to-be bow. The sangha bowed to each one of us. At least once in his or her life, everyone should be bowed to by a crowd of people.

Evening in the Lower Hamlet, Earll and I went to "undirected meditation"; a few women, Steffie, Carole, were also there in the small meditation hall. The Noble Silence was wide, deep, dark. In the black night full of stars, the villages and countryside were beautifully still.

I awoke to a small bell moving through the hamlet; someone was walking its paths and hallways, carrying and ringing the bell. Noble Silence continued through morning meditation and breakfast. Sister Annabelle Laity led chanting, and the dawn arose with gradual, soft light. A couple from Scandinavia brought fruit and crème fraîche, and made crêpes as their gift to the sisters.

The dog sleeping by the potbelly stove was named Maitrya. Maitrya is the Buddha-of-Love, who is yet to be born. Thây says that the next incarnation of the Buddha will not be an individual but a sangha.

After breakfast, when the BBC crew returned from coffee in town, Kate and her production manager, Tricia Chacon, gathered the veterans and me in the meditation hall at the Upper Hamlet. Sister Chân Không and Jerry Crawford were already sitting under the blazing lights. The rest of us joined them on the red runner leading up to the altar, Ted and Jerry in chairs, Dan, Jimmy, Sister, Earll, and I on cushions. (Hips and backs hurt from parachute jumping.) Now we were to talk story.

Sister True Emptiness said that she likes Jerry's story, which she has known for a few years, and told it on camera. I'd met Jerry and heard his story before she had, read its many rewrites. The ghost of his guerrilla woman—the one he'd stalked and shot—sat up on the gurney, and jumped inside of him. She looked straight at him, and flew into his body. "I am the woman warrior," he'd said. "I carry the woman warrior within myself. Inside, I am a woman. Part of me is a woman. The warrior woman lives within me. Would you role-play her for me?" I'd been smart and scared enough to say No.

Sister Chân Không spoke for Jerry, sometimes inhabiting his voice. "One young woman who he wound. She was wounded. She been shot. Jerry take her to hospital. When she die she look at him in very strange eyes, very—of course a lot of angry, a lot of anger and, and . . . hate. And the face of that woman follow him for more than ten or fifteen year. And every time he told the story, he cry. He cry. And he hold on to the hammock of the guerrilla soldier in his arms, and he cry, he cry." He carried the hammock that she had carried, took it with him everywhere he went, to college, to Omega. He said, "I didn't think anything about it." He had kept quitting Omega, packing and repacking his motorcycle. "Outta here. I can't hear the monk anyway. He doesn't speak loud enough." But at Thich Nhat Hanh's next lecture, Jerry would be sitting in front, on the floor, as close as he could get to Thây, trying again to hear him.

Sister Chân Không recalled the ceremony she'd invented for Jerry at Omega. "We made a board and put on it beautiful flowers, and the names of people dead in Viet Nam. Jerry wrote down guerrilla soldier. He said that he want to pray for the transformation, the liberation of that woman who die on the plane in front of him, full of anger and hate. So I help him to write—I don't know the name of the woman—but I say that you, the young woman who suffer so much in front of Jerry, we wish that you will be liberate. And then we make beautiful design to honor her and we stick on the board. And of course there's many soldier— Americ—ah, Viet Nam—veteran, who told me their story, and asked me to write a few word about the person they feel that they are guilty for, or they want to help be liberate and join them."

Sister Chân Không pronounces "Viet Nam" rhyming with "yam," the sweet potato.

I was there at that ceremony she made. Chanting "Return. Return," in Vietnamese, we carried the paper and flowers to the lake. A monk walking ahead wore on the back of his robe—across his shoulders, down to his heels—an unfurled scroll with the phonetic syllables of the chant, including the names of Kuan Yin, Avalokiteshvara, goddess of mercy, bodhisattva of compassionate listening. We chanted, "Kwoon Yum Po Saht, Kwan Ti Om." On the beach, into the fire for burning the names of the dead, Jerry put the hammock, which was by now little more than a rolled-up ball of string. The veterans stopped chanting Kwoon Yum Po

Saht, and sang "Amazing Grace." I will always remember Jerry's face and his hands and tears golden in the firelight. Sparks and fireflies all around.

"Jerry's heart is lighter, and he let go of the guerrilla woman and the hammock," Sister Chân Không said now. But I know it had not happened in a magical instant; then came years of writing and schooling. Jerry is finishing a graduate program in adult education at the University of Southern Maine. He did not correct Sister Chân Không's telling. She said the guerrilla soldier "died"; she never said "killed." He seemed curious to hear his story from the good Vietnamese nun's point of view, to let her re-vision it. She called the hammock his "souvenir." The phenomenon now known as PTSD was once called *nostalgie*, and *Heimweh*. Homesickness.

Kate's off-camera voice directed Jerry to comment on his story. He said, "I had carried her spirit for twenty-five years, and I, I didn't think it was particularly unusual that I carried this hammock with me in my, my rucksack and in my bookbag everywhere I went for twenty-five years. It was, it was with me. It was like—well, it was with me." At the burning of the hammock, "I had a great sense of grief, overwhelmed by this grief that I was experiencing for her. But after, when I went away . . . I didn't feel like I had a burden. I felt like I left the burden there, and I didn't feel like I was responsible for her death any longer."

Sister Chân Không advised, "But that souvenir still remain in your stored consciousness, is come up from time to time. And when it's come up, you have to say Hello. You say: Hello, you are there, but you are no longer a burden, you are an old friend. You say, 'Hello, my little fear.' 'Hi, my anger.' "

Sister True Emptiness talked story about her time in Viet Nam during the war. She was Sister Phuong then, and she organized and worked with the School of Youth for Social Service. "Even the Red Cross of one side shooting the Red Cross other side. I tried to bring help, especially near Ho Chi Minh Trail. I lead a team of twenty person, and we have hire five big boat, and then we brought food and medicine, everything." In the shooting, she would stop and breathe: "Every time both side fight each other, we stop, and then I sit in meditation and I followed my breath. And people jump into the river. I say that the bullet have to avoid us, we cannot avoid the bullet, because"—she laughed—"the bullet, people do not try to aim at us. But they are shooting each other, and then, and then only, the energy of goodness and beauty in us can protect us. Because we are motivate by love. We are motivate by the fact that people are dying on the other side, and we want to bring something for them." She told us what she told the social workers: "So there is something wonderful around us, a kind of energy who can protect us. We can call ourself a little part of bodhisattva Kuan Yin; Kuan Yin is bodhisattva of love. Or, if you are Christian, you can call yourself a part of Jesus, or of God. So that beauty will protect you. But you cannot avoid the bullet, the bullet should avoid you. . . . So I said like that, and then the fire start. We chant the Heart Sutra and we pull out our breath, and we chant the Heart Sutra, and the fire stop—I don't know why and how. But then we continued."

Soldiers from both sides left a village. Innocent people were wounded or dead. Sister Phuong and the social workers had few bandages; they were bringing food. She went into a house. "Two other children are crying and one baby seriously wound, with full of blood." The mother begged her to save the baby. " 'Please save my baby.' So I carry the baby and I said, 'Please go with me,' and so I walk and she walk with me, but I know that there is nothing there, nowhere to go. But on the way the baby die anyway. So in, in my heart I feel big pain, and that remain like—like that, the sense of helpless, of despair. So many children, but this child is in my care, and I feel helpless, and how many thousand of children like that, who are dying because of that war. . . . Breathing in, I know that I am breathing in. Breathing out, I know that I am breathing out."

She breathed consciously then, and she breathed consciously now.

She had an epiphany some years later in Firenze. "At that time I see that the merchant of postcard in front of the cathedral is like me. I, I feel that I'm—I am one part of her, and she smile, I smile, and we look at many birds, pigeon who fly near us. And then I feel that I am in touch with the reality as it is in that moment. . . . So I continue to walk and I enter in the cathedral. You know that I am born as a Buddhist, a Vietnamese Buddhist, so I feel very familiar to look at the Buddha statue. I feel not very familiar in the Catholic church at all, and very far away from the apostle or the angel, all the Catholic architecture.

"But that day, suddenly, I feel I enter in my own home, I enter in the cathedral, but I feel that I enter in my own home. And on the painting, these apostle—it's like my uncle, my father—where Jesus Christ is so close to me, he—I feel that he is my real—I don't know, I am him, we are so close, like father and son or, or spiritual teacher and student, I mean.

"And I look at the angel on one painting. Suddenly I saw the angel smile at me and wave at me, and just that smile, that smile of that baby I carried in my arm full of blood. And of course she die at that moment. And of course she didn't smile. But I saw the angel smile to me, like that—that very smile of the little girl—and I feel so released, and I feel that there is no pain at all. And I feel very happy at that moment. And then I know that when we practice correctly we drop all the concept, I see the realities are as one togetherness. But because we try to make a concept, we are separated: he is Christian, he is Buddhist, he is Islam, he is Western, he is non-Western, Vietnamese."

Sister Chân Không waved, waved peeping down, waved peering up, waved at us, so cute, like a bald baby herself. She was baby, angel, and herself, all at once, waving and returning waves.

Earll and I walked from the Upper Hamlet to the Lower Hamlet, about a mile, through grape fields, orchards, past old stone buildings, under linden and oak, over a hill above a lake. The hills were arcs of earth colors. A row of poplars stood on a ridge. We were a long-wedded couple walking inside a Cézanne landscape.

In the small meditation hall, the Heart Sutra hung on the corner wall opposite the door. It's Thây's Chinese calligraphy. I recognized the many "no"s and "not"s, the negative particles in the poem. Why did the Vietnamese chant the Heart Sutra during firefights, and keep a copy of it on their person? This nothing poem that the Monkey King, journeying on the Silk Road, brought from India to China. I don't understand, what is so inspirational about "No eye or ear or nose or tongue or body or mind / No form, no sound, no smell, no taste, no touch, no object of mind"? And why is it called the "Heart" Sutra? "Heart" does not appear in the poem.

At the door, we ran into Sister Annabelle Laity. I burbled away at her. She held her hand out, presenting me to the sunset, and the sunset to me. The horizon was purple and rose and gold, and the grain and grape fields and hills, also purple and gold. The poplars moved in the wind, and the cypresses held dark and still.

.   .   .

Kate had an idée fixe for a scene—walking meditation at night. At twilight, she picked us up in the van and drove into the woods. The crew had hauled a generator onto the forest floor, and plugged in the big lights. In the beams, the rain fell in heavy, slanting drops, and mists steamed. The vets and I were to do walking meditation for the BBC in the rain and the dark and the mud and the cold. "Whose idea was this?" "There isn't a tradition of walking meditation in the dark, is there?" "We don't do walking meditation in the dark." "Shouldn't've volunteered. Never volunteer." "Let's mutiny." I should never have let Kate know about walking meditation. But Buddhists *do* walk and meditate at night. I remembered Sister Chân Không singing on the steps in the moonlight at Mount Madonna. The moon and the porch light shone on her, and she taught us songs. And the burning of Jerry's hammock had been done at night; I remembered some sixty people walking on the beach in the dark, and the sparks and flames flying up into black sky and reflecting off black water. Asia has pavilions, rooms, ponds, holidays for moon-viewing, which is meditation at night.

The crew kept changing the lights as the darkness changed. Kate was coughing and sneezing. She directed us to walk from one stand of lights to the next. Earll and I led the way. I seriously walked, kept track of the breathing, said gatas, held a meditative pace, minded everything I could mind. I was not acting. Jimmy, Dan, and Jerry filed behind us, Jimmy with the hood of his coat over his head, Dan in his big-brim hat, Jerry in the peaked hat with the tartan band. We hit the mark, and turned to watch Ted, quite a ways behind, coming through the rain—he was dramatic, tall, thin, his cane moving with his stiff leg, a soldier in a romantic war movie. He was wearing a beret in honor of being in France. "Brilliant," said Kate. "Will you do it again?" We redid the walk four or five times. The rain fell steadily harder.

In between takes we stood about in the wet and cold—the crew moving and resetting the lights each time—and complained.

Ted said, "I have problems with Sister Chân Không and her generalities. I don't like her politics. I know the way the Vietnamese do things. Good-cop, bad-cop. *He*—Thây—can stay pure, preach the straight dharma, because she negotiates the dirty work."

I said that she is the necessary, ubiquitous one who gets the worldly tasks done—drives everywhere in her little car, deals with the French authorities for building permits, does the business of the community.

"What bothers you politically about her? Did her phrase 'too Communist' get to you?" She'd said that political enemies who come to Plum Village stop arguing; even those who are "too Communist" or "too anything" can't talk during the Noble Silence.

"She exaggerates," said Ted. "She likes drama. Goddamn it. Claude did not plant 'booby traps' in Plum Village."

I said, "Oh, she means Claude rigged alarms around his tent. Tin cans on string, crunchy leaves, twigs."

"She didn't say alarms; she said booby traps. She knows what a booby trap is—they blow up, they kill people. And she said that innocent villagers were forced into war by the VC, forced to take a side. There *were* VC villages. There were villages that were loyal to the North. They were not terrorized and drafted into it. And babies were not harmless. The VC booby-trapped babies. A little kid could be armed." Claude AnShin had written a story about tanks and trucks stopping for a baby in the road. The baby exploded and killed a lot of people. Ted had written a poem about candy that exploded.

Kate said again, "That was brilliant. Brilliant. Let's do it again." I pictured the silver-and-black shot she was trying for, a platoon and trees silhouetted in the spangling rain. Ted said, "It makes me nervous when a group walks close together. A platoon never walks in a bunch; they could all get blown up. A grenade or someone firing a machine gun can get people too easily." We kept saying loudly for Kate's benefit, "We're going to miss dinner." "If we miss dinner, the BBC will have to take us with them to town."

At last, Kate and Trish Chacon drove the film subjects back to the Upper Hamlet. I asked them to wait until I saw if there was any food left. Some spaghetti was at the bottom of a pot, enough for six. The rumor was that when the Italian monks cook you need your trail mix, but I made the decision that we would stay in Plum Village for dinner.

I hung up my coat and hat, and helped myself to a sixth of the spaghetti; as a kid, I shared treats six ways. I put my plate down and took off my cowboy boots. The villagers wore clogs, so much easier to slip off and on. I started up the steep, open stairs with no railing or riser boards, looked behind me, and saw the big backs of the veterans. They were still in their coats and hats. Their backs were also to one another; they were hunched over their plates of spaghetti, eating standing up. I thought of joining them. I should pull them together, organize them into a sit-down family dinner. Through the hatchway, I saw the monks dining communally. The nuns were not eating here tonight; I'd be the only woman. Earll said, "I'm staying down here." He would be loyal to his brother vets. I went on upstairs. The Italians, who were near the hatch, made room for me. At once I felt belonging, treasured. And Jimmy was already up here! There he was on the inside of the square of tables.

After dinner, Earll and I joined the nuns for meditation. Sister Annabelle led chanting in Vietnamese and in English. The Heart Sutra. This time the "no"s seemed to me the quiet opposite or complement of the jubilant "yes"es at the end of *Ulysses*, a book in which I was formally trained. "Form is emptiness, emptiness is form. / Form is not other than emptiness. / Emptiness is not other than form. / . . . in emptiness there is neither form, nor feelings, nor perceptions, / Nor mental formations, nor consciousness. / . . . No ill-being, no cause of ill-being, / No end of ill-being, and no path; / No understanding, no attainment." Bell. ". . . perfect understanding / Is the highest mantra, the unequaled mantra, / The destroyer of ill-being, the incorruptible truth. . . ." It was an especially long meditation, sitting, walking, sitting, walking, sitting, in candlelight, incense light, moonlight.

Still nary hide nor hair of Thich Nhat Hanh. He doesn't live in the hamlets. He lives many kilometers away, at the Hermitage. Thây's neglect, I feel, is like my own father's. Thây is like BaBa; Sister Chân Không is like MaMa. No wonder I put up with them. I took my mother's word for what my father was about. "Your BaBa thinks that . . ." "Thây says that . . ."

The rain stopped. Earll and I stood under the clear stars, and watched the mist unfurl through the valleys and over the hills. Not speaking, we walked into the alleys and hallways to our room, put a flashlight and a travel clock next to each of the pallets, and went to sleep.

Morning, it was Thanksgiving Day in America, and it was the thirty-third anniversary of Earll's and my wedding. Today we would see Thây. He was coming from the Hermitage to give a dharma talk. After breakfast, the men walked and rode to the Lower Hamlet. Thây and Sister Chân Không drove in. It's too cold for him, especially winters, to live in Plum Village. His childhood malaria acts up. I envied him the hermit writer's life. He built a society that fits his shyness. He can retreat from his retreat. And to stay civilized, he drops in on the village of quiet people. People trained to be quiet.

The sangha filled the rows of chairs in the larger meditation hall. Morning light shone on the stones, which were like white sea coral, and on the cement blocks and new wood. No, actually the beautiful light was coming from the BBC. The crew with their camera and sound paraphernalia stood against one wall; the big light was near the door, beaming across the room. In the very middle of the crowd, Earll and I sat behind Jerry and Ted. Beside them was another sound system; it was for simultaneous translation. The clock rang ten o'clock, chiming like a miniature Big Ben. The crowd stilled, breathed. The door, which was at the back of the hall, opened; we stood. In walked a young man, not Thây. People laughed; some bowed reverently to him as if he were Thây.

Then Thây walked in, and we made a wave of bows as he walked slowly up the aisle to his chair and table. He looked as usual, a small man in a brown habit. He's got big ears that stick out from his shaved head. He grew Buddha ears by practicing the Mindful Listening precept. The BBC and this audience had flushed him out. He'd rather be gardening and writing poems, but it was his duty to teach us. He stood straight, not ducking and loose-limbed like the Dalai Lama. He gave us a smile and a bow.

Thich Nhat Hanh announced the date and place, thus locating us in time/space. He marked this day a special day. Today's dharma talk was: "The Living Tradition of Buddhist Meditation." He spoke in Vietnamese; Sister Annabelle Laity translated into British English. She spoke with an urgent, exhorting voice.

Ted and I, and no one else, took notes, as when we were Cal students. Thây has been known to object to note-taking. The Hopis also warn visitors not to take photographs or notes. I think they're trying to get us to experience direct mouth-to-ear transmission. Thây said: "If we do not live right, we suffer a terrible consequence; we let down our ancestors." He doesn't get that Westerners don't care about ancestors in that way. They care about children. You can't appeal to Westerners via ancestors. They aren't shocked into being good lest they "betray ancestors."

Without warning, explosions—a horrible racket of pops and static— came over the earphones. Ted and Jerry jumped, and almost fell out of their chairs. Trish, who should have known better, laughed.

Thây told a fable about a student after exams. The master says to the student, "Lie down. I'll boil some millet soup for you." The student falls asleep, and in his dream, he has passed his Ph.D. He meets and works with the king. He becomes the husband of the princess. Invaders come. He fights and loses the war. Then — the master wakes him. " 'Now the soup is ready. Get up and have some.' During the time it takes the soup to boil," Thây said, "he has gone up and down." He has been gone a lifetime. "A cloud, a hair can pull us away. . . . drifting and sinking. . . . drifting and sinking . . . up and down . . ."

"Stop!"

Thây looked severely at us, at me, and said, "Stop!"

What was the word he said that Sister Annabelle translated as "stop"? *Shamata? Sunyata? Saranga?*

"Stopping here is to stop our running away from home. We want to stop . . . chasing after a goat . . . chasing after a cloud, or chasing after a butterfly. These small things cause us to give up our home, and give up our ancestors, give up our country. . . . Stop . . . our wandering. Each of us has our home — our homeland, our ancestors, our parents, our roots, our opportunity for happiness, for peace and for joy. . . . We are here seven days or ten days or three months, and that space of time is to practice putting an end to running away, putting an end as we eat, putting an end as we walk, putting an end as we work, putting an end as we sit. There isn't a moment when we do not practice returning, putting an end to running away. Our ancestors, our roots, always are calling us home . . . pushed along by some sort of force . . . the force of forgetfulness . . . the force of no-mindfulness. . . . Rest at peace in the present moment. Stop. Recognize our unwholesome habit energies. Walking meditation is a wonderful method of stopping, a practice that is stopping. . . . When you are walking, you walk, but at the same time you have stopped. . . . Walking meditation is a wonderful way to stop. . . . Walk in such a way that you've stopped. When we do walking meditation, that is a way of stopping to return to home. . . . Walking meditation is the most important, most important practice in Plum Village."

Thây was saying something paradoxical — to walk and at once to be at the stopping point. "If you live in a sangha where everybody's doing walking meditation, knows how to do walking meditation — not just once a day but all day — if we practice like that for a week, there will be a change in you . . . bit by bit, and our steps begin to become stable and free. And when in our steps there is the element of freedom, stability, we already have peace and joy, we already have happiness. We only need to walk. . . . Stability and freedom are the two characteristics of nirvana. We know that every one of us has a home, a spiritual home, and we have lost that because we have run away from it. And our practice is to bring us back to that home. . . . If you need to go fast, you can go fast. Fast in right mindfulness is not the same as fast when you are being pulled along by the force of forgetfulness."

Maybe "stop" could've been translated as "wake up." Tibetan scholars translate *shamata* as "peace abode." And *sunyata* is "emptiness."

He gave us a gata to use during walking meditation: "I have arrived, I am home / in the here, in the now. / I am solid, I am free. / In the ultimate, I dwell." He was trying to get us to live in the exact present moment, to take our place on the earth, right now. "Here, here, here, now, now, now. Returning here and now is the point, the unique point where we can be in touch with our true home, with our roots, with our ancestors, with our happiness. That point is here, that point is now."

The spiritual home is real, an actual place in this world at this very moment.

"Whether you're walking on the wooden floor or walking on the earth, or walking on the grass, all these places are your home, as long as your heart has returned to the present moment."

Thây put his hands together and bowed to us. We stood and bowed to him. He walked down the aisle and out the door. The entire sangha followed him and walked around and about Plum Village.

We had a silent lunch. Then the veterans and I went to tea with Thich Nhat Hanh. The vets named the cabin where he stays when he's at Plum Village "Thây's hootch." It's downhill from the vets' hootch. We passed the sign at the top of the stairs and path:

DO NOT GO BEYOND THIS POINT
PRIVATE

Thây's hootch had a wide deck that spanned out into the autumn air, over the valleys, toward the hills. We'd been here earlier, when Brother Sariputra led tai chi–like exercises. I sat on the edge of the deck and dangled my feet out into the Cézanne valley. The far hills were the colors of maples turning.

Inside, the cameras and lights had been set up. Thich Nhat Hanh, Sister Chân Không, and a young monk were sitting on the floor with tea things. The veterans and I sat in arcs to either side of them, Ted on a chair, the rest of us on the floor. The BBC crew and their equipment completed the circle; Carole and her friend John sat on the sofa behind the camera. (Thây and Sister Chân Không knew to invite Carole, True Grace, our friend from home.)

The attendant monk poured tea and handed each cup to Thây, who bowed and passed it on. We also bowed, accepted the tea, and passed it even to the film crew, who had to hold teacup and equipment. All was still; you could hear the hum from the camera and lights. After sipping and sitting for quite a while, Thây said, "The true miracle is that we are drinking tea together." He was exactly right—we were having a miracle. We had been through Viet Nam, and we had been through America, and out of all time and all space, and births and deaths, these particular beings meet.

I sat next to Thây, on his right. I had never been so near him. On his other side was the tea-server, and next to him, Sister Chân Không. She asked me whether Plum Village lived up to my expectations.

I said I felt at home; I loved being welcomed home. "But I expected a million daffodils—"

"In the spring."

"—spring and summertime, and winter."

"Come back in the spring for the millions of daffodils, and the plum trees in blossom."

Thây said, "You can stop time." He was very sure and serious. It was a statement of fact, and a command. I am to stop time.

Jimmy Janko said to Thây: "You spoke of the importance of not running away from one's culture, one's ancestors, one's spiritual home. Um . . . When I was a medic in Viet Nam, I went to the war with a lot of pride in my country. I felt it was the best country in the world, that we would never harm other people. I believed we represented democracy, and after I saw the really indescribable destruction, as a medic, all kinds of wounds—not only, not only people but the large areas of the earth just destroyed—I feel that . . . that I got stripped from my culture, that I no longer felt a kind of connection that could nourish me from my culture. What I want to ask you is, in your perception of American culture today, do you see something positive that perhaps I cannot see, something that might truly nourish people, and . . . something that is not just another advertisement, another . . . another plug for materialism?"

In the long pause, Thây not answering him, Jimmy laughed and said, "I can—I can just ask myself too."

Thây said, "Ask *her*." He opened his hand at me.

I answered, "Well, you know, America has produced *you*, Jimmy, it produced these people, it produced me. And we are wonderful products of American culture. And we have great ideas, such as the First Amendment in the Bill of Rights, which I see as rights to be *practiced*—speak, write, assemble, build a sangha. The First Amendment is prescriptive; they are our American Precepts."

Sister Chân Không said, "The fact that you come so far and eager to learn, to see deep, to understand deeply, to love deeply, and to live in peace and harmony—that is a hidden treasure of America. And that people like you, if you look deeper, you found. You are not the . . . the lonely people. Everywhere in the United States, many seek of hidden treasure. They learn to respect the earth, they learn to respect the ecosystem, they learn to learn many deep thing."

Jimmy spoke again, his hair sticking up high and higher: "Yeah, it's true, and we are—I think we are the freest people in the world. But I, I also feel that, with the enormous influence that we have in the world, we also—I also feel that, because of the enormous influence of American culture, that we really do cause a lot of suffering throughout the world, and that we need to be aware of that. That's not to take away what we do have, what we can build with the freedoms that we are given. They're to be used to alleviate suffering."

Thây spoke about suffering, which is the first subject of the Four Noble Truths. "America is an open society. It is—it has the ability to open itself to the world, to the other influences. It's not whole yet. So America can renew—can renew herself quite easily, more than many other societies. Ah, suffering is also very important. You need to suffer in order to learn from your suffering. We may suffer uselessly, but if we look deeply into our suffering, we can learn a lot from that."

Jerry talked again about his woman warrior, and he admitted, "I get confused a lot. I am confused now, I'm confused here, because I was walking on the—on the walk this morning, and I'm thinking very calmly, and then the shooting started. And it frightened me. And I have trouble breaking through that fear. I have trouble being calm when I have chaos going round in my head all the time. Perhaps this is not a question, it's simply to let you know that I'm, I'm trying very hard to be mindful but it doesn't—it, it doesn't always work for me."

Thây advised Jerry, "Don't try very hard to be mindful." He laughed. "Don't try very hard to be mindful. Just be in touch with what is there. The people around you, the trees, with the sky, with the leaves, everything around you. Just be in touch with them, and then you will be healed, you will have peace. You will have a joy. Don't try, don't try too hard to be mindful at all, to be something else. Just be yourself. That's what I practice also."

Suddenly Sister Chân Không got what Jerry had said, that there was actually shooting this morning. "Oh, I understand. I hear him. My insight—it was the hunters' gunshots!" I'd heard the gunshots too, and the BBC caught them on audio. We go into the country—Omega, Sebastopol, Bordeaux—for some peace and quiet, and there's shooting. "I see his point. He said that he hear the shooting of the hunter, and because of that is revive the fear of the war in the past. And so if you— you can say that: Hello, my little fear of the war, my experience again, you go back, we are in a safe area. Here's Plum Village. Is not Viet Nam in war. Here is Thây, here is Maxine, here's all your friend, and we are practicing mindfulness."

MaMa used to pull us by the ears while she chanted our address, and the names of everyone in the family. Return. Return. Frighted soul, return to your body, which is at this address and with these beloved people. She quit doing that after we were grown. She should have pulled my brother's ears to get him up off the sofa. You are not in Viet Nam. You are home. Jerry, we are drinking tea in this cabin while the sun sets gloriously behind the autumn hills. A starry night comes to the windows. Viet Nam was long ago. The hunters have left.

Ted said, "I got angry. The static on the earphones made me angry."

Thây spoke again. "We enjoy making peaceful steps, touching Mother Earth, nourishing us. Suddenly you hear the sound of the gun and the hunter. Of course, it can touch the suffering. But with many friends surrounding us, we are able to say: I suffer because of that sound, because it remind me of something in the past. Is okay, is human. You are able to practice that, but you don't want to practice that. You want to imprison yourself into the memory of the past. And if, with the sangha, the community of practice, around you, if you cannot do that, how can you do it alone? Ah, I know that man—there are many people who want to, to stick to their suffering, that has become a habit. That is not good for your health, it's not good for us, for humanity. So that kind of en-lightenment, that kind of ah, ah, reconnection is important.

"I don't say that suffering is my only raison d'être. Because suffering is not enough. We can learn a lot from suffering, but life has also the other side—wonderful, refreshing, healing. All of us have to learn to touch that aspect of life. Ah, when there is a tree dying in our garden, don't make it as if the whole garden is dying. That's not fair, that's not just, that's not wise.

"And there must be someone who remind you of that. Until the time when you yourself can remind yourself of that."

He was scolding the veterans; his voice was soft, impatient, adamant, scolding. Stop suffering. Cut it out.

Thây continued, "You are a veteran, but you are more than a vet-eran. You have to remember that. Mmm, and all of us, Vietnamese and Americans, we are war veterans. All of us have suffered. So you have to remember that you are whole human beings, not just veterans. That apply for me and for you also. Don't say: 'I am only a veteran.' I am more than that. I have to be able not only to help myself but to help my sister, my brother, my child, my society. Because I have the responsibility of a brother, a father, a teacher, a sister, a mother, I cannot just imprison myself in my own suffering. I have to transform it."

Then he said, "I ask Sister Chân Không to sing us a song."

The Vietnamese song, strange sounds of a strange language, glottal stops, bells, charged the air. I breathed sadness, romance, regret, ques-tions. I harked Sister True Emptiness as a chanteuse in an R&R bar, and as Mother in the nursery. She and Thây were reraising us, singing lulla-bies, telling us fables, retraining us: how to breathe, how to eat, how to walk.

We shouldn't have gone to war with people whose music we hadn't heard.

We sat quietly for a long while at the end of her song.

.   .   .

Ted invited each of our group of Americans and Brits to Thanksgiving dinner, his treat. "I've been poor for a long time. Now I have the money—one hundred percent Disability—to be generous." The BBC's van shuttled us to Loubès-Bernac, an old village with one restaurant. A sign over the door of a house from the Middle Ages said, "Pizza." But we were not going to have pizza. Ted and Trish had negotiated with the restaurateur for Thanksgiving dinner. The dining room was ours, lit and warmed by a huge fireplace that must have once been used for cooking. Earll and I sat together in the middle of one side of the long table, the best place for seeing and speaking with everyone. The vets and the crew interspersed themselves. Ron Brown, the soundman. Martin Patmore, the cameraman. Peter, the junior assistant, at the foot of the table. The restaurant family ran in and out, cooking and serving Thanksgiving dinner—roast chickens big as turkeys, piles of pommes frites, soup and vegetables and fruit from the gardens and fields, many kinds of cheeses (aged in the caves of Dordogne), Bordeaux wine—harvests of this place. "Happy Thanksgiving, one and all." "La jour de merci." "Merci." "Merci beaucoup." And "Happy anniversary, Maxine and Earll." "Thirty-three years!" Playing hooky from the monastery, from vegetarian meals and no-wine and no-coffee, the men shouted, "Meat!" "Wine!" "Plenty!" "Largesse!"

All of us tried to reimburse Ted, but he wanted to pay, even for the BBC, who had per diems. He didn't have enough francs. French money and American money and British money changed so many hands, I lost track of who owed whom what. I don't want to care too much for money.

In the almost-full-moonlight, we walked to the end of the empty street and the end of the village. The stone houses shone white. Martin, camera-and-light man, said that he often visited his wife's village in Ireland; it was a beautiful jewel, like this one we were walking through. Most of earth's people live on this scale. I saw my father, Rabbit in the Moon, in France too.

Earll and I rode back to Plum Village with some of the crew. I heard that the last shuttle had driven off without Jimmy. He met some people from Spain, and asked in Spanish for a ride to Village Pruniers. Meanwhile, the vets noticed that he was MIA. The Spaniards' car with Jimmy in it and the deployed BBC van passed each other. When at last everyone was regathered, Jimmy said, "No wonder we lost the war." The other vets didn't think that was funny, and he had to apologize.

I shouldn't have gone outside of Plum Village. I felt a tearing of new roots. A peacefulness had begun. I had to settle in again and reattach myself to the sangha, its inhabitants, and the slow, quiet ways.

The next dawn, when Earll and I went for meditation, the nuns were already assembled. They were in ceremonial clothing, yellow-and-red sashes across their brown habits. We sat behind them, aligned along a red runner up to the altar. Sister Annabelle led the giving of the Five Wonderful Precepts to two young women from the United States. At the calling out of their names, Toinette and Rosalind stood and walked up the red aisle. They were tall and goddesslike among the people seated on the floor, bowing to them. The building of this community, two and a half millennia of Buddhism, these many people rising so early for a ceremony hours long—all on behalf of these two young women. And "all Buddhas and bodhisattvas throughout space and time" were here too, summoned by incense. We witnessed Toinette and Rosalind vow to engage the universe morally and ethically. Bells, bells, bells. "Awaken from forgetfulness and realize our true home."

The men were probably holding this ceremony too. I doubted whether scrupulous Ted was taking the Precepts. He was still thinking it over. Earll and I had taken ours already; we'd surprised each other. Without consulting him, I vowed the Five Wonderful Precepts at Mount Madonna in Watsonville; it was just before the big fire. At Omega, I watched Thây give the Precepts to Earll, Jerry, and Dan. At Malibu, Jimmy took the first four, still allowing himself wine at dinners. I had wanted to cry, seeing Jerry—back hurting, legs hurting—prostrate himself, head to earth, humming "gratitude" to all the conditions of life.

Later, in the time of God's light, our group of veteran writers took a walk—a regular, unfilmed, nonmeditation walk—on the road that went winding uphill and downhill from the Upper Hamlet to the Lower Hamlet. There were no noises of hunters' guns. The sun was melting into blues and violets, and raying straws of gold. Limestone fences and dark tapers of evergreens edged the quilty fields. Row upon row of grape vines curved with the hills. Over a rise, we stopped and looked below on the lakes and ponds. I thought of the gata "I am water reflecting / what is real, what is true." Passing the woods where we did the night walk, we scoffed at that weird scene. "It won't make the film." "She better cut it." "She'll cut it." At the vineyards, Ted examined the winter-bare, gnarling branches, and taught us that grapes are pruned, grafted, espaliered differently here in Bordeaux from back home in Sonoma. We touched the scars of plants grafted a dozen years ago. The lovely blue on wood posts was not mere decoration but copper sulfate, to protect the grapes from mildew. California saved the grapes of Europe, which were almost wiped out from disease. The descendants of twigs that had been shipped from Italy generations ago returned and grew. "The cut branches look dead, like dry, dead sticks. But just stick them right side up in the soil, and they'll grow." Ted once worked managing a vineyard; he'd been a farmhand, an emergency-room nurse, a logger, a bicycle repairman, a bottling-plant worker, a waiter, a janitor, dishwasher, day laborer, and tree pruner. Not bad for a Berkeley grad. When I get home, I'm going to cut branches from my father's grapes, and plant them in the ashes-filled yard.

I was the BBC's last interview, which would take place in the big meditation hall in the Upper Hamlet. The low sun would slant on me sitting on the floor. The crew set up their lights at the altar. Behind me was Kuan Yin, and outside the windows behind her was the winter lotus pond, bronze and shadowy in the going light. I took off my cashmere hat, and tried smoothing my hair, and could feel it sticking up from static electricity. I braided pigtails. I kept my down jacket on—too cold to show off my Tibetan-looking sweaters. I was going on international television with not a bit of glamour on me, no lipstick, no eye makeup. I'd look like a tired ghost. I'd been at this strange place forever. The filming hadn't started when the day went dark, no more light but for the artificial TV spot and its reflections in the black windows. That light browned, and blacked out. A short. No, it's Le Grève. The national strike. The electricity in Bordeaux had been shut off in solidarity with the railroad workers. Martin, Ron, and Peter reconnected everything to the generator; the lamp emitted but a dimness.

A monk came in at a far door and tripped the circuit switch. I was in light again, everyone else in blackness. Kate did not ask me the same questions she had asked the veterans; she began with an abstract question about "nation." But I had in mind what I wanted to say no matter what she asked. Earll and Jimmy, then Jerry came in, and sat in the dark.

Umming and ahing, I said that Plum Village was a successful experiment in international community. Crossing, erasing, broadening boundaries, people had come here from all over the world—the U.K., America, Japan, Viet Nam, Scandinavia, Italy, Germany, India, Russia— I met a Russian veteran of their war in Afghanistan—and many French people, and many people of Chinese ancestry. And they were of various religious traditions—Jews, Muslims, Christians, Buddhists, Hindus, Sufis. We were living in community, living in peace.

I said that abstract terms such as "nation" put me into despair. If I had to acquire big power—get elected or crowned, take over a country, convince a lot of people of some ideology, make money, amass weapons—in order to change the world, I would give up. (The feeling is wanting to crawl away and die, and letting the world die.) Thich Nhat Hanh has promised: "Peace is every step. . . . Step into the present moment, where peace is available. . . . Peace can happen in an instant, right now. . . . With the next aware breath, be at peace." I understand: I could make one person—myself—peaceful, and somehow all of existence will change.

I felt free living here without lock and key. We were living in trust with the people in the adjoining rooms, the people in the next buildings, the people in the next hamlet, the villes and cities surrounding us. Plum Village is not a secret fortress hidden from the rest of France. We were not sequestered in a refuge apart. We didn't need lock and key, because there was nothing to steal. And we didn't have greed for things. We didn't have to buy and sell junk, buy and sell arms.

Plum Village is a product of the Viet Nam–American War. Vietnamese in diaspora settled here. A city of peace has resulted from war.

I chanted my Woman Warrior chant. I learned it from my mother, and now tried to translate it as closely as possible. It is about Fa Mook Lan, who disguised herself as a man and fought a war against the Tatars. I have told her story as a women's liberation story, and as a war story. But I now understand, it is a homecoming story. Fa Mook Lan leads her army home from war. She shows the troops herself changing back from a man to a woman, and gives them a vision of the Feminine. It is possible for a soldier to become feminine. Veterans can return to civil society; they do not have to be homeless. The chant begins with the sound of weaving. Fa Mook Lan was a weaver. "Jik jik jik" is the sound of the shuttle going back and forth across the loom. "Jik" means "to weave," "to knit," "to heal."

Jik jik jik. Jik jik jik.
Fa Mook Lan is weaving
the shuttle through the loom
when news of the draft comes.
Each family must provide one man
to be a soldier in the army.
Sparing her dear father
the wretched life of a soldier,
she disguises herself as a man,
and goes in his stead to war.
With a horse, heavy armor, and
her hand-fitting sword,
she fights wars.
She is away long years,
and many battles, so long a time
that her father and mother grow old and die.
At the head of her army, giving chase,
and being chased,
she suffers wounds; blood drips red
from the openings of her armor.
Her army, chasing and
being chased, passes
her home village six times, back
and forth past her home,
but she cannot stop to place offerings
on the graves. At last, the invaders
flee the country, the war is done.
Fa Mook Lan leads her army to her home village,
and orders them to wait for her in the square.
Indoors, she takes off man's armor.
She bathes, dresses herself in pretty silks,
and reddens her cheeks and lips.
She upsweeps her long black hair,
and adorns it with flowers.
Presenting herself to the army, she says,
I was the general who led you.
Now, go home. By her voice,
the men recognize their general—

a beautiful woman.
You were our general?! A woman.
Our general was a woman. A beautiful woman.
A woman led us through the war.
A woman has led us home.
Fa Mook Lan disbands the army.
Return home. Farewell.
Beholding—and becoming—Yin, the Feminine,
come home from war.
Jik jik jik. Jik jik jik.

There is such a story in the West too. After twenty years of traveling to the war, fighting the war, destroying the other's city, and traveling home, Odysseus could not stop warring. He killed the men who had taken over his house; he killed a dozen women servants. He drafted his twenty-year-old son, Telemachus, and his still-capable father, Laertes. Three generations went to war against every neighbor. But suddenly, a beautiful woman appears. She is Athena, the Hope of Soldiers. "Now, hold!" she shouts. "Break off this bitter skirmish; end your bloodshed, Ithakans, and make peace. Odysseus, master of land ways and sea ways, command yourself. Call off this battle now." At her words, the warriors on all sides lay their weapons down. Their hearts are glad, and together they vow peace.

Now, hold.

Of all that Thây said in the last few days, the one hard-to-believe assertion is: "You can stop time." I am to stop time. On camera, telling it, I started to cry. (The veterans say, "You never cry." Jimmy said, "You cried when you talked about time.") I have to stop time. The difference between my father dead and my father alive was but a moment. My father and I used to wind the grandfather clock at the gambling house. Time is everywhere moving, moving through and around, and causing all things. I want to but can't take ahold of time. Untraceable element. Invisible, untouchable, maybe unreal, like silence, like peace and silence. The responsibility for stopping time is mine, and I don't know how to do it.

My mother is so old. I may have already seen her for the last time. I need to go home.

. . .

On a Sunday, the veterans and I met for what I had announced would be the last time, the Day of Aloha. We would consider disbanding the veterans' writing workshop, and each one going on to found a new sangha.

Almost everybody who'd ever come to the veteran writers' group came to the gathering at Green Gulch Farm. We sat in the largest circle we ever had—about forty people, moving this way and that way to see one another around the columns of the meeting hall.

I pointed out the benefits of parting, of bringing these workshops to a close. "Look at this turnout. You know we're ending, so you show up. You're here to appreciate the last dear moments, and to say goodbye. We need a deliberate goodbye. Saying goodbye to one another, we'll say goodbye to the Viet Nam–American war. We're detaching ourselves from that war. We're ending it." Viet Nam—a war, a state of mind, now just another place.

Ted had brought white limestone rocks from Plum Village; he put them in the middle of the floor. "Enough for everyone." He and Dan had traveled in France until their money ran out. Jerry, back in Alfred, Maine, has worked out the time difference, and all day today, he's meditating when we're meditating and writing when we're writing. I have photos of Dan standing beside the giant bell of Plum Village; monks are all around him and the bell—everybody smiling.

The veteran writers did not want this meeting to be the last. Tom Currie hid, lying down on the floor in back of the sofa next to the pot-belly stove.

Therese said that she was not able to be a leader anymore, or to make the phone calls and do the mailings. "I'll support *you* organizing new sanghas." Mo Nerli said, "You are welcome to meet at my house." Jimmy said that this large a number of people is obviously too large for a writing group. "We need to make groups of manageable sizes." Miki suggested staying in contact via a phone tree, and explained what a phone tree is. Scott volunteered to do mailings. Miki said, "Let's take up a collection for postage." She rushed about with a hat. People pulled bills out of their wallets. Bob Golling said, "We aren't ending the work-shops; we're transforming them. They're changing shape." I held on to silence to keep from saying, Okay, I won't abandon you. We will be together for the rest of our lives. All you single men and all you single women, look at one another amorously, why won't you? Date. Marry.

The veterans had to have a last fight.

Woman Vet said, "I read that in Bosnia ninety-two percent of the children feel they're going to die, and they want to die. I'm thinking about joining a demonstration against sending troops to Bosnia." Our very own patriotic Woman Vet, a cop, is going on a peace demonstration.

Somebody started reminiscing about meeting the North Vietnamese veterans. "We reconciled with them."

Somebody else said, "But not with the peace activists. We could never reconcile with *them.*"

A chorus of people said, "No. No reconciliation with the peace activists." "Yeah, I'm still mad at the peaceniks."

I asked, "Do you mean that you are reconciled with the enemy but not with your fellow Americans? Why?"

Woman Vet said, "Betrayal. They betrayed us."

Even Mike, even Keith said, "Betrayal."

I argued, "It seems odd to me that you can feel close to the North Vietnamese vets—instant rapport with Thai and Khue—but can't get together with our own American peace activists."

Lee said, "I, I thought we'd gotten past this."

Keith said, "I feel bad about them. The betrayers."

"But, Keith," I said, "you're talking about yourself. You're a war veteran *and* a peace activist. Reconciliation isn't with other, unknown people. It's yourself with yourself."

Woman Vet said, "The yuppies, the betrayers—my sister—partied at college while we were doing the grunt work, and sacrificing our lives."

"But," I said, "you'd be reconciling with your own sister, not some anonymous peacenik."

"Irreconcilable," said Keith. "I feel angry at the very word 'reconciliation.' "

Jade said, "I don't believe in forgiveness. Forgiveness is not my problem."

I panicked; they were refusing to have an easy goodbye. They wanted a divorce fight. They were angry at me for being a peacenik, and for leaving them. Betrayer.

I groped for a point of agreement. "But you do agree with the *need* for reconciliation?" They nodded, doubtfully. I pointed to the drawing of Avalokiteshvara on the wall; it had been painted by children. She has many hands—even her hands have hands—and an eye in each hand. "That is the bodhisattva of compassionate listening, whom we've been invoking. Here is what she looks like." Therese took the picture down and held it in the middle of the circle. "We have asked her again and again to help us be like her. To be compassionate and to listen. To listen 'without judgment.' "

Lee, with tears, said, "As a peace activist, I work hard to understand you veterans' point of view. I try to know you as individuals. Please see me as an individual. Peace activists made sacrifices too, went to jail, got kicked out of the family. I got my father's will with my name crossed off." Lee's father disowned him for some years, "till the war went bad."

Lee stopped talking then, and read. In his piece, a woman drove away from the prison and left her man behind. The young man, young during the war, carried pieces of antipersonnel bombs to meetings and protests. Vietnamese in Paris had given him this evidence that Honeywell, Litton Industries, American corporations, were manufacturing and delivering weapons. Lee had been willing to sail a medical-supply ship into Haiphong Harbor, and chance getting blown up, to prove that our government was lying about not mining the DMZ. It was Vietnamese who talked the peace activists out of making such a sacrifice. Please, no more self-immolation: "We need you alive to make peace." Lee ended his reading to silence.

Ellen rang the bell. Another person started to read. Ted interrupted: "She rang the bell before we could put our hands together for Lee." The war veterans applauded Lee Swenson, resister.

Time has lengthened. The day is now long enough so that forty people read.

At last the vets got up to leave, gathered their stuff, milled. They'd forgotten that we always end the day in meditation. I couldn't believe it—they thought that we would end our years together without ceremony. And I'd earlier announced hugging meditation. I rang the Bell of Mindfulness and said, "I have a last thing to teach you." Scott said,

"Damn! The hug. I thought you were kidding about hugging." People took their seats again.

I asked Jimmy to help me demonstrate what we'd learned at Plum Village. He and I stood in a spot of overhead light. I said, "Hugging meditation is an American contribution to Buddhist ritual. Thich Nhat Hanh invented it at a civil-rights and peace march. An exuberant Black woman gave him a tremendous hug. She didn't know you weren't supposed to hug monks. Thây stood there like a stick, not hugging her in return. Mulling over what he should have done, he invented hugging meditation. Now he would hug an American vet, and say, 'When you hug one Vietnamese person, you hug all Vietnamese people.' I say, 'When you hug Americans, who are from everywhere, you hug all the people of the earth.' "

Jimmy and I turned toward and looked at each other, noticing at least one wonderful quality of the being who stood before us. We smiled and bowed. A lotus for you, Buddha-to-be. We stepped toward each other, put our arms around this dear person, and hugged, breathing three mindful breaths, then parted, and bowed again. Jimmy and I went up to other people, and bowed, and hugged. Like snowball dance in high school. Soon, everybody was hugging everybody. Jeremiah "Psycho Dog," ex–gang member, and Woman Vet, cop. Lee and everybody who'd said, Betrayer. Hug and let go. Keith and Earll did a walk toward each other like a couple of Marx brothers; Keith held his arms out—and walked straight past Earll toward somebody he liked better. It was so funny, they did it again. Ann Marks hugged saying, "I don't hug. I'm not a hugger." We became a mass of loving humanity. Laughing and talking too. Before Mike and I hugged, he wanted to talk. "I didn't get to throw you the Trust Ball. Could you give me your thoughts on me?" I confessed that I'd kept seeing him as Wittman Ah Sing, but now know that he is not a jumpy monkey. "You're a solid citizen, using statistics and logic and evidence to substantiate peace. Your peace and your faithful true love for our country, for us, for Jade, fill me with hope. You have the most amazing full life, better than any imagined character's. You've done it all. You were in the army *and* in a commune, lived in the U.S. *and* Canada, you've been a hippie *and* a soldier. You're a free spirit and a householder, a black belt and a pacifist. What a wonderful life!" Mike's Chinese name, pronounced somewhat like "Michael," means "Mankind Has"; the first character is one that the Chinese use for "people," as in the People's Republic. Mike's name is like the vow that Ngok Fei the Patriot's mother cut on his back: "First Save the Nation." Jade asked for words about her. She needs feelings to be said, the meanings of the silent hug explicitly voiced. I told her I love hugging her, same-same height as me. I trust a person I can see eye to eye. Richard Gilman and Scott are so tall, they got on their knees to hug me. My democratic self was taken aback. Tom said, "I don't have a sangha." I called out his name to be invited to one. Tom added a kiss to the hugging. At last, everybody having hugged and been hugged, as far as I could see, the group went outside. But there, under the black winter sky and the stars, was Ted alone. I said, "Aha. You're not getting away unhugged." I gave him a good hug, forgot the bowing, and felt him hug back.

In the writing of this Book of Peace, Mother died. The days and nights of her dying, the San Joaquin flooded. The silver-and-white dragons—fog dragons, cloud and rain dragons, river dragons—came for her, fellow dragon. Up in an airplane, her granddaughter, Cher Nicolas, a teacher, saw her walking on top of the clouds. Brave Orchid was smiling, meeting Father, who was smiling too, holding open a shawl for her. Ancestors surrounded them. They walked all together into the sky.

I had been able to tell Mother that I built a sangha. I pronounced it Soo Hong, the name of the community house she wanted.

In a war dream, my army lays down guns and missiles. We walk toward the other army with our arms open. We walk into Gatling guns, rocket launchers, and hard bullets and missiles, and are unharmed because we are permeable. I touch another, he or she touches me, and love courses through crowds. Peace yet new, an assassin comes with a closed basket, carrying snakes and explosives. I walk toward him, and touch him, hold his hand. The weapons change into nothing. The lid opens. The basket is a singing mouth.

We have built a different house on the site of the burned one. My brother Norman designed it crannied with reading nooks. Its lines "swoop" with the hills. On the grounds and the neighboring lot, which we bought, we have planted sixty trees. Three are redwoods from seed, and four are loquats from seed. There are also volunteers—yucca, Texas privet, coyote, unkillable bamboo, and the heart-leafed katsura.

If the world, time and space, and cause-and-effect accord with my mother's teachings—her Tao—then we have stopped wars years hence. We made myriads of nonwars. We have ended wars a hundred years from now. The war against Iraq, which began the same year as the Oakland-Berkeley fire, is still occurring. But the peace we make also continues, and fans, and lives on and on.

EPILOGUE

The veteran writing workshop did not break up after all. We had a place to go after the terrorist attacks; we met on September 22, 2001. The theme of the gathering was "Return." As in "Here we go again." The veterans expressed the same feelings and thoughts that other Americans did, including: Let's get 'em back. Tom Currie said, "I told you so. Time passes and it has come to this. Those terrorists are out to kill me, me personally. I take it personally. Evil exists. I have seen it." Keith Mather said, "We don't completely return to the same place. This is bad. I've never been here before. I may leave again for Canada. I can't bear to be in this country when it's at war." But on the whole, our sangha remains stable. Peace leads us. Moral principles do not change. A moral principle is neither relative nor conditional; it does not depend on the time, circumstance, or situation. Pauline Laurent said she hears the wounded calling her name, and her compassion goes to the terrorists too. This day, though we are tired, scared, old, we renewed our dedication to one another and to the work that we must do.

On October 22, the tenth anniversary of the fire in the Oakland-Berkeley hills, I spoke at a rally in support of Barbara Lee, the only member of Congress to vote against giving the President unlimited war powers. Her constituents, people of the Ninth District, gathered to give her support. She surprised us, showed up despite threats. We chanted, "Thank you. Thank you." And "Barbara Lee for President." She said, smiling, "Thank you." We answered, "Thank *you*. Thank *you*." Another surprise: Kelly Campbell, sister-in-law of Craig Amundson, who had been killed at the Pentagon, walked across the platform and gave Barbara Lee an armful of flowers. She spoke on behalf of her family. "Craig would not want his death to be a cause for war. Violence will not bring

Craig back; it will not make America safe from terrorist attacks, and will not make for a safer world. I want to say Thank you, Barbara, for being the voice of reason during these days of tragedy." They hugged with the flowers between them; it would have made a beautiful picture—the Black woman in a bright-red coat, the pale White woman in a blue hat. But by the time the news of the rally reached the East Coast, there was no mention of Kelly Campbell.

Nor is there much about Peaceful Tomorrows, an organization formed by families of people who were killed in the attacks on the World Trade Center and the Pentagon. The group is urging Congress and the President to make financial restitution to Afghanis who lost relatives, homes, and businesses to American bombing.

Immediately after the terrorist attacks, firefighter Ray Gatchalian flew to New York. He said the same thing that he said at the Oakland-Berkeley hills fire. "I believe we should take people there. We should take them in buses and give them an opportunity to see this and say, 'When we decide to send our military and our bombs into a country, this is what we're deciding to do.' So think hard before you decide to destroy people in another country." I am so relieved; it's not true that 9/11 changed everything. No recanting.

Shepherd Bliss of the family that gave Fort Bliss its name—he is an organic farmer near Sebastopol, our workshop's permanent home—wrote an essay, *America on the Warpath: A Nation's Soul at Risk*. It has been published by Amal Press, a Muslim publisher in England. He said, "As the divisions between America and the Muslim world increase, I want to do anything that I can to find common ground. Rumi, a Muslim poet who was born in what is today Afghanistan, writes: 'Out beyond ideas of wrongdoing and rightdoing, / there is a field. / I'll meet you there.' And as the old book says, 'Thou shalt not kill.' "

Yigal Gelben Ben-Haim returned to Israel, where he wrote from a kibbutz: "I'm sorry but I no longer can write a good enough English (four years now that I am using only Hebrew). Here in Israel Peace is very elusive. In Haifa I am very busy being with my new family (Dan and Tanya) but hope to find time for a writing veterans group here." In Judaism, there is also a tradition of meditation; it's called *hitbonenut*. Its practitioners look deeply, look with great attention. He invites us to Israel. "Come visit me. We'll go to Hamutal, the land of the killing, and there take a moment to remember the ancient Biblical story of the sacrifice. 'And God came out from above and stopped the senseless killing.' "

Jimmy Janko went to Viet Nam to do research for his novel, and met and married Chanpidor. With our borders being sealed, the INS put obstacles in the way of Jimmy's bringing his wife to the U.S. He has to prove what has heretofore been self-evident—that he really is an American citizen.

On the Veterans Day after 9/11, Ted Sexauer and peace activists Judy and Charlie Liteky and Clare Morris—the dear one for whom Ted has been waiting—were at Fort Benning, Georgia, to protest the School of the Americas, renamed the Western Hemisphere Institute for Security Cooperation. Ted quoted Charlie in poem form:

> "The Vietnam war is not over.
> It is being carried on in other places
> by other means. The policy of the United States
> is to keep the third world
> third. We take what is not ours.
> And the United States is
> us, each of us responsible."

Next, Ted went to Iraq with Voices in the Wilderness. His goal is to be a connection between the people of his hometown, Sonoma, and the people of Iraq. The only photograph he carried with him was one of our veteran writers group.

In Hawai'i, there will soon open America's first Buddhist high school. Pieper Toyama, who will be the principal of the Pacific Buddhist Academy, said, "We're going to develop happy, successful students who make peace. Peace education will cut across the entire academic curriculum. Coming at a time like this, it makes even more sense."

At a demonstration in the spring, in San Francisco, Earll and I mustered with the Buddhists, who sat meditating in three or four rows on the grassy hill overlooking the excitement. We made an area of peace. On the march we walked with Doug Howerton, survivor of MOVE. He brought his fourteen-year-old son, Shan—his first peace march. I asked Shan if demonstrating is doing any good, stopping war. He said, "It will slow it down."

One of Bob Golling's six sons, Joe, has been charged with malicious mischief for writing antiwar slogans on the Questa College, San Luis Obispo, campus. The judge fined him $100, plus $118 to the school for the removal of graffiti. Joe is not to carry chalk—his implement of damage—on his person for a year. So Joe makes peace films for cable access television.

On International Women's Day, I was one of the women dressed in pink who called and sang for peace in front of the White House. "Bush says Code Red. We say Code Pink." The spirit of Yin—a feeling of peace and love—suffused everyone, including counterdemonstrators and police officers. Never before had I experienced such nonviolence. Thousands of women tried to send our good feelings and protection all the way to the Iraqi children. The police carefully arrested two dozen women, including me and my sister writers—Rachel Bagby, Susan Griffin, Alice Walker, and Terry Tempest Williams. The charge: "Stationary demo in a restricted zone (White House sidewalk)." But first, the police arrested the journalists—Kirsten Michel, a filmmaker, and Amy Goodman of Pacifica Radio—and took away their camera and audio equipment, and cell phones. We had been talking live via cell phone on independent radio stations all over the country. Amy said, "If an event—an arrest—is not witnessed and photographed by the media, it did not happen." The police lines that blocked off Pennsylvania Avenue turned away journalists from the *Washington Post*, the *New York Times*, and ABC television; we heard this sad news from people who had made their way through or around the police.

The images of peace are ephemeral. The language of peace is subtle. The reasons for peace, the definitions of peace, the very idea of peace have to be invented, and invented again.

Children, everybody, here's what to do during war: In a time of destruction, create something. A poem. A parade. A community. A school. A vow. A moral principle. One peaceful moment.

Permissions Acknowledgments

Grateful acknowledgment is made to the following for permission to reprint previously published material:

Bishop Museum: Excerpt from *Na Hana A Ka Po 'e Kahiko: The Works of the People of Old* by Samuel Kamakau. Reprinted by permission of the Bishop Museum.

Renny Christopher: Excerpts from *Viet Nam and California* by Renny Christopher. Reprinted by permission of the author.

Curbstone Press: Excerpts from *Shopping Cart Soldiers* by John Mulligan. Reprinted by permission of Curbstone Press, distributed by Consortium.

Farrar, Straus and Giroux, LLC.: Excerpt from the poem "Two Villages" from *Begin Again: Collected Poems* by Grace Paley. Copyright © 2000 by Grace Paley. Excerpt from *The Collected Stories* by Grace Paley. Copyright © 1994 by Grace Paley. Excerpt from the poem "Keeping Quiet" from *Extravagaria* by Pablo Neruda, translated by Alastair Reid. Translation copyright © 1974 by Alastair Reid. Reprinted by permission of Farrar, Straus and Giroux, LLC.

Grey Fox Press: Excerpts from *Ring of Bone* by Lew Welch. Copyright © 1973 by Lew Welch. Reprinted by permission of Grey Fox Press.

Ludlow Music, Inc.: Excerpt from the song lyric "This Land Is Your Land" words and music by Woody Guthrie. TRO-Copyright © 1956 (renewed) 1958 (renewed) 1970 (renewed) by Ludlow Music, Inc., New York, New York. Reprinted by permission of Ludlow Music, Inc.

Ted Sexaurer: Excerpts from *Mercy Lives Inside the Wire* by Ted Sexaurer. Reprinted by permission of the author.

Shambhala Publications, Inc.: Excerpts from *Open Secret* by Rumi, edited by John Moyne and Coleman Barks. Reprinted by permission of Shambhala Publications, Inc., Boston, www.shambhala.com.

Simon & Schuster Adult Publishing Group: Excerpts from *Viet Rock* by Megan Terry. Copyright 1967 by Megan Terry. Reprinted by permission of Simon & Schuster Adult Publishing Group.

Universal-Songs of Polygram Int., Inc., on behalf of Black Pig Publ.-Festival Music PTY., Ltd.: Excerpt from the song lyric "X X X," words and music by Joseph Bonavia, Edward Stemac, Matthew Healy. Copyright © by Universal-Songs of Polygram Int., Inc., on behalf of Black Pig Publ.-Festival Music PTY., Ltd. (BMI). International copyright secured. All rights reserved. Reprinted by permission of Universal-Songs of Polygram Int., Inc., on behalf of Black Pig Publ.-Festival Music PTY., Ltd.

A NOTE ABOUT THE AUTHOR

Maxine Hong Kingston is Senior Lecturer for Creative Writing at
the University of California, Berkeley. For her memoirs and fiction, *The Woman Warrior*, *China Men*, *Tripmaster Monkey*, and
Hawai'i One Summer, Kingston has earned numerous awards,
among them the National Book Award, the National Book Critics Circle Award for Nonfiction, the PEN West Award for Fiction, an American Academy and Institute of Arts and Letters
Literature Award, and a National Humanities Medal from the
National Endowment for the Humanities, as well as the rare title
of "Living Treasure of Hawai'i."

A NOTE ON THE TYPE

The text of this book was set in Electra, a typeface designed by
W. A. Dwiggins (1880–1956). This face cannot be classified as
either modern or old style. It is not based on any historical model,
nor does it echo any particular period or style. It avoids the
extreme contrasts between thick and thin elements that mark
most modern faces, and it attempts to give a feeling of fluidity,
power, and speed.

Composed by Creative Graphics, Inc.,
Allentown, Pennsylvania

Printed and bound by Berryville Graphics,
Berryville, Virginia

Book design by Dorothy Schmiderer Baker